D1283801

OXFORD STUDIES IN ANCIENT DOCUMENTS

General Editors
Andrew Meadows Alison Cooley

OXFORD STUDIES IN ANCIENT DOCUMENTS

This innovative new series offers unique perspectives on the political, cultural, social, and economic history of the ancient world. Exploiting the latest technological advances in imaging, decipherment, and interpretation, the volumes cover a wide range of documentary sources, including inscriptions, papyri, and wooden tablets.

Teos and Abdera

Two Cities in Peace and War

MUSTAFA ADAK
PETER THONEMANN

OXFORD
UNIVERSITY PRESS

UNIVERSITY PRESS

Great Clarendon Street, Oxford, OX2 6DP,
United Kingdom

Oxford University Press is a department of the University of Oxford.
It furthers the University's objective of excellence in research, scholarship,
and education by publishing worldwide. Oxford is a registered trade mark of
Oxford University Press in the UK and in certain other countries

© Mustafa Adak and Peter Thonemann 2022

The moral rights of the authors have been asserted

First Edition published in 2022

Impression: 1

Published in the United States of America by Oxford University Press
198 Madison Avenue, New York, NY 10016, United States of America

British Library Cataloguing in Publication Data

Data available

Library of Congress Control Number: 2021945587

ISBN 978–0–19–284542–9

DOI: 10.1093/oso/9780192845429.001.0001

Printed in Great Britain by
Bell & Bain Ltd., Glasgow

Preface

The rich and varied epigraphic record of the city of Teos in northern Ionia has been dramatically enriched by recent excavations at the site, conducted since 2010 under the aegis of the University of Ankara. Over the past decade, the number of known inscriptions from Teos has increased from *c.*300 to *c.*500, and every season's campaign brings significant new finds. The most remarkable document discovered in recent years is a long honorific decree of Abdera for the *dēmos* of Teos, dating to the mid-160s BC (Chapter 1, **Document 1**). The new inscription invites a reassessment of the uniquely close relationship between Teos and her daughter-city Abdera over a period of almost four centuries, from the original Teian settlement at Abdera in the 540s BC to the Roman sack of Abdera in 170 BC and its aftermath. We hope that readers will share our excitement in retracing the long shared history of Teos and Abdera, in times of both peace and war.

It is a pleasure to thank the many colleagues and institutions that have supported our work. Musa Kadıoğlu and his excavation team provided a splendid environment to work on the inscriptions preserved on site at Teos. Erkan Taşdelen gave invaluable technical assistance in the decipherment of the new Abdera decree, as well as many other inscriptions. Serkan Örnek drew the maps of Ionia and Thrace. The directorate of the Archaeological Museum at İzmir kindly allowed Mustafa Adak to work on the relevant inscriptions from Teos now housed in the museum, and Maria Chryssafi gave a hospitable welcome to Peter Thonemann at the site and museum of Abdera. Denis Rousset generously provided photographs of Philippe Le Bas's squeeze of Dirae I (Chapter 3, **Document 2**) at the Fonds Louis Robert, and the British Library provided access to the epigraphic manuscripts of William Sherard. Peter Thonemann's work on this book was made possible by a Senior Research Fellowship from the British Academy/Leverhulme Trust. For advice on specific textual or interpretative problems, we are grateful to Hariclea Brecoulaki, Charles Crowther, Patrice Hamon, Philip Kinns, Christina Kokkinia, Stephen Lambert, Leah Lazar, John Ma, Andrew Meadows, Maria-Gabriella Parissaki, Robert Parker, Selene Psoma, P. J. Rhodes, Bert Smith, and the anonymous readers for the Press. We owe a particular debt of gratitude to Christopher Jones for his assistance and encouragement throughout. Appropriately, this book has been a collaboration across national borders, and it is a pleasure to put on record the ἀνέλλειπτος ὁμόνοια which has characterized our work together.

Mustafa Adak
Peter Thonemann
Akdeniz Üniversitesi, Antalya
Wadham College, Oxford

Contents

List of Illustrations

Abbreviations

AE	*L'Année épigraphique*
Agora	*The Athenian Agora: Results of Excavations Conducted by the American School of Classical Studies at Athens*. Princeton, NJ, 1953–.
Barrington Atlas	R. J. A. Talbert, *Barrington Atlas of the Greek and Roman World* (3 vols). Princeton, NJ and Oxford.
BE	*Bulletin épigraphique*, annually in *REG*.
BMC Phrygia	B. V. Head, *A Catalogue of the Greek Coins in the British Museum: Catalogue of the Greek Coins of Phrygia*. London, 1906.
BNJ	I. Worthington (ed.), *Brill's New Jacoby Online*, 2nd edn, <https://referenceworks.brillonline.com/browse/brill-s-new-jacoby-2>.
CGRN	*Collection of Greek Ritual Norms*, <http://cgrn.ulg.ac.be>.
CH	*Coin Hoards*. London, 1975–2002 (vols I–IX); New York, 2010 (vol. X).
CID IV	F. Lefèvre, *Corpus des inscriptions de Delphes, Tome IV: Documents amphictioniques*. Paris, 2002.
CIG	A. Boeckh, *Corpus Inscriptionum Graecarum* (4 vols). Berlin, 1828–77.
CIL	*Corpus Inscriptionum Latinarum*.
CITh III	P. Hamon, *Corpus des inscriptions de Thasos, III: Documents publics du quatrième siècle et de l'époque hellénistique*. Athens.
CNG	*Classical Numismatic Group* (auction catalogues).
CPI I	A. K. Bowman, C. V. Crowther, S. Hornblower, R. Mairs, and K. Savvopoulos, *Corpus of Ptolemaic Inscriptions, Volume 1: Alexandria and the Delta (Nos. 1–206), Part I: Greek, Bilingual, and Trilingual Inscriptions from Egypt*. Oxford, 2021.
FD III	*Fouilles de Delphes, Tome III: Épigraphie*. Paris, 1909–85.
FGrHist	F. Jacoby, *Die Fragmente der griechischen Historiker*. Berlin and Leiden, 1923–.
GEI	*Greek Economic Inscriptions*, <http://geionline.sns.it>.
IAph2007	J. Reynolds, C. Roueché, and G. Bodard, *Inscriptions of Aphrodisias*, <http://insaph.kcl.ac.uk/iaph2007>.
I.Beroia	L. Gounaropoulou and M. Hatzopoulos, Ἐπιγραφὲς Κάτω Μακεδονίας. Α΄ Ἐπιγραφὲς Βεροίας. Athens, 1998.
I.Cret.	M. Guarducci, *Inscriptiones Creticae* (4 vols). Rome, 1935–50.
I.Délos	*Inscriptions de Délos* (7 vols). Paris, 1926–72.
I.Didyma	A. Rehm, *Didyma II. Die Inschriften*. Berlin, 1958.
I.Eleusis	K. Clinton, *Eleusis: The Inscriptions on Stone* (2 vols). Athens, 2005–8.

I.Ephesos	H. Wankel, R. Merkelbach, et al., *Die Inschriften von Ephesos* (7 vols). *IGSK* 11–17. Bonn, 1979–81.
I.Erythrai	H. Engelmann and R. Merkelbach, *Die Inschriften von Erythrai und Klazomenai* (2 vols). *IGSK* 1–2. Bonn, 1972–3.
IG	*Inscriptiones Graecae.*
IGBulg.	G. Mihailov, *Inscriptiones Graecae in Bulgaria repertae* (5 vols in 6). Sofia, 1958–97.
IGRR	R. Cagnat, *Inscriptiones Graecae ad Res Romanas Pertinentes* (3 vols). Paris, 1906–27.
IGUR	L. Moretti, *Inscriptiones Graecae Urbis Romae* (4 vols). Rome, 1968–90.
I.Iasos	W. Blümel, *Die Inschriften von Iasos* (2 vols). *IGSK* 28. Bonn, 1985.
I.Ilion	P. Frisch, *Die Inschriften von Ilion. IGSK* 3. Bonn, 1975.
I.Iznik	S. Şahin, *Katalog der antiken Inschriften des Museums von Iznik (Nikaia)* (2 vols in 4). *IGSK* 9–10. Bonn, 1979–87.
I.Kallatis	A. Avram, *Inscriptions grecques et latines de Scythie Mineure III. Callatis et son territoire.* Bucharest and Paris, 1999.
I.Kaunos	Chr. Marek, *Die Inschriften von Kaunos.* Munich, 2006.
I.Knidos	W. Blümel, *Die Inschriften von Knidos I. IGSK* 41. Bonn, 1992.
I.Kyme	H. Engelmann, *Die Inschriften von Kyme. IGSK* 5. Bonn, 1976.
I.Lampsakos	P. Frisch, *Die Inschriften von Lampsakos. IGSK* 6. Bonn, 1978.
I.Laodikeia	T. Corsten, *Die Inschriften von Laodikeia am Lykos. I. IGSK* 49. Bonn, 1997.
I.Magnesia	O. Kern, *Die Inschriften von Magnesia am Maeander.* Berlin, 1900.
I.Mylasa	W. Blümel, *Die Inschriften von Mylasa* (2 vols). *IGSK* 34–5. Bonn, 1987–8.
I.Oropos	B. Petrakos, Οἱ Ἐπιγραφὲς τοῦ Ὠρωποῦ. Athens, 1997.
IOSPE I²	V. Latyshev, *Inscriptiones antiquae orae septentrionalis Ponti Euxini graecae et latinae, I: Inscriptiones Tyriae, Olbiae, Chersonesi Tauricae* (2nd edn). St Petersburg, 1916.
*IOSPE*³	*Inscriptiones antiquae orae septentrionalis Ponti Euxini graecae et latinae* (3rd edn), <http://iospe.kcl.ac.uk/index.html>.
I.Pergamon	M. Fränkel, *Die Inschriften von Pergamon* (2 vols). Berlin, 1890–5.
I.Perge	S. Şahin, *Die Inschriften von Perge* (2 vols). *IGSK* 54, 61. Bonn, 1999–2004.
I.Pisid.Cen.	G. H. R. Horsley and S. Mitchell, *The Inscriptions of Central Pisidia. IGSK* 57. Bonn, 2000.
*I.Priene*²	W. Blümel and R. Merkelbach, *Die Inschriften von Priene. IGSK* 69. Bonn, 2014.
I.Prusa ad Olympum	T. Corsten, *Die Inschriften von Prusa ad Olympum* (2 vols). *IGSK* 39–40. Bonn, 1991–3.

IScM I	D. M. Pippidi, *Inscriptiones Scythiae Minoris graecae et latinae, I: Inscriptiones Histriae et vicinia*. Bucharest, 1983.
ISE III²	F. Canali de Rossi, *Iscrizioni storiche ellenistiche, III: Decreti per ambasciatori greci al senato* (2nd edn). Rome, 2006.
I.Selge	J. Nollé and F. Schindler, *Die Inschriften von Selge*. IGSK 37. Bonn, 1991.
I.Sestos	J. Krauss, *Die Inschriften von Sestos und der thrakischen Chersones*. IGSK 19. Bonn, 1980.
I.Side	J. Nollé, *Side im Altertum* (2 vols). IGSK 43–4. Bonn, 1993–2001.
I.Strat.	M. Ç. Şahin, *Die Inschriften von Stratonikeia* (2 vols in 3). IGSK 21–2. Bonn, 1981–90.
IThrakAig	L. D. Loukopoulou, M. G. Parissaki, S. Psoma, and A. Zournatzi, Ἐπιγραφὲς τῆς Θρᾴκης τῆς Αἰγαίου. Athens, 2005.
IvO	W. Dittenberger and K. Purgold, *Die Inschriften von Olympia*. Berlin, 1896.
Kühner–Gerth	R. Kühner and B. Gerth, *Ausführliche Grammatik der griechischen Sprache, II Teil: Satzlehre* (3rd edn). Hanover and Leipzig, 1898.
LGPN	*A Lexicon of Greek Personal Names.*
LIMC	*Lexicon Iconographicum Mythologiae Classicae.*
Lindos II	C. Blinkenberg, *Lindos. Fouilles et recherches, 1902–1914, Vol. II: Inscriptions* (2 vols). Copenhagen and Berlin, 1941.
LSJ	H. G. Liddell and R. Scott, *A Greek-English Lexicon*, revised by H. Stuart Jones and R. McKenzie.
MAMA	*Monumenta Asiae Minoris Antiqua.*
Milet	*Milet. Ergebnisse der Ausgrabungen und Untersuchungen seit dem Jahre 1899.*
OGIS	W. Dittenberger, *Orientis Graeci inscriptiones selectae* (2 vols). Leipzig, 1903–5.
PMG	D. L. Page, *Poetae Melici Graeci*. Oxford, 1962.
RE	*Paulys Real-Encyclopädie der classischen Altertumswissenschaft.*
Robert, *Hellenica*	L. Robert, *Hellenica. Recueil d'épigraphie, de numismatique et d'antiquités grecques* (13 vols in 12). Paris, 1940–65.
Robert, *OMS*	L. Robert, *Opera Minora Selecta. Épigraphie et antiquités grecques* (7 vols). Amsterdam, 1969–90.
Roma	*Roma Numismatics* (auction catalogues).
RPC	*Roman Provincial Coinage*, <https://rpc.ashmus.ox.ac.uk>.
Sardis VII 1	W. H. Buckler and D. M. Robinson, *Sardis, Vol. VII: Greek and Latin Inscriptions, Part 1*. Leiden, 1932.
SEG	*Supplementum Epigraphicum Graecum.*
SGO	R. Merkelbach and F. Stauber, *Steinepigramme aus dem griechischen Osten* (5 vols). Munich and Leipzig, 1998–2004.
SNG Cop.	*Sylloge Nummorum Graecorum.*

StV IV	R. M. Errington, *Die Staatsverträge des Altertums IV: Die Verträge der griechisch-römischen Welt von ca. 200 v. Chr. bis zum Beginn der Kaiserzeit*. Munich, 2020.
Syll.[1]	W. Dittenberger, *Sylloge Inscriptionum Graecarum* (2 vols). Leipzig, 1883.
Syll.[2]	W. Dittenberger, *Sylloge Inscriptionum Graecarum* (2nd edn, 3 vols). Leipzig, 1898–1901.
Syll.[3]	W. Dittenberger, *Sylloge Inscriptionum Graecarum* (3rd edn, 4 vols). Leipzig, 1915–24.
TAM	*Tituli Asiae Minoris.*
ThesCRA	*Thesaurus cultus et rituum antiquorum* (8 vols). Los Angeles, 2004–14.
Tit. Calymnii	M. Segre, 'Tituli Calymnii', *ASAtene* 22–3 (N.S. 6–7), 1944–5, 1–248.
Welles, *RC*	C. B. Welles, *Royal Correspondence in the Hellenistic Period: A Study in Greek Epigraphy*. Oxford, 1934.

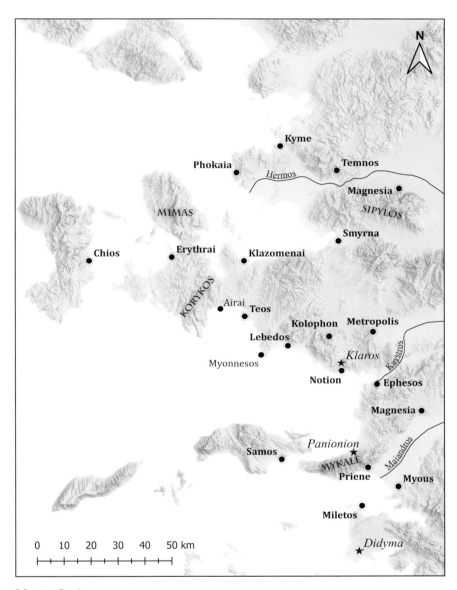

Map 1. Ionia

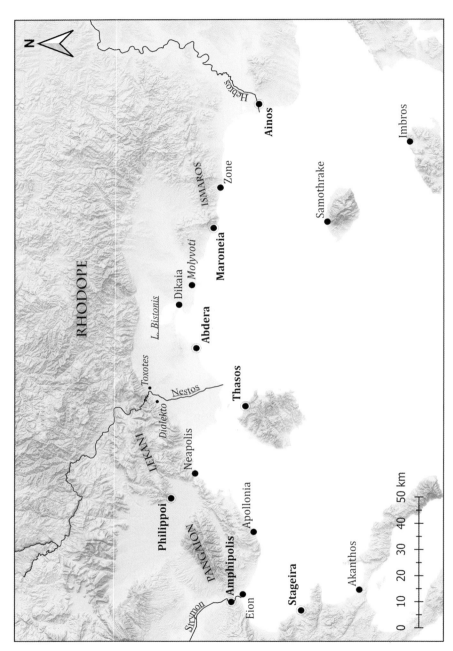

Map 2. Aegean Thrace

Prologue
The Fall of Abdera, 170 BC

In his account of events during the second year of the Third Macedonian War, Livy recounts the arrival in Rome, probably in late summer 170 BC, of a delegation from the free city of Abdera, on the Aegean coast of Thrace (43.4.8–13):

> Weeping before the senate-house, they protested that their city had been captured and plundered by Hortensius. They said that the reason for the destruction of the city was the following: that when he ordered them to furnish 100,000 *denarii* and 50,000 *modii* of wheat, they had requested a deferral while they sent ambassadors to the consul Hostilius and to Rome. But hardly had the ambassadors reached the consul when they heard that their city had been captured, the leading men beheaded, and the rest of the population enslaved. The senate judged the affair to be an outrage, and they passed the same decree about the Abderites as they had done concerning the Koroneans the previous year, and ordered the praetor Q. Maenius to pronounce it as an edict before the assembly. Two ambassadors, C. Sempronius Blaesus and Sex. Iulius Caesar, were sent to restore the Abderites to freedom, and these same men were instructed to announce to both the consul Hostilius and the praetor Hortensius that the senate had resolved that an unjust war had been waged against the Abderites, and that all those who had been enslaved were to be sought out and restored to freedom.

The treatment of Abdera by the praetor L. Hortensius (admiral of the Roman fleet in 170 BC) was not atypical of the behaviour of Roman commanders in Greece during the early years of the war against Perseus. The previous year, as Livy says, the campaign in Greece had been waged 'with excessive cruelty and greed by the consul Licinius and the praetor Lucretius' (43.4.5). The Boiotian city of Haliartos (which chose to resist the Romans) was razed to the ground; the neighbouring cities of Thisbe and Koronea, which surrendered without a fight, were treated with exemplary harshness, including the enslavement of at least part of the cities' populations (a decision subsequently reversed by the

Teos and Abdera: Two Cities in Peace and War. Mustafa Adak and Peter Thonemann, Oxford University Press.
© Mustafa Adak and Peter Thonemann, 2022. DOI: 10.1093/oso/9780192845429.003.0001

senate).[1] Autumn 170 BC also saw the arrival in Rome of a delegation from Chalkis in Euboia, Rome's chief naval base in the Aegean, complaining that both Lucretius and Hortensius had ruthlessly plundered their city, as well as kidnapping many free persons and selling them into slavery (Livy 43.7.5–8.10).

The siege and destruction of Abdera in summer 170 BC are also described— from a rather different perspective—in an isolated fragment from the lost thirtieth book of Diodoros (30.6):

> When Eumenes' troops were besieging the city of Abdera and despaired of capturing it by force, they sent in secret to a certain Python, a leading man among the Abderites, who was defending the key position with two hundred of his own slaves and freedmen. Having won him over with various promises, they were admitted within the walls thanks to his assistance, and gained control of the city. This Python, who had betrayed his city, although he received a moderate reward, continued to have the destruction of his city before his eyes, and lived out the rest of his life in despondency and regret.

Diodoros here attributes the sack of Abdera to Rome's ally Eumenes II of Pergamon, who had seized the opportunity of Rome's war with Perseus to try (not for the first time) to extend his domains westwards from the Hellespont into coastal Thrace. Late in the first year of the war, as Livy tells us, Eumenes' general Korrhagos had launched a campaign from the Hellespontine region against Perseus' ally King Kotys of Thrace; along with a Thracian dynast by the name of Autlesbis, Korrhagos had seized a region called 'Marene', probably somewhere east of the river Hebros near Eumenes' territories on the northern shore of the Propontis.[2] By summer 170 BC, to judge from Diodoros, Korrhagos had succeeded in pushing as far west as Abdera, where he seems to have met up with Hortensius' fleet. The presence of an Attalid army may well account for the apparent reluctance of the Abderites to welcome Hortensius with the enthusiasm he clearly expected: the Abderites may have feared (rightly or wrongly) that they were about to be handed over to Eumenes as a

---

[1] Livy 42.63.3–12 and *Per.* 43; Zonar. 9.22.6; Gruen 1984, I 297–8; Ferrary 1988, 175–7; Burton 2017, 134. For the extant *s.c. de Thisbensibus* (October 170 BC) and the fragmentary *s.c. de Coronaeis* (probably late autumn 171 BC), see Sherk 1969, 26–33, nos. 2–3 (translated in Sherk 1984, nos. 20–1), with Burton 2017, 207–9.

[2] Livy 42.67.4–5, with Gruen 1984, I 557–8; Hatzopoulos and Loukopoulou 1987, 65. Korrhagos is almost certainly identical to the Attalid *stratēgos* of the Hellespontine region honoured by an unknown city (Apollonia on the Rhyndakos?) in the early 180s BC: *I.Prusa ad Olympum* 1001, with Holleaux 1924, 48–50.

prize of war.³ Whether the primary responsibility for the sack of Abdera rests with Hortensius (as Livy states) or with Eumenes' forces (as Diodoros implies) is ultimately unknowable; from the Abderite perspective, it was the Roman senate who were in a position to reverse the decision, and hence it was to them that they appealed for redress in the late summer of 170 BC.

The senate, as we have seen, was appalled by Hortensius' actions. C. Sempronius Blaesus and Sex. Iulius Caesar were sent to Thrace to restore the Abderites to freedom, and to seek out and liberate those of the Abderites who had been sold into slavery.⁴ For Livy, the story essentially ends there: Abdera reappears in his narrative only in passing, in his account of the post-war settlement of 167 BC, when the status of Abdera and her neighbours Maroneia and Ainos as free cities was confirmed by the Roman senate.⁵ But for us, the sack of Abdera in summer 170 BC is only the beginning. Thanks to an extraordinary new epigraphic discovery from the city of Teos in western Asia Minor, the full story of the slow and painful recovery of Abdera in the years after the Roman sack can now be told for the first time.

---

³ The Abderites had good reason to fear Pergamene ambitions in coastal Thrace: in 185 BC, Eumenes II had requested the cities of Maroneia and Ainos as a reward for services rendered in the war against Antiochos (Livy 39.27: *praemia belli*), and Attalos II repeated the request in 167 BC (Polyb. 30.3.3; Livy 45.20.2): see Dmitriev 2010.

⁴ Bielman 1994, 305.

⁵ Livy 45.29.6. For the treaties of alliance struck by Rome with Maroneia and Ainos at this point, see *IThrakAig* E168 (English translation, Bagnall and Derow 2004, no. 49); a reference to Abdera is restored in line 7 by R. M. Errington, *StV* IV 664.

1

Abdera and Teos after the Third Macedonian War

The New Inscription (Document 1)

In summer 2017, the Turkish team currently excavating the site of Teos in Ionia uncovered a large fragment (Fragment **B**) of a tapered white marble *stēlē* in the *temenos* of the temple of Dionysos, a few metres from the south-west corner of the temple (Fig. 1.1).[1] The stone is broken above and below, but preserved almost intact at left and right; the inscribed text is largely in a good state of preservation. Ninety-three lines of Greek are preserved in whole or in part, and a *vacat* below the final surviving line (**B93**) shows that we have the original end of the text. As the excavators swiftly recognized, the new fragment belongs to an inscribed *stēlē* of the mid-second century BC, the upper part of which was discovered in the south-western part of the *temenos* of the Dionysos-temple in 1966, but not fully published until 1997 (Fig. 1.2).[2] The 'old' fragment (Fragment **A**) consists of the uppermost part of the *stēlē*, topped with an elaborate gabled pediment, with twenty-seven lines of text preserved in whole or in part. Thanks to the regular tapering of the *stēlē*, it is possible to estimate with reasonable accuracy how much text has been lost between the two surviving fragments of the inscription (*c.*14–16 lines); the entire original text must therefore have been around 135 lines long (Fig. 1.3). The original height of the *stēlē* cannot be determined with certainty, since we do not know how much uninscribed space there was at the base of the shaft, but our best guess is that the *stēlē* was originally around 2.5m–2.75m in height.[3] The rear

---

[1] A brief announcement of the discovery in Kadıoğlu et al. 2019, 60.

[2] Herrmann 1971, 76–7 (lines 1–3 only); Marek 1997 (whole text). The findspot of Fragment **A** is reported to have been 'not far' from the findspot of the fragments of the famous Antiochos III dossier (Herrmann 1971, 76), around 20m from the south-west corner of the Dionysos-temple (Herrmann 1965, 31–2).

[3] Total height of Fragments **A**+**B**: 1.03m+1.17m. On the basis of the tapering of the *stēlē*, the gap between the lowest part of Fragment **A** and the top of Fragment **B** can be estimated as *c.*0.195m (the gap is *c.*0.31m at the sides of the *stēlē*). The absolute minimum for the original height of the *stēlē* is therefore 2.395m, but the original bottom is certainly not preserved; the *stēlē* can hardly have been less than 2.50m tall, and *c.*2.75m is distinctly more likely.

Teos and Abdera: Two Cities in Peace and War. Mustafa Adak and Peter Thonemann, Oxford University Press.

Fig. 1.1. Document 1, Fragment **B**.
Photo: Teos excavation archive.

of the shaft is roughly worked. The sheer size and weight of the two main surviving fragments suggests that they are unlikely to have moved far from their original context, a hypothesis which received welcome confirmation in 2018 by the discovery in the south-western part of the *temenos* of the Dionysos-temple of a further small fragment from the upper left corner of the pediment (see Figs 1.2–1.3).

Fig. 1.2. Document 1, Fragment **A**.
Photo: Teos excavation archive.

The lettering of the inscription is broadly compatible with a date in the mid-second century BC (Figs 1.4–1.8). The mason evidently did not employ guide-lines in the upper part of the inscription, with the result that there are some unusually wide interlinear spaces early in the text (particularly between lines **A9** and **A10**), and a few lines wander up and down in alarming fashion (particularly lines **A13–15**). The height and breadth of the individual letters also fluctuate wildly in the opening lines of the text: the mason squeezed sixty-five letters into line **A5**, but a mere forty-three letters into line **A16**. The lettering becomes considerably more regular from around line **A20** onwards, and traces of interlinear guidelines can frequently be seen on Fragment **B**. Most letters have marked serifs at the apices. *Alpha* has a broken cross-bar, and the right diagonal (which often descends less sharply than the left) frequently does not reach the bottom of the letter-space. *Delta* is typically rather broad and flat, and the ends of the lower horizontal stroke usually project outwards to the left and right. The central horizontal of the *epsilon* is short, and the lower horizontal (which often extends further to the right than the upper horizontal)

Fig. 1.3.   Document 1, Fragments **A+B**.

Photo: Teos excavation archive.

Fig. 1.4.   Document 1, lines **A4–27**.

Photo: Teos excavation archive.

Fig. 1.5.   Document 1, lines **B1–32**.

Photo: Teos excavation archive.

Fig. 1.6.   Document 1, lines **B25–58**.
Photo: Teos excavation archive.

Fig. 1.7.   Document 1, lines **B42–75**.
Photo: Teos excavation archive.

Fig. 1.8. Document 1, lines **B62–93**.
Photo: Teos excavation archive.

sometimes curves slightly downwards. The form of the *mu* varies a great deal: the right and left strokes are sometimes vertical, sometimes quite broadly splayed. The lower right-hand angle of the *nu* is usually slightly elevated. The sizes of *omicron* and *theta* vary widely (sometimes full height, sometimes considerably smaller); *theta* has a short horizontal bar in the centre, detached from the outer loop. The two verticals of *pi* are usually of the same length, and the upper horizontal extends considerably outwards beyond the two verticals. The upper and lower strokes of *sigma* are usually horizontal, but sometimes splay outwards slightly. *Omega* is generally elevated, with a small upper loop and very broad horizontal strokes to right and left. The overall impression is somewhat scruffy, with the same letter often varying significantly in height and breadth. The closest Teian parallel for the lettering is the law establishing an educational foundation at Teos with an endowment left by Polythrous son of Onesimos, usually dated to the first half of the second century BC (Fig. 1.9); the two texts may have been inscribed by the same mason.[4]

---

[4] *Syll.*³ 578 (translation in Austin 2006, no. 139); photograph of fr. a, lines 1–34, in Ma 2007b, 224, fig. 26. The Polythrous inscription displays the same distinctive fluctuation in letter-sizes from line to

Fig. 1.9. Endowment of Polythrous, lower part (Sığacık castle). *Syll.*[3] 578, fr. b, lines 35–68.

Photo: Teos excavation archive.

Document 1: Honorific Decree of Abdera for the Teians

Two non-joining fragments of a tapering white marble *stēlē*, **A** (upper part: broken below) and **B** (lower part: broken above and below). At top, gabled pediment with palmette acroteria at the apices; in the tympanum, right-facing reclining griffin in deep relief; dentils in the bedmould of the cornice; at the top of the shaft, decorative entablature. Lines 1–3 within an elaborate ivy-wreath, carved in low relief within an inset circular panel.

Fragment **A**: H. 1.03m; W. 0.655m (gable); 0.53m (top of shaft); 0.55m (below); Th. 0.265–0.270m.

Fragment **B**: H. 1.17m; W. 0.58m (above); 0.602cm (middle; width at bottom unknown); Th. 0.28m (above), 0.295m (below).

Letters: 0.013m (lines 1–3); 0.008–0.009m (from line 4). Interlinear space: 0.004–0.005m.

Total height (reconstructed): +2.395m.

line, particularly in the upper part of the text; the cross-bar of the *alpha* in the Polythrous inscription is usually curved, sometimes straight, sometimes broken.

Fragment A: discovered near the temple of Dionysos at Teos in 1966. Ed. Herrmann 1971, 76–7 (lines 1–3 only); (*BE* 1971, 64 [*parasēmon*]); Marek 1997 (whole text); (*BE* 1998, 352 [Ph. Gauthier]; *SEG* 47, 1646; *SEG* 49, 1536; *AE* 2000, 1383 [with French translation]; *IThrakAig* E6). Cf. Eilers 2002, 118–19 (date); Loukopoulou and Parissaki 2004, 308–9 (context); Bloy 2012, 197–8 (context).

Fragment B: discovered near the temple of Dionysos at Teos in 2017 (Kadıoğlu et al. 2019, 60); unpublished.

Date: *c*.165 BC (historical context).

Fragment A

(*in wreath*)
ὁ δῆμος
ὁ Ἀβδηριτῶν
τὸν δῆμον.

ἐπειδὴ Τήϊοι, πατέρες ὄντες τῆς πόλεως ἡμῶν, τὴν προγονικὴν εὔνοιαν ο̣ὐ̣

5 λόγοις, ἔρ̣[γοις] δὲ τηρεῖν προαιρούμενοι, πειρῶνται πρὸς ὑπέρθεσιν ἀεὶ τῶν εἰς ἡ- ν.
μᾶς εὐεργεσιῶν ἁμιλλώμενοι τὴν ἑαυτῶν σπουδὴν καὶ φιλοτιμίαν ἀκατάπαυστον πρὸς τὸν δῆμον ἡμῶν διαφυλάξει̣ν, ἀθάνατον παρασκευά[ζον]-
τες, ὅσον ἐφ’ ἑαυτοῖς, τὴν ἐκ τῆς ὁμονοίας ἑκατέραις ταῖς πόλεσιν π[εριγε]νο-
μένην εὐδοξίαν, ὑπερβολὴν εὐεργεσιῶν οὐθενὶ βεβουλημένοι ἀ̣π̣[ολιπεῖ]ν

10 τῶν [ἐ]πὶ τὰ παραπλήσια δεδωκότων ἑαυτοὺς δήμων, ΩΙΓΑΝ[- - c.7 - -]
[- - c.7 - -]ΘΕΙ φιλανθρωπίας ἀπαραστόχαστον τὴν Τηΐων εἰ̣[ς] ἡμᾶς Ε[- - c.7 - -]
[- c.5 - τὴ]ν ἁ̣δρότητά (?) τε καὶ [- -?τοῖς ἀνθρώ]-
π̣οις καὶ κοινῆι ταῖς πόλεσι̣ν ἐ̣κ̣τ̣ε̣θεικότων αὐτῶν τὴν πρὸς τοὺς σ̣[υγ]-
γενεῖς ἑαυτῶν ἀπροφάσιστον σπουδήν· κ̣αὶ [.]ΑΛ[- - - c.11 - - -]

15 οἱ τῆς πόλεως καιροὶ τῆς παρ’ ἐκείνων ἐνεδεήθησαν [βοηθεί]-
α̣ς καὶ ἡ τύχη τοῖς τοῦ δήμου πράγμασιν ἀγνωμόνως [?διέ]-
κ̣ε̣ι̣τ̣ο̣ κ̣αὶ περίβολος μόνον τειχῶν ἡ πόλι̣ς ἀπ[- - c.7 - -, τῶν]
δὲ ἐνοικούντων οἱ μὲν εἰς τὸν πόλεμον ἀνήλωσαν [- c.6 -],
οἱ δὲ αἰχμάλωτοι γενόμενοι ΑΙΣΣΗΝΣΑΝΕΙΧ[- - c.10 - -]

20 [. .]Τ̣Α̣Η̣[. .]Α̣Ν ἀποβεβληκότες, τότε ἐπὶ ταῖς κο̣ι̣[ναῖς χρείαις? - c.4 -]
[- c.3 -]ΠΑΣΑΝ[…]ΣΥΝ δ̣ι̣ακούσαντες ΕΚΛΕΠ[- - c.17–19 - -]
[τ]ὴν ἀγορὰν καὶ [τοὺ]ς ναοὺς τῶν θεῶν κα̣ὶ̣[- - - c.17–19 - - -]
[- c.4 -]Α̣ προσκρίνοντες τοῖς ΕΙΣ[- - - - c.24–6 - - - -]
[- c.3 -]ΤΩΝΒΙΟ[- c.3 -] συνπενθεῖν κα̣ὶ̣[- - - - c.24–6 - - - -]

25   [- c.5 -]ΙΣΛΛ[. .]καὶ ἐν ταῖς δυστυ[χίαις? - - - - c.21–3 - - - -]
      [- - c.10–12 - -]ΑΙ τὴν πόλιν ἡμ[ῶν - - - - - c.26–8 - - - - -]
      [- - - c.17–19 - - -]ΣΤ[- - - - - - c.31–3 - - - - - -]

      (c.14–16 lines missing)

      Fragment B

      [- - - - - - - - - - - - - - c.40–2 - - - - - - - - - - - - - - -ἡ]μῖν ἐν τῶι
      [- - - - - - - - - - - c.33–5 - - - - - - - - - - - -]Ι[.]άμενοι τὴν χάριν ΠΕ- ν.
      [- - - - - - - - - - c.30–2 - - - - - - - -] παρ' αὐτοῖς καὶ κατορθώσαν-
      [τες - - - - - - - c.23–5 - - - - - -]ΕΝ ἄνευ λύτρων ἐποίησαν ΑΦΕ-
5   [- - - - - - - c.21–3 - - - - - - ἐφ'] ὅσον ἰσχύοσαν, πάλιν ἐπὶ τὴν ἀρχαί-
      [αν - - - - - c.15 - - - κατ]άστασιν, συλλέγοντες ἐκ παντὸς τόπου
      [- - - - - c.16 - - - - -]Σ καὶ ἀναπέμποντες ἐπὶ τὰς πατρώιους ἑ⟨σ⟩τίας
      [καὶ τὴν ἐξ ἀρχῆς] πολιτείαν· οὐ μόνον δὲ ἐπὶ τοσοῦτον ἡ φιλαγαθία τὴν
      [ἀπὸ τῆς συ]γγενείας εὔνοιαν προσφερομένη τὴν κοινὴν πρὸς τὸν
10   [δ]ῆμ[ον] ἡμῶν φιλοστοργίαν ἐπὶ τῆς κατ' ἰδίαν ἑκάστωι βοηθείας ν.
      τῶν ἐπταικότων ἀπεδείκνυτο, ἀλλ' ἐπειδή τινα μὲν ὁ χρόνος ν.
      καθείρηκει τῶν τειχῶν, ἃ δ' ἡ τοῦ πολέμου περίστασις διέφθαρκ[ε],
      παραπλησίως δὲ καὶ ναοὶ θεῶν ἐπανορθώσεως προσδεόμεν[οι]
      οὐθένα τῶν πολιτῶν εἰς τὴν ἐπισκευὴν εἶχον τὸν χρήσοντα
15   τοῖς πολίταις, διαλο⟨γ⟩ισάμενος ὁ τῶν Τηίων δῆμος διότι προγονι-
      κῶν θεῶν πρόνοιαν ποιήσεται καὶ κοινὴν πᾶσιν Ἀβδηρίταις βοήθει-
      αν ἔσται προσενηνεγμένος ἐπιδοὺς εἰς τὴν τῶν τειχῶν ἐπα-
      νόρθωσιν τὴν ἑαυτοῦ φιλαγαθίαν, προήκατο χρημάτων ἀναποδότων πλῆ-
      θος, ὅσο[ν] ἰσχύειν αὐτῶι τότε ἐδίδοσαν οἱ καιροί, δεικνὺς ὡς οὐ τῆ[ι]
20   πολυπληθίαι τῶν ὑπαρχόντων τὴν ἑτοιμότητα τῆς χορηγία[ς]
      ὑπομένειν, τῆι δὲ εὐνοίαι πρὸς πᾶν τὸ παρακαλούμενον ἀνέλλει - ν.
      πτον τὴν φιλο[τι]μίαν παρέχεται· τοῦ χρόνου δὲ προκόψαντος καὶ τῆ[ς]
      πόλεως ἡμῶν ἤδη πρὸς βελτίονα κατάστασιν ἐρχομένης διὰ τὸ κα[ὶ]
      πλῆθος ἤδη μέτριον ἠθροῖσθαι πολιτῶν, πολλῆς τε δαπάνης γινομέ-
25   νης εἰς τὴν τῆς χώρας ἐξεργασίαν καὶ διὰ τοῦτο θλιβομένων τοῖς
      βίοις τῶν ἀνθρώπων καὶ ἀπροσόδων γινομένων, πέμψαντος πά-
      λιν πρὸς Τηίους τοῦ δήμου καὶ παρακαλοῦντος εἰς βοῶν καταγορασ-
      μὸν ἑαυτῶι προχορηγῆσαι διάφορα, Τήιοι τῶι μὲν πλουτεῖν λειπόμε-
      νοι, τῶι δὲ εὐνοεῖν πάντας ἀνθρώπους ὑπεράγοντες, προέχρησαν ἄτο-
30   κα τάλαντα πέντε εἰς ἔτη πέντε, βουλόμενοι κατὰ μηθὲν ἐλλιπῆ τῶν
      συμφερόντων τὸν δῆμον ἡμῶν γενέσθαι· ἐπιβάντων δὲ καὶ Μαρωνιτῶν
      ἐπὶ τὴν πάτριον ἡμῶν χώραν οὐκ ἐπιβαλλόντως καὶ παραγενομένων ν.

εἰς ἀμφισβήτησιν ὑπὲρ αὐτῆς, ληφθέντος κατὰ δόγμα τῆς συνκλήτου
κριτοῦ τοῦ Ἐρυθραίων δήμου, αἰσθόμενοι Τήϊοι καταφρονουμένους ἡ-
35 μᾶς διὰ τὴν στενοχωρίαν τῶν βίων οὐ προήκαντο, ἀλλ᾿ἴδια νομίσαντες
ἑαυτῶν εἶναι τὰ διὰ τῶν ἰδίων προγόνων κρατηθέντα καὶ κατοικισθέν- ν.
τα, ἀξίως καὶ μεγαλομερῶς ἐπέδωκαν ἑαυτούς, πάσῃ προθυμίαι καὶ φιλαγα-
[θ]ίαι χρησάμενοι, πρὸς τὸν ἀγῶνα τὸν ὑπὲρ ταύτης τῆς χώρας, ἐπέλεξάν
τε γὰρ ἐξ ἑαυτῶν συνέδρους χάριν τῆς τῶν δικαίων ἐρεύνης τοὺς νοεῖν
40 τε καὶ προσκαρτερῆσαι δυναμένους ἀπερισπάστως τοῖς πρὸς τὸν ν.
ἐξετασμὸν παρατεθησομένοις δικαίοις, εἵλοντό τε καὶ τὸν ἐροῦντα ἐπὶ τῆς κρίσεως τὰ δίκαια καὶ πᾶσαν ὅλως τὴν ὑπὲρ τοῦ ἀγῶνος ἀ-
νελάβοσαν φροντίδα, διαλαβόντες δὲ καὶ μὴ ἱκανὴν ἑνὸς ἀνδρὸς ὑπάρχειν
δύναμιν διὰ τὸ μέγεθος τοῦ ἀγῶνος καὶ τὸ πλῆθος τῶν ἀποδείξεων, ἔ- ν.
45 πεμψαν εἰς Μίλητον τὸ ἐλλεῖπον δοκοῦν τῆι καθ᾿ ἑαυτοὺς σπουδῆι καὶ ν.
φιλοτιμίαι προσαναπληροῦντες ἀπὸ ξένης καὶ τὸν συναντιληψόμενον ν.
ἐν τῶι ἀγῶνι μετεπέμψαντο καὶ χάριν ἰδίαν αἰτησάμενοι καὶ μισθὸν πα- ν.
ρ᾿ ἑαυτῶν ὅσον ᾔτησεν ἐκτείναντες, καὶ τὸ συνέχον, τῆς τῶν θεῶν καὶ Τηΐων εὐνοίας ἅμα τοῖς δικαίοις προσγενομένης, κατώρθωσεν ὁ δῆμος ἡμῶν ἐν τῆι
50 πρὸς Μαρωνίτας κρίσει, ἀθάνατον ὑπόμνημα τῆς πρὸς τοὺς συνγενεῖς εὐνοίας διὰ τῶν ἔργων πᾶσιν ἐ⟨κ⟩θέντων ἀνθρώποις Τηΐων καὶ πρὸς ὑπερβο- ν.
[λὴ]ν εὐεργεσιῶν οὐθενὶ τόπον ἀπολειπόντων· ν. ἵνα οὖν καὶ ὁ παρ᾿ ἡμῶν δῆ-
[μο]ς ἀξίως ἐφ᾿ ὅσον ἰσχύει τιμῶν φαίνηται τοὺς ἑαυτὸν εὐεργετήσαν- ν.
[τας·] τ[ύχ]ηι ἀγαθῆ· δεδόχθαι τῆι βουλῆι καὶ τῶι δήμωι τῶι Ἀβδηριτῶν· ἐπῃ-
55 [νῆσθαι Τηΐου]ς ἐπὶ τῆι αἱρέσει καὶ εὐνοίαι ἧι ἔχοντες διατελοῦσι πρὸς τὸν
[δῆμον ἡμ]ῶν, ν. στῆσαι δὲ καὶ εἰκόνα χαλκῆν κολοσσικὴν τοῦ Δήμου τοῦ
[Τηΐων ἐπὶ τῆς] ἀγορᾶς ἐν τῶι ἐπιφανεστάτωι τόπωι, τῆι μὲν δεξιᾶι σπέν-
[δοντα κανθάρω]ι, τῆι δὲ ἀριστερᾶι ἀπηρεισμένον ἐπὶ τὴν στήλην ἐν ἧι γε-
[γράψεται τόδ]ε τὸ ψήφισμα, ἔστω δὲ καὶ κιόνιον παρεστηκὸς ἐκ τῶν εὐωνύ-
60 [μων, ἐφ᾿ οὗ ἐπ]έστω Νίκη στεφανοῦσα τὸν Τηΐων Δῆμον κισσοῦ στε-
[φάνωι· κατὰ πρ]όσωπον δὲ τῆς εἰκόνος βωμὸς κατασταθήτω ἐφ᾿ οὗ θυέ-
[τω ὁ γυμνασίαρ]χος ἐν τῶι Ἀνθεστηριῶνι μηνὶ τῆι τρεισκαιδεκάτηι ἱερεῖον ν.
[καὶ ἀγῶνα τιθ]έτω, κατευχομένου τοῦ ἱεροκήρυκος διδόναι τὰ ἀγαθὰ τοὺς
[θεοὺς Τηΐοις καὶ] Ἀβδηρίταις, καλείσθω δὲ ὁ δῆμος ὁ Τηΐων εἰς προεδρίαν, συγ-
65 [τελούντων ἡμῶν λ]αμπάδα τῶν παίδων καὶ ἀνδρῶν, καὶ τοῖς νικήσασιν διαμερίζε-
[σθω τὰ κρέα τοῦ ἱερ]είου, ἵνα μὴ μόνον παρὰ τοῖς ἐν ἡλικίαι τῶν πολιτῶν ὑπάρχου-
[σιν, ἀλλὰ καὶ παρὰ τ]οῖς νεωτέροις ἐπίσημος ἡ τιμὴ τοῦ Τηΐων ὑπάρχῃ δήμου
[καὶ προτρέπωνται] πάντες ἀπὸ τῆς πρώτης nac. 6 ἡλικίας τῆι πρὸς τοὺς εὐ-
[εργέτας εὐχαριστίαι· τὸ] δὲ ἐσόμενον{ον} ἀνάλωμα εἰς τὴν θυσίαν καὶ τὸν ἀγῶνα ἀπο-
70 [γραψάμενος ὁ γυμνα]σίαρχος λαβέτω ἀπὸ τῆς τραπέζης, ἐπιμελὲς δὲ ποι- ν.
[ησάτω τὸ λοιπὸν ὁ ἀ]εὶ γυμνασίαρχος· καὶ ἵνα πρὸ τοῦ ἀγῶνος ἀναγορεύῃ ὁ ἱερο- ν.

[κῆρυξ διότι στεφανοῖ] ὁ δῆμος τὸν Τηΐων δῆμον χρυσῶι στεφάνωι καὶ εἰκόνι χαλκῇ
[ἀρετῆς ἕνεκεν καὶ ε]ὐνοίας τῆς εἰς ἑαυτόν· ἵνα δὲ καὶ ἐν Τέῳ πᾶσα ἡλικία πα-
[ρακολουθῆι ταῖς τιμαῖ]ς, οἱ νομοφύλακες ἀεὶ κατ᾽ ἐνιαυτὸν αἱρείσθωσαν ἄνδρας
75 [(number) ἐμ μηνὶ Ἀπα]τουριῶνι τοὺς ἀποδημήσοντας εἰς Τέω καὶ θύσοντας
[ὑπὲρ τοῦ δήμου ἡμῶν βο]ῦν ἐμ μηνὶ Λευκαθεῶνι χαριστήρια τῶι Τηΐων Δήμωι,
[τὰ δὲ κρέα οἱ πρεσβεύσο]ντες τοῖς τε νέοις καὶ παισὶν μερισάτωσαν τοῖς νι-
[κήσασιν (?) τὰ Λευκάθεα, εἰς δὲ τὴ]ν τιμὴν τοῦ βοὸς διάφορον χορη⟨γη⟩σάτωσαν οἱ
νομοφύ-
[λακες ἀπὸ τῆς τραπέζης· δια]πέμψαι δὲ Τηΐοις πυρῶν μεδίμνους χιλίους ν.
80 [καὶ τόπον αἰτησάσθων οἱ πεμ]φθέντες ἄνδρες ἐν τῶι ἱερῶι τοῦ Διονύσου ἢ
[(?) ἐν τῆι ἀγορᾶι ἐν ὧι στήσουσι] στήλην λευκοῦ λίθου ἐν ἧι ἀναγεγράφθω τόδ[ε]
[τὸ ψήφισμα· τὸ δὲ γενόμενον] ἀνάλωμα εἰς τὴν κατασκευὴν τῆς στή[λης]
[καὶ τὴν ἀναγραφὴν τοῦ ψηφίσμα]τος τὸ συνκριθὲν χορηγείτωσαν οἱ νομ[οφύλα]-
[κες (?) ἀπὸ τῶν εἰς τὰς πρεσβείας· ἵνα δὲ] καὶ Τήϊοι παρακολουθῶσιν τοῖς ὑφ᾽ ἡμ[ῶν ἐψη]-
85 [φισμένοις, ἀποστειλάτωσαν οἱ με]τὰ ἱερέα Σχησίστρατον νομοφ[ύλακες]
[τὸ ἀντίγραφον τοῦ ψηφίσματος πρὸ]ς τὸν Τηΐων δῆμον· τὴν δὲ ἐπιμ[έλειαν]
[(e.g.) τῆς τε ἀναστάσεως τῆς εἰκόνος] καὶ τῶν ἄλ[λ]ων τῶν δηλου[μένων (e.g.) ἐν τῶι]
[ψηφίσματι - - - c.12–14 - - - ποιησάσθ]ωσαν οἱ αὐτοὶ νομοφ[ύλακες - - c.7 - -]
[- - c.9–11 - - - τὸ δὲ ψήφισμα τόδε εἶναι] εἰς εὐχαριστίαν τ[οῦ δήμου· εἱρέθησαν]
90 [πρεσβευταὶ - - - - - - c.20–2 - - - - - - -ὁ] πρεσβύτερος, Ἀθ[ηνα- - - - c.11–13 - - - -]
[- - - - - - - - - - - - c.32–4 - - - - - - - - - - -]νος ὀκτωκαιδ[εκάτηι - - - - - c.11–13 - - - - -]
[- - - - - - - - c.26–8 - - - - - - - - ὁ πρεσβύτ]ερος, Ἀθην[α- - - - - - - -c.19–21 - - - - - - - -]
[- - - - - - - - - - - - c.33–5 - - - - - - - - - - - - -]μηνὸς Ε[- - - - - - - - - c.21–3 - - - - - - - - -]

vacat

Critical Notes

A4–5 εὔνοιαν | ἐ[ν] λόγοις ἔρ[γοις] τε M(arek 1997). **A5** π[ειρῶ]νται M. **A7**
διαφυλάσ[σειν] M. **A7–8** παρα[σκευάζον]|τες M. **A8–9** π[εριγενο]|μένην
εὐδοξ[ίαν] M.; π[εριγιγνο]|μένην Herrmann (SEG). **A9** *ΕΥΔΟΞΙ*ᴬ*Ν lapis.*;
οὐθὲν βεβουλημένοι κα[ταλείπ]ειν M.; *οὐθενὶ lapis.* **A11** [- -]ει φιλανθρωπίας
[...6–8...]*ΣΤΟΝ* τῶν Τηΐων [- -] M. **A12** [- -]οτητα τε καὶ [- -] M. **A13**
[πεποιη]κότων M. **A14** σπουδὴν καὶ φιλοτιμίαν [- -] M. **A16** [- -] ἡ
τύχη...ἀγνώμ[ων - -] M. **A17** [- -]περίβολος μόνον τειχῶν ἐπολ[- -] M. **A17–18**
[τ[ῶ]ν ἐνοικούντων M. **A18** ἀναλώσ[αντες - -] M.; *ΑΝ*ᴴ*ΛΩΣΑΝ lapis.* **A19**
γενόμενοι ἀ[- -] M. **A20** ἐλευθερίαν ἀποβεβληκότες το[- -] M. **A21** [- -]
διακούσαντες [- -] M. **A22** τὴν ἀγορὰν καὶ τοὺς ναοὺς τῶν θεῶν [- -] M. **A23**
[- -] προσκρίνοντες τοῖς [- -] M. **A24** [- -]*ΘΕΙΝ ΚΑΙ*[- -] M. **A25** [- -]εν τοῖς

λοιποῖς [- -] M. **A26** [- -]την πολ[- -] M. **B7** *ΕΤΙΑΣ* lapis. **B8** *ΦΙΛΑΓΑΘ¹Α* lapis. **B15** *ΔΙΑΛΟΠΙΣΑΜΕΝΟΣ* lapis. **B51** *ΕΧΘΕΝΤΩΝ* lapis. **B69** *ΕΣΟΜΕΝΟΝΟΝ* lapis. **B78** *ΧΟΡΗΣΑΤΩΣΑΝ* lapis.

Translation

A 'The *dēmos* of the Abderites (honours) the *dēmos* (of the Teians). Since the Teians, being the fathers of our city, having resolved to maintain their ancestral goodwill not in (5) words but in deeds, attempt to preserve unceasing their eagerness and generosity towards our *dēmos* by striving always to add to their benefactions towards us, thereby rendering eternal, as far as is in their power, the glory that has accrued to both cities through their like-mindedness, and wishing to leave no opportunity for exceeding them in benefactions to any of (10) those *dēmoi* that have dedicated themselves to comparable ends, [(?) by which all might recognize, by the (?) magnit]ude of their generosity, the inestimable [(?) goodwill] of the Teians towards us, [...] strength (?) and [...for m]en and in common for the cities, with them having exhibited eagerness without excuses towards their kinsmen; and [...e.g. when] (15) the city's circumstances called for [assistance] from them, and fortune was cruelly [disposed] to the affairs of the *dēmos*, and the city [was left as] a mere circuit of walls, and of the inhabitants, some in the war expended [their lives?], and others, having become captives, [e.g. were enslaved...] (20) having lost [...]; then, in the face of this common [need,...] hearing [...] the agora and the temples of the gods [...] judging [...] to join in grieving [...] (25) in our misfortunes [...] our city [...]' (*c*.14–16 lines missing)

B '...us in the...gratitude/favour...among them, and succeeding...without ransom, they made...(5)...as far as they were able, back to their former... [con]dition, collecting from every place...and sending them back to their ancestral hearths [and their former] state of citizenship. Yet not only within these limits did their excellence of character, bringing to bear the goodwill that comes from kinship, show collective (10) affection for our *dēmos* in their individual assistance to each of those who were in distress, but since the passage of time had brought down some parts of the walls, and other parts the crisis of war had destroyed; and likewise also the temples of the gods, though in need of reconstruction, had found none of the citizens who would lend the citizens (what was needed) for their repair—(15) the Teian *dēmos*, reckoning both that they would have care for their ancestral gods and that they would have provided collective assistance to all the Abderites by committing their excellence of character towards the reconstruction of the walls, handed over a large sum of money which did not need to be repaid, as much as the present circumstances then permitted them to be able to do, showing how (20) they provide their generosity unfailingly, not through an abundance of property to sustain a ready supply of income (?), but rather through goodwill in the face of every request. When time had passed, and our city was now returning to a better condition because of the fact that a moderately large body of citizens had now been gathered together, but great expense (25) was being incurred for the cultivation of the territory, and for this reason the people were being oppressed in their livelihoods and had no revenues, the *dēmos* sent once again to the Teians and called on them to advance us a sum of money for the purchase of oxen, the Teians, although lacking in wealth, but outstripping all other men in goodwill, advanced us (30) five talents without interest over five years, wishing that in no respect our *dēmos* should be lacking in what is beneficial. And when the Maroneitai encroached upon our ancestral territory, although it did not pertain to them, and entered into a dispute over it, and when the *dēmos* of Erythrai was appointed as judge by decision of the senate, the Teians, perceiving that we were being treated (35) contemptuously because of the poverty of our livelihoods, did not abandon us, but considering as their own possessions the lands conquered and settled by their own ancestors, they dedicated themselves worthily and magnificently to the lawsuit over this stretch of land, employing all enthusiasm and excellence of character; for also they selected from among themselves commissioners for the sake of seeking out the legal claims, those able both to understand and (40) to persist without distraction in the face of the legal claims that would be put forward in the enquiry, and they also appointed a person who would present their claims at the hearing, and they completely took on in all respects the care of the lawsuit; and when they perceived that the ability of a single man was insufficient given the scale of the lawsuit and the volume of depositions, they sent (45) to Miletos, to supplement from a foreign city what seemed to be lacking to their own eagerness and ambition, and requested someone who would join in taking on the lawsuit, requesting a private favour (from Miletos) and providing whatever fee he demanded from their own resources—and most importantly, with the goodwill both of the gods and the Teians being added to our legal claims, our *dēmos* was successful against the Maroneitai (50) in the judgement, with the Teians having set up through their actions an eternal memorial for all men of their goodwill towards their kin, and leaving space for no one else to surpass them in benefactions. And therefore, in order that it should be clear that our *dēmos* honours worthily—insofar as it is able—those who confer benefactions upon it, with good fortune, be it resolved by the *boulē* and *dēmos* of the Abderites, to (55) praise the Teians for the disposition and goodwill which they continue to hold towards our *dēmos*, and to erect a colossal bronze statue of the *Dēmos* of the [Teians], on the agora in the most prominent spot, pouring a libation [with a kantharos] with the right hand, and with the left hand/arm leaning on the *stēlē* on which this decree shall be inscribed; and let there be a small column standing by on the left-hand side, (60) [on which] let there be placed a Nike crowning the *Dēmos* of the Teians with an ivy-wreath; and [in fr]ont of the statue let an altar be erected, on which let the [gymnasiar]ch sacrifice a victim on the thirteenth day of the month Anthesterion and [hold a contest], with the sacred herald praying that the [gods] should give good things to the [Teians and] Abderites, and let the *dēmos* of the Teians be called to a front seat when [we] (65) hold the torch-race of boys and adults, and let the [meat of the vic]tim be distributed to the victors, in order that not only among those of the citizens who have reached adulthood, [but that also among] the younger ones the honour conferred on the *dēmos* of the Teians might be conspicuous, [and that] all from the earliest age [should be inspired to gratitude] towards their benefactors; and let the gymnasiarch in[voice] the future expenses for the sacrifice and the contest (70) and draw them from the public bank, and let each gymnasiarch in office [in future] have care for this. And in order that before the contest the sacred herald might announce that the *dēmos* crowns the Teian *dēmos* with a gold crown and a bronze statue for the sake of its virtue and goodwill towards them, and in order that also in Teos people of every age [might learn of these honours], let the *nomophylakes* in office each year choose (75) [(number)] men [in the month] Apatourion who will travel to Teos and sacrifice [on behalf of our *dēmos* a b]ull in the month Leukatheon as a thank-offering to the *Dēmos* of the Teians, [and let the ambassad]ors distribute [the meat] to the young men and boys who are victorious [(?) at the Leukathea], and let the *nomophylakes* provide the money for the price of the bull [from the public bank]; and send to the Teians 1,000 *medimnoi* of wheat. (80) And let the men who have been sent [request a spot] in the sanctuary of Dionysos or [(?) in the agora in which they can set up] a *stēlē* of white marble, on which let this [decree] be inscribed, and let the *nomophylakes* provide the agreed expenditure [incurred] for the making of the *stēlē* [and the inscription of the dec]ree [from the funds reserved for embassies. And so that] the Teians too might learn of the [things decreed] by us, (85) let the *nomophylakes* in office in the year after the priesthood of Schesistratos [send a copy of the decree t]o the Teian *dēmos*. And let the same *nomophylakes* have respon[sibility for (e.g.) the erection of the statue] and the other things laid out [(e.g) in the decree... and let this decree be for the purpose of (showing)] the gratitude of [the *dēmos*. The following ambassadors (90) were chosen: (name) son of (name) the] elder; Ath[ena- son of (name)...] on the eighteenth (of the month) [- - ; (name) son of (name) the el]der, Athen[a- son of (name)...] of the month....'

Commentary

The right-facing griffin in the pediment is the characteristic *parasēmon* or civic blazon of both Teos and Abdera: the griffin appears on the coinage of both Teos and Abdera, and is also present on amphora-stamps, tiles, and seals at Abdera (sometimes facing right, sometimes left).[5] Here the primary signification of the griffin is surely Teos, the community honoured in the decree. The placement of a civic *parasēmon* in the pediment is characteristic of decrees of the second century BC: near-contemporary examples are found at Olympia (proxeny decree for a Tenedian, late III/early II BC), Panamara (decree for a Rhodian *epistatēs*, early II BC), Athens (decree for a taxiarch, 163/2 BC), and perhaps Kyme (date uncertain).[6]

The surface of Fragment **A** is extremely worn. Peter Herrmann despaired of being able to make anything of the text aside from the 'heading' in the wreath, and in his 1997 *editio princeps* Christian Marek emphasized the extreme difficulty of deciphering the inscription.[7] Only after extensive study of the stone in good light, with the help of several excellent photographs, have we been able to improve on Marek's readings in a handful of places, and many uncertainties remain. Fig. 1.4 above shows the condition of the stone; the drawing in Fig. 1.10 indicates what we believe we have been able to decipher with reasonable confidence. As will be clear from both the photograph and the drawing, the size and spacing of the lettering are distinctly uneven. As noted in the introduction to this chapter, the stonemason left a larger than usual interlinear space between lines **A9** and **A10**, and the latter parts of lines **A15–17** are unusually widely spaced. The reader ought therefore not to place

---

[5] Herrmann 1971, 76–7 and n. 7; Killen 2017, 191–2 (Abdera), 248–9 (Teos); also 149 n. 1613 (shared *parasēmon* indicating colony–mother-city link).
[6] Olympia/Tenedos: Minon 2007, no. 34; Killen 2017, 220 Tene k1. Panamara/Rhodes: *I.Strat.* 9; Killen 2017, 261 Rho Ik1. Athens: *Agora* XVI 295; Killen 2017, 181 Athe IXk1. Kyme: Killen 2017, 221 Kyme Ik1.
[7] Herrmann 1971, 76–7; Marek 1997, 169.

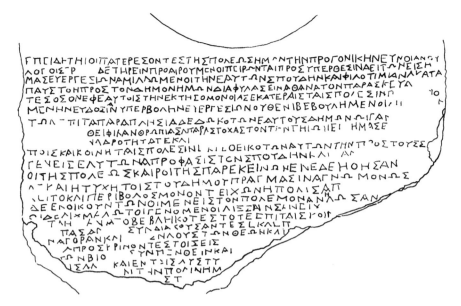

Fig. 1.10. Document 1, lines **A4–27**.
Drawing: Peter Thonemann.

too much weight on our estimates of the number of letters missing in the various lacunae, particularly at line-ends.

A1–3

ὁ δῆμος | ὁ Ἀβδηριτῶν | τὸν δῆμον.

'The *dēmos* of the Abderites (honours) the *dēmos* (of the Teians).'

These words cannot have stood at the head of the Abderite copy of the decree (**B59–60**): a decree erected at Abdera could hardly have failed to specify the identity of the *dēmos* being honoured (the Teians). The elaborate wreath of ivy-leaves and flowers around **A1–3** (Fig. 1.11; cf. **B60–1**) is closely paralleled on the reverse of a near-contemporary tetradrachm struck at Teos in the name of the Artists of Dionysos (Fig. 1.12): in both instances, the ends of the ivy-stalks at the rear of the wreath are simply overlaid on top of one another, not tied in a knot; the sides of the wreath bear symmetrical patterns of

Fig. 1.11. **Document 1**, lines **A1–3**, in ivy-wreath.

Photo: Teos excavation archive.

Fig. 1.12. Tetradrachm in the name of the Dionysiac Artists (*c*.170–145 BC). 16.87g.

Numismatica Ars Classica NAC AG, Auction 116, Lot 182.

ivy-leaves; and two ivy-flowers are set at the very front of the wreath, so as to sit above the brow of the wearer.[8]

---

[8] NAC Auction 116 (01/10/19), Lot 182; Lorber and Hoover 2003, dating the issue *c*.155–145 BC; Psoma 2007, 239, favours an earlier date, *c*.170–160 BC. A very similar ivy-wreath (with flowers only at the very front of the head, over the brow) is worn by Dionysos on the obverse of the Artists of Dionysos

A4–5

ἐπειδὴ Τήϊοι, πατέρες ὄντες τῆς πόλεως ἡμῶν, τὴν προγονικὴν εὔνοιαν οὐ
5 λόγοις, ἔρ[γοις] δὲ τηρεῖν προαιρούμενοι,…

'Since the Teians, being the fathers of our city, having resolved to maintain their ancestral goodwill not in words but in deeds,…'

Like the near-contemporary Abderite decree for Amymon and Megathymos (**Document 6** below, c.166 BC) the decree has no prescript, but launches straight in to the considerations.[9] The general shape of the opening clause is standard for Hellenistic decrees affirming a kinship or colonial relation between two cities: compare e.g. *Milet* I 3, 141 (Miletos and Kios, c.228 BC), lines 6–7, ἐπειδὴ Κιανοὶ ἄποικοι ὄντες τῆς πόλεως; *SEG* 23, 489 (*SEG* 41, 545: Paros and Pharos, shortly after 219 BC), lines A.29–30, ἐπει[δὴ δὲ Φάριοι ἄποικοι ὄντες] τῆς ἡμετέρας πόλεως; *IG* XII 4, 1, 222 (decree of Kamarina recognizing Koan *asylia*, 242 BC), lines 9–10, ἐπειδὴ οἱ Κῶιοι συνοικισταὶ ἐγένοντο τᾶς πόλιος ἁμῶν. The description of the Teians as 'fathers of our city' (πατέρες ὄντες τῆς πόλεως ἡμῶν) is not quite without parallel in epigraphic texts (*pace* Marek 1997, 171). As Philippe Gauthier already noted (*BE* 1998, 352), the same term is used in a decree of Chersonesos (reign of Antoninus Pius) honouring the people of Herakleia Pontike, the mother-city of Chersonesos, for sending an embassy to the emperor on their behalf: the Herakleotai are described as τοὶ εὐσεβέστατοι πατέρες, 'our most pious fathers'.[10] Nonetheless, the use of a kinship term to describe the relationship between colony and mother-city is striking and unusual: the normal word to

---

tetradrachm (Fig. 1.12), as also on the Dionysos-portrait on the obverse of the new mid-second-century tetradrachm in the name of the Teians (*Roma* XVII [18/03/19], Lot 451; see Chapter 6 below).

[9] The slightly later Abderite honorific decrees for Philon of Akanthos, Marcus Vallius M.f., C. Apustius M.f., and P. Apustius C.f. (*IThrakAig* E7–E10) all begin with the single word νομοφυλάκων; but this probably indicates that the decrees were recorded in the archive of the *nomophylakes*, rather than being proposed by them (Boffo 2012, 25–6). On the functions of the *nomophylakes* at Abdera, see below, on B73–6.

[10] *IOSPE*³ III 25 (previously *IOSPE* I² 362), lines 1.3–4. Later in the same decree (line 1.20) Herakleia is described as [τὰν πρό]γονον ἁ[μῶν μητρόπο]λιν, 'our ancestral mother-city'. In another decree of the same period, *IOSPE*³ III 24 (previously *IOSPE* I² 357), a citizen of Herakleia is honoured for showing goodwill towards the city of Chersonesos 'such as good fathers show towards loving sons' (οἷα πατέρων ἀγαθῶν πρὸς υἱοὺς φιλοστόργους, line 6), and in the decree of Lampsakos for their ambassador Hegesias (*I.Lampsakos* 4: 196 BC), the Massaliots are described as their 'brothers' (Μασσαλιήτας εἶναι ἡμῖν ἀδελφ[ούς], line 26), on the grounds that both cities were founded by Phokaia. See Robert 1937, 247–51; and the Epilogue below.

use in this context would be οἰκισταί or perhaps κτίσται.[11] No doubt the Abderites wished to emphasize both the intimacy of the relationship and (in the context of the assistance provided by the Teians) the subordinate position of Abdera vis-à-vis her mother-city: see further the Epilouge below. The determination to preserve an ancestral relationship of mutual goodwill (προγονικὴ εὔνοια) is a standard trope of Hellenistic interstate diplomacy;[12] for the general shape of the phrase here, see for example *I.Priene*² 114 (Erythrai and Priene, early II BC), line 19, προαιρούμενος διαφυλάσσειν τὴν πρὸς τὸ πλῆθος ἡμῶν εὔνοιαν.

The notion of showing goodwill 'not in words but in deeds' (οὐ λόγοις, ἔρ[γοις] δέ; misread by Marek as ἐ[ν] λόγοις ἔρ[γοις] τε) is a fairly common sentiment, but the phraseology here is idiosyncratic; compare *IG* XII 2, 45 (Mytilene), ἔργωι δὲ πλέον ἢ λόγωι; A. Bernand 1992, no. 41 (Aphroditopolis, 57 BC), [τὴν σπουδὴ]ν μὴ διὰ λόγων δεδειχὼς ἀ[λλὰ δι᾽ ἔργων]. For this strongly adversative use of δέ (οὐ x; y δέ), compare **B19–21**, οὐ τῆι[ι] πολυπληθίαι…τῆι δὲ εὐνοίαι.[13] The compounds συντηρεῖν and διατηρεῖν are more common than the simple τηρεῖν in this context, but for the uncompounded verb see e.g. *IG* V 2, 265 (Mantineia, I BC), lines 3–4, καὶ αὐτὰ τειρεῖν ἐξελομένα τὰν τῶν προγόνων ἀρετάν; Rigsby 1996, no. 155 (Eranna and Teos), lines 22–4, 31–2, ἁ πόλις τῶν Ἐρωνίων καὶ πρότερον τετήρηκεν τὰν πρὸς Τηίους φιλίαν καὶ εὔνοιαν…καὶ τηρήσει τὴν φιλίαν καὶ ἐπὶ πλεῖον αὐξήσει.[14]

A5–7

5   πειρῶνται πρὸς ὑπέρθεσιν ἀεὶ τῶν εἰς ἡ- ν.
μᾶς εὐεργεσιῶν ἁμιλλώμενοι τὴν ἑαυτῶν σπουδὴν καὶ φιλοτιμίαν ἀκατάπαυστον πρὸς τὸν δῆμον ἡμῶν διαφυλάξειν,…

---

[11] Curty 1995, 220–3.

[12] e.g. *IG* II³ 1, 870 (Athens and Spartokos III, 285/4 BC), lines 27–9, [προαιρούμεν]ος διαφυλάττειν τὴν [εὔνοιαν τὴν εἰς τὸν δῆμ]ον τὴν παραδεδομένην [αὐτῶι παρὰ τῶν προγόνω]ν; a similarly elaborate phraseology (the details of which cannot restored with confidence) in the first Teian decree for Antiochos III and Laodike (*SEG* 41, 1003, I: *c*.203 BC), lines 4–6, κ[αὶ δια]φ[υ]λάσσων…[τὴ]ν ἑαυτῶι διὰ προ[γόνω]ν ὑπάρχουσα[ν εὔ]νοιαν κα[ὶ - -]τασθαι προαιρούμενος πολαπλασ[ι .]ν.

[13] Similarly e.g. Osborne and Rhodes 2017, no. 141 (Athens, *c*.435 BC), lines 32–3, ἐκέ[ν]ο[ις] δὲ μὲ ἐπιτάττοντας, κελεύοντας δὲ ἀπάρχεσθαι; Denniston 1954, 166–7.

[14] The phrase [ἐπὶ τῶι τηρεῖν τὴν πατρικὴν] ἀρετήν is plausibly restored in the Abderite decree for C. Apustius M.f. (*IThrakAig* E9, line 18) by Holleaux 1914, 66; Wilhelm 1921a, 26.

'(They) attempt to preserve unceasing their eagerness and generosity towards our *dēmos* by striving always to add to their benefactions towards us,...'

The idea of a contest (ἅμιλλα) to outdo one's predecessors in benefactions is a standard feature of the hortative clauses of Hellenistic honorific inscriptions (e.g. *I.Perge* 11, ἵνα δὲ καὶ οἱ ἄλλοι... [π]ειρῶνται ἁμιλλᾶσθαι πρὸς φιλοδο[ξί]αν), here used of the Teians' contest with their own ancestors; for the idea of striving to 'surpass/exceed' (ὑπερτίθεσθαι) one's own previous good deeds, see e.g. *I.Mylasa* 105, lines 13–14, προαιρούμενος μὴ μόνον ἐν τοῖς προειρημένοις φιλοδοξ[εῖν, ἀλλὰ καὶ] ὑπερτίθεσθαι τὰς πρότερον εὐεργεσίας.[15] The term ἀκατάπαυστος, 'unceasing, incessant' (A6–7), seems not otherwise to appear in Hellenistic epigraphy, but the word is occasionally found in contemporary historiography (Polyb. 4.17.4, 15.25.9; Diod. Sic. 11.67.7). The author of this text had a particular fondness for rare *alpha*-privative adjectives: cf. ἀπαραστόχαστον (**A11**), ἀπροφάσιστον (**A14**), ἀναποδότων (**B18**), ἀνέλλειπτον (**B21–2**), ἀπροσόδων (**B26**), ἀπερισπάστως (**B40**).[16] In **A7**, Marek read διαφυλάσ[σειν]; examination of the stone shows that the true reading must be the future infinitive διαφυλάξειν.[17] The future infinitive is also found in a very similar context in the decree for Polemaios from Klaros (*SEG* 39, 1243), lines V.16–18, [ἐπαγγέλλεται] πειρᾶσθαι καθ' ὑπέρθεσιν ἀνέλλιπτον παρέξεσθαι τὴν ἑαυτοῦ σπουδήν, 'he promises to attempt to provide his eagerness without fail, in a manner not to be surpassed'.

A7–10

ἀθάνατον παρασκευά[ζον]-
τες, ὅσον ἐφ' ἑαυτοῖς, τὴν ἐκ τῆς ὁμονοίας ἑκατέραις ταῖς πόλεσιν π[εριγε]νο-
μένην εὐδοξίαν, ὑπερβολὴν εὐεργεσιῶν οὐθενὶ βεβουλημένοι ἀπ[ολιπεῖ]ν
10   τῶν [ἐ]πὶ τὰ παραπλήσια δεδωκότων ἑαυτοὺς δήμων,...

'Thereby rendering eternal, as far as is in their power, the glory that has accrued to both cities through their like-mindedness, and wishing to leave no opportunity for exceeding them in benefactions to any of those *dēmoi* that have dedicated themselves to comparable ends,...'

---

[15] For the verb ἁμιλλᾶσθαι, see Robert, *OMS* II, 1063; for ὑπερτίθεσθαι, Wilhelm 1915, 59; Wilhelm 1932, 38; Robert and Robert 1989, 56.
[16] Polybios shows the same tendency: Foucault 1972, 28.
[17] Again, a similar tendency in Polybios: Foucault 1972, 159.

The conception of the glory (εὐδοξία, **A9**)[18] which derives to both cities through their like-mindedness (ὁμόνοια, **A8**) has no close parallels in Hellenistic epigraphy, although pairs of cities often prided themselves on their long-term preservation of mutual *homonoia*: see e.g. *IG* VII, 207 (Aigosthena and Siphai, late III BC), lines 8–11, ὅπως ὢν φανερὸν ἴει ὅτι τὰν ὁμόνοιαν διαφυλάττι τὰν ἐκ τῶν προγόνων παρδοθεῖσαν ἁ πόλις Ἡγοσθενιτάων πὸτ τὰν πόλιν Σιφείων; *TAM* II, 555 (Curty 1995, no. 78: Roman imperial period), [Ξ]ανθίων ἡ πόλις... Τλωέων τὸν δῆμον τὸν συνγενῆ ἐπὶ τῇ διηνεκεῖ ὁμονοίᾳ.[19] At the end of line **A7**, we could restore either παρασκευά[ζον]|τες or παρασκευά[σαν]|τες, and in lines **A8–9**, the present participle π[εριγιγ]νο|μένην is also possible (suggested by P. Herrmann in his note on *SEG* 47, 1646); note the use of present participles elsewhere in this run of clauses (προαιρούμενοι, ἁμιλλώμενοι). In line **A8**, the phrase 'as far as is in their power' (ὅσον ἐφ' ἑαυτοῖς) is a standard way of qualifying generalizations or hyperbolic statements in Hellenistic honorific epigraphy: e.g. *IG* XII 4, 1, 109 (Kos: decree for Onasandros, II BC), line 22, παραίτιος γενόμενος, ὅσον ἐφ' ἑαυτῷ, τᾶς σωτηρίας; similarly *Milet* I 9, 368 (*c*.100 BC), βουλόμενοι συντηρῖν, ὅσον ἐφ' ἑαυτοῖς, τὸ ἀξίωμα τῆς γερουσίας. The author of the decree was fond of qualifications with ὅσον: cf. **B5**, **B19**, **B53**. In line **A9**, Marek incorrectly read οὐθέν. The true construction is ὑπερβολὴν εὐεργεσιῶν βούλεσθαι ἀπολιπεῖν οὐθενὶ τῶν δήμων, 'wish to leave to no (other) *dēmos* any possibility of surpassing them in benefactions', with the aorist infinitive ἀπολιπεῖν, not Marek's present infinitive καταλείπειν; the verb ἀπολείπειν is used in a similar context at **B51–2**, πρὸς ὑπερβολὴν εὐεργεσιῶν οὐθενὶ τόπον ἀπολειπόντων. This construction is a favourite of Polybios: the closest analogies are Polyb. 34.6.15, μηδενὶ καταλιπεῖν ὑπερβολὴν ἀνοίας τῶν ἐπιγινομένων, 'to leave no possibility for any future writer of surpassing him in foolishness', and 12.26b.5, ὥστε μὴ καταλιπεῖν ὑπερβολὴν τοῖς μειρακίοις... πρὸς τὰς παραδόξους ἐπιχειρήσεις, 'so as to leave no possibility even for children... of surpassing him in the paradoxes he ventures on'.[20] This construction (and sense of ὑπερβολή, 'opportunity of surpassing') is rare in Greek epigraphy: compare e.g. *I.Strat.* 295a.3–4 = 295b.3–4, εὐσεβῶς καὶ φιλοτείμως ἱερατεύων

---

[18] In **A9**, the mason originally inscribed *EYΔΟΞΙΝ*; the *alpha* has been squeezed into the interlinear space above the *iota* and *nu*. The same mode of inserting a correction at **A18** (*AN^HΛΩΣAN*); **B8** (*ΦΙΛΑΓΑΘ^IA*).

[19] For *homonoia* between cities in the Hellenistic world, see Robert, *OMS* VI, 290–1; Thériault 1996, 72–4 ('souvent des relations d'amitié entre deux villes, et plus particulièrement entre cités parentes'); Messerschmidt 2003, 56. Cf. also perhaps *I.Priene*² 112 (Priene and Magnesia, late III BC), lines 27–8, διαφυλάσσοντα τὴν ὁ[μ]ό[νοιαν καὶ τὴν φιλ]ίαν τὴν ὑπάρχουσαν ταῖς πόλεσι πρὸς ἀλλ[ή]λας (the restoration questioned by Holleaux 1907, 384).

[20] Without the dative indirect object, Polyb. 3.12.3, 4.11.1, 6.56.8, 15.16.1, 16.23.4, 16.25.6, 18.12.4, 30.18.5.

ὡς μηδεμίαν καταλιπεῖν ὑπερβολὴν μηδενί; SEG 30, 82 (Athens: decree for M. Ulpius Eubiotos Leuros, c. AD 230), line 29, οὐδεμίαν ὑπερβολὴν εὐνοίας τῆς περὶ τὴν πατρίδα οὐδενὶ καταλείποντα.[21] The phrase οἱ ἐπὶ τὰ παραπλήσια δεδωκότες ἑαυτοὺς δῆμοι (line **A10**) has no close parallels; for the sense of (ἐπι)διδόναι ἑαυτόν, 'dedicate oneself (to something)', cf. *I.Magnesia* 53 (Klazomenai, c.207–205 BC), lines 47–50, τούς τε προγόνους αὐτῶν ... εἰς ἅπαν τὸ συμφέρον ταῖς δεηθείσαις τῶν πόλεων ἐπιδεδωκότας ἑαυτοὺς προθύμως.

A10–14

10   ΩΙΓΑΝ[- - c.7 - -]
[- - c.7 - -]ΘΕΙ φιλανθρωπίας ἀπαραστόχαστον τὴν Τηΐων εἰ[ς] ἡμᾶς Ε[- - c.7 - -]
[- c.5 - τὴ]ν ἁδρότητά (?) τε καὶ [-?τοῖς ἀνθρώ]-
ποις καὶ κοινῆι ταῖς πόλεσιν ἐκτεθεικότων αὐτῶν τὴν πρὸς τοὺς σ[υγ]-
γενεῖς ἑαυτῶν ἀπροφάσιστον σπουδήν· ...

'[(?) by which all might recognize, by the (?) magnit]ude of their generosity, the inestimable [(?) goodwill] of the Teians towards us, […] strength (?) and [...for m]en and in common for the cities, with them having exhibited eagerness without excuses towards their kinsmen;…'

Lines **A10–12** are extremely difficult to read, and the syntactical structure of this section is far from clear. The Teians, having been the subjects of the clauses in lines **A4–10**, appear in the genitive in **A11**, and again in **A13**. A new clause presumably begins after δῆμων in **A10**, but we are unable to offer a plausible reconstruction of the syntax. The stone appears to carry ΩΙΓΑΝ[- -], which could conceivably be the beginning of a phrase such as ὧι πάν[τες], 'by which all might (see/recognize?)…'. At the start of line **A11**, we presumably have a dative noun on which the genitive φιλανθρωπίας depends (e.g. [μεγέ]θει φιλανθρωπίας). The reading of the adjective ἀπαραστόχαστον in **A11** is certain. This adjective is unattested elsewhere, but the formation is perfectly regular; the adjective ἀκαταστόχαστος appears in ancient lexica and glosses, and the verb παραστοχάζεσθαι is found in Greek medical texts (e.g. Soranos *Gynaecology* 1.20.2, quoting Diokles). Here it must mean 'beyond estimating', 'inestimable'; the sense of the whole clause is presumably

---

[21] Cf. also *CID* IV, 86, lines 15–16 = *CID* IV, 87, lines 13–14; Hatzopoulos and Loukopoulou 1992–6, I 77–80, K2, lines 13–14.

something like 'by which all might recognize, by the magnitude of their generosity, the inestimable goodwill of the Teians'. At the start of **A12**, Marek read only the end of a feminine abstract noun [- -]οτητα; we were able to make out the fuller reading [- -]ν ἁδρότητα (the *nu*, *delta*, and *rho* are certain, the *alpha* very probable). The *nu* is either the end of the definite article [τὴ]ν or an adjective or participle agreeing with ἁδρότητα. The noun ἁδρότης or ἁδροτής (from ἁδρός, 'strong, fine') appears nowhere else in Greek epigraphy, and is very rare in literary texts; the closest parallel for the present usage is in Epicurus' *Letter to Herodotos* (Diog. Laert. 10.83), where he claims that the student of Epicurean physical theory 'will achieve an incomparable superiority over other men' (ἀσύμβλητον αὐτὸν πρὸς τοὺς λοιποὺς ἀνθρώπους ἁδρότητα λήψεσθαι).

In **A13**, Marek restored [πεποιη]κότων, but the *theta*, *epsilon*, and *iota* of ἐκτεθεικότων are clear on the stone; the same verb appears in **B50–1** (ἀθάνατον ὑπόμνημα τῆς πρὸς τοὺς συγγένεις εὐνοίας . . . ἐ⟨κ⟩θέντων). The normal verbs for 'bringing to bear' or 'exhibiting' an enthusiastic disposition (σπουδή) are προσφέρεσθαι, εἰσφέρεσθαι, ἀποδεικνύναι, and ποιεῖσθαι; for the use of τιθέναι and related compounds, cf. e.g. *I.Kyme* 13 (Archippe), VI lines 21–2, κατατιθεμένην τὴν ἑαυτῆς φιλοτιμίαν εἰς τὰ κάλλιστα; Jacobsthal 1908, 279–81, no. 2 (*c.*133 BC), lines 7–8, πᾶσαν μὲν ἀσχολίαν ὑπερθέμενος. At the end of line **A14**, the clause probably finishes with σπουδήν, with the following καί introducing a new clause; the traces after the καί are incompatible with Marek's reading σπουδὴν καὶ φιλοτιμίαν [- -], and we suspect that Marek may have inadvertently printed a hypothetical restoration καὶ [φιλοτιμίαν] as if it were legible on the stone.

A14–20

        καὶ [.]ΑΔ[- - - *c.11* - - -]
15 οἱ τῆς πόλεως καιροὶ τῆς παρ' ἐκείνων ἐνεδεήθησαν [βοηθεί]-
    ας καὶ ἡ τύχη τοῖς τοῦ δήμου πράγμασιν ἀγνωμόνως [?διέ]-
    κειτο καὶ περίβολος μόνον τειχῶν ἡ πόλις ἀπ[- - *c.7* - -, τῶν]
    δὲ ἐνοικούντων οἱ μὲν εἰς τὸν πόλεμον ἀνήλωσαν [- *c.6* -],
    οἱ δὲ αἰχμάλωτοι γενόμενοι ΑΙΣΣΗΝΣΑΝΕΙΧ[- - *c.10* - -]
20 [. .]ΤΑΗ[. .]ΑΝ ἀποβεβληκότες, . . .

'And [. . . e.g. when] the city's circumstances called for [assistance] from them, and fortune was cruelly [disposed] to the affairs of the *dēmos*, and the city [was left as]

a mere circuit of walls, and of the inhabitants, some in the war expended
[their lives?], and others, having become captives, [e.g. were enslaved...] having
lost [....]'

The narrative of the sack of Abdera in 170 BC begins at line **A14**; the precise
syntactical connection to the preceding lines is unclear (we might have
expected something like καὶ ἐπεί vel sim. at the end of line **A14**). Despite the
fragmentary state of this part of the inscription, it is clear that the Abderites
were studiously vague about the cause of the disaster that befell their city in
170 BC: note the euphemistic references to 'circumstances' (καιροί) and 'fortune' (τύχη).[22] The inhabitants of Pharos likewise did not identify Rome as the
agents of their city's destruction in 219 BC when appealing for help from
Paros and others.[23] In **A15**, the verb ἐνεδεήθησαν suggests the restoration
[βοηθεί]|ας (already proposed by Marek); cf. e.g. IG XII 6 1, 12 (Samos: hon-
ours for the doctor Diodoros, c.198/7 BC), lines 30–1, τῶν [ἀεὶ ἐνδ]εομένων
τῆς β[οηθεί]ας. The phraseology in line **A16** has no epigraphic parallels. For
the idea of the 'cruelty' (ἀγνωμοσύνη) of fortune, compare Dem. De cor. 207
(τῇ τῆς τύχης ἀγνωμοσύνῃ); Dem. Epist. 2.5; Diod. Sic. 13.29.6; for ἀγνωμόνως
διακεῖσθαι (here 'behave harshly'), cf. ἀγνωμόνως ἔχειν in Isoc. Antid. 227;
Dem. 2.26.

Lines **A17–20** appear to be describing the effects of the sack of Abdera on
both the physical fabric and the population of the city, but the syntax is not
entirely clear. In line **A17**, the words περίβολος μόνον τειχῶν are quite clear
on the stone. We assume that the sense of this line is that 'the city (ἡ πόλις)
[was left] as a mere circuit of walls', i.e. everything inside the wall-circuit was
destroyed; at the end of **A17** we would then need a verb in the indicative such
as ἀπ[ελείφθη].[24] In lines **A18–19**, two groups of Abderite sufferers in the war
are distinguished. The first group (**A18**) are said to have 'expended' something
(ἀνήλωσαν) 'in/for the war' (εἰς τὸν πόλεμον), no doubt their 'lives' (hence
restore perhaps [τοὺς βίους] at the end of the line).[25] The second group (**A19**)

---

[22] οἱ καιροί = '(critical) circumstances', Boulay 2014, 342–4. For τύχη as a euphemism for military
disaster, cf. I.Mylasa 602 (Sherk 1969, no. 60, 31 BC), lines 7–8, περὶ τῆς κατ[ασχού]σης ὑμᾶς τύχης; cf.
also SEG 47, 891 (Beroia, II/I BC), lines 6–7, εἰ καὶ ἡ τύχη διὰ τοὺς καιροὺς αὐτῶν [sc. τῶν προγόνων]
ἥττων ἦν.

[23] SEG 23, 489 (SEG 41, 545), with Derow 1991; see further Epilogue below (pp. 227–30).

[24] We know of no close parallels for the phraseology. For the destruction of cities, see
Boulay 2014, 261–3.

[25] In **A18**, the mason originally inscribed ΑΝΛΩΣΑΝ, and subsequently squeezed the eta into the
interlinear space just above the top left corner of the lambda; similar corrections in **A9** (ΕΥΔΟΞΙ^ΑΝ);
B8 (ΦΙΛΑΓΑΘ^ΙΑ). For ἀναλῶσαι τὸν βίον, cf. e.g. Diod. Sic. 13.29.1, τοὺς ὑπὲρ τῆς κοινῆς ἐλευθερίας
τοὺς ἰδίους ἀναλώσαντας βίους. [τοὺς βίους] does, however, seem long for the lacuna; perhaps
[σώματα]? Cf. Thuc. 2.64.3; Dem. 18.66.

were taken captive and (presumably) enslaved; once again we need a verb in the indicative in the latter half of the line, e.g. ἀπήχθησαν, as Marek suggests.[26] As Marek noted (1997, 173), these lines correspond very well to Livy's account of the sack of Abdera in 170 BC, when the leading citizens were executed and the remainder sold into slavery (Livy 43.4.9: *principes securi percussos, sub corona ceteros uenisse*). Marek's reading of the first word of line **A20** (ἐλευθερίαν) cannot be confirmed from the surviving traces on the stone; we are unable to suggest a convincing alternative.[27]

A20–7

20   τότε ἐπὶ ταῖς κοι[ναῖς χρείαις? - c.4 -]
[- c.3 -]ΠΑΣΑΝ[...]ΣΥΝ διακούσαντες ΕΚΛΕΠ[- - c.17–19 - -]
[τ]ὴν ἀγορὰν καὶ [τοὺ]ς ναοὺς τῶν θεῶν κα[ὶ[- - - c.17–19 - - -]
[- c.4 -]Α προσκρίνοντες τοῖς ΕΙΣ[- - - - c.24–6 - - - -]
[- c.3 -]ΤΩΝΒΙΟ[- c.3 -] συνπενθεῖν κα[ὶ[- - - - c.24–6 - - - -]
25 [- c.5 -]ΙΣΔΔ[. .]καὶ ἐν ταῖς δυστυ[χίαις? - - - - c.21–3 - - - -]
[- - c.10–12 - -]ΑΙ τὴν πόλιν ἡμ[ῶν - - - - - c.26–8 - - - - -]
[- - - c.17–19 - - -]ΣΤ[- - - - - - c.31–3 - - - - - -]

'then, in the face of this common [need,…] hearing […] the agora and the temples of the gods […] judging […] to join in grieving […] in our misfortunes […] our city [….]'

Continuous sense cannot be recovered for these lines. The word τότε in line **A20** seems to mark the point when the Teians once again become the grammatical subject. In the face of the 'common need' of the Abderites (**A20**, ἐπὶ ταῖς κοι[ναῖς χρείαις], cf. *IOSPE* I² 39 [Olbia, II AD], lines 6–7, ἔν τε γὰρ ταῖς κοιναῖς χρείαις αὐθαιρέτως λειτουργῶν; Polyb. 4.15.4, πρὸς τὰς κοινὰς χρείας), the Teians hear (**A21**, διακούσαντες) of the disaster that has befallen the 'agora and temples of the gods' (**A22**); the Teians then make a judgement about the circumstances (**A23**), and join in grieving the fate of Abdera (**A24**) in her misfortunes (**A25**). It is not clear whether these lines describe any concrete measures taken by the Teians to support the Abderites, or whether they simply describe the grief that the Teians felt in the wake of the sack.

[26] On the vocabulary of enslavement in Greek inscriptions, see Robert, *Hellenica* XI–XII, 134–8; Ducrey 1999, 29–46 (esp. 40–1, on ἀπάγειν); Boulay 2014, 266–8.
[27] For the verb ἀποβάλλειν in this context, cf. *I.Mylasa* 602 (Sherk 1969, no. 60: 31 BC), lines 12–14, πολλοὺς μὲν αἰχμαλώτο[υς] ἀποβαλῖν, πολίτας οὐκ ὀλίγους μὲν φονευθέντας κτλ.

Thanks to the regular tapering of the *stēlē*, we can fairly accurately estimate the gap between the lowest part of Fragment **A** and the top of Fragment **B** as 0.195m (the gap is *c.*0.31m at the sides of the *stēlē*). With letter-heights typically around 0.008–0.009m, and an interlinear space of around 0.004–0.005m, the missing text between **A** and **B** can be estimated at around 14–16 lines. The missing lines probably provided a chronological narrative of some concrete measures taken by the Teians immediately after the sack of Abdera, e.g. the shelter of Abderite refugees at Teos, as well as Teian efforts to seek out those Abderites who had been sold into slavery; Fragment **B** seems to begin with Teian diplomatic activities linked to the release of Abderite captives.

B1–4

[- - - - - - - - - - - - - *c.*40–2 - - - - - - - - - - - - - - - -ή]μῖν ἐν τῶι

[- - - - - - - - - - *c.*33–5 - - - - - - - - - - - -]Ι̣[.]ά̣μενοι τὴν χάριν ΠΕ- ν.

[- - - - - - - - - *c.*30–2 - - - - - - - -] παρ' αὐτοῖς καὶ κατορθώσαν-

[τες - - - - - - - *c.*23–5 - - - - - -]ΕΝ ἄνευ λύτρων ἐποίησαν ΑΦΕ-

'...us in the...gratitude/favour...among them, and succeeding...without ransom, they made....'

In line **B2**, before the letters -*MENOI*, the lower right-hand serif of a diagonal stroke is visible; we therefore have the end of an aorist participle, -ά̣μενοι, no doubt governing the noun τὴν χάριν.[28] The subject of the participle can only be the Teians. The verb κατορθοῦν (**B3**) is generally used of success in an embassy or a lawsuit (cf. **B49**); combined with the phrase ἄνευ λύτρων, 'without ransom' (**B4**), this suggests that the Teians have successfully appealed to a higher authority for the release without ransom of the captives taken at the time of the sack of Abdera (**A19**).[29] This higher authority can only be the Romans, and it is conceivable that the phrase παρ' αὐτοῖς, 'among them' (**B3**), refers to an embassy to Rome ('them' = the Romans). At the end of line **B4**, it is very likely that the letters *AΦE* are the beginning of the infinitive ἀφε[θῆναι] or the

---

[28] Conceivably [ἐξαιτ]η[σ]ά̣μενοι τὴν χάριν, 'having asked this favour'; cf. line **B47**, χάριν ἰδίαν αἰτησάμενοι (Teos asks a favour of Miletos); *Syll.*³ 748 (Gytheion, 71 BC), line 15, ἰδίαν χάριν ἐξαιτησάμενοι, of a favour asked of two Roman legates.

[29] Cf. *Milet* I 3, 148 (treaty between Miletos and Magnesia, early II BC), lines 67–9, τοὺς δὲ ὑπεράγοντας αἰχμαλώτους τοὺς Μιλησίων χαριζόμενος ὁ δῆμος ὁ Μαγνήτων ἔδωκεν [ἄν]ευ λύτρου Ῥοδίοις. On the term λύτρα, see Bielman 1994, 259–65.

noun ἄφε[σιν], 'release'; cf. *IG* II³ 1, 877 (Athens, 283 BC), lines 20–1, [ὅσοι δ]ὲ αἰχμάλωτοι ἐγένοντο, ἐμφανίσας τῶι βα[σιλεῖ καὶ] λαβὼν αὐτοῖς ἄφε[σ]ιν.[30] It is naturally highly tempting to connect this putative embassy to Rome with Livy's account of the Abderite embassy to Rome in late summer or autumn 170 BC. As Livy informs us, the Abderite ambassadors successfully persuaded the Roman senate that an unjust war had been waged against Abdera; the senate appointed two legates, C. Sempronius Blaesus and Sex. Iulius Caesar, to restore the freedom of the city of Abdera, and to seek out and liberate all those Abderites who had been enslaved.[31] It is true that Livy describes this as an embassy from Abdera alone, but it is perfectly possible that some Teian ambassadors might have assisted with this embassy; compare the Teian embassy to Rome on Abdera's behalf in late 167 BC (Chapter 5 below, **Document 6**).

B5–8

5   [- - - - - - - c.21–3 - - - - - - ἐφ'] ὅσον ἰσχύοσαν, πάλιν ἐπὶ τὴν ἀρχαί-
     [αν - - - - - c.15 - - - κατ]άστασιν, συλλέγοντες ἐκ παντὸς τόπου
     [- - - - - c.16 - - - - -]Σ καὶ ἀναπέμποντες ἐπὶ τὰς πατρώιους ἑ⟨σ⟩τίας
     [καὶ τὴν ἐξ ἀρχῆς] πολιτείαν· ...

'...as far as they were able, back to their former... [con]dition, collecting from every place...and sending them back to their ancestral hearths [and their former] state of citizenship....'

These lines recount the process by which the Teians, insofar as they were able ([ἐφ'] ὅσον ἰσχύοσαν, B5), restored the Abderite captives to their former condition (πάλιν ἐπὶ τὴν ἀρχαί|[αν ... κατ]άστασιν, B5–6), collecting them from far and wide (συλλέγοντες ἐκ παντὸς τόπου, B6) and sending them back to their ancestral homes (ἀναπέμποντες ἐπὶ τὰς πατρώιους ἑ⟨σ⟩τίας, B7) and restoring

---

[30] No close parallels fall to hand for the phrase ἐποίησαν ἀφε[θῆναι], 'they brought it about that they were released', but for the construction, cf. e.g. *I.Mylasa* 109 (I BC), lines 16–17, ἐποίησεν εὐεργε[τικώ]τερον διατεθῆναι [sc. τὸν ἄνδρα] πρὸς τὸν σύμπαντα δῆμον. For ἄφεσις and ἀφίημι in this context, Bielman 1994, 255–7.

[31] Livy 43.4.11–12: *legati duo, C. Sempronius Blaesus Sex. Iulius Caesar, ad restituendos in libertatem Abderitas missi. iisdem mandatum, ut et Hostilio consuli et Hortensio praetori nuntiarent, senatum Abderitis iniustum bellum inlatum conquirique omnes, qui in seruitute sint, et restitui in libertatem aecum censere.* An embassy from Chalkis arrived at Rome at around the same time, also complaining about Hortensius' behaviour (Livy 43.7.4–43.8.7); the senate likewise decreed that any free Chalkidians who had been enslaved should be restored to liberty (43.8.7: *si qui in seruitutem liberi uenissent, ut eos conquirendos primo quoque tempore restitutendosque in libertatem curaret* [sc. Hortensius]). See Burton 2017, 140.

their Abderite citizen-rights (πολιτείαν, **B8**). The limiting clause [ἐφ'] ὅσον ἰσχύοσαν (also in **B53**, ἐφ' ὅσον ἰσχύει; cf. **B19**) seems not to be precisely paralleled elsewhere, but the phrase is semantically identical to the common ἐφ' ὅσον ἦσαν δυνατοί: cf. especially *IG* XII 7, 36 (Arkesine: honours for Timessa, II BC), lines 12–15, [τ]ὴν πᾶ[σα]ν σπουδὴν ἐποήσατο εἰς τ[ὸ ἀνασ]ωθῆναι τοὺς πολίτας πάντας [τοὺς ἀχθ]έντας, ἐφ' ὅσον ἐστὶν δυνατή.[32] The standard verb for 'restoring' someone or something to a former condition would be ἀποκαθιστάναι; the phraseology ἀποκαθιστάναι... ἐπί/εἰς κατάστασιν is paralleled in the first Teian decree for Antiochos III and Laodike, *SEG* 41, 1003, I (*c.*203 BC), lines 10–11, ἀποκατέστησε τὰ πράγματα εἰς συμφέρουσαν κατάστασιν.[33] The natural position for the verb is immediately before the limiting clause [ἐφ'] ὅσον ἰσχύοσαν (**B5**), and so we might conjecturally restore lines **B4–6** as follows: ἐποίησαν ἄφε[σιν καὶ ἀποκατέστησαν αὐτοὺς, ἐφ'] ὅσον ἰσχύοσαν, πάλιν ἐπὶ τὴν ἀρχαί[αν... κατ]άστασιν, 'they procured their release, and restored them, as far as they were able, back to their former... condition'. It is unclear what stood in the lacuna at the start of **B6**; it may simply have been an elaborate participial phrase qualifying [κατ]άστασιν, e.g. ἐπὶ τὴν ἀρχαί[αν αὐτοῖς ὑπάρχουσαν κατ]άστασιν.

Lines **B6–8** move on to a new stage in the restoration of Abdera, the gathering and transport homewards of the citizen population from their various places of exile. The inscription tells us nothing about the practicalities of how this was done; one might compare the vagueness with which Solon, four centuries earlier, describes his restoration of Athenians who had been sold into slavery abroad.[34] At the start of **B7**, we presumably have a passive participle denoting the Abderites who had been sold into slavery, e.g. [τοὺς ἀπαχθέντα]ς. The phrase τὰς πατρώιους ἑ⟨σ⟩τίας, 'their ancestral hearths' (**B7**), is effectively just an elevated way of saying 'their homes'; when the exiled Elateians were received by the Stymphalians in the 190s BC, the Stymphalians are said to have welcomed them 'into their own homes': *SEG* 25, 445, line 3, ὑπεδέξαντο

---

[32] The normal form of the aorist would be ἴσχυσαν; compare ἐδεικνύοσαν in *Syll.*[3] 826E (Delphi, 125 BC), line D2.

[33] e.g. *I.Kallatis* 7 (253 BC), lines 23–5, ἀπ[οκα]τασταθέντων αὐτῶι τῶν πραγμάτ[ων ε]ἰς τὰν ἐξ ἀρχᾶς διάθεσιν; *Syll.*[3] 543 (Philip V to Larisa, 215 BC), lines 34–5, παρακαλῶ ὑμᾶς... τοὺς μὲν κεκριμένους ὑπὸ τῶν πολιτῶν ἀποκαταστῆσαι εἰς τὴν πολιτείαν; *SEG* 37, 859 (Zeuxis to Herakleia, *c.*196–193 BC), C13–14, σπεύδοντες οὖν καὶ αὐτοὶ τὸν δῆμον εἰς τὴν ἐξ ἀ[ρχῆ]ς διάθεσιν ἀποκαταστα θῆναι; *I.Priene*[2] 70 (I BC), lines 17–18, τὸ τῶν νέων ἀποκατέστησεν εἰς τὴν ἀρχαί[αν] τάξιν σύστεμα; *Syll.*[3] 814 (Nero's oration at the Isthmia, AD 67), lines 42–3, ἀποκατέστησεν εἰς τὴν ἀρχαιότητα τῆς αὐτονομίας καὶ ἐλευθερίας. Cf. also *I.Ilion* 32 (date uncertain: Antiochos I or III), lines 11–12, τὴν βασιλείαν εἰς τὴν ἀρχαίαν διάθεσιν κατέστησεν.

[34] Solon Fr. 36 West, lines 8–12: πόλλους δ' Ἀθήνας πατρίδ' ἐς θεόκτιτον | ἀνήγαγον πραθέντας, ἄλλον ἐκδίκως, | ἄλλον δικαίως, τοὺς δ' ἀναγκαίης ὑπὸ | χρειοῦς φυγόντας, γλῶσσαν οὐκέτ' Ἀττικὴν | ἱέντας, ὡς ἂν πολλαχῇ πλανώμενους.

ἔ[κ]αστος ἐπὶ τὰν ἰδί[αν] ἑστίαν.³⁵ The treatment of the adjective πατρῷιος as two-termination is unusual, but far from unparalleled (LSJ, s.v., citing examples from Aeschylus and Euripides). The noun πολιτείαν in line B8 must be grammatically parallel to ἑ⟨σ⟩τίας in line B7. πολιτεία here ought to mean 'citizenship', 'possession of citizen-rights', rather than 'constitution', as e.g. in Philip V's second letter to Larisa, *Syll.*³ 543 (215 BC), lines 34–5, παρακαλῶ ὑμᾶς ... τοὺς μὲν κεκριμένους ὑπὸ τῶν πολιτῶν ἀποκαταστῆσαι εἰς τὴν πολιτείαν. We therefore suggest restoring [καὶ τὴν ἐξ ἀρχῆς] πολιτείαν, 'and to their former state of citizenship', as apparently in Ager 1996, no. 65 (Thaumakoi, III/II BC), lines 1–2, ἀπο[δοῦναι αὐτοῖς ... τὴ]ν ἐξ ἀρχῆς πολιτεία[ν].

B8–11

οὐ μόνον δὲ ἐπὶ τοσοῦτον ἡ φιλαγαθία τὴν

[ἀπὸ τῆς συ]γγενείας εὔνοιαν προσφερομένη τὴν κοινὴν πρὸς τὸν

10   [δ]ῆμ[ον] ἡμῶν φιλοστοργίαν ἐπὶ τῆς κατ' ἰδίαν ἑκάστωι βοηθείας ν.

τῶν ἐπταικότων ἀπεδείκνυτο, ...

'Yet not only within these limits did their excellence of character, bringing to bear the goodwill that comes from kinship, show collective affection for our *dēmos* in their individual assistance to each of those who were in distress, ...'

These lines are highly elaborate in both syntax and vocabulary: the core idea is that the *collective* affection (τὴν κοινὴν ... φιλοστοργίαν) of the Teians for the Abderites has manifested itself in the assistance of *individual* Abderites (τῆς κατ' ἰδίαν ... βοηθείας). The phrase ἐπὶ τοσοῦτον, 'to this extent, within these limits', appears nowhere else in this sense in Hellenistic epigraphy, but is a favourite of Polybios (more than sixty instances, often in the form ἐπὶ τοσοῦτον ἡμῖν εἰρήσθω, 'this is as much as I will say about that'). The verb προσφέρεσθαι, 'bring a certain quality to bear', is very common in Hellenistic honorific epigraphy, but always with the honorand as its subject; we are unable to locate any other examples where one abstract moral quality (ἡ φιλαγαθία, B8) brings another moral quality to bear (τὴν ... εὔνοιαν, B8–9). The goodwill (εὔνοια) that derives from a kinship-relation (συγγένεια) is a standard trope of Hellenistic

---

³⁵ For the phrase πατρῷα ἑστία, cf. e.g. Soph. *El.* 881; Eur. *Alc.* 738; *I.Eleusis* 271 (*c.*76 BC), line 22; *TAM* V 3, 1418 (Philadelphia, III AD), line 47.

kinship diplomacy.[36] The euphemism οἱ ἐπταικότες (**B11**), literally 'those who have stumbled', also appears in the Iasian decree for Antiochos III and Laodike (*I.Iasos* 4 [*c*.196 BC], line 44, [πο]λλοῖς δὲ ἐπταικόσιν βοηθοῦντος), in a decree of the Xanthians dating to 206/5 BC (*SEG* 38, 1476, lines 60–1, δεινὸν δ᾽ἡγουμένης εἶναι τοὺς συγγενεῖς ἐπταικότας περιιδεῖν), and in the decree for Polemaios from Klaros (*SEG* 39, 1243, line III.51, with Robert and Robert 1989, 44); it is often used by Polybios of those who have suffered misfortune (e.g. 3.48.4, 24.10.11).

B11–15

ἀλλ᾽ ἐπειδή τινα μὲν ὁ χρόνος ν.
καθείρηκει τῶν τειχῶν, ἃ δ᾽ ἡ τοῦ πολέμου περίστασις διέφθαρκ[ε],
παραπλησίως δὲ καὶ ναοὶ θεῶν ἐπανορθώσεως προσδεόμεν[οι]
οὐθένα τῶν πολιτῶν εἰς τὴν ἐπισκευὴν εἶχον τὸν χρήσοντα
15 τοῖς πολίταις,...

'But since the passage of time had brought down some parts of the walls, and other parts the crisis of war had destroyed; and likewise also the temples of the gods, though in need of reconstruction, had found none of the citizens who would lend the citizens (what was needed) for their repair,...'

The narrative now jumps forward to a point when the Abderite exiles have returned and are planning the reconstruction of their ruined city. It is note-worthy that the city's first priorities are its fortifications and sanctuaries; it is possible that Rome's war with Perseus was still underway at this point. Parts of the wall-circuit have been brought down by the passage of time, and other parts by the Roman sack of 170 BC. The rhetorical variation τινα μὲν...ἃ δέ (**B11–12**) seems to have no epigraphic parallels,[37] but Polybios is notably fond of this kind of variation: cf. especially 14.1.13, ὁ Πόπλιος ἀεί τινας μὲν τῶν πραγματικῶν, οὓς δὲ καὶ στρατιωτικῶν... ἐξέπεμπε; also 5.105.7, τινὲς μὲν πρὸς Καρχηδονίους, οἱ δὲ πρὸς Ῥωμαίους ἐπρέσβευον; similarly 7.18.2, 11.16.7, 15.27.9, 39.4.4.[38] The verb καθείρηκει (**B12**) is an awkward attempt to form the pluperfect of καθαιρεῖν (perhaps a confusion with the pluperfect of ἐρεῖν?).

---

[36] e.g. *SEG* 38, 1476 (Xanthos, 206/5 BC), lines 30–2, παραδεικνύοντες τὴν ἐκ παλαιῶν χρόνων συνωικειωμένην πρὸς ἡμᾶς εὔνοιαν διὰ τὴν συγγένειαν.
[37] It is possible that a contrast of this kind should be restored in *IGRR* IV, 292 (Pergamon: decree for Diodoros Pasparos, I BC), lines 4–5, οὓς δὲ ἀπολωλεκέναι τοὺς βίους.
[38] Foucault 1972, 89–90.

The phrase ἡ τοῦ πολέμου περίστασις (**B12**) is well paralleled in Hellenistic epigraphy: cf. e.g. *SEG* 26, 1817 (Arsinoe-Taucheira, II/I BC), lines 21–2, κατὰ τὰν τῶ πολέμω περίστασιν; *I.Sestos* 1 (honours for Menas, shortly after 133 BC), lines 25–6, ἔν τε ταῖς πολεμικαῖς περιστάσεσιν; *I.Cret.* III iv 9 (Itanos, 112/111 BC), line 137.[39] The city's temples were similarly (παραπλησίως, **B13**; cf. **A10**) in need of reconstruction; for the phrase ἐπανορθώσεως προσδεῖσθαι, cf. e.g. *IG* II² 968 (II BC), line 47, τά τε ἐν ἀκροπόλει προσδεόμε[να ἐργασία]ς; *IGBulg.* I² 45 (Odessos), lines 28–9, τινα τῶν τειχῶν ἐπ[ισκευῆς προσδεόμ]ενα; similar phrases also appear in the Ptolemaic synodic decrees of 217 BC (Raphia: *CPI* I, 144 [Pithom], lines 13–14: τὰ προσδεόμενα ἐπανορθώσεως ἀνενεώσατο) and 196 BC (Memphis: *CPI* I, 126 [Rosetta], line 34, τά τε προσδεόμενα ἐπισκευῆς προσδιωρθώσατο).[40] In **B14**, as Christopher Jones points out to us, τὸν χρήσοντα must mean 'who would lend money' (cf. προέχρησαν, **B29**); cf. LSJ s.v. χράω (B), 'lend in a friendly way' (ctr. δανείζω), citing Arist. *Eth. Nic.* 1162b33, οὐ δεδωκὼς ἀλλὰ χρήσας. The repetition τῶν πολιτῶν…ταῖς πολίταις (**B14–15**) is clumsy. It is very striking that the city assumes that the 'default' way to fund urgent public works of this kind is by state borrowing from members of the citizen body, but we have good parallels for the (re)construction of city walls being funded or part-funded by loans from individuals or groups of individuals, as at Oropos in the late fourth or early third century BC (primarily citizens?) and again in the late third century BC (primarily foreigners); at Odessos in the late third century BC (an individual); and at Olbia *c.*200 BC (an individual citizen).[41]

B15–18

15   διαλο⟨γ⟩ισάμενος ὁ τῶν Τηΐων δῆμος διότι προγονι-
κῶν θεῶν πρόνοιαν ποιήσεται καὶ κοινὴν πᾶσιν Ἀβδηρίταις βοήθειαν ἔσται προσενηνεγμένος ἐπιδοὺς εἰς τὴν τῶν τειχῶν ἐπανόρθωσιν τὴν ἑαυτοῦ φιλαγαθίαν,…

'The Teian *dēmos*, reckoning both that they would have care for their ancestral gods and that they would have provided collective assistance to all the Abderites

---

[39] Robert, *OMS* VI, 639–40; Boulay 2014, 337–9.

[40] For the term ἐπανόρθωσις, see Robert, *Hellenica* XI–XII, 517–19, 541; Migeotte 1992, 232 n. 134.

[41] Migeotte 1984, 357–62; the relevant instances are his nos. 8 (*I.Oropos* 302), 9 (*I.Oropos* 303), 39 (*IGBulg.* I² 35), and 44 (*Syll.*³ 495).

by committing their excellence of character towards the reconstruction of the walls,…'

The Teians 'reason that' (διαλογίζεσθαι…διότι) they can best show care (πρόνοια) for the gods and provide aid (βοήθεια) for the Abderites through committing (ἐπιδούς) themselves to the rebuilding of the walls; the participle ἐπιδούς (B17) is a circumstantial participle expressing the means by which the main actions (showing care/aiding) will be performed.[42] The verb διαλογίζεσθαι ('reckon, calculate') appears to be otherwise unattested in this sense in Greek epigraphy.[43] The Teians' two stated aims here are to assist the entire Abderite citizen body in common (B16–17, κοινὴν πᾶσιν Ἀβδηρίταις βοήθειαν, echoing the phraseology of B9–10, τὴν κοινὴν πρὸς τὸν δῆμον ἡμῶν φιλοστοργίαν) and, more particularly, to have care for their ancestral gods (προγονικοὶ θεοί): the ancestral gods of the Teians are assumed to be identical to the gods of Abdera (see Chapters 3 and 4 below). The future perfect (ἔσται προσενηνεγμένος, B17) is very rare in Greek epigraphy, but cf. e.g. I.Knidos 31 (Piracy Law, c.100 BC), V.33–4, ὅστις…[κα]ταλελυμένος ἔσται. The verb ἐπιδιδόναι is usually used of devoting oneself to something (ἑαυτὸν ἐπιδιδόναι) or of contributing money (χρήματα ἐπιδιδόναι); it is seldom used of the commitment of a moral quality, but cf. I.Priene² 70 (third decree for Zosimos, I BC), lines 12–13, ἐπέδωκε τὸν ἑαυτοῦ [ζῆλον εἰς] τε τὴν τοῦ τόπου φι[λοδο]ξίαν.

B18–19

πϱοήκατο χϱημάτων ἀναποδότων πλῆ-
θος, ὅσο[ν] ἰσχύειν αὐτῶι τότε ἐδίδοσαν οἱ καιϱοί,…

'(They) handed over a large sum of money which did not need to be repaid, as much as the present circumstances then permitted them to be able to do,…'

In concrete terms, the Teians' contribution towards the rebuilding of the walls of Abdera took the form of a gift of cash; for the verb προΐημι in this context, cf. I.Priene² 64 (decree for Moschion, late II BC), lines 107–8, προήκατο εἰς ταῦτα

---

[42] Kühner–Gerth II 84, 86–7.

[43] For διαλογίζεσθαι…(δι)ότι, 'reckon/reason that something is the case', cf. e.g. Dem. 23.26 (διελογίζετο ὅτι πάντα τὰ τοιαῦτ'ὀνόματα…αἰτιῶν ὀνόματ'ἐστίν); [Dem.] 25.25 (διαλογισάμενος…ὅτι ἔξεστι καὶ λέγειν καὶ ποιεῖν μέχρι παντὸς ὅ τι ἂν βούληταί τις).

μετὰ τἀδελφοῦ δραχμὰς Ἀ[λε]ξανδρείας κτλ.⁴⁴ This gift is explicitly described as not needing to be repaid (ἀναποδότων, **B18**), in contrast to the interest-free loan that the Teians provided some time later (προέχρησαν ἄτοκα, **B29–30**); these two different kinds of financial subvention are often contrasted in honorific epigraphy, e.g. *SEG* 44, 940 (Miletos, 6/5 BC), lines B7–8, [ἃ μὲν τούτ]ων παρ᾽ ἀτοῦ προ[δανε]ίζων ἄτοκα, ἃ δὲ χαρ[ιζόμενος ἀν]απόδοτα.⁴⁵ The Abderites are studiously vague about the sum of money concerned (χρημάτων … πλῆθος, **B18–19**);⁴⁶ given that they later specify the size of the Teians' interest-free loan (five talents, **B30**), we may guess that the sum was not in fact large (Chapter 4 below). One recalls the long series of excuses which the Xanthians offered to the city of Kytenion in 206/5 BC when explaining why they were unable to provide more than 500 drachms towards the rebuilding of the walls of Kytenion (*SEG* 38, 1476, lines 52–7): 'since not only have the public monies been spent and a mass of debts incurred, and it is impossible to impose a levy on the citizens because of the budget which has been decreed for a nine-year period, and the wealthiest citizens have recently made great contributions because of the pressing circumstances (διὰ τοὺς περιστάντας καιρούς)'.⁴⁷ In line **B19**, the Teians are said to have provided 'as much as the present (sc. difficult) circumstances then permitted them to be able to do' (ὅσο[ν] ἰσχύειν αὐτῶι τότε ἐδίδοσαν οἱ καιροί). The form of words has no close parallels: the nearest analogy known to us is found in the decree of Paros (probably *c.*218 BC) responding to the appeal of her colony Pharos for assistance after the Roman sack of 219 BC, where the Pharians are said to call on the Parians 'to help them in the reconstruction of the city, inasmuch as we are in a position to do so', [βοηθῆσαι αὐτο]ῖς εἰς ἐπανόρθωσιν τῆς [πόλεως καθ᾽ ὅσον ἂν εὐκ]αιρῶμες.⁴⁸

---

⁴⁴ Robert 1962, 271–2; Migeotte 1984, 297.

⁴⁵ Similarly *I.Didyma* 142 (II BC), line 19; *I.Priene*² 88 (*c.*200 BC); Migeotte 1984, no. 101 (Halikarnassos, III BC), lines 18–21.

⁴⁶ For the vague χρημάτων πλῆθος, cf. *IG* XII 4, 1, 99 (Halasarna, II BC), line 14; *IG* XII 5, 860 (Tenos, I BC), lines 12 and 26; *SEG* 39, 1244 (decree for Menippos, late II BC), line II.16.

⁴⁷ Bousquet 1988, 44–5, comparing an early second-century decree of Theangela in which the people of Hyllarima apologize for only being able to send 300 drachms to their kinsmen at Theangela because of their difficult financial circumstances: Robert 1936, 92–3 (Curty 1995, 178–9, no. 72; Debord and Varinlioğlu 2018, 33–4, T5), lines 10–12, ἀπολογίζονται δ[ὲ τὴν ὑπάρχουσα]ν περὶ αὐτοὺς κατὰ τ[ὸν καιρὸν κατάστ]ασιν.

⁴⁸ *SEG* 23, 489 (*SEG* 41, 545), lines A35–6, with Derow 1991, 264 (date not certain: conceivably mid-II BC, Eckstein 1999, 415–18; the Epilogue below). Derow compares the phrase κατὰ τὸ εὔκαιρον βοηθείτω, 'let x help inasmuch as is possible', the form of words for mutual military assistance found in Rome's treaties with Kibyra and Maroneia of 174 and 167 BC respectively (Meier 2019, 9–40, Exemplar 2(b) line 4 [Kibyra: *StV* IV 632], esp. 34–5 for the Latin equivalent; *IThrakAig* E168, lines 33 and 36 [Maroneia: *StV* IV 664]).

B19–22

δεικνὺς ὡς οὐ τῆ[ι]
20 πολυπληθίαι τῶν ὑπαρχόντων τὴν ἑτοιμότητα τῆς χορηγία[ς]
ὑπομένειν, τῆι δὲ εὐνοίαι πρὸς πᾶν τὸ παρακαλούμενον ἀνέλλει- ν.
πτον τὴν φιλο[τι]μίαν παρέχεται·...

'Showing how they provide their generosity unfailingly, not through an abundance of property to sustain a ready supply of income (?), but rather through
goodwill in the face of every request....'

The syntax of these lines is extremely difficult. We take the main clause to be
δεικνὺς ὡς... ἀνέλλειπτον τὴν φιλο[τι]μίαν παρέχεται, '(the Teian *dēmos*) showing
how it provides its generosity unfailingly'; the sense is similar to A5–7,
πειρῶνται... τὴν ἑαυτῶν σπουδὴν καὶ φιλοτιμίαν ἀκατάπαυστον πρὸς τὸν δῆμον
ἡμῶν διαφυλάξειν, '(the Teians) attempt to preserve unceasing their eagerness
and generosity towards our *dēmos*', with ἀνέλλειπτος φιλοτιμία in B21–2 having essentially the same force as φιλοτιμία ἀκατάπαυστος in A6–7.[49] This main
clause is qualified by two datives of means: οὐ τῆι πολυπληθίαι τῶν
ὑπαρχόντων... τῆι δὲ εὐνοίαι πρὸς πᾶν τὸ παρακαλούμενον, 'not through abundance of resources, but through goodwill in the face of every request'; cf. Diod.
Sic. 9.30.1, τὴν μὲν γὰρ νίκην ἀρετῇ καὶ οὐ πολυπληθίᾳ χειρῶν περιγίνεσθαι, 'the
victory came about through courage, and not through abundance of manpower'. The phrase πρὸς πᾶν τὸ παρακαλούμενον, 'in the face of every/any
request', is a favourite of Polybios: e.g. 15.4.8, διακούσας... διότι πρὸς πᾶν τὸ
παρακαλούμενον ἑτοίμως ἔχοιεν, 'hearing that they were ready to comply with
every request' (similarly 1.83.3, 4.51.2, 24.15.2, 29.27.6); in Hellenistic epigraphy, compare *I.Délos* 1517 (*c.*154 BC), lines 24–5, προθύμως ἑαυτὸν εἰς πᾶν
τὸ παρακαλούμενον ἐπιδίδωσιν. The difficulty lies in construing the phrase τὴν
ἑτοιμότητα τῆς χορηγία[ς] ὑπομένειν (B20–1). The general sense of the words
τὴν ἑτοιμότητα τῆς χορηγία[ς] can be determined by comparison with a
famous passage of Polybios, 6.50.6, οὐ μικρὰ πρὸς τὸ καθικέσθαι τῆς πράξεως
ταύτης συμβαλλομένης αὐτοῖς τῆς εὐπορίας καὶ τῆς ἑτοιμότητος τῆς κατὰ τῆς
χορηγίας, 'no small contribution to the achievement of this feat [sc. the

---

[49]   The adjective ἀνέλλειπτος (unattested in literary texts) is synonymous with the more common
ἀνελλιπής (Robert and Robert 1989, 28). It appears twice in the decree for Polemaios from Klaros
(*SEG* 39, 1243, lines II.9–10, ἀνελείπτως, and V.17–18, πειρᾶσθαι... ἀνέλλιπτον παρέξεσθαι τὴν ἑαυτοῦ
σπουδήν), once at Priene (*I.Priene*² 69 [I BC], lines 90–1, [ἀ]νέλ[λειπτο]ς), once at Hierokaisareia in
Lydia (*TAM* V 2, 1269 [(?) I BC], ἀνελλείπτως), and once at Nîmes (*IG* XIV, 2498, ἀνενλείπτως).

conquest of the whole world] was made by the ease of procurement and ready availability of their (material) resources'. We have tentatively assumed that the infinitive ὑπομένειν ('endure, withstand') depends on the substantival participle ὑπαρχόντων in **B20** (τῶν ὑπαρχόντων... ὑπομένειν, 'resources (lying ready) to sustain'), and that τὴν ἑτοιμότητα is the direct object of ὑπομένειν; the sense would be that the Teians do not have sufficient abundance (πολυπληθία) of property (τὰ ὑπάρχοντα) to sustain (ὑπομένειν) a ready supply (ἑτοιμότης) of income (χορηγία). But the syntax is very strained, and the assumed sense of ὑπομένειν ('underwrite') is not well paralleled; readers may well be able to find a better solution.

B22–6

τοῦ χρόνου δὲ προκόψαντος καὶ τῆ[ς]

πόλεως ἡμῶν ἤδη πρὸς βελτίονα κατάστασιν ἐρχομένης διὰ τὸ κα[ὶ]

πλῆθος ἤδη μέτριον ἠθροῖσθαι πολιτῶν, πολλῆς τε δαπάνης γινομέ-

25 νης εἰς τὴν τῆς χώρας ἐξεργασίαν καὶ διὰ τοῦτο θλιβομένων τοῖς

βίοις τῶν ἀνθρώπων καὶ ἀπροσόδων γινομένων,...

'When time had passed, and our city was now returning to a better condition because of the fact that a moderately large body of citizens had now been gathered together, but great expense was being incurred for the cultivation of the territory, and for this reason the people were being oppressed in their livelihoods and had no revenues,...'

The narrative now jumps forward an unspecified period of time, to a point when a moderately large body of citizens had resettled the site of Abdera and were seeking to bring their land back under cultivation. The verb προκόπτειν in the sense 'advance, progress (temporally)' (**B22**) is virtually unattested in Greek epigraphy (and rare in Greek literature more generally): the closest analogy is in the decree for Aristagoras from Istros, *IScM* I, 54 (I BC), lines 17–18, [τῇ] τε ἡλικίᾳ προκόπτων.[50] For the notion of the city attaining a 'better condition' (βελτίονα κατάστασιν, **B23**), compare the Pergamene decree conferring cult honours on Attalos III (*OGIS* 332, lines 55–6), ὅπως εἰς βελτίονα καὶ εὐδαιμονεστέραν παραγίνηται κατάστασιν τὰ κοινὰ τοῦ

---

[50] Cf. e.g. Joseph. *BJ* 4.298, τῆς νυκτὸς προκοπτούσης; Robert, *OMS* V, 430 n. 36; Gray 2013, 246–7.

πολιτεύματος.[51] The phrase πλῆθος ... ἠθροῖσθαι (**B24**) is a favourite of Polybios: cf. e.g. 3.18.8, πλῆθος ἀνθρώπων διαφερόντων εἰς αὐτὴν [sc. τὴν πόλιν] ἠθροῖσθαι; also 1.44.5, 3.42.4, 3.92.8, 15.30.9, 16.13.2, 23.1.1. The Abderites were incurring much expense in the attempt to recultivate their land (εἰς τὴν τῆς χώρας ἐξεργασίαν, **B25**); compare *IG* II³ 1, 1160 (*c*.215 BC), [τῆς χώρας διὰ] τοὺς πολέμους ἀργοῦ καὶ ἀσπόρου οὔ[σης αἴτιος ἐγέ]νετο τοῦ ἐξεργασθῆναι καὶ σπαρῆναι [χρήματα πορί]σας, 'when the land was lying idle and unsown because of the wars, he was responsible for them being cultivated and sown by providing money'.[52] The verb θλίβεσθαι, 'be oppressed' (**B25–6**), is very common in the context of economic suffering in the wake of military conflict: for the oppression of one's 'livelihood' (θλιβομένων τοῖς βίοις), cf. the decree for Aristagoras from Istros, *IScM* I, 54 (I BC), line 28, τεθλειμμένων τῶν ἰδιωτικῶν βίων.[53] The adjective ἀπρόσοδος (**B26**), 'not revenue-bearing', is exceptionally rare in this sense (LSJ cites only a passage from Philodemos' *On Property Management*, col. XI line 7); the only other epigraphic instance comes in the Thasian decree for Epie, *SEG* 18, 343 (I BC/I AD), lines 24–5, ἱερωσύνης [ἦν] οὐδεμία ὑφίσταται διὰ τὸ ἀπρόσοδον τε αὐτὴν εἶν[αι καὶ π]ολυδάπανον, 'a priesthood which no one is willing to take on since it brings no revenues and many expenses'.

B26–8

πέμψαντος πά-
λιν πρὸς Τηΐους τοῦ δήμου καὶ παρακαλοῦντος εἰς βοῶν καταγορασ-
μὸν ἑαυτῶι προχορηγῆσαι διάφορα, ...

'The *dēmos* sent once again to the Teians and called on them to advance us a sum of money for the purchase of oxen, ...'

The Abderites ask the Teians to lend them a sum of money for the purchase of oxen. The noun καταγορασμός, 'purchase' (**B27–8**) is virtually unattested in literary texts (only Diod. Sic. 16.13.3), but is fairly common in Hellenistic

---

[51] Similarly *I.Iasos* 4 (Laodike to Iasos, *c*.196 BC), lines 9–11, προτέθειται συναύξειν τὸ πολίτευμα καὶ εἰς βελτίονα διάθεσιν ἀγαγεῖν; *I.Didyma* 142 (II BC), line 21, ἐμ βελτίονι γενέσθαι καταστά[σει]; see further Gauthier 1989, 84 n. 7. τὴν ἀρχαί[αν ... κατ]άστασιν already in **B5–6**.

[52] Cf. also *I.Sestos* 1 (honours for Menas, shortly after 133 BC), lines 54–7: in the course of incursions by Thracians and other wars, 'everything in the fields was carried off, and most of the land was unsown'.

[53] See the numerous parallels collected by Drew-Bear 1972, 449–50; also Robert and Robert 1989, 103.

epigraphy, usually of the purchase of grain (*I.Kallatis* 26, line 10; *IG* XII 9, 900A [Chalkis], line c.2; *I.Didyma* 488, line 29) or slaves (*SEG* 33, 1039 [Kyme: Archippe], lines 69, 74). The compound προχορηγῆσαι (**B28**), 'loan, advance', is otherwise attested only in a precisely contemporary decree of Magnesia on the Maeander (*c.*175–160 B C), where it refers to a short-term cash advance by a civic magistrate: *I.Priene*[2] T 4a (Ager 1996, no. 120 I), lines 29–32, [τὸ δὲ ἀνάλωμα τὸ εἰς] ταῦτα προχορηγησάτω Παυσανίας ὁ νεωκόρος τῆς Ἀ[ρ]τεμίδος τῆς Λευκο[φρυηνῆς, κομι]σάσθω δὲ ἐκ τῶν ἐσομένων προσόδων κτλ.[54] The oxen that the Abderites are seeking to purchase are surely draft-oxen for arable cultivation (cf. **B25**, εἰς τὴν τῆς χώρας ἐξεργασίαν), known in the Hellenistic period as οἱ ἐργάται βοῦς ('working oxen') or οἱ ἀροῦντες ('ploughers'), as opposed to βοῦς ἀγελαῖαι ('herd-cows'), reared for milk and meat.[55] The loss of draft-animals in wartime could cause cities major economic difficulties; in 279/8 B C, after the ravaging of the territory of Kyzikos during the war between Antiochos I and Antigonos Gonatas, Philetairos of Pergamon granted the Kyzikenes tax-exemption on any draft-oxen they purchased in his territory and exported back to Kyzikos: *OGIS* 748, lines 8–12, ἀτέλειαν [sc. ἔδωκεν]...βοῶν ὧν ἀγοράσαντες ἐκ τῆς αὐτοῦ ἐξηγάγοντο. The text does not make it clear whether the oxen are to be purchased by the city of Abdera, or by the individual Abderite proprietors who were 'oppressed in their livelihoods' (**B25–6**).

B28–31

Τήϊοι τῶι μὲν πλουτεῖν λειπόμε-
νοι, τῶι δὲ εὐνοεῖν πάντας ἀνθρώπους ὑπεράγοντες, προέχρησαν ἄτο-
30 κα τάλαντα πέντε εἰς ἔτη πέντε, βουλόμενοι κατὰ μηθὲν ἐλλιπῆ τῶν
συμφερόντων τὸν δῆμον ἡμῶν γενέσθαι·...

'The Teians, although lacking in wealth, but outstripping all other men in good-will, advanced us five talents without interest over five years, wishing that in no respect our *dēmos* should be lacking in what is beneficial....'

---

[54] See further Wilhelm 1921a, 32–3; Samitz 2019, 288–92. The prefix προ- is very common in the vocabulary of loans: see Migeotte 1980.

[55] Chandezon 2003, 99–100, 210; for ἐργάται and ἀροῦντες, see the late fourth-century *sympoliteia* between Teos and a neighbouring community (Robert, *OMS* VII, 319–32; Chandezon 2003, no. 53), lines 4–5.

The Teians respond to this request by advancing the Abderites an interest-free loan of five talents for five years. The phraseology of **B28–9** has no close parallels in Greek epigraphy; the overall sense is very similar to that of **B19–22** (the Teians are not wealthy, but their goodwill is second to none). The verb λείπεσθαι is regularly used in the sense 'fall short', usually with ἐν + dat. (as in the stock phrase ὅπως ὁ δῆμος φαίνηται μὴ λειπόμενος ἐν χάριτος ἀποδόσει); for the plain dative, as here, cf. e.g. *SEG* 47, 891 (Beroia, II/I BC), lines 7–8, ἐσπούδασεν μὴ λειφθῆναι ἀρετῇ. The verb ὑπεράγειν, 'surpass', is exceptionally rare: the only close epigraphic parallels are found in two Pergamene honorific inscriptions of the late second century BC, *I.Pergamon* 252 line 20, ὑπεράγουσαν ἐπιστροφὴν ἐποήσατο, and Jacobsthal 1908, 375–9, no. 1, lines 16–17, ὑπε[ρά]γουσαν πρόνοιαν ἐποήσατο. The verb προχρᾶν (**B29**) is very often used of loans to communities;[56] the term is precisely synonymous with προχορηγεῖν (**B28**), and is here used only for the sake of variation. The sum of five talents is within the normal range for loans (with or without interest) between city-states in the Hellenistic period: in 283/2 BC, the Knidians lent a total of twelve talents and ten minas of Rhodian silver (raised by public subscription) to the city of Miletos, of which three talents were interest-free (over a one-year term) and the remainder subject to interest at a low rate of 6 per cent per annum (over a three-year term); in the early second century BC, the small city of Thisbe lent between 5,000 and 10,000 drachms to her neighbour Chorsiai.[57] However, the term of five years is startlingly generous for an interest-free loan: the interest-free part of the Knidians' early third-century loan to Miletos had to be repaid within one year, as did the interest-free loan of 1,000 gold staters granted by Dionysios to Istros in the third century BC (*IScM* I, 19) and Protogenes' interest-free loan of 300 gold staters to Olbia (*Syll.*[3] 495, lines 69–70).[58] There is no reliable way of estimating how many draft-oxen the Abderites could have purchased for five talents. In various different parts of the Greek world (Athens, Delos, Kos) cattle purchased for sacrifice seem typically to have cost 50–100 drachms a head in the late Classical and Hellenistic periods, with particularly impressive specimens costing up to 600 drachms.[59] At the other end of the spectrum, Polybios tells us that draft-oxen in Spain could be

---

[56] e.g. *SEG* 29, 1216 (Kyme, III/II BC), line 14; *IG* XII 6, 1, 11 (III BC), lines 35, 39; *I.Erythrai* 28 (III BC), lines 40, 47; *I.Ephesos* 1382 ((?) I BC), line 8; Migeotte 1984, 201 and index IV s.v. προχράω.

[57] Miletos and Knidos: *Milet* I 3, 138 (Migeotte 1984, no. 96); Thisbe and Chorsiai: Migeotte 1984, no. 11. The massive loan of one hundred talents provided by Rhodes to Argos at some point in the early Hellenistic period (Migeotte 1984, no. 19) is unique in our epigraphic evidence. See further Migeotte 1984, 364–6.

[58] Migeotte 1984, 385–6.   [59] Rosivach 1994, 95–106; *ThesCRA* I, 101–3.

purchased for 10 drachms a head (34.8.8).⁶⁰ Coastal Thrace offered excellent conditions for cattle-breeding, but the sheer number of oxen that the Abderites were seeking to purchase would have pushed up prices; e.g. at 50 drachms a head, five talents would be sufficient to purchase six hundred animals. For the general sense of the clause in **B30–1** (κατὰ μηθὲν ἐλλιπῆ... γενέσθαι), compare *SEG* 44, 872 (Halikarnassos), lines 12–15, τὴν ἄλλην ἐκ προγόνων ἀρετὴν καὶ μεγαλιότητα κατὰ μηδὲν ἐνλιπῆ γενηθῖσαν; *I.Sestos* 1 (shortly after 133 BC), lines 50–1, βουλόμενος... κατὰ μηθὲν ἐνλείπειν τῆι πρὸς τὸ πλῆθος εὐνοίαι; *I.Iasos* 22, lines 36–40, βουλόμενος κατὰ μηθὲν ἐνλε[ίπειν ὅσ]ων... ἐπήνγελται; *I.Priene*² 64 (late II BC), lines 54–5, σπεύδων... κατὰ μηδὲν ἐνλείπειν.

B31–4

ἐπιβάντων δὲ καὶ Μαρωνιτῶν
ἐπὶ τὴν πάτριον ἡμῶν χώραν οὐκ ἐπιβαλλόντως καὶ παραγενομένων ν.
εἰς ἀμφισβήτησιν ὑπὲρ αὐτῆς, ληφθέντος κατὰ δόγμα τῆς συνκλήτου
κριτοῦ τοῦ Ἐρυθραίων δήμου, ...

'And when the Maroneitai encroached upon our ancestral territory, although it did not pertain to them, and entered into a dispute over it, and when the *dēmos* of Erythrai was appointed as judge by decision of the Senate, ...'

The decree now moves on to a new topic, the alleged seizure of part of the ancestral territory of Abdera by the neighbouring city of Maroneia and the ensuing arbitration of the dispute by the *dēmos* of Erythrai; the account of this dispute occupies the remainder of the considerations (B31–52). It is likely enough that the seizure of Abderite land occurred in the immediate aftermath of the Roman sack of Abdera in 170 BC, but there is no way of knowing how many years intervened before the arbitration was actually heard (see further Chapter 5 below). The verb ἐπιβαίνειν (B31) is used of an illicit encroachment onto someone else's land in a spurious Amphiktyonic decree inserted in Dem. *De cor.* 154, ἐπειδὴ Ἀφισσεῖς ἐπιβαίνουσιν ἐπὶ τὴν ἱερὰν χώραν καὶ σπείρουσι καὶ βοσκήμασι κατανέμουσιν; cf. also *I.Priene*² 132 (190s BC), lines 148 and

---

⁶⁰ App. *Mith.* 78 and Plut. *Luc.* 14.1 tell us that during Lucullus' march into Pontos in 72 BC, oxen seized as booty were sold at the ridiculously low price of 1 drachm a head.

163 (of Samian encroachment on Prienian territory).⁶¹ The claim that the Maroneitai had encroached onto Abderite 'ancestral territory' (**B32**, τὴν πάτριον ἡμῶν χώραν) is closely paralleled in the decree for Amymon and Megathymos (**Document 6** below, Chapter 5), where Kotys is similarly said to have laid claim to (part of) the ancestral territory of Abdera (line 9, ἠτεῖτ[ο τὴν π]άτριον ἡμῶν χώραν; also line 6, πρεσβείας . . . ὑπὲρ τῆς πατρίου [χώρας]).⁶² The adverb ἐπιβαλλόντως is otherwise unattested epigraphically (or in Greek literature before Late Antiquity), but the verb ἐπιβάλλειν is commonly found in the sense 'belong to/pertain to'; a fairly close analogy for the sense here is found in *I.Priene²* 67 (honours for Krates, I BC), lines 139–40, where *publicani* encroach on [τῶν μ]ηδὲν ἐπιβαλλόντων ἑαυτοῖς τόπων, 'places which do not pertain to them'; for the use of the term in interstate disputes, see e.g. Ager 1996, no. 167 (dispute between Skarphai and Thronion, II BC), lines 15–16, ἐξιδιάζεσθα[ι θέ]λεις ἀδίκως τὸ ἐμὶν ἐπιβάλλον μέρος τᾶς ἱερομναμοσύνας.

The two parties appealed to the Roman senate, who appointed the *dēmos* of Erythrai to hear the case (**B33–4**). In the second century BC, the senate usually delegated arbitrations between Greek cities to a neutral third party.⁶³ When the dispute was over territorial boundaries (as here), the senate sometimes stipulated that the land was to belong to whichever state possessed it at the point when they entered into alliance or friendship with Rome, but we do not know whether that rule was applied in this instance (see Chapter 5 below). For the phraseology of **B33–4**, compare the Milesian arbitration between Sparta and Messene (*c.*138 BC), *Syll.*³ 683 (Ager 1996, no. 159; Camia 2009, no. 3), lines 49–52, εἰσήχθη ἡ κρίσις κατὰ . . . τὸ δόγμα τῆς συ[γκλ]ήτου π[ερὶ τοῦ] ἐπαμφιλλό[γου] κτλ., and the Magnesian arbitration between Itanos and Hierapytna (*c.*111 BC), *I.Cret.* III iv 9 (Ager 1996, no. 158 II; Camia 2009, no. 10 II), lines 9–10, κεχειροτονημένων καὶ αὐτῶν ὑπὸ τοῦ δήμου δικάσαι Κρησὶν Ἰτ[ανίοις τε κα]ὶ Ἱ[ερ]απυτνί[οις κατὰ τὸ γεγο]νὸς ὑπὸ τῆς συγκλήτου δόγμα.⁶⁴ In the contemporary dossier recording the settlement of a land-dispute

---

⁶¹ The verb is also used simply of 'setting foot' in forbidden territory, as in the late fourth-century tyrants' dossier from Eresos (Rhodes and Osborne 2003, no. 83), §vi line 38, [αἰ δ]έ κέ τις . . . ἐπιβαίνων ἐπὶ τὰν γᾶν τὰν Ἐρεσίων.

⁶² Cf. also *OGIS* 228 (Rigsby 1996, 102–5, no. 7: Delphi, privileges for Smyrna from Seleukos II), lines 8–9, τάν τε ὑπάρχουσαν αὐτοῖς χώραν βεβαιοῖ, καὶ τὰν πάτριον ἐπαγγέλλεται ἀποδώσειν; Robert, *Hellenica* XI–XII, 513–14.

⁶³ Ager 1996, 26–9; Camia 2009, 197–9; add now also *SEG* 60, 15699 (Rousset 2010; *StV* IV, 675), lines 91–4 (Knidos arbitrates between the Lykian League and Termessos by Oinoanda, *c.*160–150 BC).

⁶⁴ The Itanos–Hierapytna dossier also features the appointment of a *dēmos* as κριτής (cf. **B33–4**, ληφθέντος . . . κριτοῦ τοῦ Ἐρυθραίων δήμου): *I.Cret.* III iv 9 (Ager 1996, no. 158 *II*), lines 18–20, τῆς δὲ συγκλήτου . . . δούσης κριτὴν αὐτ[οῖς τὸν ἡμέτερ]ον δῆ[μον]; cf. also the senate's appointment of the Knidian *dēmos* as *kritēs* in the territorial dispute between the Lykian League and Termessos by Oinoanda, *SEG* 60, 1569, lines 93–4, ἔλαβον παρὰ τῆς συγκλήτου τὸν Κνιδί[ων δῆμ]ον κριτήν.

between Priene and Magnesia by a Mylasan tribunal (*c*.175–160 BC), the senate instructs the *praetor* M. Aemilius M.f. to appoint a free city as arbitrator, ideally one acceptable to both parties, but failing that, whichever free city the *praetor* may choose: *I.Priene*² T 4b (Ager 1996, no. 120 II; Camia 2009, no. 7 II), lines 14–15, ὅπως Μάαρκος Αἰμύλιος Μαάρκου υἱὸς στρατηγὸς δ[ῆμον ἐ]λεύθερον κριτὴν δῶι ὃς ἂν ἐν αὐτοῖς ὁμόλογος γενηθῇ, 'the *praetor* M. Aemilius M.f. is to appoint a free *dēmos* as judge, whichever is agreed by the two parties'. It is likely enough that a similar procedure was followed on this occasion. Erythrai had been granted the status of a free city after the peace of Apameia (Polyb. 21.45.6) on the basis of the goodwill they had shown towards Rome during the war with Antiochos (Livy 37.8.5, 37.11.14, 37.12.10); the Erythraians are later found arbitrating between the city of Priene and Roman *publicani* (*I.Priene*² 67, lines 125–7, 146: late 90s BC). Erythrai's geographical location may also be relevant, lying as it did between Teos to the east and Chios (the supposed mother-city of Maroneia: pseudo-Skymnos, *FGrHist* 2048 T1, lines 676–8) to the west; the Romans might reasonably have felt that Erythrai would have been particularly likely to take an unprejudiced view in a dispute between the daughter-cities of Teos and Chios.[65]

The actual hearing may well have taken place at Erythrai; in the late 90s BC, an Erythraian tribunal heard a dispute between the city of Priene and Roman *publicani* in the theatre at Erythrai: *I.Priene*² 67 (honours for Krates, I BC), lines 124–7, ἀ[πο]δεδειγμένος καὶ αὐτὸς ἔκδικος…[ἀποδημ]ήσας εἰς Ἐρυθράς… [δικαιο]λογήσας ὑπὲρ τῆς πόλεως ἐν τῶι θεάτρωι τῶι Ἐρυθραίων.

B34–8

αἰσθόμενοι Τήϊοι καταφρονουμένους ἡ-
35 μᾶς διὰ τὴν στενοχωρίαν τῶν βίων οὐ προήκαντο, ἀλλ' ἴδια νομίσαντες
ἑαυτῶν εἶναι τὰ διὰ τῶν ἰδίων προγόνων κρατηθέντα καὶ κατοικισθέν- ν.
τα, ἀξίως καὶ μεγαλομερῶς ἐπέδωκαν ἑαυτούς, πάσῃ προθυμίαι καὶ φιλαγα-
[θ]ίαι χρησάμενοι, πρὸς τὸν ἀγῶνα τὸν ὑπὲρ ταύτης τῆς χώρας,…

'The Teians, perceiving that we were being treated contemptuously because of the poverty of our livelihoods, did not abandon us, but considering as their

---

[65] On the motives underlying the choice of arbitrator, Camia 2009, 198.

own possessions the lands conquered and settled by their own ancestors, they dedicated themselves worthily and magnificently to the lawsuit over this stretch of land, employing all enthusiasm and excellence of character;...'

The Teians' motivations for assisting the Abderites once again are described at length. We ought perhaps to be sceptical of the claim that the Abderites 'were being treated contemptuously' (καταφρονουμένους, B34) in the arbitration because of their poverty.[66] The term στενοχωρία, 'poverty, distress', is rather rare in Hellenistic epigraphy: cf. *I.Sestos* 1 (honours for Menas, shortly after 133 BC), line 103, διὰ τὴν ὑπάρχουσαν περὶ τὰ κοινὰ στενοχωρίαν; *SEG* 37, 859B (Zeuxis to Herakleia, *c.*196–193 BC), lines 12–14, τῆς γεγενημένης στενοχω[ρία]ς περὶ τὴν πόλιν ἐκ τῶν ἐπάνω χρόνων διὰ τοὺς πολέμους καὶ τὰς κα[ταφθ]οράς; *IG* VII, 190 (Pagai, mid-first century BC), line 19, διὰ τὸ στενο[χωρεῖ]σθαι τὰ κοινὰ πράγματ[α τᾶς π]ό[λιος]. For βίων στενοχωρία, 'poverty of livelihoods', cf. Polyb. 31.31.2, στενοχωρίας μὲν ὑπαρχούσης καθάπαξ ἐπὶ τῶν κατ᾿ ἰδίαν βίων, 'when one is experiencing temporary impoverishment of one's private livelihood'. The use of the verb προέσθαι in the sense 'betray, abandon' (B35), is common in literary texts (LSJ s.v. προΐημι B.II.1–2). The description of the Teians' emotional commitment to the maintenance of the territory of Abdera as originally conquered and settled by them (B35–7) has no epigraphic parallels: for the epic struggles of the sixth-century Teian colonists to drive out the Paionians from the plain of Xanthi and extend their territory as far as Mt Lekani, see Pind. *Pae.* 2.57–79 (discussed in Chapter 2 below), especially lines 59–61, τοὶ σὺν πολέμῳ κτησάμ[ενοι] χθόνα πολύδωρον ὄλ[βον] ἐγκατέθηκαν, 'those who won in warfare the land rich in gifts established (for their descendants) a store-house of prosperity'. Note the emphatic repetition of ἴδια...ἰδίων (B35–6): the land conquered by the Teians' ancestors continues to be, in a sense, the Teians' 'own' land. For the phrase ἐπιδίδοναι ἑαυτὸν πρὸς ἀγῶνα (B37–8), 'dedicate oneself to a lawsuit', cf. *I.Pergamon* 536 (I BC), lines 6–7, ἐπιδόντα δὲ ἑατὸν καὶ εἰς Ῥώμην ὑπὲρ τῆς πατρίδος ἐπὶ τοὺς τῶν ἡγουμένων ἀγῶνας.[67]

---

[66]   The closest epigraphic parallel comes in the third-century AD petition of Skaptopara to Gordian III: Hauken 1998, no. 1, A: 5, lines 70–3, προιόντων δὲ τῶν χρόνων πάλιν ἐτόλμησαν ἐπιφύεσθαι ἡμεῖν πλεῖστοι ὅσοι τῆς ἰδιωτίας ἡμῶν καταφρονοῦντες, 'as time passed, those numerous people who despise our private status have again ventured to assault us'.

[67]   See further Robert 1937, 51–2, 56–7; for ἀγών of a land-dispute, cf. Robert 1945, no. 11 (Sinuri), lines 7–8.

B38–43

$$ἐπέλεξάν$$

τε γὰρ ἐξ ἑαυτῶν συνέδρους χάριν τῆς τῶν δικαίων ἐρεύνης τοὺς νοεῖν
40 τε καὶ προσκαρτερῆσαι δυναμένους ἀπερισπάστως τοῖς πρὸς τὸν ν.
ἐξετασμὸν παρατεθησομένοις δικαίοις, εἵλοντό τε καὶ τὸν ἐροῦν-
ταἐπὶ τῆς κρίσεως τὰ δίκαια καὶ πᾶσαν ὅλως τὴν ὑπὲρ τοῦ ἀγῶνος ἀ-
νελάβοσαν φροντίδα, . . .

'For also they selected from among themselves commissioners for the sake of
seeking out the legal claims, those able both to understand and to persist without
distraction in the face of the legal claims that would be put forward in the enquiry,
and they also appointed a person who would present their claims at the hearing,
and they completely took on in all respects the care of the lawsuit; . . .'

The Teians provide the Abderites both with a group of σύνεδροι ('advisors,
commissioners') to help them prepare their case (**B38–41**), and with an advocate to present their case at the hearing (**B41–2**), thereby taking on the entire
burden of the lawsuit (**B42–3**). For Teian legal specialists in the second century
BC, see—in addition to the decree for Amymon and Megathymos (**Document
6** below, Chapter 5)—*SEG* 47, 745 (Larissa: Teian judges requested by the
Thessalian *koinon*).[68] The variation ἐπέλεξάν τε γὰρ . . . εἵλοντό τε καί (**B38,
B41**) does not reflect any difference in the process of selecting the relevant
Teian legal specialists, but is simply rhetorical variation for its own sake
(cf. προχορηγῆσαι . . . προέχρησαν, **B28–9**).[69] The task of the Teian σύνεδροι
was apparently to help prepare the dossier of evidence supporting the
Abderite claim to the land, which would be presented at the enquiry
(ἐξετασμός, **B41**). We know of no close parallel for the use of the term
σύνεδρος for—in effect—a member of a legal team, but similar vocabulary is
used in the decree for Amymon and Megathymos (**Document 6** below,
Chapter 5), where the two Teians give useful advice at the 'synedriai which
took place concerning the territory' (lines 15–19), apparently meetings at
Abdera where the Abderite case was put together. For χάριν + gen. expressing

---

[68] For a third-century Teian judge, see *I.Iasos* 608 (*c.*270–261 BC, decree of Bargylia for the judge
Tyron of Teos).

[69] The verb αἱρεῖσθαι (**B41**) is used of the Teian selection of Amymon and Megathymos as ambassadors (**Document 6** below), lines 9–10, ο[ἱ] αἱρέθεντες πρεσβευταί; for ἐπιλέγειν (LSJ s.v. II), *OGIS*
309 (Teos, II BC), line 9, τὰς παρθένους τὰς ἐπιλεγείσας ὑπὸ τοῦ παιδονόμου; *Milet* I 3, 145 (200/199
BC), line 72, οἱ ἐπιλεγέντες ὑπ'αὐτῶν [sc. τῶν παιδονόμων] παῖδες.

purpose ('for the purpose of *x*'), cf. **Document 6** below, lines 16–17, ἐπίνοιαν π[αρέσχ]οντο χάριν τοῦ μηθὲν π[α]ραλειφθῆναι τῶν δυναμ[ένων ἐπα]νορθῶσαι τὰ πράγματα.[70] For the characterization of the Teian *synedroi* as 'those able both to understand and to persist' (τοὺς νοεῖν τε καὶ προσκαρτερῆσαι δυναμένους, **B39–40**), cf. *IG* XII 6, 1, 128 (Samos, *c.*200 BC), [το]ὺς ἀγαθοὺς καὶ ἀξίους ἄνδρας [καὶ δ]υναμένους ὠφελεῖν τῶν νέων [τοὺς] φιλομαθοῦντας. The verb προσκαρτερῆσαι appears in a judicial context in *IG* XII 4, 1, 57, lines 5–6, and *IG* XII 4, 1, 59, lines 19–21 (second-century Koan decrees for *dikastagōgoi*), ποτικαρτερήσας καὶ τᾶι δικαστοφυλακίαι ἐκτενῶς καὶ δικαίως; *SEG* 26, 677 (II BC: decree of Peparethos for judges from Larisa), lines 31–2 (with Crowther 1997, 352), ἐκτε[νῶς καὶ δικαίως τῇ δικαστείᾳ προσ]-καρτεροῦντες. The earliest literary attestations of the adjective ἀπερίσπαστος, 'without distraction', are in Polybios;[71] the only epigraphic instance (in the sense 'continually') is in the letter of Antiochos III on the appointment of an *archiereus* at Daphne (189 BC), Welles, *RC* 44, lines 14–16, ὅπως τὸν ἐπίλοιπον χρόνον τοῦ βίου ἀπερισπάστως ἐν εὐσταθείαι τοῦ σώματος γένηται.

In **B41–2**, the phrase τὸν ἐροῦντα ἐπὶ τῆς κρίσεως τὰ δίκαια, 'a person who would present their claims at the hearing', is an elaborate periphrasis for the role of advocate (ἔκδικος, συνήγορος, σύνδικος), often denoted in Hellenistic epigraphy with the verb δικαιολογεῖν/δικαιολογεῖσθαι.[72] We have several other Hellenistic instances of cities employing advocates from foreign cities to plead their case in interstate arbitrations.[73] So in the 290s BC, the small city of Kalymna brought in a certain Hekatonymos of Miletos to act as advocate alongside two Kalymnians in a dispute with Kos, adjudicated by judges from Knidos (*Tit. Calymnii* 7); around 179 BC, Delphi employed an Athenian advocate, Apollodoros, to represent them in a dispute with Amphissa (*FD* III

---

[70] Robert and Robert 1983, no. 35 (Amyzon, II BC), lines 5–8, [σπου]δὴν καὶ πρόνοιαν ποιούμενος διατετέλεκε[ν περὶ τῶν τ]ῶ[ι] δήμωι συνφερόντων χάριν τῆς ἐπαυξήσε[ως τῶν κ]οινῶ[ν] πραγμάτων. The first-century honorific decree of Halikarnassos published by Cousin and Diehl 1890, 97–9, no. 4, features three successive purpose-clauses expressed with χάριν + gen. (lines 8–12).

[71] e.g. 4.18.6, οὔτε γὰρ πρὸς τοὺς διὰ τῆς πύλης εἰσπίπτοντας οἷοί τ᾽ἦσαν βοηθεῖν ἀπερισπάστως διὰ τοὺς πρὸς τὰ τείχη προσβάλλοντας.

[72] For δικαιολογοῦντες/δικαιολογούμενοι in Hellenistic epigraphy (Savalli-Lestrade 2012, 143 n. 7), cf. e.g. *FD* III 4, 69 (Daulis honours Hermias of Stratonikeia, early I BC), lines 19–20, δικαιολογηθέντ[α ὑπὲρ τοῦ δ]άμου ἐπὶ τῶν ἀγειμένων; *I.Priene²* 67 (honours for Krates, I BC), lines 126–7, ἔκδικος...[δικαιο]λογήσας ὑπὲρ τῆς πόλεως ἐν τῶι θεάτρωι τῶι Ἐρυθραίων; *I.Priene²* 132 (Rhodian arbitration, 190s BC), lines 13–14, δικαιολογησα[μένω]ν τῶν αἱρεθέντων ὑπὸ μὲν Σαμίων; *I.Priene²* T 4a (Magnesia, *c.*175–160 BC), line 22, δικαιολογηθέντων. On σύνδικοι, Wilhelm 1912, 251; Wilhelm 1942, 33–4; Fournier 2007.

[73] Savalli-Lestrade 2012, 142–6.

2, 89; Rousset 2002, 74–6, no. 2); and around 190 BC, Apollodoros of Priene (who had already acted as advocate in the Prienean dispute with Samos) seems to have served as advocate of the city of Phokaia in a dispute with Smyrna (*I.Priene*² 101). The aorist form ἀνελάβοσαν (**B42–3**), with -οσαν for -ον, is common in documents of the second century BC: cf. e.g. *I.Priene*² T 4c (*c.*175–160 BC), lines c11 (ἐλέγοσαν), c24 (διακατείχοσαν); *I.Cret.* III iv 10 (112/111 BC), line 91 (προσήλθοσαν).⁷⁴

B43–8

διαλαβόντες δὲ καὶ μὴ ἱκανὴν ἑνὸς ἀνδρὸς ὑπάρχειν
δύναμιν διὰ τὸ μέγεθος τοῦ ἀγῶνος καὶ τὸ πλῆθος τῶν ἀποδείξεων, ἔ- ν.
45 πεμψαν εἰς Μίλητον τὸ ἐλλεῖπον δοκοῦν τῆι καθ' ἑαυτοὺς σπουδῆι καὶ ν.
φιλοτιμίαι προσαναπληροῦντες ἀπὸ ξένης καὶ τὸν συναντιληψόμενον ν.
ἐν τῶι ἀγῶνι μετεπέμψαντο καὶ χάριν ἰδίαν αἰτησάμενοι καὶ μισθὸν πα- ν.
ρ' ἑαυτῶν ὅσον ᾔτησεν ἐκτείναντες, …

'And when they perceived that the ability of a single man was insufficient given the scale of the lawsuit and the volume of depositions, they sent to Miletos, to supplement from a foreign city what seemed to be lacking to their own eagerness and ambition, and requested someone who would join in taking on the lawsuit, requesting a private favour (from Miletos) and providing whatever fee he demanded from their own resources,…'

The Teians procure an additional professional advocate from Miletos to represent the Abderites at the hearing; for another 'international' Milesian advocate of this kind, see *Tit. Calymnii* 7 (the *synēgoros* Hekatonymos of Miletos, *c.*300–296 BC), with Savalli-Lestrade 2012, 143–4, 166–7. For the verb διαλαβεῖν (**B43**) in the sense 'judge, reckon' (LSJ s.v. III.6), see Robert, *OMS* II, 1060–1; Robert and Robert 1989, 51, citing *I.Priene*² 64 (decree for Moschion, late II BC), lines 91–2, διαλαβ[ὼν κ]οινὴν εἶναι τὴ[ν] οὐσίαν πάντων τῶν πολιτῶν. For ἱκανὴν…δύναμιν, 'sufficient ability' (**B43–4**), cf. Polyb. 7.16.2, διὰ τὸ δοκεῖν ἑκάτερον ἱκανὴν δύναμιν ἔχειν καὶ τόλμαν πρὸς τὴν

---

⁷⁴ For ἀναλαβεῖν φροντίδα ὑπέρ τινος, cf. *IThrakAig* E180 (Maroneia, 40s AD), lines 22–5, ἀναγκαιότατον δέ ἐστιν καὶ ἡμᾶς πᾶσαν εἰσενέγκασθαι φροντίδα ὑπὲρ τοῦ μήτε νῦν μήτε ἄλλοτέ ποτε… συνβῆναι κατὰ μηδένα τρόπον ἐλασσωθῆναι ἡμῶν τὴν ἐλευθερίαν.

ἐπινοουμένην πρᾶξιν, 'because both seemed to have sufficient ability and courage for the projected undertaking'. For the phrase τὸ ἐλλεῖπον ἀναπληροῦν, 'make up the deficiency' (**B45–6**), cf. Polyb. 38.15.5, οἷς δ᾽ ἂν ἐλλείπῃ τὸ τῶν παρατρόφων πλῆθος, ἀναπληροῦν ἔδει τὴν ἑκάστοις καθήκουσαν μοῖραν ἐκ τῶν ἄλλων οἰκέτων, 'those who had insufficient home-bred slaves had to make up the deficiency in their share from their other slaves'; Dion. Hal. *Ant. Rom.* 8.87.3, ἵνα τὸ ἐλλιπὲς ἀναπληρωθῇ τῶν λόχων; Diod. Sic. 37.21.1, τὸ τοῦ πλήθους ἐλλιπὲς τῇ τῆς ἀρετῆς ὑπερβολῇ προσανεπλήρουν; Dio Cass. 56.35.4. For ἀπὸ ξένης ('from abroad', **B46**), cf. *SEG* 41, 625 (Phanagoreia), τοὺς ἀπὸ ξένης στρατιώτας; Jacobsthal 1908, 379–81, no. 2 (Pergamon), lines 13–14, τοὺς παραγινομένους ἀπὸ ξένης. Instances of συναντιλαμβάνεσθαι ('join in providing assistance', **B46**) are collected and analysed by Robert 1936, 93; Robert and Robert 1983, 135 n. 24, 189; add *SEG* 59, 1407 (Kyme, III bc), line A9; *IG* XII 4, 1, 94 (Kos, late III bc), lines 8–9. The Teians requested the services of this advocate as a 'private favour' from Miletos (**B47**, cf. *Syll.*³ 748, Gytheion, 71 bc, line 15, ἰδίαν χάριν ἐξαιτησάμενοι); it is unclear what is being alluded to here (a previous favour done by the Teians for Miletos?). At any rate, the Milesian advocate insisted on being paid (**B47–8**), and the Teians picked up the bill.[75]

B48–52

κ
αὶ τὸ συνέχον, τῆς τῶν θεῶν καὶ Τηΐ-
ων εὐνοίας ἅμα τοῖς δικαίοις προσγενομένης, κατώρθωσεν ὁ δῆμος ἡμῶν ἐν τῆι
50 πρὸς Μαρωνίτας κρίσει, ἀθάνατον ὑπόμνημα τῆς πρὸς τοὺς συνγενεῖς εὐνοίας διὰ τῶν ἔργων πᾶσιν ἐ⟨κ⟩θέντων ἀνθρώποις Τηΐων καὶ πρὸς ὑπερβο- ν.
[λὴ]ν εὐεργεσιῶν οὐθενὶ τόπον ἀπολειπόντων· …

'And most importantly, with the goodwill both of the gods and the Teians being added to our legal claims, our *dēmos* was successful against the Maroneitai in the judgement, with the Teians having set up through their actions an eternal memorial for all men of their goodwill towards their kin, and leaving space for no one else to surpass them in benefactions.…'

---

[75] The term μισθός is regularly used of the fees charged by skilled professionals such as doctors (*IG* XII 4, 1, 109 [Kos, II bc], line 28; *IG* XII 1, 1032 [Karpathos, II bc], line 14) and philosophers (*IG* XII 6, 1, 128 [Samos, *c.*200 bc], line 22).

The Abderites briefly note their success in the lawsuit, and give a final summary of the Teians' benefactions. The adverbial phrase τὸ συνέχον, 'most importantly' (**B48**), is not found elsewhere in Greek epigraphy; it is, however, a favourite of Polybios, used to mark the most significant point in a list of clauses or attributes. For example in his account of the peace treaty at the end of the First Illyrian War (228 BC), Teuta agrees to pay tribute (or an indemnity), to withdraw from Illyria except a few places, 'and most importantly' (καὶ τὸ συνέχον), which particularly concerned the Greeks, not to sail beyond Lissos with more than two unarmed ships (2.12.3).[76] For the conception of divine favour contributing to success in a lawsuit (**B48–9**), compare the contemporary decree of Magnesia on the Maeander (*c.*175–160 BC) concerning their victory over Priene in a land-dispute, *I.Priene*[2] T 4a (Ager 1996, no. 120 I), lines 11–12, τῶν δὲ θεῶν μετὰ τῆς τοῦ σ[τρατηγοῦ δικαι]οσύνης ἐπιτεθεικότων τέλος τῆι κρίσει καὶ νενικηκότος πάλιν τοῦ δή[μου ἡμῶν], 'with the gods and the justice of the *praetor* putting an end to the lawsuit, and with our *dēmos* being victorious again'; for the combination of divine and human agency, cf. *OGIS* 305 (Delphi recognizes Panathenaia and Eumeneia at Sardeis, 160s BC), lines 10–11, Σαρδιανοὶ διαφυγόντες [τὸν μέγιστον] κίνδυνον μετά τ[ε τᾶς τ]ῶν [θεῶν] εὐν[ο]ίας καὶ [μετὰ τᾶς τοῦ β]ασιλέος Εὐμένεος ἀρετᾶς. In lines **B50–2**, the decree comes full circle, and the language closely echoes the opening lines of the decree (**A4–14**): for ἀθάνατον ὑπόμνημα τῆς πρὸς τοὺς συγγενεῖς εὐνοίας... ἐ⟨κ⟩θέντων (**B50–1**), cf. ἀθάνατον παρασκευά[ζον]τες... εὐδοξίαν (**A7–9**) and ἐκτεθεικότων αὐτῶν τὴν πρὸς τοὺς σ[υγ]γενεῖς ἑαυτῶν ἀπροφάσιστον σπουδὴν (**A13–14**); for πρὸς ὑπερβο[λὴ]ν εὐεργεσιῶν οὐθενὶ τόπον ἀπολειπόντων (**B51–2**), cf. ὑπερβολὴν εὐεργεσιῶν οὐθενὶ βεβουλημένοι ἀπ[ολιπεῖ]ν (**A9**).[77] For the idea of leaving an 'eternal memorial' (ἀθάνατον ὑπόμνημα, **B50**) of the Teians' goodwill, compare *IG* XII 9, 236 (Eretria, *c.*100 BC), lines 14–17, βουλόμενός τε τῆς ἑαυτοῦ καλοκἀγαθίας τε καὶ εὐνοίας ἧς ἔχει πρὸς τὸν δῆμον ἀθάνατον ὑπόμνημα καταλείπειν; *SEG* 33, 1039 (decree for Archippe, II BC), lines 21–3, κατατιθεμένην τὴν ἑαυτῆς φιλοτιμίαν εἰς τὰ κάλλιστα καὶ πρὸς ἐπιφάνειαν καὶ μνήμην ἀθάνατον ἀνήκοντα; Cousin and Diehl 1890, 97–9, no. 4 (Halikarnassos, I BC), lines 10–11, χάριν τοῦ τὴν μνήμην μένειν ἀθάνατον τῶν ὑπὲρ τῆς πατρίδος ὑπ᾽αὐτοῦ κατωρθωμένων.

---

[76] Similarly Polyb. 2.52.4, 3.51.13, 6.16.4, 9.37.1, 10.45.5, 15.2.3, 21.16.9, 22.21.4, 23.7.6, 23.16.9, 30.2.7; Cic. *Att.* 9.7.1.

[77] For τόπον τινὶ ἀπολείπειν, cf. Polyb. 1.88.2, τὸ μὴ καταλείπεσθαι σφίσι τόπον ἐλέους μηδὲ συγγνώμης; 30.8.3, παρὰ τοῖς ἐπιγενομένοις μηδ᾽ἔσχατον ἐλέῳ καὶ συγγώμῃ τόπον καταλιπεῖν.

B52–6

ἵνα οὖν καὶ ὁ παρ' ἡμῶν δῆ-
[μο]ς ἀξίως ἐφ' ὅσον ἰσχύει τιμῶν φαίνηται τοὺς ἑαυτὸν εὐεργετήσαν- ν.
[τας·] τ[ύχ]ηι ἀγαθῆ· δεδόχθαι τῆι βουλῆι καὶ τῶι δήμωι τῶι Ἀβδηριτῶν· ἐπη-
55 [νῆσθαι Τηΐου]ς ἐπὶ τῆι αἱρέσει καὶ εὐνοίαι ἧι ἔχοντες διατελοῦσι πρὸς τὸν
[δῆμον ἡμ]ῶν,...

'And therefore, in order that it should be clear that our *dēmos* honours worthily—
insofar as it is able—those who confer benefactions upon it, with good fortune, be
it resolved by the *boulē* and *dēmos* of the Abderites, to praise the Teians for the
disposition and goodwill which they continue to hold towards our *dēmos*,...'

The purpose clause in **B52–3** is largely formulaic: cf. e.g. *I.Iasos* 153 (Samothrake,
II BC), lines 20–2, [ὅπως] οὖγ καὶ ὁ δῆμος φαίνηται τοὺς εὐεργετοῦντας αὐτὸν
τιμῶν ἀξίω[ς] διὰ πάντος (but close variants are legion). The phrase ὁ παρ'
ἡμῶν δῆ[μο]ς (= ὁ ἡμέτερος δῆμος) is paralleled in a first-century Delphic
decree, *Syll.*[3] 699 (*c.*100 BC), lines 12–13, καθάπερ ἐψάφισται αὐτοῖς τό τε
κ[οι]νὸν τῶν Ἀμφικτιόνων καὶ ἁ παρ' [ἁ]μῶν πόλις; for the qualification ἐφ'
ὅσον ἰσχύει, cf. [ἐφ'] ὅσον ἰσχύοσαν (**B5**; also **A8, B19**). At the start of **B55**, we
would normally expect to find τὸν δῆμον τὸν Τηΐων as honorand, but the
author of the decree generally favoured the plain ethnic Τήϊοι (**A4, B27, B28,
B34, B48, B51, B79, B84**) over ὁ δῆμος ὁ Τηΐων (**B15, B64, B67, B72, B86**).[78]
The honorific formula in **B54–6** is effectively identical to that found in the
Abderite decree for Philon of Akanthos, *IThrakAig* E7 (II BC), lines 13–16,
ἐπηνῆσθαι Φίλωνα Πύθωνος Ἀκάνθιον ἐπὶ τῆι εὐνοίαι καὶ τῆι αἱρέσει ἧι ἔχων
διατελεῖ πρὸς τὸν δῆμον ἡμῶν.

B56–61

στῆσαι δὲ καὶ εἰκόνα χαλκῆν κολοσσικὴν τοῦ Δήμου τοῦ
[Τηΐων ἐπὶ τῆς] ἀγορᾶς ἐν τῶι ἐπιφανεστάτωι τόπωι, τῆι μὲν δεξιᾶι σπέν-
[δοντα κανθάρω]ι, τῆι δὲ ἀριστερᾶι ἀπηρεισμένον ἐπὶ τὴν στήλην ἐν ἧι γε-
[γράψεται τόδ]ε τὸ ψήφισμα, ἔστω δὲ καὶ κιόνιον παρεστηκὸς ἐκ τῶν εὐωνύ-

---

[78] For the bare ethnic in such clauses, cf. e.g. *I.Cret.* I xxiv 1 (Priansos, II BC), δεδόχθαι τᾶι πόλει
ἐπαινέσαι Τήϊος; *I.Magnesia* 97 (II BC), lines 68–9, δεδόχθαι τῶι δήμωι ἐπηινῆσθαι μὲ[ν Τηΐους];
I.Knidos 219 (early II BC), lines 23–4, δεδόχθαι τῶι δά[μωι· ἐπαινέ]σαι Μάγνητας ἀρετᾶς ἕνεκε[ν].

60 [μων, ἐφ᾽οὗ ἐπ]έστω Νίκη στεφανοῦσα τὸν Τηΐων Δῆμον κισσοῦ στε-
    [φάνωι·…

'And to erect a colossal bronze statue of the *Dēmos* of the [Teians], on the agora in
the most prominent spot, pouring a libation [with a kantharos] with the right
hand, and with the left hand/arm leaning on the *stēlē* on which this decree shall
be inscribed; and let there be a small column standing by on the left-hand side,
[on which] let there be placed a Nike crowning the *Dēmos* of the Teians with an
ivy-wreath;…'

This remarkable personification of the Teian *Dēmos* is discussed further in
Chapter 6 below. The agora was the normal setting for honorific statues of all
kinds in Hellenistic cities (Ma 2013, 75–9); as it happens, we have no other
direct evidence for statues in the agora of Abdera, but the Abderite copy of the
decree for Amymon and Megathymos was likewise to be erected on the agora,
in the most prominent spot (**Document 6** below, Chapter 5, lines 36–7: ἐν τῶι
ἐπιφανεστάτωι τόπωι τῆς ἀγορᾶς); by contrast, the second-century Abderite
decree for Philon of Akanthos was to be erected in the sanctuary of Dionysos
at Abdera, 'where the inscribed honours for other *proxenoi* are', with a second
copy to be erected in the most prominent spot of the agora at Akanthos
(*IThrakAig* E7, lines 28–31, 39–40). The statue was made of bronze, and was
'colossal' (κολοσσικός, **B56**), i.e. of greater than human size;[79] for its probable
height, see Chapter 6 below. The lengthy description of the statue has no epigraphic parallels. The statue was depicted pouring a libation with its right hand
(**B57–8**, τῆι μὲν δεξιᾶ σπέν[δοντα]); the restoration [κανθάρω]ι in **B58** ('with a
kantharos') is based on the assumption that the statue was in part modelled
on the cult-statue of Dionysos at Teos (see further Chapter 6 below).

B61–4

κατὰ πρ]όσωπον δὲ τῆς εἰκόνος βωμὸς κατασταθήτω ἐφ᾽ οὗ θυέ-
[τω ὁ γυμνασίαρ]χος ἐν τῶι Ἀνθεστηριῶνι μηνὶ τῆι τρεισκαιδεκάτηι ἱερεῖον ν.
[καὶ ἀγῶνα τιθ]έτω, κατευχομένου τοῦ ἱεροκήρυκος διδόναι τὰ ἀγαθὰ τοὺς
[θεοὺς Τηΐοις καὶ] Ἀβδηρίταις,…

---

[79] κολοσσικός/κολοσσιαῖος = 'oversize': Dickie 1996; Badoud 2011; Bresson 2012, 211–12, 216–17;
Ma 2013, 250–1. For other statues of the personified *Dēmos* described as 'colossal', cf. *SEG* 33, 1035
(Kyme), lines 2–4; *SEG* 55, 1503 (Xanthos).

'And [in fr]ont of the statue let an altar be erected, on which let the [gymnasiar]ch sacrifice a victim on the thirteenth day of the month Anthesterion and [hold a contest], with the sacred herald praying that the [gods] should give good things to the [Teians and] Abderites,...'

For the erection of an altar opposite a statue (**B61**, [κατὰ πρ]όσωπον δὲ τῆς εἰκόνος), cf. *SEG* 58, 1220 (Labraunda: decree of the second half of the third century BC, reinscribed in the late second century), in which an altar was to be set up opposite a statue of the dynast Olympichos, probably in the agora at Mylasa (lines 8–9, ἱδρύσασθαι δὲ [καὶ αὐτῶι ἀπέναν]τι τῆς εἰκόνος βωμὸν λευκοῦ λίθου);[80] cf. also the decree of Aigai in honour of Seleukos I and Antiochos I (shortly after 281 BC), in which an altar of Seleukos and Antiochos was to be set up 'opposite the temple': *SEG* 59, 1406A [*CGRN* 137], lines 11–12, ἱδρύσασθαι [δ]ὲ καὶ βωμὸν τοῦ ναοῦ κατεναντίον. For κατὰ πρόσωπον, 'opposite', cf. *I.Ephesos* 2222A, 4357; the phrase is a favourite of Polybios (fifty-five instances, often contrasted with ἀπ' οὐρᾶς, κατὰ νώτου). The decree leaves it unclear to which deity or deities the altar is dedicated (see further Chapter 6 below): its location suggests that it was dedicated to the *Dēmos* of the Teians (and note the sacrifice to the *Dēmos* of the Teians at **B76** below) but the sacred herald's prayer at **B63–4** (associated with the sacrifice on the altar) is directed to the 'gods'.

The restorations at the start of lines **B62** and **B63** (θυέ[τω ὁ γυμνασίαρ]χος... [καὶ ἀγῶνα τιθ]έτω) are guaranteed by **B69–70**, where the gymnasiarch is instructed to draw the expenses for the sacrifice (θυσίαν) and the contest (ἀγῶνα) from the public bank at Abdera. The gymnasiarch was often responsible for the performance of sacrifices associated with athletic contests: at Kolophon, the gymnasiarch performed an annual sacrifice on the birthday of Athenaios, associated with athletic contests of *neoi*, ephebes, and *paides* (*SEG* 56, 1227 [Klaros, *c.*180–160 BC], lines 11–13), and in the gymnasiarchic law from Beroia (as elsewhere), the gymnasiarch sacrifices to Hermes at the beginning of the annual Hermaia (*I.Beroia* 1, lines B45–6).[81] The sacrifice and contest are to take place on the thirteenth day of Anthesterion (**B62**), a

---

[80] For the location of this statue and altar, cf. Marek and Zingg 2018, 125–6 (the 'sacred agora' at Mylasa); cf. also *CGRN* 150.

[81] Cf. also e.g. Eretria, *IG* XII 9, 234, lines 15–16, 28–9 (Hermes) and *IG* XII 9, 235, lines 13–14 (Hermes and Herakles); *I.Sestos* 1 (honours for Menas, shortly after 133 BC), lines 35–6, 62–3. At Miletos, the gymnasiarchs sacrificed to the *Dēmos* of the Romans and Roma on entering and leaving office (*Milet* I 7, 203, b19–28: late II BC), as well as sacrificing annually to Hermes and Herakles and 'Hero Antiochos' (*Milet* I 9, 368: *c.*100 BC). See further Gauthier and Hatzopoulos 1993, 95–8; Schmitt Pantel 1997, 367–70; Curty 2015, 249–60.

day which is all but certain to have fallen during the Abderite festival of the Anthesteria (a spring 'new wine' festival of Dionysos), in February/March.[82] At Athens, the Anthesteria lasted three days (11–13 Anthesterion); at Kyzikos, the Anthesteria were celebrated over at least two days (12 and 13 Anthesterion), and at Miletos, the Anthesteria lasted at least two days (dates unknown).[83] At Teos, around the turn of the era, a *thiasos* of Dionysiastai honoured Hediste, priestess of Dionysos, by declaring 13 Anthesterion as sacred and renaming it after her; it is overwhelmingly likely that this day fell during the Teian Anthesteria.[84] The Anthesteria was a particularly appropriate occasion to celebrate the close relations between Abdera and Teos, since it was a 'shared' festival between the two cities: in the fifth-century Teian Dirae, the Anthesteria was one of the three festivals celebrated at both cities at which curses were pronounced.[85]

The sacred herald (ἱεροκῆρυξ) is well attested at both Abdera and Teos; his duties included the proclamation of honours, and, as here, the performance of public prayers.[86] The wording of the prayer at B63–4 is conventional: compare *I.Priene*² 65 (decree for Herodes, *c.*120 BC), lines 197–200, κατευξάμενος... πάντα τὰ ἀγαθὰ διδόναι τοὺς θ[εοὺς καὶ τοῖς πο]λίταις [πᾶσι] καὶ γυ[ν]αιξὶ καὶ τοῖς τέκνοις; Le Guen 2001, no. 39 (Aneziri 2003, D2: Teos, late III BC), lines 1–5, [εὔχεσθαι... τὸν ἱε]ροκήρυκα [ἐν τ]αῖς ἐκλησίαις γίνεσθαι τἀγαθὰ καὶ τῶι κοινῶι τῶ[ν περὶ τ]ὸν Διόνυσον τεχνιτῶν; IG XII 4, 1, 291 (Kos, *c.*180 BC), ἐπὶ δὲ ταῖς θυσίαις ἐπευχέσθ[ων πάντα τὰ ἀγαθὰ γί]νεσθαι τῶι τε δάμῳ τῶι Κώιων καὶ βασ[ιλεῖ Ἀριαράθηι κτλ.].[87] For the restoration [*Τηΐοις* καὶ] Ἀβδηρίταις in B64 (bare ethnics, without the definite article), cf. *I.Magnesia* 80 (Rigsby 1996, 270–2, no. 125b: Antioch in Pisidia (?), *c.*207–205 BC), lines 13–16, το[ὺς δὲ ἱερεῖ]ς καὶ τὰς ἱερε[ί]ας... εὔξασθαι... [γίνε]σθ[α]ι

---

[82] For the place of Anthesterion in the Teian calendar, see Adak and Stauner 2018, 14–16; Adak and Thonemann 2020, 14–15.

[83] Athens: Mikalson 1975, 113–14. Kyzikos: *SEG* 28, 953, lines 52–3, with Sève 1979, 356 and Carbon 2014, 153. Miletos: *I.Didyma* 236A, 258. Thuc. 2.15.4 claims that the Anthesteria were celebrated by all the Ionians. On the Athenian Anthesteria, see in particular Humphreys 2004, 223–74; Parker 2005, 290–326. At Smyrna in the Roman imperial period, the Anthesteria featured a ship-procession representing the return (*katagōgia*) of Dionysos: Burkert 1983, 200–1; Graf 1985, 386–7; Merkelbach 1988, 75.

[84] *SEG* 4, 598, lines 15–16. For the consecration of particular days in honour of civic benefactors, cf. Robert, *Hellenica* II, 58–60; *SEG* 39, 605 (Morrylos), lines 18–22, with Hatzopoulos and Loukopoulou 1989, 44–6.

[85] Document 3 (Chapter 3 below), D1–8.

[86] Proclamation of honours at Abdera: below, B71–2; Document 6 (Chapter 5 below), line 31; *I.ThrakAig* E7, lines 24–5; E8, lines 23–4; E9, line 26. At Teos: *SEG* 44, 949, I line 10. Prayers: Le Guen 2001, no. 39; Aneziri 2003, D2 (Teos, probably late III BC: for the date, see below, Chapter 4), lines 1–5. See Robert 1937, 41 (prayers); Gauthier 2006, 485 n. 11 (proclamation of athletic victors).

[87] Cf. Robert, *OMS* I, 29; *OMS* II, 1072; Robert 1937, 40.

κοιν[ῆ[ι πάντα τὰ ἀγαθ[ὰ] Ἀ[ντιοχεῦ]σίν τε καὶ Μάγνησιν; *IG* XII Suppl. 3
(Mytilene, II BC), lines 24–6, [εὖ]χεσθαι δὲ καὶ τὸν ἱεροκάρυ[κα γίνεσθαι τὰ
ἄγαθα Θεσσά]λοισι, ἐπεί κε τᾶι πόλι τᾶι Μ[υτιληνάων εὔχηται].[88]

B64–9

καλείσθω δὲ ὁ δῆμος ὁ Τηΐων εἰς προεδρίαν, συγ-
65 [τελούντων ἡμῶν λ]αμπάδα τῶν παίδων καὶ ἀνδρῶν, καὶ τοῖς νικήσασιν διαμερίζε-
[σθω τὰ κρέα τοῦ ἱερ]ε̣ίου, ἵνα μὴ μόνον παρὰ τοῖς ἐν ἡλικίαι τῶν πολιτῶν ὑπάρχου-
[σιν, ἀλλὰ καὶ παρὰ τ]οῖς νεωτέροις ἐπίσημος ἡ τιμὴ τοῦ Τηΐων ὑπάρχῃ δήμου
[καὶ προτρέπωνται] πάντες ἀπὸ τῆς πρώτης *vac.* 6 ἡλικίας τῆι πρὸς τοὺς εὐ-
[εργέτας εὐχαριστίᾳ·...

'And let the *dēmos* of the Teians be called to a front seat when [we] hold the torch-
race of boys and adults, and let the [meat of the vic]tim be distributed to the victors, in order that not only among those of the citizens who have reached
adulthood, [but that also among] the younger ones the honour conferred on the
dēmos of the Teians might be conspicuous, [and that] all from the earliest age
[should be inspired to gratitude] towards their benefactors;...'

It is now clarified that the contest organized by the gymnasiarch was a torch-
race (λαμπάς) for two age-classes, 'boys' (παῖδες) and 'men' (ἄνδρες), subsequently described periphrastically as 'the younger ones' (οἱ νεώτεροι, **B67**, i.e.
boys) and 'those of the citizens who have reached adulthood' (οἱ ἐν ἡλικίαι τῶν
πολιτῶν ὑπάρχοντες, **B66–7**, i.e. men).[89] At the start of B65, the restoration
συγ[τελούντων ἡμῶν] is not certain, since nowhere else in this decree do the
Abderites simply describe themselves as 'we' (ἡμῶν); however, the verb
συντελεῖν is certainly what is required here, as the standard verb for 'holding'
a contest.[90]

---

[88] Similarly *I.Magnesia* 73b (Rigsby 1996, 252–3, no. 108), lines 14–16, ἐπευ[χ]ομέ[νους
γί]ν〈ε〉σ〈θ〉αι τὰ ἀ[γαθὰ τῶι τε] δή[μ]ωι ἡμῶν καὶ τῶι Μαγν[ήτων].
[89] The same distinction (οἱ ἐν ἡλικίαι...οἱ νεώτεροι) in a decree of Pergamon dating to 133 BC
(*OGIS* 338, lines 21–2: former royal slaves); for οἱ ἐν ἡλικίαι = 'those who are of age', i.e. adults, cf. *SEG*
49, 855 (Amphipolis), A11, B27–8; *SEG* 41, 1003 (Teos), II line 23, with parallels collected by
Herrmann 1965, 60 n. 18; Chankowski 2010, 69–71. In the new ephebarchic law from Amphipolis
(Lazaridou 2015, lines 6–7, with Hatzopoulos 2015–16, 149–51), the ephebarch is to place on his
register 'all those from the register of *paides* who are of age and have not yet served as ephebes' (τοὺς ἐν
ἡλικίᾳ ὄντας πάντας καὶ μήπω ἐφηβευκότας ἐκ τῆς ἀπογραφῆς τῶν παίδων); the cut-off age is 18.
[90] e.g. *SEG* 56, 1227 (Klaros, *c.*180–160 BC), lines 13, 14, 26–7, 28–9, 32–3.

Torch-races are widely attested in the Hellenistic world, sometimes as relays, sometimes with individual competitors.[91] These races were typically organized by the gymnasiarch, whether the torch-race formed part of a festival restricted to members of the gymnasium (as at the Hermaia at Beroia) or a larger civic festival (as at an unidentified civic festival at Koresia on Keos).[92] The race was often associated with a specific altar, as here; at Delphi, for example, the race was run from the gymnasium to an altar of Hermes, and the winner lit the fire on the altar with his torch.[93] The two age-classes for whom the torch-race was organized at Abdera (*paides* and *andres*) are also attested as the two age-classes that competed in the torch-race at the Delian Apollonia in the third century BC; however, at Delos, the older age-class can also be described as *neaniskoi*, indicating that the athletic age-class of *andres* is in fact synonymous with the age-class of *neoi* or *neaniskoi*, and that is probably also the case here (cf. **B77** below).[94] In the second century BC, the *neoi* in the Teian gymnasium may well have held torch-races associated with the hero Dionysas, to judge by the existence of a room called the *lampadeion* in the hero's sanctuary (Adak and Stauner 2018, lines 21–2).

For the distribution of sacrificial meat to victors in an associated athletic contest (**B65–6**), compare again *SEG* 56, 1227 (Klaros, *c*.180–160 BC), lines 18–20: an annual sacrifice on the birthday of Athenaios, with part of the meat distributed as prizes to the victors of athletic contests of *neoi*, ephebes, and *paides*.[95] Similarly, at Miletos around 100 BC, the gymnasiarchs distributed part of the meat from the sacrifices of two oxen to 'Hero Antiochos' as prizes to ephebes and *neoi* in the gymnasium (*Milet* I 9, 368, lines 14–17), and at Kos, the meat from a sacrifice to Hermes Enagonios was to be distributed among all the *paides* who participated in a torch-race, with the left shank reserved for the victor (*IG* XII 4, 1, 298, lines A58–62).

The purpose of the sacrifice and contest is said to be in order to render the honours to the Teian *dēmos* 'conspicuous' (ἐπίσημος) to people of all ages at

---

[91] Gauthier and Hatzopoulos 1993, 109–10; Gauthier 1995; Baker and Thériault 2017, 455–8; Chankowski 2018.

[92] Chankowski 2018, 60–4, on *I.Beroia* 1, B59, and *IG* XII 5, 647, lines 21–3.

[93] *Syll.*³ 671A, lines 15–16. At Athens, torch-races were run from the altar of Prometheus at the Academy to the Great Altar on the Acropolis: Deubner 1932, 211–13; Chankowski 2018, 56–7.

[94] Compare *IG* XI 2, 203, line 65 and *IG* XI 2, 274, line 25 (*paides* and *andres*) with *IG* XI 2, 287, line 132 (*paides* and *neaniskoi*). *Andres* and *neoi* are similarly used interchangeably of an athletic age-class in the decree of Sestos for Menas, *I.Sestos* 1, lines 36–7, 79, 81–2. See Chankowski 2010, 94, with other examples; Kennell 2013, 227–8; Chankowski 2018, 65–8.

[95] Paul 2018, 330.

Abdera (**B66–7**),[96] and to encourage the Abderites from the youngest age to look on the Teians with gratitude (**B68–9**). At the start of **B69**, the restoration τῆι πρὸς τοὺς εὐ[εργέτας εὐχαριστίᾳ] seems certain: 'gratitude towards one's benefactors' is a standard trope of Hellenistic honorific decrees: cf. e.g. *Milet* VI 3, 1039 (decree for Eirenias, 167–164 BC), lines I.12–13, ὥστε τὴν μὲν τοῦ πλήθους εἰς τοὺς εὐεργέτας εὐχαριστίαν φανερὰν πᾶσιν καταστῆσαι.[97] At the start of **B68**, it seems likely that we should restore the verb προτρέπεσθαι, which is very commonly used in honorific decrees of the exhortation to others to imitate their virtuous predecessors; individuals are often praised for their protreptic role in urging the young towards virtue.[98] Elsewhere, προτρέπεσθαι usually takes a preposition (ἐπὶ τὰ κάλλιστα, πρὸς ἀρετήν); the plain dative, as restored here, seems to have no epigraphic parallels. The notion that a sacrifice and contest might have a protreptic educational function (here teaching future generations gratitude towards the Teians) is closely paralleled in the second Teian decree for Antiochos III (*c.*203 BC): on the first day of the Teian year (1 Leukatheon), when the ephebes enter adulthood, the ex-ephebes are to sacrifice to the king, the Charites, and Memory, 'so that they do not start to handle any of the common affairs before returning thanks to the benefactors, and so that we may accustom (ἐθίζωμεν) our offspring to consider everything of lesser significance than the returning of thanks.'[99]

In **B68**, the lengthy *vacat* between πρώτης and ἡλικίας is a puzzle. Perhaps the stone-cutter laid out the inscription on the stone in pencil (more precisely, with a charcoal stick or lead strip) before inscribing it,[100] accidentally duplicated either πρώτης or ἡλικίας at this point, realized his error when he came to cut the letters, and decided simply to leave the resulting space blank rather than having to redo the layout of the final twenty-five lines of the inscription.

---

[96] Cf. *SEG* 37, 1006 (Adramytteion, II BC), [ὅ]πως τούτων οὕτως συντελ[εσθέντων ἦι ἐπ]ίσημος ἡ παρὰ τοῦ δήμου χά[ρις πᾶσι τοῖς αὐτ]ὸν εὐεργετοῦσιν.

[97] Similarly e.g. *IG* XII 9, 899 (Chalkis), lines 4–6, ὅπως οὖν … οἵ τε λοι[ποὶ εἰδότες τὴν τῆ]ς πόλεως εὐχαριστίαν εἰς τοὺς εὐεργέτας ζηλωταὶ [γίνωνται τῶν ὁμοίω[ν]; *I.Erythrai* 31, lines 7–9; *I.Mylasa* 101, lines 62–3; *I.Mylasa* 121, lines 5–6; etc.

[98] Robert, *OMS* I, 620–2, and above all Gray 2013, 248–53, citing e.g. the actions of Menas of Sestos in urging the *neoi* towards 'practice and love of exertion' (προτρεπόμενος εἰς ἄσκησιν καὶ φιλοπονίαν τοὺς νέους, *I.Sestos* 1 lines 38–9, 70–1).

[99] *SEG* 41, 1003, II (Ma 2002, 311–17, no. 18), lines 40–2, with Ma 2002, 221–2; Chaniotis 2005b, 194–9; Chankowski 2010, 298–300; cf. also *Milet* I 3, 139 (Miletos and Ptolemy II, *c.*262 BC), lines 47–51: on leaving the ephebate, young men are to swear to preserve the friendship and alliance with the Ptolemies.

[100] Charcoal or lead: Tsakirgis 2015.

B69–71

τὸ] δὲ ἐσόμενον{ον} ἀνάλωμα εἰς τὴν θυσίαν καὶ τὸν ἀγῶνα ἀπο-
70 [γραψάμενος ὁ γυμνα]σίαρχος λαβέτω ἀπὸ τῆς τραπέζης, ἐπιμελὲς δὲ ποι- ν.
[ησάτω τὸ λοιπὸν ὁ ἀ]εὶ γυμνασίαρχος·

'And let the gymnasiarch in[voice] the future expenses for the sacrifice and the contest and draw them from the public bank, and let each gymnasiarch in office [in future] have care for this.'

The phraseology here is closely paralleled in the contemporary decree for Amymon and Megathymos, when arrangements are being made for the financing of the erection of a copy of the decree at Teos (**Document 6** below, Chapter 5, lines 44–7): [τὸ δ]ὲ γενόμενον ἀνάλωμα εἴς τε τὴν στήλην καὶ τὴν ἀναγ[ραφὴν τοῦδε] τοῦ ψηφίσματος ἀπογραψάμενοι τῆι πόλει οἱ πρεσβε[υταί, ὅπως δ]ιαμείβωνται, κομισά[σ]θωσαν ἀπὸ τῆς τραπέζης, 'as for the expense incurred for the *stēlē* and the inscription of [this] decree, let the ambassadors invoice it to the city, so that they might be reimbursed, and let them draw it from the public bank'. In both instances, the procedure seems to be that the relevant officials (the gymnasiarch in one case, the ambassadors to Teos in the other) pay the expenses out of their own pocket; they then invoice (ἀπογράψασθαι) the expenses to the city, and are reimbursed from the public bank at Abdera.[101] The procedure seems to have been a standard one in Hellenistic cities: for example, at Kyme, the publication costs of an honorific inscription are to be advanced by the *stratagoi*, who are subsequently reimbursed from whichever fund the *damos* may decree (*SEG* 19, 1216, honours for Epigonos of Tarentum: τὸ δὲ εἰς ταῦτα ἐσσόμενον ἀνάλωμα προχρῆσαι τοῖς στραταγοῖς, κομίσσασθαι δὲ ἐκ πόρω ὧ κε ὁ δᾶμος ψαφίσσηται).[102] In lines B70–1, it is not certain whether we should restore the aorist ποι[ησάτω], on the analogy of λαβέτω in the previous clause, or the present ποι[είτω] (as suggested to us by Patrice Hamon).

---

[101] For the public bank at Abdera, Bogaert 1969, 118–19.
[102] For the procedure, see Samitz 2019.

B71–3

καὶ ἵνα πρὸ τοῦ ἀγῶνος ἀναγορεύῃ ὁ ἱερο- ν.
[κῆρυξ διότι στεφανοῖ] ὁ δῆμος τὸν Τηΐων δῆμον χρυσῶι στεφάνωι καὶ εἰκόνι χαλκῇ
[ἀρετῆς ἕνεκεν καὶ ε]ὐνοίας τῆς εἰς ἑαυτόν· …

'And in order that before the contest the sacred herald might announce that the
dēmos crowns the Teian *dēmos* with a gold crown and a bronze statue for the sake
of its virtue and goodwill towards them,…'

The presence of a purpose clause here (ἵνα…ἀναγορεύῃ) is surprising; one
would expect a third-person imperative (ἀναγορευέτω). The wording of the
proclamation is formulaic: compare the decree for Amymon and Megathymos
(**Document 6** below, Chapter 5), lines 31–3, τὴν ἀναγγελίαν ποιουμέν[ου τοῦ
ἱερο]κήρυκος διότι ὁ δῆμος στεφανοῖ χρυσῶι στεφάνωι Ἀ[μύμονα Ἐ]πικούρου
Τήϊον ἀρετῆς ἕνεκεν καὶ εὐνοίας τῆς εἰς ἑα[υτόν]. The paradoxical phraseology
'to crown with a statue' is widespread in Hellenistic honorific epigraphy
(Robert, *OMS* VI, 92; Ma 2013, 31–8). Note that the gold crown mentioned in
B72 has not in fact previously been listed among the honours for the Teian
dēmos; it is unlikely to be identical to the ivy-wreath with which Nike crowns
the bronze statue of the *Dēmos* of the Teians (**B60–1**), which was presumably
also of bronze.

B73–6

ἵνα δὲ καὶ ἐν Τέῳ πᾶσα ἡλικία πα-
[ρακολουθῆι ταῖς τιμαῖ]ς, οἱ νομοφύλακες ἀεὶ κατ' ἐνιαυτὸν αἱρείσθωσαν ἄνδρας
75 [(number) ἐμ μηνὶ Ἀπα]τουριῶνι τοὺς ἀποδημήσοντας εἰς Τέω καὶ θύσοντας
[ὑπὲρ τοῦ δήμου ἡμῶν βο]ῦν ἐμ μηνὶ Λευκαθεῶνι χαριστήρια τῶι Τηΐων Δήμωι,…

'And in order that also in Teos people of every age [might learn of these honours],
let the *nomophylakes* in office each year choose [(number)] men [in the month]
Apatourion who will travel to Teos and sacrifice [on behalf of our *dēmos* a b]ull in
the month Leukatheon as a thank-offering to the *Dēmos* of the Teians,…'

The decree now turns to the process by which the Teian *dēmos* will be
informed of the honours voted by the Abderites: an annual embassy to Teos
to sacrifice at (probably) the Teian Leukathea (**B74–9**), a gift of 1,000

medimnoi of grain (**B79**), and the erection of a copy of the decree at Teos (**B80–6**). The Abderites are concerned that people of 'every age' at Teos (πᾶσα ἡλικία, **B73**)—not just adults who attend the Teian assembly—should learn of the Abderites' decision, and in order to ensure this, they stipulate that part of the sacrificial meat should be distributed to victors in the age-class of *paides* at the Teian Leukathea (**B77**).[103] The verb in the lacuna at the start of **B74** is almost certainly παρακολουθεῖν, 'learn of, become acquainted with', regularly used in this context where an honouring community wishes another community to be aware of what they have voted. The verb is used both with the dative and the accusative: so in an Eretrian decree for Milesian judges (*Milet* I 3, 154, lines 25–6), we read ἵνα δὲ καὶ Μιλήσιοι παρακολουθήσωσιν τήν τε τῶν ἀνδρῶν καλοκαγαθίαν καὶ τὰ παρ' [Ἐρετριέων φι]λάνθρωπα, while in a contemporary Methymnaian decree for Milesian judges (*Milet* I 3, 152, lines *B*49–50), we read ὅππως δὲ καὶ Μιλάσιοι παρακολούθωσι τᾷ τῶ δάμω εὐχαριστίαι. The dative is used in **B84** below, and hence that is probably what we have here; the remainder of the lacuna in **B74** is short (*c*.6–8 letters), and we should presumably restore either [ταῖς τιμαῖ]ς or simply [τούτοι]ς.[104]

The annual envoys to Teos are to be appointed each year by the *nomophy-lakes* at Abdera. In the second century BC, the Abderite board of *nomophylakes* was responsible, among other things, for appointing ambassadors (**Document 6** below, lines 38–9; *IThrakAig* E7, lines 34–5) and reimbursing their expenses (**Document 6** below, lines 47–8; **B78–9**; **B82–4**), commissioning statues (*IThrakAig* E9, lines 29–30), managing the inscribing of decrees (**Document 6** below, lines 34–7; *IThrakAig* E7, lines 28–9, and E8, lines 31–3) and providing official copies of decrees (*IThrakAig* E9, lines 41–3; **B85–6**). Four Abderite decrees (*IThrakAig* E7–10) begin with the single word νομοφυλάκων: this probably indicates that the *nomophylakes* were responsible for the archiving of public documents.[105]

In a fragmentary Abderite decree of *c*.246/5 BC, recognizing the Aitolian penteteric Soteria at Delphi (*IThrakAig* E5), we find a board of *timouchoi* performing functions closely parallel to those performed by the second-century Abderite board of *nomophylakes*, including the appointment of ambassadors and the provision of travel-expenses. Conversely, *timouchoi*

---

[103] For πᾶσα ἡλικία denoting 'people of every age', cf. e.g. *I.Kaunos* 30 (honours for Agreophon, *c*. AD 100), lines 16–17, φιλοστόργως δὲ καὶ φιλοκάλως προσφερόμενος πάσῃ ἡλικίᾳ.

[104] For παρακολουθεῖν τιμάς/τιμαῖς, cf. e.g. *IG* XII 6, 1, 153 (Samos, II BC), lines 16–17, [ὅπως δὲ καὶ Θάσιοι παρακολουθῶ]σιν ταῖς ἐψηφισμέναις ὑπὸ τοῦ δήμου [τιμαῖς]; *SEG* 26, 677 (Peparethos, II BC), lines 70–1, [ὅ]πως δὲ καὶ Λαρισαῖοι παρακολου[θήσωσι τὰς ἐψηφισμένας τι]μά[ς].

[105] Fröhlich 2004, 243 n. 47; Boffo 2012, 25–6; Faraguna 2015, 148.

are absent from second-century decrees of Abdera, and it therefore seems very likely that the Abderite board of *timouchoi* was replaced by a new board of *nomophylakes* at some point between the 240s and 160s BC.[106] We know that the *timouchoi* were the chief executive magistrates at Teos in the early fifth century BC, and they continue to appear at Teos alongside a board of *stratēgoi* down through the Hellenistic period (*nomophylakes* are not attested at Teos).[107] Precisely when and why the Abderites chose to abandon this magistracy (which evidently dated back to the original mid-sixth-century Teian colonization) is unknown. However, we also find a board of *nomophylakes* proposing decrees at the neighbouring city of Maroneia in the later Hellenistic period, and boards of *nomophylakes* appear as the chief civic magistrates (alongside *stratēgoi*) at the Macedonian royal foundations of Kassandreia and Demetrias. It therefore seems possible that the replacement of the *timouchoi* by *nomophylakes* at Abdera should be attributed to Macedonian influence at Abdera under Philip V or Perseus, but certainty is impossible.[108]

As we shall see (commentary to lines **B90–3** below), it is unclear whether the Abderites appointed two or three envoys each year; the number was given in the lacuna at the start of **B75**. The specification that the envoys are to be appointed in the month Apatourion is presumably because this is not a one-off appointment, but a regular annual office. The closest parallel known to us is in the decree of Antioch in Persis recognizing the *asylia* of Magnesia on the Maeander and the Panhellenic status of the Magnesian Leukophryeneia (*c*.207–205 BC): the Antiocheis resolve to appoint annual *theōroi* to the Leukophryeneia on a specified date in the month Herakleion, 'when the other annual civic magistrates are appointed': *I.Magnesia* 61 (Rigsby 1996, 257–60, no. 111), lines 64–71, [ἀποστεῖλαι δὲ καὶ θεωροὺς] εἰς Μαγνησία[ν τοὺς θύσοντας Ἀρτέμιδι Λευκο]φρυηνῆι… [αἱρεῖσθαι δὲ τοὺς θεωροὺς τῆι - - τοῦ Ἡρα]κλείου μηνὸς [ὅταν καὶ αἱ ἄλλαι ἀρχαὶ αἱ πολιτικαὶ] σταθῶσιν. Around 9–10 letters are missing at the start of line **B75**, which seems too long for either of the possible numbers of envoys ([δύο] or [τρεῖς]). It is therefore likely that these envoys were designated as *theōroi*, in which case we could most easily restore here οἱ νομοφύλακες … αἱρείσθωσαν ἄνδρας [θεωροὺς δύο ἐμ μηνὶ Ἀπα]τουριῶνι τοὺς ἀποδημήσοντας κτλ.

---

[106] *IThrakAig* pp. 170, 191.

[107] Gottlieb 1967, 18–28; Rhodes with Lewis 1997, 394; Adak and Stauner 2018, 20; see further Chapter 3 below.

[108] *Nomophylakes* as proposers of decrees at Maroneia: *IThrakAig* E171–2. At Kassandreia and Demetrias: Hatzopoulos 1996, I 157–9; Faraguna 2015, 150–1.

The month-name 'Apatourion' (here attested for the first time at Abdera) derives from the festival of the Apatouria, celebrated by the majority of Ionian cities, and by many other cities across the Greek world.[109] The Athenian Apatouria (far the best known) was a phratry-festival, and it is likely that elsewhere too the festival was closely associated with extended kinship-groups.[110] The month Apatourion is attested in numerous Ionian cities of the Aegean and their colonies, including Teos.[111] So far as we can tell, it seems normally to have fallen in the autumn (October/November), and to have corresponded to the Athenian month Pyanepsion, in which the Athenian Apatouria festival took place. That the Teian month Apatourion fell in the autumn receives some confirmation from the Teian 'pirates inscription', dating around 300 BC. The inscription includes a chronologically ordered list of persons who made a loan to the city; those who made a loan on the last day of the month Trygētēr are immediately followed by those who did so on the first and second days of Apatourion. The name of the month Trygētēr appears to be connected with the grape harvest (Chapter 2 below), which takes place in Ionia during September, strongly suggesting that the Teian month Apatourion should indeed be placed around October.[112]

It is not certain why the annual appointment of the envoys occurred in the Abderite month Apatourion. As we have seen, the month Apatourion almost certainly fell in the autumn (October/November), around nine months before the annual journey of the Abderite envoys to Teos in the summer month Leukatheon (assuming that our reconstruction of the Teian calendar below is broadly correct). It is tempting to suppose that Apatourion was the first month of the Abderite year, and that the appointment of the year's envoys was undertaken by the *nomophylakes* as one of their first acts in office. There is nothing intrinsically impossible about this: Apatourion seems to have been the first month of the year at the neighbouring city of Thasos, as perhaps also at the Phokaian colony of Lampsakos.[113] At Teos, however, the civic year is known with certainty to have begun in mid-summer, with the month

---

[109] Prevalence in Ionia: Hdt. 1.147.2; Herda 2006, 47. Wide geographic spread: Lambert 1993, 268 n. 105; Braund 2018, 235–42 (Black Sea). The following discussion draws on our recent study of the Teian calendar, Adak and Thonemann 2020.

[110] Lambert 1993, 143–89; Parker 2005, 458–61; Humphreys 2018, II 569–89. The absence of a month-name Apatourion at Athens may suggest that the festival was an Ionian 'import' to Attica (Connor 1993, 197).

[111] See Trümpy 1997, 21–2; 290 (index).

[112] *SEG* 44, 949 (with Meier 2017 and Hamon 2018), lines 69–102; for the sequence Trygētēr–Apatourion, Adak and Stauner 2018, 14–15; Adak and Thonemann 2020, 9–13 (publishing a new fragment of the 'pirates inscription').

[113] Thasos: Salviat 1992, accepted by P. Hamon in his commentary on *CITh* III 9 (though note the doubts of Trümpy 1997, 65–72). Lampsakos: Trümpy 1997, 109. At Athens, the 'phratry year' began

Leukatheon (see below). We would naturally have expected that this would also be the case for their daughter-city of Abdera, but it is possible that the start of the year at the two cities had fallen out of step at some point between the sixth and the second centuries B C.[114] It is conceivable that this change occurred during a period of Macedonian control at Abdera (see above, on the *nomophylakes*), since the first month of the Macedonian calendar (Dios) also fell in October.

The month-name Leukatheon is attested at Teos, Erythrai, Chios, Lampsakos, and Magnesia on the Maeander; its presence at the Teian colony of Abdera hence comes as no surprise. At Chios, and probably elsewhere, Leukatheon seems to fall around the time of the summer solstice, roughly corresponding with the Athenian month Hekatombaion (Trümpy 1997, 103–5). At Teos, in contrast to Abdera, it is absolutely clear that Leukatheon was the first month of the civic year.[115] In the second Teian decree for Antiochos and Laodike (*c.*203 B C), incoming civic officials are to offer sacrifices to the king, the Charites, and Memory on the first day (*noumenia*) of the month Leukatheon, as are the outgoing ephebes and their gymnasiarchs.[116] In decrees of the late fourth and late third centuries, the month Leukatheon marks the beginning of financial privileges that the Teian state granted to external groups for a fixed number of years;[117] the month Leukatheon also served as the starting-date of contracts, as in the recently published lease-decree of the hero-sanctuary of Dionysas by the Teian *neoi*.[118]

Each year, the Abderite envoys are instructed to sacrifice a 'thank-offering' (χαριστήρια, B76) at Teos to the *Dēmos* of the Teians, consisting of a bull ([βο]ῦν). The decree does not make it clear whether the victim was purchased at Teos or (less likely) brought by the envoys from Abdera (for the purchase of the bull, see B78–9). In restoring the start of line B76, we have assumed that

with the Apatouria festival, in the Athenian month Pyanepsion, corresponding to the Ionian Apatourion: Humphreys 2018, II 582–3.

[114] Salviat 1992, 263–4, assumes something similar for the calendars of Paros and her colony Thasos.

[115] Herrmann 1965, 67; *BE* 1973, 77 (p. 71); Trümpy 1997, 106; Adak and Thonemann 2020, 3–6.

[116] *SEG* 41, 1003 II (Ma 2002, 311–17, no. 17), lines 33–44; cf. also line 21, where the budget for a new annual sacrifice to the king by the Teian *symmoriai* has to be settled by Day 4 Leukatheon, i.e. by the fourth day of the new civic year.

[117] Robert and Robert 1976, 175–88 (*SEG* 26, 1305), lines 20–1 (confirmed from autopsy [Adak]): [εἶν]αι δὲ αὐτοῖς τὴν ἀτέλειαν δέκα ἔτεα· ἄρχε[ιν δὲ τῆς ἀτελείας] μῆνα Λευκαθεῶνα καὶ πρύτανιν Ἀρίστιππον (on the historical context, see now Adak 2021); *SEG* 2, 580 (Aneziri 2003, D2), lines 18–20: δεδόσθαι δὲ αὐτοῖς καὶ ἐπο[χὴ]ν ἔτη πέντε ἀπὸ μηνὸς Λευκαθεῶνος καὶ πρυτ[άνεως] Μητροδώρου.

[118] Adak and Stauner 2018 (with Jones 2019), lines 8–9, ἄρξει τῆι μισθώσε[ι] μὴν Λευκαθεῶν καὶ πρύτανις Ἑστιαῖος; similarly, in lines 45–6, we are told that the lessee had to have the contract inscribed within a year ἀπὸ μηνὸς Λευκαθεῶνος τοῦ ἐπὶ πρυτάνεως Ἑστιαίου.

the text specified that the sacrifice was to be performed on the Abderites' behalf, as in *IG* XII 7, 506 (decree of the League of Islanders recognizing the Ptolemaieia, probably 280/79 BC), lines 53–6, ἑλέσθαι … θεωροὺς τρεῖς, οἵτινες ἀφ[ικ]όμενοι εἰς Ἀλεξάνδρειαν θύσουσίν τε ὑπὲρ τοῦ [κ]οινοῦ τῶν νησιωτῶν Πτολεμαίωι Σωτῆρι.[119] The chief civic festival at Teos during the month Leukatheon was the Leukathea festival, apparently held over several days around Day 20 of Leukatheon, and that is almost certainly the occasion of the sacrifice mentioned here: see further below.

B77–9

[τὰ δὲ κρέα οἱ πρεσβεύσο]ντες τοῖς τε νέοις καὶ παισὶν μερισάτωσαν τοῖς νι-
[κήσασιν (?) τὰ Λευκάθεα, εἰς δὲ τὴ]ν τιμὴν τοῦ βοὸς διάφορον χορη⟨γη⟩σάτωσαν οἱ νομοφύ-
[λακες ἀπὸ τῆς τραπέζης· δια]πέμψαι δὲ Τηΐοις πυρῶν μεδίμνους χιλίους ν.

'[And let the ambassad]ors distribute [the meat] to the young men and boys who are victorious [(?) at the Leukathea], and let the *nomophylakes* provide the money for the price of the bull [from the public bank]; and send to the Teians 1,000 *medimnoi* of wheat.'

At the start of **B77**, [οἱ θεωρήσο]ντες seems too short for the lacuna, and hence we have assumed that the envoys were here designated as [οἱ πρεσβεύσο]ντες. Just as at Abdera, the sacrificial meat is to be distributed to the athletic victors (**B65–6**), here designated as belonging to the age-classes of *neoi* and *paides*. As at Abdera, there is no mention of the ephebic age-class (although the Teian ephebate is well attested elsewhere);[120] it is possible that the Leukathea (if that is the festival concerned here) did not include ephebic contests precisely because the Leukathea fell shortly after the transitional moment when ephebes at Teos became full adult citizens, on the first day of the month Leukatheon.[121]

At the start of **B78**, we presumably have an indication of the festival and athletic contest at which the sacrifice occurs (in **B76** the sacrifice is simply

---

[119] For more examples of *theōroi* sacrificing 'on behalf of' their home communities, see Rutherford 2013, 214.

[120] Chankowski 2010, 487–91 (list of testimonia); Catling and Kanavou 2013.

[121] *SEG* 41, 1003, II (Ma 2002, 311–17, no. 17), lines 37–44, with Herrmann 1965, 67; Graf 1985, 406.

stated to occur 'in the month Leukatheon').[122] This is overwhelmingly likely to be the Teian festival of the Leukathea. The Teian Leukathea is strictly only attested in an honorific decree of the Teian *symmoria* of the Echinadai (second century B C), in which the crowns decreed for the preceding year's four *prostatai* of the *symmoria* are to be proclaimed at the Leukathea festival (τοῖς Λευκαθέοις).[123] The chronological placement of the festival within the month Leukatheon seems to be indicated by a second honorific decree of the same *symmoria* for the previous year's *prostatai*, passed on Day 20 of the month Leukatheon; it therefore seems likely that the Leukathea lasted for several days, including Day 20.[124] The festival is almost certainly also mentioned in the second Teian decree for Antiochos and Laodike, where the priest of the royal cult is instructed to preside over rituals performed to the king 'just as the priest of Poseidon presides at the [Leukath]ea'.[125] Given the close mythical relationship between the maritime goddess Leukathea and Poseidon, there is nothing surprising about the idea that the Teian priest of Poseidon might have served as the chief cultic official at the Teian Leukathea.

The prominent place of the cult of the goddess Leukathea at Teos may well be a reflection of her role in the early mythical history of the city. From the Archaic period onwards, the Teians attributed their city's foundation to the Minyan Athamas of Orchomenos, a descendant of Athamas son of Aiolos.[126] The goddess Leukathea was generally identified with Ino, wife of the elder Athamas, and hence she could naturally have been seen by the Teians as their own semi-divine ancestor. Ino–Leukathea's role as ancestral mother-figure to the Teians would have been further corroborated by her close links with Dionysos, the chief city-god of Teos; in one version of the myth of Dionysos' childhood, he was said to have been reared by his maternal aunt Ino–Leukathea after the death of his mother Semele (Pherekydes of Athens, *BNJ* 3

---

[122] This is not strictly certain: we could, in principle, have a specification of which athletic event was concerned ([τὴν διαδρομήν], [τὴν λαμπάδα], etc.). But it would be surprising for the festival to go unnamed here.

[123] *CIG* 3066 (Michel 1900, no. 1007), lines 24–6; cf. Adak and Stauner 2018, 10 with n. 25; Adak and Thonemann 2020, 3–6.

[124] *SEG* 35, 1152; the decree was almost certainly passed during the festival, as correctly noted by Şahin 1985, 15.

[125] *SEG* 41, 1003, II, lines 16–17. Herrmann 1965, 58, wondered about restoring a reference to a [Poseid]ea festival (not otherwise attested at Teos); the restoration [Λευ|καθ]έοις was suggested by the Roberts in *BE* 1968, 451, and is accepted by Graf 1985, 406 n. 17, and by Ma 2002, 314.

[126] The earliest attestation comes from Anakreon (*PMG* 463), as quoted by Strabo 14.1.3; in more detail, Pherekydes of Athens, *BNJ* 3 F 102; Pausanias 7.3.6; cf. Olding 2007, 142–4. In the late first century A D, the Teian Ti. Claudius Philistes was honoured as a 'new Athamas': Robert, *OMS* VI, 448; Herrmann 2000. For a likely depiction of Athamas on the Antonine bronze coinage of Teos, see *RPC* IV.2 1006 (temp.).

F 90d 2; Apollod. *Bibl.* 3.4.3).[127] It is possible—though far from certain—that Ino–Leukathea was depicted on the frieze of the Teian temple of Dionysos (Fuchs 2018, 152–3).

In the Greek world more generally, the cult of the goddess Ino–Leukathea seems to have been strongly associated with 'initiatory' or maturation rituals for children and adolescents.[128] Gymnastic contests of *paides* may have been particularly central to festivals in honour of Leukathea, to judge from a story preserved by the mythographer Konon in connection with the founding of the oracle at Didyma, in which the goddess Leukathea orders the Milesians to establish a gymnastic *agōn* for *paides* in her honour.[129] This would nicely explain why the Abderites choose the Leukathea (rather than, say, the Teian Dionysia) as the festival at which they were to make their annual thank-offering to the *Dēmos* of the Teians. The stated aim of this thank-offering is precisely 'in order that also in Teos people **of every age** [might learn of these honours]' (**B73–4**); the Abderites therefore chose to link their annual embassy with the Teian festival which had a particularly close association with younger age-groups and (perhaps) initiation- and maturation-rituals.

The *nomophylakes* are instructed to provide the cash (διάφορον, **B78**, cf. **B28**) for the purchase of the bull; for the verb χορηγεῖν in this context, cf. **B83** below and *IThrakAig* E9 (honours for C. Apustius), line 31.[130] The verb is used in an identical sense in one of the second-century Teian honorific decrees of the *symmoria* of Echinos for their *prostatai*: *CIG* 3066 (Michel 1900, no. 1007), lines 11–12 (payment for sacrificial animals: cf. Adak and Stauner 2018, 10 n. 25). In restoring the start of line **B79**, we have assumed that the funds for the purchase of the bull are to come from the same source as the funds for the purchase of the sacrificial victim at the Abderite Anthesteria (**B69–70**).

---

[127] For the association between Ino–Leukathea and Dionysiac ritual, see also *I.Magnesia* 215a (Harland 2014, 344–50, no. 143): Magnesia imports three maenads from Thebes 'from the race of Ino daughter of Kadmos'. See further Henrichs 1978, esp. 123–37.

[128] Graf 1985, 405–7; Bremmer 1999, 187; Herda 2006, 48 n. 236; S. Blakely's commentary on Conon, *BNJ* 26 F 1.33. On cults of Ino–Leukathea, see also Henrichs 1978, 137–43; Krauskopf 1981; Burkert 1983, 178–9; Larson 1992, 123–5; on the orthography of her name (Leukathea/Leukothea), Trümpy 1997, 104.

[129] Conon, *BNJ* 26 F 1.33. The cult of Leukathea is not otherwise attested at Miletos, but there is no reason to doubt the existence of this *agōn*: Fontenrose 1988, 154–5.

[130] The restorations of lines 29–33 proposed by Wilhelm 1921a, 32–3 (accepted in *IThrakAig*; doubted by Samitz 2019, 297–9) are overcomplex, and involve the introduction of a magistrate unattested at Abdera, the *oikonomos*; we prefer to restore [τὸ δὲ ἔργον ἐγδό]τωσαν οἱ νομοφύλακε[ς οἱ μετὰ ἱερέα (name)]τον Σωτηρίχου, χορηγή[σαντος τὸ εἰς ταῦτα ἀνάλωμα] τοῦ ἐπὶ τῶν χρημάτων [ἐκ τοῦ περιγινομένου ἀργυ|ρ|ίου ἀπὸ τῶν πεσουμένω[ν προσόδων], 'let the *nomophylakes* in office in the year after the priesthood of [name] son of Soterichos award the contract for the work, with the official in charge of the money providing the funds for this out of the accrued silver from the revenues which will come in'; the basic structure of lines 31–3 was correctly perceived by Holleaux 1914, 65–7.

The Abderites also resolve to send the Teians 1,000 *medimnoi* of wheat (**B79**);[131] the brevity of this clause leaves it unclear whether this is to be an annual or a one-off gift, and whether it is in any way associated with the festival at which the sacrifice is to be performed. At any rate, the combination of these two thank-offerings—the bull and the grain—is particularly appropriate given the Teians' assistance in the purchase of draft-oxen for the cultivation of Abderite territory (**B24–31**); the Abderites seem to have selected a package of honours which reflected some of the specific benefactions provided by the Teians, which led to the revival of Abderite arable cultivation after the disaster of 170 BC.

B80–4

80   [καὶ τόπον αἰτησάσθων οἱ πεμ]φθέντες ἄνδρες ἐν τῶι ἱερῶι τοῦ Διονύσου ἢ
[(?) ἐν τῆι ἀγορᾶι ἐν ὧι στήσουσι] στήλην λευκοῦ λίθου ἐν ἧι ἀναγεγράφθω τόδ[ε]
[τὸ ψήφισμα· τὸ δὲ γενόμενον] ἀνάλωμα εἰς τὴν κατασκευὴν τῆς στή[λης]
[καὶ τὴν ἀναγραφὴν τοῦ ψηφίσμα]τος τὸ συνκριθὲν χορηγείτωσαν οἱ νομ[οφύλα]-
[κες (?) ἀπὸ τῶν εἰς τὰς πρεσβείας·...

'And let the men who have been sent [request a spot] in the sanctuary of Dionysos or [(?) in the agora in which they can set up] a *stēlē* of white marble, on which let this [decree] be inscribed, and let the *nomophylakes* provide the agreed expenditure [incurred] for the making of the *stēlē* [and the inscription of the dec]ree [(?) from the funds reserved for embassies.]'

The Abderite envoys are to request permission from the Teians to erect a copy of the decree at Teos, either in the sanctuary of Dionysos—where the decree was in fact set up—or (if our restoration at the start of **B81** is correct) in the agora at Teos. For 'requesting a spot' at a foreign city for the erection of an inscription or statue (Ma 2013, 72–4), see e.g. Le Guen 2001, no. 45 (Aneziri 2003, D10: decree of the Dionysiac Artists for the *aulētēs* Kraton, *c*.171 BC), lines 36–8, [ἀποστεῖλαι δὲ πρεσβευτὰς] δύο πρὸς τον δῆμον τὸν Τηίων οἵτινες αἰτήσονται τόπον ἐν τῶι [θεάτρωι ἐν ὧι σταθήσεται] ἡ εἰκὼν Κράτωνος; IG XI 4, 1022 (Delos, III BC), lines 2–4, [οἱ Χῖοι] ἀποστείλαντες πρεσβευτὴν [πρὸς ἡμᾶς αἰτοῦνται τ]όπον ἐν τῶι ἱερῶι ὅπου σταθήσετα[ι ἡ στήλη ἐν ἧι εἰσιν

---

[131] The infinitive [δια]πέμψαι is the first infinitive (as opposed to third-person imperative) we have had since **B56**, στῆσαι.

ἀν]αγεγραμμέναι αἱ τιμαί. The single letter *eta* at the end of line **B80** must indicate that the Abderites decided, unusually, to give the Teians a choice of location, either the sanctuary of Dionysos or (perhaps) the agora; contrast the decree for Amymon and Megathymos (**Document 6** below, line 43), where the Abderites asked merely that the Teian copy of the decree should be erected 'in the most prominent spot'. For the restoration [ἐν ὧι στήσουσι] στήλην (**B81**), cf. Michel 1900, no. 534 (Kyzikos, III BC), lines 13–14, τόπον αἰτοῦνται ἐν τῆι ἀγορᾶι ἐν ὧι στήσουσι τὴν εἰκόνα; SEG 46, 1519 (Apollo Pleurenos, shortly after 188 BC), lines 14–15, ἵνα παραδείξῃ μοι τόπον ἐν ᾧ στήσω τὴν στήλην.

The basic sense of **B82–4** is clear enough: the *nomophylakes* are to provide the money for the erection of the *stēlē* at Teos. The first words of line **B84** presumably specified where the *nomophylakes* are to draw the funds from. However, it is not clear whether the *nomophylakes* provide this money in advance, or whether the ambassadors are only reimbursed after their return from Teos. In the contemporary decree for Amymon and Megathymos (**Document 6** below, Chapter 5), lines 44–7, the latter procedure was followed: the ambassadors themselves paid for the erection of the *stēlē* at Teos, invoiced their expenses to the city of Abdera on their return, and received the money back from the public bank. Whether that was also the process followed in this case depends on how we interpret τὸ συνκριθέν (sc. ἀνάλωμα), 'the agreed expenditure', in **B83**.[132] This phrase could either signify the *projected* cost 'agreed' at Abdera in advance of the embassy ('you are not to spend more than *x* drachms on the *stēlē*') or the *actual* cost eventually 'agreed' by the ambassadors with the craftsmen at Teos ('we ended up agreeing to spend *x* drachms on the *stēlē*'). Either way, it seems more likely that, as in **Document 6** below, the ambassadors initially paid out for the *stēlē* and were only reimbursed by the *nomophylakes* after their return to Abdera.

The ultimate source of the money provided by the *nomophylakes* (the lacuna at the start of **B84**) cannot be determined with certainty. The restoration [ἀπὸ τῆς τραπέζης] is too short for the lacuna. It seems more likely that we are dealing with one of the special 'earmarked' funds attested at Abdera: we hear in other documents of payments being made 'from the fund reserved for

---

[132] The verb συνκρίνειν is rare in Hellenistic epigraphy. It is elsewhere used of decisions in which several parties or several considerations are involved: Gauthier 1989, 31, citing examples from Sardeis, Kyme, Priene, and Ilion (add SEG 45, 1508 [Bargylia], A17, B4, and the Kanopos synodic decree of 238 BC, CPI I, 119 [Tanis], lines 71–2 = CPI I, 129 [Kom el-Hisn], line 61), none closely parallel to this passage.

embassies' (**Document 6** below, line 48, ἀπὸ τῶν εἰς τὰς πρεσβείας) and 'from the fund reserved for sacrifices' (*IThrakAig* E7, lines 32–3, ἀπὸ τῶν εἰς τὰς θυσίας).[133] We have tentatively preferred the former.

B84–9

ἵνα δὲ] καὶ Τήϊοι παρακολουθῶσιν τοῖς ὑφ᾽ ἡμ[ῶν ἐψη]-
85 [φισμένοις, ἀποστειλάτωσαν οἱ με]τὰ ἱερέα Σχησίστρατον νομοφ[ύλακες]
[τὸ ἀντίγραφον τοῦ ψηφίσματος πρὸ]ς τὸν Τηΐων δῆμον· τὴν δὲ ἐπιμ[έλειαν]
[(e.g.) τῆς τε ἀναστάσεως τῆς εἰκόνος] καὶ τῶν ἄλ[λ]ων τῶν δηλου[μένων (e.g.) ἐν τῶι]
[ψηφίσματι - - - c.12–14 - - - ποιησάσθ]ωσαν οἱ αὐτοὶ νομοφ[ύλακες - - c.7 - -]
[- - c.10 - - · τὸ δὲ ψήφισμα τόδε εἶναι] εἰς εὐχαριστίαν τ[οῦ δήμου· ...

'[And so that] the Teians too might learn of the [things decreed] by us, let the *nomophylakes* in office in the year after the priesthood of Schesistratos [send a copy of the decree t]o the Teian *dēmos*. And let the same *nomophylakes* have respon[sibility for (e.g.) the erection of the statue] and the other things laid out [(e.g.) in the decree...and let this decree be for the purpose of (showing)] the gratitude of [the *dēmos*.]'

For the purpose-clause in **B84–5**, cf. **B74–5** above, with commentary. The formulation in line **B85** ([οἱ με]τὰ ἱερέα Σχησίστρατον νομοφ[ύλακες]) indicates that this decree must have been passed towards the end of the year at Abdera, and it is the following year's board of *nomophylakes* who are to be responsible for sending a copy of the decree to Teos.[134] The eponymous magistrate at Abdera was the priest of Dionysos: cf. **Document 6** below, lines 34–5 (οἱ δὲ νομοφύλακες οἱ ἐπὶ ἱερέως Ἡρα[- c.7 -]); *IThrakAig* E8, lines 31–2 (οἱ νομοφύλακες οἱ ἐπὶ ἱερέως Διονύσου; cf. lines 26–7, δεδόσθαι δὲ αὐτῶι καὶ ἀτέλειαν μετὰ ἱερέα Διόνυσον);[135] in *IThrakAig* E9, lines 30–1, we should

---

[133] At Miletos we find 'those in charge of the public bank' (οἱ ἐπὶ τῆς δημοσίας τραπέζης) making payments ἀπὸ τῶν εἰς τὰ τειχοποϊκὰ ἐξειρημένων (*Milet* I 3, 143A, lines 37–9; 144A, lines 5–7 (restored); 146A, lines 48–50; 147, lines 64–6) and treasurers (ταμίαι) making payments ἀπὸ τῶν εἰς τὰ κατὰ ψηφίσματα ἐξειρημένων (*Milet* I 3, 146A, lines 56–8; 147, lines 51–3); for a similar formulation at Kolophon, cf. *I.Priene*² 116, line 9, ἀπὸ τῶν εἰς τὴν διοίκησιν. Cf. Bogaert 1969, 256–7, 261–2.

[134] The *nomophylakes* were also responsible for providing a copy of the decree (ἀντίγραφ[ον τοῦ ψηφίσματος]) for C. Apustius and P. Apustius to the honorands: *IThrakAig* E9, lines 41–3.

[135] The god Dionysos acted as his own eponym: Robert, *Hellenica* II, 56; Sherk 1991, 225; Chryssanthaki 2001, 392.

restore οἱ νομοφύλακε[ς οἱ μετὰ ἱερέα (*name*)]τον Σωτηρίχου (with the priest's patronym included).

The personal name Σχησίστρατος is otherwise unattested, and names in Σχησι- are in fact exceptionally rare: the only other example is the name Σχησίπολις, twice attested on Thasos in the fourth century BC (*LGPN* I, s.v.). However, an Abderite mint-magistrate of the late fourth or early third century BC bore the name Σχη(-); it is likely enough that his name was Σχη(σίστρατος) or Σχη(σίπολις).[136]

In lines **B86–8**, the same board of *nomophylakes* (that of the following year) are instructed to take responsibility (τὴν δὲ ἐπιμ[έλειαν . . . ποιησάσθ]ωσαν) for something. The words ϙαὶ τῶν ἄλ[λ]ων τῶν δηλου[μένων], 'and of the other things laid out' (**B87**) indicates that they are being instructed to take on the management of certain actions specified earlier in the decree; hence in **B87–8** we should presumably restore τῶν δηλου[μένων ἐν τῶι | ψηφίσματι] *vel sim*. At the start of **B87**, a single action must therefore be specified as the most important responsibility of the *nomophylakes*, evidently one which is mentioned earlier in the decree but for which responsibility has not yet been assigned; this can only be the construction and erection of the monumental bronze statue of the *Dēmos* of the Teians (**B56–61**), and we therefore restore [τῆς τε ἀναστάσεως τῆς εἰκόνος]. For the phraseology, compare e.g. Michel 1900, 544, with Wilhelm 1921a, 45–8 (Themisonion, 67/6 BC), lines 57–9, τὴν δ[ὲ ἐπιμέλειάν] τε τῆς ⟨στ⟩άσεως τῆς εἰκόνος καὶ τῆς σ[τήλης ποιεῖ]σθαι τοὺς ἐν ἐκείνωι τῶι καιρῶι στρ[ατηγούς].

In **B89**, the clause [τὸ δὲ ψήφισμα τόδε εἶναι] ᾖς εὐχαριστίαν τ[οῦ δήμου] is a standard concluding formula for honorific decrees at Abdera: cf. **Document 2** below, lines 48–9; *IThrakAig* E7, lines 40–1 (longer version: τὸ δὲ ψήφισμα τόδε εἶναι εἰς εὐχαριστίαν τῶν εὐνοούντων τῶι δήμωι); *IThrakAig* E9, line 44. These kinds of standardized 'labels' often appear at the end of Hellenistic decrees, usually with reference to the 'salvation' (εἰς σωτηρίαν) or 'protection' (εἰς φυλακήν) of the city, although other formulations are found; e.g. at Julio-Claudian Miletos, a decree is labelled as 'for the purpose of (showing) piety towards the gods and the Augusti and (ensuring) the continuation of the city' (*Milet* I 3, 134, lines 33–5, ταῦτα δὲ εἶναι εἰς εὐσέβειαν τῶν τε θεῶν καὶ τῶν Σεβαστῶν καὶ διαμονὴν τῆς πόλεως).[137]

---

[136] Masson 1984, 55; Chryssanthaki-Nagle 2007, 202, 210 (*c*.311–280 BC).
[137] Gschnitzer 1983; Rhodes with Lewis 1997, 522–3.

B89–93

εἱρέθησαν]

90 [πρεσβευταὶ - - - - - - c.20–2 - - - - - - - ὁ] πρεσβύτερος, Ἀθ[ηνα- - - - c.11–13 - - - -]

[- - - - - - - - - - - c.32–4 - - - - - - - - - - -]νος ὀκτωκαιδ[εκάτηι - - - - - c.11–13 - - - - -]

[- - - - - - - - c.26–8 - - - - - - - ὁ πρεσβύτ]ερος, Ἀθην[α- - - - - - - -c.19–21 - - - - - - - -]

[- - - - - - - - - - - - c.33–5 - - - - - - - - - - - - -]μηνὸς Ε[- - - - - - - - - c.21–3 - - - - - - - - -]

vacat

'[The following ambassadors were chosen: (name) son of (name) the] elder; Ath[ena- son of (name)...] on the eighteenth (of the month) [- - ; (name) son of (name) the el]der, Athen[a- son of (name)...] of the month....'

The names of the ambassadors ((?) or *theōroi*) selected are appended after the end of the decree proper, as in the decree for Amymon and Megathymos (**Document 6** below, lines 49–50: ε[ἱρέθησα]ν πρεσβευταὶ Ἡρακλείδης Ἀλκίφρονος, Ἀλκ[ίφρων Δη]μητρίου). The first ambassador's name stood in the lacuna at the start of **B90** (c.21–3 letters, a plausible length for name + patronym); this first ambassador was designated [ὁ] πρεσβύτερος, 'the elder', to distinguish him from a younger homonym: cf. e.g. *IG* XII 6, 1, 152–3 (Samos, c.200–150 BC), where the single ambassador to Thasos was Ζηνόδοτος Ἀριστομάχου ὁ νεώτερος. The second ambassador's name stood at the end of **B90**; he may well have been called Ἀθήναιος, a name which is well attested at Abdera (*LGPN* IV, s.v. **25–8**).

Lines **B91–3** are an unsolved puzzle. **B93** is certainly the last line of the inscription (there is a blank space below the surviving letters). In the middle of line **B91**, we clearly have a date (the eighteenth of the month); we then appear to have another date in the middle of line **B93**. Between these two dates, we seem to have the *same* list of ambassadors repeated for a second time (line **B92**). We are unable to offer a convincing explanation for this repetition of the list of names; nor is it clear what the dates in lines **B91** and **B93** represent. It is worth noting that our decree—very unusually—stipulated the month in which the Abderite envoys to Teos were to be selected (lines **B74–5**: οἱ νομοφύλακες ἀεὶ κατ' ἐνιαυτὸν αἱρείσθωσαν ἄνδρας [(number) ἐμ μηνὶ Ἀπα]τουριῶνι), no doubt because this was not a one-off appointment of ambassadors, but a recurring annual appointment of *theōroi* to the Teian Leukathea (see the commentary on **B74–5** above). It is therefore possible that the date in **B91** represents the date on which the first annual group of envoys was appointed; if that were correct, the central part of **B91** could then be restored [μηνὸς Ἀπατουρίω]νος ὀκτωκαιδ[εκάτηι]. But that still leaves it unclear why the envoys' names were (apparently) repeated in lines **B92–3**— were the same men perhaps appointed a second time as envoys, in the second year of the annual Abderite *theōria* to the Teian Leukathea? Given the uncertainty about the structure of these lines, it is best to remain agnostic as to whether there were two or three envoys in total (i.e. whether a third envoy was named at the start of line **B91**).

This extraordinary new text recounts, in exquisite detail, the terrible fate of Abdera during the Third Macedonian War (**A14–27**); the various forms of assistance provided by the city of Teos in the reconstitution of the citizen body, urban fabric, and rural territory of Abdera over a period of (apparently) several years (**B1–52**); and the extraordinary honours conferred in return on the Teians by the grateful Abderites (**B52–89**). It is unclear exactly how many years had elapsed since the destruction of Abdera (precisely dated to summer 170 BC) by the time this decree was passed: note the unspecified passage of time in **B22**, τοῦ χρόνου... προκόψαντος, 'when time had passed'. It is hard to believe that the resolution of the territorial dispute between Abdera and Maroneia (**B31–52**) could have occurred before the Roman settlement of Macedonia in 167 BC, but it is also unlikely that the Abderites waited too long to raise their grievances over their lost territory. Our best guess is that the hearing over the Abdera–Maroneia dispute was held fairly soon after the settlement of 167 BC, and that our inscription should be placed shortly thereafter, most likely in 166 or 165 BC. (This raises thorny problems about the chronological relationship between this decree and the Abderite decree for the Teians Amymon and Megathymos, **Document 6** below, which almost certainly dates to 166 BC: see our discussion in Chapter 5.)

In the chapters that follow, we explore various aspects of the historical background, context, and significance of the new decree (hereafter **Document 1**). In Chapters 2 and 3, we look back at the origins of the 'kinship' between Abdera and Teos (**A4, B9, B15–16, B36, B50**) that underlay the repeated Abderite appeals to Teos in the years after 170 BC. We will look first at the foundation of Abdera by Teian settlers in the mid-sixth century BC (Chapter 2), and then at the strikingly close relations that persisted between the two cities into the fifth century BC and beyond (Chapter 3). Our most important documents for the ongoing institutional links between the two cities in the Classical period are the famous 'Teian Dirae', two large and difficult inscriptions from Teos of (probably) the 470s BC. Earlier editions of these two texts are unsatisfactory in various ways, and the precise character of the relations that they assume between Teos and Abdera has (so we argue) been seriously misunderstood; we therefore offer a full re-edition of both texts in Chapter 3 (**Documents 2** and **3**). In Chapters 4 and 5, we turn to look at Teos and Abdera in the 170s and 160s BC. The first part of Chapter 4 is concerned with the Hellenistic temple and cult of Dionysos at Teos, and we take the opportunity to publish two interesting new Hellenistic inscriptions from the *temenos* of the Dionysos-temple at Teos (**Documents 4** and **5**); the second part of the chapter explores the status of Teos in the decades after the treaty of Apameia in 188 BC. In Chapter 5, we move back to Abdera, and in particular the territorial disputes with the Thracian king Kotys and the neighbouring city of Maroneia that blew up in the wake of the sack of 170 BC. The dispute with Kotys has long been known, thanks to an inscription from Teos recording Abderite honours for two Teian ambassadors to Rome, Amymon and Megathymos; we provide a new edition of this text (**Document 6**), along with a revised interpretation of its historical context, in the light of the new decree. In Chapter 6, we look in detail at one of the most remarkable features of the Abderite honours for Teos, a monumental statue of the personified *Dēmos* of the Teians at Abdera and its associated cult (**B56–73**). The Epilogue draws these threads together to assess the significance of the new decree for our understanding of interstate diplomacy in the second century BC. But that is a long way ahead: let us begin at the beginning.

2

'The Lands Conquered and Settled by Their Ancestors'

Archaic Teos and the Foundation of Abdera

Archaic Teos and its colonies

The earliest ceramic evidence for settlement at Teos dates to the Protogeometric period (tenth century BC); there is at present no sign of an earlier Bronze Age occupation phase.[1] Our knowledge of the early history of Teos remains extremely patchy, but the recent Turkish excavations at the site have amply demonstrated the city's prosperity throughout the Archaic period. Of particular importance is the recent discovery, to the west of the Hellenistic wall-circuit, of a group of kiln wasters dating to the sixth and fifth century BC, evidently from a local Teian pottery workshop. NAA analysis of these kiln wasters has demonstrated beyond reasonable doubt that a large and widespread body of North Ionian ceramics of the eighth to sixth century BC, 'North Ionian Group B' ('Bird Bowl Workshops'), must be attributed to Teos.[2] This ceramic group, including the well-known 'North Ionian bird kotylai', is very widely distributed across the Aegean and western Asia Minor, as well as the Black Sea, Sicily, and Egypt (Naukratis and Thebes). A fragment of a drinking-song by the Lesbian poet Alkaios (c.600 BC) refers specifically to wine-drops flying from 'Teian drinking-cups', suggesting that Teian drinking-ware was proverbial in aristocratic sympotic contexts; it is a pleasing coincidence that perhaps the best-known surviving drinking-cup from the Archaic Greek world, 'Nestor's Cup' from Pithekoussai, is now known to have been made in a Teian workshop.[3] In addition to finewares, substantial quantities of trade

---

[1] Kadıoğlu, Özbil, Kerschner, and Mommsen 2015, 348; Kadıoğlu 2019, 295.
[2] Kerschner 2014, 109–10; Kadıoğlu, Özbil, Kerschner, and Mommsen 2015, 349–53; Kadıoğlu 2019, 297–300, with the distribution map at 299.
[3] Alkaios F322 Lobel/Page, quoted by Ath. 11.481a: 'λάταγες ποτέονται κυλίχναν ἀπὺ Τηίαν', ὡς διαφόρων γινομένων καὶ ἐν Τέῳ κυλίκων, '"The wine-drops fly from Teian kylichnai", for excellent kylikes are also found at Teos'. Nestor's Cup: Kerschner 2014, 109–10. For a group of Late Geometric

Teos and Abdera: Two Cities in Peace and War. Mustafa Adak and Peter Thonemann, Oxford University Press.

amphorae were produced at Teos between the late seventh and mid-sixth century, virtually all identified specimens of which derive from the northern Black Sea and Egypt.[4] At Berezan, where several sixth-century amphora assemblages can be closely dated, Teian amphorae are absent from contexts of the second half of the sixth century, suggesting that Teian exports might perhaps have been sharply interrupted by the dramatic political events of the 540s BC (see further below).[5]

The chief export-commodity of Teos in the Archaic period must certainly have been wine. The territory of Teos has no major perennial rivers, and the only continuous stretch of flat arable land is a narrow strip of low-lying territory between modern Seferihisar and Bademler.[6] Local cereal-production must always have been relatively limited, and the city's dependence on imported grain is a recurring leitmotif in Teian history: in the early fifth century BC, the Teians proclaimed public curses against 'whoever prevents grain from being imported into the land of Teos by any device or means, either by land or sea, or pushes grain which has been imported away again', and at the time of the attempted synoikism of Teos and Lebedos by Antigonos the One-Eyed (c.302 BC), the Teians and Lebedians were seriously concerned about how to secure sufficient grain-imports in future, since the Teians 'do not produce enough'.[7] By contrast, the hilly hinterland of Teos is exceptionally well-suited to vine-cultivation, whose abundance is most vividly attested by the five thousand jars of wine prepared by the Teians in autumn 190 BC to supply the fleet of Antiochos III (Livy 37.27.3). Very unusually, Teian wine-production was directly reflected in the civic calendar: the autumn month *Trygētēr*, 'vintage-month', is attested only at Teos.[8] The city's chief deity was the god Dionysos, whose Hellenistic cult-statue depicted the god pouring wine from a kantharos; according to Diodoros, 'the Teians offer as a visible sign (*tekmērion*) that the god was born among them the fact that right up to the present day, at fixed times, a spring of exceptionally sweet-smelling wine appears of its own accord

---

drinking wares (one krater and twenty-three kotylai) discovered near the north harbour of Teos (Sığacık), see İren and Ünlü 2012 (the attribution to a burial context is indecisive).
[4] Sezgin 2012, 283–92; Sezgin 2017 (with catalogue).   [5] Chistov 2018, 87–9.
[6] A large number of wells and cisterns can still be seen in the hinterland of Teos, some of them built from ancient spolia. The fullest accounts of the geography of Teian territory are to be found in Robert and Robert 1976 and Strang 2007, 18–42; a short but evocative sketch in Ma 2007b, 216–20; see now also Adak 2021.
[7] Curses: Dirae I, lines 47–51 (**Document 2**, Chapter 3 below). Synoikism: Welles, *RC* 3 (c.302 BC), lines 72–101 (note line 78, οὐ γὰρ ποεῖν ὑμᾶς ἱκανόν); see further Boehm 2018, 96–102; Adak 2021.
[8] *SEG* 44, 949 (with Meier 2017 and Hamon 2018), line 70; Şahin 1994, 27–8 and 34 ('Monat der Winzer'); Adak and Stauner 2018, 14; Adak and Thonemann 2020, 9–12.

out of the earth in their city'.[9] It is no coincidence that the work of the city's most famous poet, Anakreon of Teos, was very largely dedicated to sympotic and Dionysiac themes.[10]

Teian overseas commerce with Egypt in the late seventh and early sixth centuries BC is particularly well attested. Teos is named by Herodotos as one of the nine Greek cities involved in the foundation of the Hellenion at Naukratis (2.178), probably in the early years of the sixth century BC, and the abundant inscribed pottery-fragments from Naukratis include five dedications (to Aphrodite and Apollo) by individuals designated as 'Teians'.[11] Teian pottery is notably well represented among ceramic finds from Naukratis.[12] In 591 BC, a Teian mercenary serving in the army of Psammetichos II carved his name on the leg of the statue of Rameses II at Abu Simbel—this man, Helesibios, is in fact the earliest Teian known to us by name.[13] One of the most startling indications of Teos' links with Egypt in the pre-Persian period is the 'Apries Amphora' (probably mid-sixth century BC), almost certainly discovered at Egyptian Thebes, which is now known to be the product of a Teian workshop. This amphora carries a depiction of two boxers facing one another across a prize dinos on a stand; on the neck, the amphora bears a cartouche band carrying the names of the pharaoh Apries, indicating that at least one Teian vase-painter was able to come up with a plausible pastiche of hieroglyphic Egyptian.[14]

The urban layout of Archaic Teos is currently only very poorly known, although the picture is changing fast thanks to the ongoing Turkish excavations. Herodotos' account of the Persian siege of Teos makes it clear that the city must have been walled in the mid-sixth century BC (1.168), but no traces

[9] Cult-statue: see Chapter 6 below. Wine-miracle: Diod. Sic. 3.66.2, discussed further in Chapter 4 below. The attempt of Hahland 1950, 85, to identify a depiction of this miracle in the frieze of the Teian Dionysos-temple is doubted by Fuchs 2018, 149; the wine-miracle may be depicted on a Hellenistic relief of uncertain provenance in the İzmir Archaeological Museum, Inv. 241 (Hahland 1950, 85–7; Fuchs 2018, 149 and 157 fig. 2).

[10] Bernsdorff 2020; for Anakreon's views on appropriate modes of wine-drinking, Palmisciano 2019. We note here a remarkable inscription discovered in secondary use in the city wall near the south harbour of Teos, to be published shortly. The text consists of thirty lines of elegiac verse, inscribed on a 1.5m high block of grey marble, which appear to be a (parodic?) verse epitaph for a woman who is attacked at length for her sexual debauchery. The new text includes at least one verse which also appears in the corpus of Theognis of Megara (Theognis line 460, 'she often finds another harbour at night'). The genre of 'blame poetry' (*psogos*) is widely attested in the Archaic Greek world, associated in particular with Archilochos and Hipponax (also in a few fragments of Anakreon), but we have no other examples of such poems preserved on stone. The letter forms seem considerably earlier than those of the Teian Dirae (Chapter 3 below), and the text probably dates to the late sixth century BC.

[11] Möller 2001, 168–9, with Demetriou 2017, 53–5. For the tombstone of a Teian at Naukratis in the Hellenistic period, see É. Bernand 1969, no. 2.

[12] Schlotzhauer and Villing 2006 ('North Ionian Group B').

[13] Meiggs and Lewis 1969, 7b.

[14] Bailey 2006; Spier, Potts, and Cole 2018, 97 (A. Villing).

of this Archaic wall-circuit, or of its presumed Classical successors, have yet been located.[15] A recent extensive geomagnetic survey of the central urban area, between the low hill (the 'acropolis') in the northern part of the site and the south harbour, found no trace of a grid-plan: in contrast to many other Ionian cities, the urban layout of Teos seems to have developed organically, with no subsequent 'Hippodamian' reorganization of the urban space.[16] The most impressive monumental structure currently known from pre-Hellenistic Teos is a 100-foot temple (*hekatompedon*), perhaps dating to the late eighth or seventh century BC, whose foundations were discovered on the 'acropolis' in 1995; this temple measured 38.46m by 7.3m, making it slightly larger than the first *hekatompedon* in the Samian Heraion.[17] This early temple seems to have had a lavish late Archaic successor in the Ionic order, several architectural elements from which have been recovered in the course of recent excavations at Teos; this late Archaic temple (dated by the excavators to the third quarter of the sixth century) seems also to have been located on the acropolis or in its immediate vicinity.[18] The only other part of the Archaic city known to us is the extensive Archaic necropolis which sprawled over the plateau to the west and north-west of the city (today largely occupied by holiday homes); sporadic rescue excavations conducted by the Museum of İzmir, as yet not fully published, have uncovered painted 'Klazomenian' sarcophagi and grave pithoi of the Archaic and Early Classical periods in this area.

The ancient literary tradition knew of no large-scale Teian overseas migrations (Naukratis aside) before the foundations of the Teian daughter-cities of Abdera in Aegean Thrace and Phanagoreia in the Kimmerian Bosporos, both of which are conventionally dated to the 540s BC. Ancient authors agree that the trigger for both enterprises was the Persian conquest of Ionia at some point in the mid- to late 540s BC (*c.*546–542 BC). According to Herodotos, 'Harpagos captured their walls with a siege-mound, and the entire population embarked on their ships and sailed off to the Thraceward region, where they founded the city of Abdera'; the Teians thereby evaded the 'enslavement'

---

[15] On the later Hellenistic wall-circuit, see now Taşdelen and Polat 2018; Hülden 2020, 188–90. Parts of the Hellenistic city wall were made of brick rather than stone, and that may also have been the case in the Archaic period. The city wall was rebuilt by the Athenians 'on the landward side' (Thuc. 8.16.3), but pulled down again in 411 BC; the anecdote in Aen. Tact. 18.13–19 assumes that the city was walled in the mid-fourth century BC.

[16] Kadıoğlu et al. 2018, 62–3, maps 1–2.

[17] Tuna 1997, 219–22; Crielaard 2009, 66. A large multi-phase structure immediately to the east, measuring 9.56m by 18.2m, was identified by Tuna as an altar associated with the *hekatompedon*.

[18] Kadıoğlu, Özbil, Kerschner, and Mommsen 2015, 353–62; see also Chapter 4 below. The excavators also refer (361) to a homogenous find of ceramic drinking vessels from the acropolis, dating *c.*639–590 BC, which they believe to derive from a sacred context.

inflicted by the Persians on the rest of Ionia.[19] Similarly, a late literary source (Arrian, writing in the early second century AD) claims that the Teian foundation of Phanagoreia in the Kimmerian Bosporos was driven by the desire to escape 'the *hybris* of the Persians'.[20]

It is hard to judge how much truth underlies this 'catastrophist' picture of Teian colonial activity. The archaeology shows no sign of a mid-sixth-century break in settlement at Teos, making it difficult to accept Herodotos' claim that the 'entire population' of Teos migrated to Abdera.[21] Even if the foundations at Abdera and Phanagoreia do indeed date to the 540s, that need not mean that they were in any sense 'refugee' settlements; the heart-warming notion of freedom-loving Teians fleeing Persian 'enslavement' looks suspiciously like a *post eventum* construction of the post-Persian Wars period.[22] Still more fundamentally, the traditional conception of 'Archaic Greek colonization' as a state-led enterprise, involving the foundation of new cities at precisely definable historical moments as a result of one-off mass migrations from single mother-cities, has met with sustained criticism in recent scholarship. In a classic paper, Robin Osborne showed that the archaeology of early Greek 'colonies' in the West typically shows no trace of a single moment of foundation, nor do we find the kind of wholesale 'mimicking' of the material culture of a mainland Greek city which we might expect from state-led enterprises.[23] Certainly for the eighth and seventh centuries BC, and probably for the sixth century too, we ought instead to be thinking about a gradual process of mobility by individuals and small groups, the incremental effects of which were retrospectively reconceptualized as one-off acts of 'colonization' by specific mother-cities.

The case for seeing Phanagoreia as a Teian refugee settlement—or indeed as a state-driven 'Teian colony' at all—is particularly fragile. Phanagoreia occupies a splendid site on the northern shore of the Taman peninsula in the Kimmerian

---

[19] Hdt. 1.168–9; very similar accounts (no doubt drawn from Herodotos) in Strabo 14.1.30 (Τήϊοι, τὴν πόλιν ἐκλιπόντες, εἰς Ἄβδηρα ἀπῴκησαν, Θρακίαν πόλιν, οὐ φέροντες τὴν τῶν Περσῶν ὕβριν), and pseudo-Skymnos, FGrHist 2048 T1, lines 670–1 (Τήϊοι δὲ τὴν πόλιν συνῴκισαν φυγόντες ὑπὸ τὰ Περσικά).

[20] Arrian, FGrHist 156 F71: Φαναγόρεια, ἣν ἔκτισε Φαναγόρας ὁ Τήϊος, φεύγων τὴν τῶν Περσῶν ὕβριν.

[21] Destruction-levels associated with the Persian conquest of the 540s are attested at the neighbouring cities of Erythrai, Smyrna, and Phokaia: see, most conveniently, Hansen and Nielsen 2004, 1075 (Erythrai), 1091 (Phokaia), 1099 (Smyrna) (L. Rubinstein).

[22] Braund 2018, 112: 'It is a wholly unsatisfactory habit of modern scholarship to rely on these relationships with non-Greeks [i.e. Lydians and Persians] as the major stimulus to overseas settlement from Ionia'. For Ionian prosperity under Persian rule, see Georges 2000.

[23] Osborne 1998. The subsequent bibliography is vast: a helpful overview can be found in Donnellan, Nizzo, and Burgers 2016.

Bosporos, on the Asiatic side of the Kerch straits.[24] As it happens, the earliest Greek pottery from Phanagoreia is consistent with an initial settlement in the 540s BC, but there is no good reason to think that the city's foundation was in any sense 'triggered' by the Persian conquest of Ionia.[25] The foundation of Phanagoreia in fact fits perfectly neatly into a much longer-term pattern of Greek contacts with and settlement on the Taman peninsula, going back at least to the late seventh century BC.[26] Were it not for the late literary traditions linking the foundation of Phanagoreia with Teos, no one would ever have guessed that Phanagoreia was a Teian foundation at all.[27] There is no sign of cultural or institutional contacts between Phanagoreia and Teos in later periods, and the material culture of Phanagoreia in the late sixth and fifth centuries shows no particularly close ties with northern Ionia.[28] None of that is to say that Teian settlers were not involved in the establishment of Phanagoreia: it is perfectly possible that the 'Phanagoras' after whom the city was named was indeed a Teian, as Arrian claims.[29] But it requires a major leap of faith to conceive Phanagoreia as a state-driven 'Teian colony', let alone as a colony founded by refugees fleeing the Persians.

For Abdera, as we will see, the situation is considerably more complex.

The Foundations of Abdera

The name Abdera (Greek, τὰ Ἄβδηρα) is not Greek. The existence of a homonymous Phoenician foundation in southern Spain suggests that the name may be of Punic origin, but there is no archaeological or literary

---

[24] Hansen and Nielsen 2004, 950–1 (A. Avram, J. Hind, and G. Tsetskhladze); Tsetskhladze 2007; Povalahev 2008, 182–91; Povalahev and Kuznetsov 2011; Povalahev and Kuznetsov 2012; Povalahev 2014; Fornasier 2016, 66–7. For the spectacular recent discovery of a fragmentary Old Persian inscription from the site, apparently dating to the reign of Darius I (perhaps a *pierre errante*), see Shaverbi 2019.

[25] Morgan 2004, 1, 17–18.   [26] Kerschner 2006; Schlotzhauer and Zhuravlev 2013.

[27] The tradition appears first in pseudo-Skymnos (second century BC or later), *FGrHist* 2048 F17b, lines 885–6, Φαναγόρεια…ἣν Τηΐους λέγουσιν οἰκίσαι ποτέ, 'Phanagoreia, which they say the Teians once settled'—note the hesitant 'they say'. Strabo does not mention Teos in his discussion of Phanagoreia (11.2.10). Kuznetsov 2000–1 argues, on minimal evidence, that Phanagoreia was in fact founded by Teians from Abdera.

[28] Dan et al. 2016, 112–16. For patterns of Phanagoreian overseas trade in the late sixth and fifth centuries, see Monakhov and Kuznetsova 2017.

[29] Arrian, *FGrHist* 156 F71; Malkin 1985, 121–3. The name Phanagoras is attested at Keos, Karystos, Thasos, Mytilene, Delos, Athens, Klazomenai, Erythrai, Smyrna: *LGPN*, s.v.

evidence for an early Phoenician settlement at the site of Thracian Abdera.[30] The Abderites believed that the city was named after a mythological hero by the name of Abderos, first attested in Pindar's second *Paean*, which dates to the early fifth century BC.[31] Pindar describes him as the son of Poseidon and the Naiad Thronia, and addresses him with the epithet χαλκοθώραξ, 'with bronze breastplate', suggesting that his cult had a warlike character.[32] The standard ancient version of the myth of Abderos seems to go back to the late fifth-century mythographer Hellanikos of Lesbos. According to Hellanikos, Abderos was a son of Hermes from Opountian Lokris, beloved by Herakles. During Herakles' campaign against Diomedes the king of the Bistones, Abderos was briefly left to look after Diomedes' mares, by whom he was torn apart; Herakles subsequently founded Abdera at the site of Abderos' tomb.[33] For both Pindar and Hellanikos, Abderos seems to have been a native of Opountian Lokris: Pindar identifies Abderos' mother as Thronia, the eponym of the Lokrian city of Thronion.[34] We know of no further historical links between Abdera and Lokris.

The hero Abderos was later the recipient of cult at Abdera. In his *Imagines*, Philostratos says that the Abderites celebrated athletic contests in honour of Abderos, which (tactfully) did not include horse-races.[35] A dedication of the late fourth century BC from Abdera informs us of a cult of '*Hērōs Mesopolitēs Epēnōr*', 'the hero in the middle of the city, the brave one', plausibly identified by the first editors with the eponym Abderos.[36] The opening lines of Pindar's second *Paean* strongly imply that it was originally performed during a choral procession that began at a shrine of Abderos, and ended at a shrine of Apollo Derenos and Aphrodite; it is likely enough that Abderos had a hero-shrine in the centre of Abdera, which served as the focal point for processions and athletic games.[37] An Athenian decree of 345 BC in honour of three Abderite brothers carried a painted depiction of the hero Abderos in the pediment

---

[30] Isaac 1986, 76–7; Graham 1992, 44–5; Chryssanthaki 2001, 386. For the alleged Phoenician foundation of Thasos, see Hdt. 6.47.1.

[31] The date of Pind. *Pae.* 2 is wholly uncertain: Radt 1958, 17–19; Graham 1992, 63–4; Rutherford 2001, 275. We suggest below some historical reasons to favour a date in the second half of the 470s or later.

[32] Pind. *Pae.* 2, lines 1–2, [Ναΐδ]ος Θρονίας Ἄβδηρε χαλκοθώραξ [Ποσ]ειδᾶνός τε παῖ; Rutherford 2001, 262, 264–5.

[33] Hellanikos Fr. 105 (Fowler), with Apollod. *Bibl.* 2.96–7; discussion in Fowler 2013, 287–8.

[34] Similarly, in the *Tabula Albana*, Abderos is said to be the son of a certain 'Thronikos': *BNJ* 40 F 1a, lines 86–9; see Radt 1958, 13 n. 4.

[35] Philostr. *Imag.* 2.24–5.   [36] *IThrakAig* E16; D. Kallintzi and Veligianni 1996.

[37] Pind. *Pae.* 2, lines 3–5 (the chorus-leader is speaking): [σέθ]εν...[παι]ᾶνα [δι]ώξω [Δη]ρηνὸν Ἀπόλλωνα πάρ τ' Ἀφρο[δίταν]; Radt 1958, 26–32. The shrine of Apollo Derenos may well have been an extramural sanctuary at which processions terminated: Dougherty 1994, 215–17; Rutherford 2001, 265–7.

(labelled Ἄβδηρος; the image is lost), and Abderos may also have been depicted on a very fragmentary fourth-century document relief from Athens.[38]

The earliest Greek settlement at Abdera is said by Herodotos to have been a Klazomenian colony, founded by a certain Timesios. Discussing the Teian 'foundation' of Abdera in the 540s BC, he says that 'before them (the Teians), the city had been founded by Timesios of Klazomenai, but he got no benefit from it, and was driven out by the Thracians; he is today honoured as a hero by the Teians at Abdera'.[39] Ancient chronographic sources placed the date of Timesios' foundation around 654 BC, and this fits well with ceramic finds from the archaic cemeteries at Abdera, the earliest of which date around 650 BC.[40] The Klazomenian settlement at Abdera was laid out on a large scale, some 600m to the north of the current shoreline, with an impressive wall-circuit (4–4.5m thick, faced with rough-worked stones of different sizes) enclosing an area of around 107.5 hectares (the 'North Enclosure'); this wall can be firmly dated to the third quarter of the seventh century BC (Fig. 2.1).[41] A deep embayment (now silted up) immediately to the west of the North Enclosure provided access to the sea, as indicated by the remains of a later ship-shed at the north-west corner of the North Enclosure and a breakwater at the south-west corner.[42] Three cemeteries associated with the Klazomenian colony have been excavated, at Ammolofos, Palaiochora, and Chortolivado, all dating between 650 and 570 BC. A curiosity of these seventh- and early sixth-century cemeteries at Abdera is the massive over-representation of infants and young children (86.4 per cent of the 309 individuals buried at Ammolofos, 100 per cent of the twenty-two at Palaiochora, and 47.6 per cent of the forty-two at Chortolivado);[43] some have taken this to reflect particularly high infant mortality at the Klazomenian colony (the result of poor diet and malarial epidemics), but more recent scholarship has rejected this on methodological grounds.[44]

Perhaps the most important result of the excavations of the North Enclosure and the seventh- and early sixth-century cemeteries at Abdera is to have demonstrated beyond any reasonable doubt that Herodotos' picture of a

[38] *IG* II³ I, 302, with Lambert 2006, 118. Document relief: Lawton 1995, 156, no. 179.

[39] Hdt. 1.168.

[40] Eusebius' date of 654 BC: Miller 1970, 25–6; see also Chryssanthaki 2001, 386–8. Earliest ceramic finds: Skarlatidou 2004, 254; Skarlatidou 2010, 356–7.

[41] Koukouli-Chrysanthaki 2004, 237–40; K. Kallintzi 2012, 132–6.

[42] Koukouli-Chrysanthaki 2004, 244–7; Tiverios 2008, 92; Baika 2013.

[43] K. Kallintzi and Papaikonomou 2010, 133–4.

[44] Agelarakis 2004; Skarlatidou 2004, 257–8; Skarlatidou 2010, 358–65 (high infant mortality); rejected by K. Kallintzi and Papaikonomou 2010, 140–1.

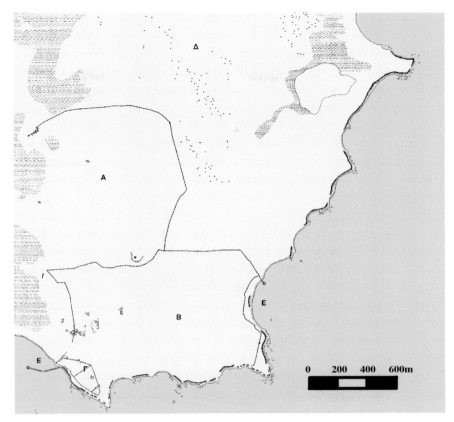

Fig. 2.1. Site-plan of Abdera. *A* = North Enclosure, *B* = South Enclosure,
Γ = Byzantine acropolis, *Δ* = cemeteries, *E* = harbours (modern).
*The copyright of the image belongs to the Greek Ministry of Culture and Sports; the monument is under
the authority of the Greek Ministry of Culture and Sports/Ephorate of Antiquities of Xanthi.*

short-lived and unsuccessful Klazomenian colonial endeavour at Abdera is
false. The Klazomenian colony clearly survived (if perhaps not in a very prosperous state) through the late seventh and early sixth centuries; although the
mortuary evidence tails off in the 570s, stray finds from the North Enclosure
seem to imply continuity of settlement through the second quarter of the
sixth century.[45] The colony seems to have maintained close links with
Klazomenai and with northern Ionia more generally, as indicated by large
quantities of East Greek pottery and Chian amphorae in the late seventh- and

---

[45] Koukouli-Chrysanthaki 2004, 241; Tiverios 2008, 92–6. Isaac 1986, 79–80 suggested a period of
Thasian settlement at Abdera between the 'failed' Klazomenian colony and the arrival of the Teians,
but this was rejected by Graham 1992, 48, and finds no support in the ceramic finds from Abdera.

early sixth-century cemeteries.[46] When the Teians arrived at Abdera in the mid-sixth century, they settled alongside an existing population of Klazomenian origin; indeed, the late sixth- and early fifth-century mortuary record at Abdera strongly suggests that this pre-Teian population group persisted at Abdera, with burial practices that remained strongly distinct from those of the new Teian settlers.[47]

As we have seen, Herodotos regards the Teian settlement at Abdera as a single event, a Teian 'mass migration' apparently dating between c.546 and 542 BC, depending on when precisely we place the conquest of Ionia by Harpagos.[48] Whether or not this picture of a single one-off population-movement is strictly correct (see above), the arrival of a new wave of settlers in the mid- to late sixth century is very clearly visible in the archaeology of Abdera. In the last quarter of the sixth century BC, the wall-circuit of the North Enclosure was rebuilt in a different style (2.7–3.0m thick, with isodomic blocks on the exterior face); around the same date, a new extra-mural sanctuary to a female deity was established just outside the north-west corner of the wall-circuit.[49] Entirely new burial practices appear at Abdera in the late sixth century and continue down through the Classical period, characterized by the covering of burials with a tumulus and (in stark contrast to the 'Klazomenian' cemeteries) the complete absence of new-borns and infants under six months.[50]

The extent of the territory of Abdera in the sixth century BC and later periods cannot be determined with certainty (see further Chapter 5 below).[51] The sole fixed point is the river Nestos, today some 16km to the west of Abdera (although its course may well have changed since antiquity), which lay within Abderite territory in Herodotos' day.[52] To the east, the limit of Abderite territory in the Archaic and Classical periods was presumably the western shore of Lake Bistonis, 12km to the north-east of Abdera; the city may also have controlled the area immediately north of Lake Bistonis, as far east as the Kompsatos River.[53] There is no way of knowing how far inland the city's

---

[46] Dupont and Skarlatidou 2005, 78–80.
[47] K. Kallintzi 2004, 271–9; K. Kallintzi 2006, 145–6; K. Kallintzi and Papaikonomou 2010, 134–6: continuity of 'Klazomenian' mortuary practices at the Chortolivado cemetery, in contrast to the tumulus-burials associated with the Teian colonists.
[48] Hdt. 1.168; see above.
[49] Koukouli-Chrysanthaki 2004, 242–4; K. Kallintzi 2012, 133–4; Baika 2013, 272.
[50] K. Kallintzi 2004, 274–6; K. Kallintzi 2006, 144–5; K. Kallintzi and Papaikonomou 2010, 134–5.
[51] Excellent summary of the evidence in *IThrakAig* pp. 167–8; see also Chryssanthaki 2001, 384, and Skarlatidou 1990 for the evidence for ancient settlements in the wider territory of Abdera.
[52] Hdt. 7.126; also Paus. 6.5.4 (drawing on Herodotos).
[53] A fourth-century BC epitaph from Porto Lagos, at the mouth of Lake Bistonis, has been plausibly attributed to Abdera: *IThrakAig* E80. Pseudo-Skymnos, *FGrHist* 2048 T1, lines 672–5, implies that the territory of Abdera extended from the Nestos to Lake Bistonis. Pseudo-Skylax, *Periplous* §67, states

territory extended. The sandstone-quarries in the low range of hills between the modern villages of Avdira and Mandra, 7km north-east of ancient Abdera, seem first to have been exploited in the late sixth century BC, after the Teian refoundation.[54] To the north, it is tempting to suppose that Abderite territory in the Classical period encompassed the entire coastal plain as far as modern Xanthi and the foothills of Mt Rhodope, some 23km to the north. At some point during the reign of Hadrian, perhaps *c.* AD 131/2, Abdera had a stretch of her ancestral territory 'restored' to her, on the left bank of the Nestos around the modern village of Toxotes (23km north-west of Abdera), close to the spot where the Nestos descends into the plain of Xanthi from the Nestos gorge.[55] Given that Abdera seems to have been at the peak of her prosperity in the late sixth and fifth centuries BC (to judge from her abundant silver coinage), it is likely enough that the area around Toxotes, in the far north-west of the plain of Xanthi, was already part of her territory in the late sixth century BC.

Aside from Pindar's second *Paean* (discussed below), our best evidence for relations between Teos and Abdera in the late sixth century derives from the silver coinages struck by the two cities. Teos' first silver coinage consists of an issue on the Lydo-Milesian standard (stater of *c.*14.2g), known from a single stater, 2 drachms, 8 hemidrachms, and numerous small fractions. These coins show a right-facing griffin on the obverse (full-length on the staters, a *protome* on the drachms and fractions) and a square incuse on the reverse.[56] The date of this coinage is uncertain, but is most plausibly placed in the 540s or 530s BC. Shortly thereafter, most probably *c.*530–520 BC, Teos switched to minting on the lower Aiginetan weight-standard (stater of *c.*12.2g), with the same obverse and reverse types; this weight-standard then persisted at Teos throughout the rest of the Archaic and Classical periods.[57] It seems to have been precisely around the time of this change of weight-standards at Teos (*c.*530–520 BC) that Abdera began minting her own abundant silver coinage, with very similar types to Teos—albeit with the griffin on the obverse facing left, rather than right—but apparently on a different, local weight-standard (perhaps 'reduced Chian', with a stater of *c.*14.9g).[58] The precise relationship between the late

that the river 'Koudetos' (probably the modern river Kompsatos) was the boundary between Abdera and Dikaia: see further Chapter 5 below.
[54] K. Kallintzi 2004, 285.   [55] *IThrakAig* E78 and E79, discussed further in Chapter 5 below.
[56] Matzke 2002, 43–6 ('Series A') and 48 (stater, 'Type By'); the correct weight-standard in Kagan 2006, 54–5. Teos may already have struck an issue of electrum coins at some point in the first half of the sixth century BC, but the attribution is uncertain (Matzke 2002, 43, nos. 16–21, 23–4).
[57] Kagan 2006, 54–5; van Alfen 2014, 638–9; Psoma 2016, 96–7.
[58] For the earliest coinage of Abdera, see Kagan 2006 (with a start date *c.*530 BC); Chryssanthaki-Nagle 2007, 97–107 (*c.*520). For the weight-standard ('reduced Chian'), Psoma 2015, 179–82 (though note the doubts of Wartenberg 2015, 351–2).

Archaic coinages of the two cities is therefore rather difficult to assess. The very close overlap in types and chronology suggests that we might be dealing with co-operative minting of some kind, but the use of different weight-standards shows that the two coinages cannot have been intended to circulate together (although it is possible that the large Abderite 'octodrachms', weighing around 31g, were intended to circulate at par with five Teian drachms, on a Aiginetan drachm-standard of 6.1g).[59] It would be fascinating to know whether the two cities' coinages were minted from the same sources of silver, but to our knowledge the relevant metal-analyses have not yet been undertaken.

Pindar's Second *Paean*

The early years of the Teian settlement at Abdera seem to have been characterized by heavy warfare against neighbouring peoples. The best evidence for this comes in a difficult and controversial passage of Pindar's second *Paean*, which is usually thought to describe events shortly after the Teians' arrival at Abdera.[60]

χρὴ δ᾽ ἄνδρα τοκεῦσι⟨ν⟩ φέρειν
βαθύδοξον αἶσαν.

τοὶ σὺν πολέμῳ κτησάμ[ενοι]
60   χθόνα πολύδωρον ὄλ[βον]
ἐγκατέθηκαν, πέραν Ἀ[θόω] Παιόνων
αἰχματᾶν [λαοὺς ἐλάσαντε]ς
ζαθέας τρόφου· ἀλλὰ [βαρεῖα μὲν]
ἐπέπεσε μοῖρα· τλάντ[ω]ν
65   δ᾽ἔπειτα θεοὶ συνετέλεσσα[ν].
ὁ δὲ καλόν τι πονή[σ]αις
εὐαγορίαισι φλέγει·
κείνοις δ᾽ὑπέρτατον ἦλθε φέγγος
ἄντα δ[υ]σμενέων Μελαμ-
70   φύλλου προπάροιθεν.

---

[59]   van Alfen 2014, 639; for the possible relationship between the Abderite 'octodrachms' and the Aiginetan standard at Teos, Kagan 2006, 54; Psoma 2015, 179.
[60]   Pind. *Pae.* 2, lines 57–79, with Radt 1958, 55–75; Graham 1992, 49–51, 62–3; Rutherford 2001, 270–3. We follow Rutherford's text, with a different punctuation in lines 60–1.

ἰὴ ἰὲ Παιάν, ἰὴ ἰέ· Παιὰν
   δὲ μήποτε λείποι.

[ἀ]λλά μιν ποταμῷ σχεδὸν μολόντα φύρσεν
βαιοῖς σὺν ἔντεσιν
75 ποτὶ πολὺν στρατόν· ἐν δὲ μηνὸς
   πρῶτον τύχεν ἆμαρ·
ἄγγελλε δὲ φοινικόπεζα λόγον παρθένος
εὐμενὴς Ἑκάτα
   τὸν ἐθέλοντα γενέσθαι.

'A man must give his ancestors their fitting share of profound glory. Those who won in warfare (60) the land rich in gifts established a store-house of prosperity, driving beyond Athos the hosts of Paionian spearmen, away from their holy mother. But a heavy fate befell them; and at last the gods helped them fulfil their task, (65) as a reward for their endurance. He who completes a noble labour blazes bright with praises; and so it was for these men that the brightest light shone against their enemies, (70) before Mt Melamphyllon. Iē ie Paian, iē ie; may Paian never abandon us. But he (Apollo) confounded him (sc. the Paionian enemy?), as he came on near the river, facing a great host (75) with just a few weapons; it happened on the first day of the month. The kindly red-footed maiden Hekate had previously proclaimed word of this, the word that longed to come true.'

The 'ancestors' being praised here (line 57) are likely to be the original Teian settlers at Abdera; the events described in the following lines would then fall in the years immediately following the Teians' arrival in Thrace.[61] The most natural way of reading lines 59–63 is as a description of the original carving out of Teian/Abderite territory on the mainland north and west of the site of Abdera. Through warfare, the Teian settlers won their 'rich territory' (χθόνα πολύδωρον, line 60), thereby establishing prosperity for the new colony (ὄλ[βον] ἐγκατέθηκαν, lines 60–1), by driving the Paionians away from the vicinity of the city (ζαθέας τρόφου, line 63) and beyond Athos (πέραν Ἀ[θόω], line 61). The presence of Paionians in the coastal plain of Xanthi in the mid-sixth century has been doubted, but we know from Herodotos that there were Paionians living around Lake Prasias, east of Mt Pangaion in the plain of Philippi, in the sixth century BC, and there is nothing problematic about the

---

[61] Radt 1958, 56–7.

idea that Paionian settlement might originally have extended still further to the east, beyond Mt Lekani.[62] We can of course hardly suppose that the territory of Abdera ever stretched as far west as Mt Athos, but it is quite possible that an initial phase of warfare against the previous Paionian inhabitants of the coastal plain of Xanthi could have involved their successful expulsion as far as (say) Mt Vertiskos, the range of hills to the east of the river Strymon (here considered, naturally enough, as a northern extension of the Athos mountain range).[63] This victory seems then to have been followed by a military disaster of some kind, probably a renewed assault on Abdera by the Paionians (lines 63–4),[64] before a final Teian/Abderite triumph in the foothills of Mt Melamphyllon (lines 68–70).

The following lines (73–9) are very obscure, but seem to refer to a major Teian/Abderite victory on the banks of a river (line 73). Someone—probably the god Apollo—defeats someone else (Paionians? Sapaioi?), apparently against great odds, fighting with only a few weapons against a great army (lines 73–5).[65] The victory was won on the first day of the month, in fulfilment of a prophecy by Hekate (lines 75–9). This whole passage seems to be closely connected to the preceding narrative, and it seems very likely that these lines are a continuation of the account of the victory of Mt Melamphyllon discussed in lines 68–70.[66] If so, we would be looking for a place near Abdera where a river runs close to the foot of a mountain-range. The obvious candidates are the river Nestos and the modern Mt Lekani, in the far north-west of Abderite territory. The battle could well have been fought somewhere to the south-west of modern Toxotes (see above), where the river Nestos descends out of its gorge into the plain of Xanthi.

---

[62] Zannis 2014, 273–86. For Paionians around Lake Prasias, Hdt. 5.15.3, and for Paionian settlement in the lower Strymon valley, Hdt. 5.1.2 and 5.13.2. Scepticism: e.g. Archibald 1998, 86; Hornblower 2013, 93–6. For the identification of Lake Prasias with Lake Datos near Philippi (today dried up), see the brilliant study of Hatzopoulos 2008 (followed by Zannis 2014, 148–51), accepting extensive early Paionian settlement in the lower Strymon and east of Pangaion.

[63] In lines 60–1, Rutherford (2001, 258–61) implausibly takes ὄλ[βον] ἐγκατέθηκαν πέραν Ἀ[θόω] as a single phrase, 'stored up wealth beyond Mount Athos', implying that the Abderites conquered and incorporated territory beyond Athos; the correct interpretation in Graham 1992, 49.

[64] That seems to be the implication of the ancient scholia on line 63, [ὑ]π[έ]ρ [τὸ]ν Ἄθω ἐκβληθέντες οἱ ἐνοικο[ῦ]ντ[ε]ς ἐπῆλθον ⟨ἀ⟩μυνούμ[ενοι το]ὺς ἐκβαλόντας καὶ ἐνί[κησ]αν, 'the inhabitants (i.e. the Paionians), having been driven out beyond Athos, returned and attacked those who had driven them out (i.e. the Teians), and defeated them'.

[65] Since Apollo was the subject of the preceding lines (71–2), and can also be plausibly identified with the 'brightest light' (ὑπέρτατον φέγγος) of line 68, he is probably also the subject of the verb φύρσεν in line 73. Note that the aorist φύρσεν is an emendation of the transmitted future φύρσει (Rutherford 2001, 273). Graham (1992, 63) assumes that the great army (πολὺν στρατόν, line 75) belonged to the victorious Abderites, and it was the defeated Thracians who had only a few weapons (βαιοῖς σὺν ἔντεσιν, line 74); but this would hardly be something for the Abderites to boast about.

[66] Thus essentially Führer 1967, 62–5, followed, tentatively, by Rutherford 2001, 272–3; contra, Radt 1958, 65–75; and Graham 1992, 63–4, separating this battle from the preceding section and dating it to the post-Persian War period.

If this is correct, then something else falls into place. No mines have yet been identified in the 'core' territory of Abdera, but the city's abundant silver coinage of the late sixth to the early third centuries BC surely requires the Abderites to have had access to silver mines somewhere along the coast of Aegean Thrace.[67] The obvious place to look is the eastern parts of Mt Lekani, south-west of Xanthi on the right bank of the river Nestos, where we know there to have been intensive mining for metals during antiquity.[68] At the eastern foot of Mt Lekani, on the right bank of the Nestos near the modern village of Dialekto, 25km north-west of Abdera (6km south-west of Toxotes), a substantial Archaic and Classical settlement has been identified; ceramic finds suggest that the site was first occupied in the late sixth century BC.[69] The site has previously been considered as part of the Thasian *peraia*, but it is surely equally plausible to see it as an Abderite outpost associated with the exploitation of the silver mines of the eastern slopes of Mt Lekani. We might recall Herodotos' clear statement that the Nestos flows *through* the territory of Abdera, indicating that Abdera controlled territory on the right bank of the Nestos: this is perhaps more likely to have been along the foot of Mt Lekani than in the marshy coastal regions further to the south, where the Nestos was generally impassable.[70]

On this hypothesis, the beginnings of Abdera's silver coinage around 530–520 BC would then reflect the securing of access to the mines of Mt Lekani thanks to the great victory at Mt Melamphyllon (an ancient name for Mt Lekani?) at some point between the 540s and the 520s BC.[71] The great prosperity of late Archaic and Classical Abdera depended not only on her vast but marshy agricultural territory in the plain of Xanthi itself, but on the mineral resources of the mountains west of the Nestos.[72] It is hardly surprising that, in the 490s or 480s BC (whenever we choose to date Pindar's second

---

[67] Chryssanthaki 2001, 390; K. Kallintzi 2004, 285; Hansen and Nielsen 2004, 873 (L. Loukopoulou). Radt 1958, 58, followed by Graham 1992, 49–50, sees a reference to precious metals in the adjective πολύδωρον in Pind. *Pae.* 2, line 60. Chryssanthaki-Nagle 2007, 88, supposes that Abdera procured its silver through commerce with its neighbours (Thracians north of Rhodope; Thracians and Thasians around Pangaion and Lekani).

[68] For ancient mining installations in and around Mt Lekani, see Koukouli-Chryssanthaki 1990; Parissaki 2000–3, 357–8; Zannis 2014, 189–92 (esp. 192, for the mines around Makrychori in the eastern part of Mt Lekani).

[69] Zannis 2014, 170. The site at Dialekto was eventually succeeded by the nearby Roman settlement at Topeiros.

[70] Hdt. 7.126, with Zannis 2014, 519.

[71] For the date, Kagan 2006, 57–8 (*c*.530); Chryssanthaki-Nagle 2007, 97–103 (*c*.520). A start date of *c*.530–520 BC for the coinage fits well with the earliest ceramics from the settlement at Dialekto in the eastern foothills of Mt Lekani.

[72] For the instability of the Nestos River in its lower courses, cf. Theophr. *Hist. pl.* 3.1.5; Strabo 7.1.44; Zannis 2014, 167.

Paean), it was the winning of the crucial western flank of the plain of Xanthi, in particular the strip of land between the Nestos and Mt Lekani, that the Abderites were most concerned to celebrate and commemorate.[73]

All this is necessarily somewhat speculative. At any event, Pindar's second *Paean* provides us with a vivid picture of the wars of conquest conducted by the Teian settlers against the previous Paionian inhabitants of the plain of Xanthi. The rich territory of Abdera (χθὼν πολύδωρος, line 60) was won by means of a series of grim battles against the Paionians, initially driven back to the Strymon River, then returning to reconquer part of their lost territory, and finally driven out of the plain of Xanthi by the Abderites' victory (against great odds) at Mt Melamphyllon. We can hardly doubt that it was the Teian settlers, not the original Klazomenian colonists under Timesios, who were responsible for the greater part of these conquests. As we have seen, as late as the second century BC, the Abderites were still intensely concerned to maintain their hard-won territory at the borders originally laid down by the sixth-century Teian settlers (**Document 1**, lines B35–7).

One final passage in Pindar's second *Paean* deserves attention. At an earlier point in the poem, the chorus sings: 'I belong to a new-born *polis*: I gave birth to my mother's mother, when she was struck down by enemy fire' (νεόπολίς εἰμι· ματρὸς δὲ ματέρ᾽ ἐμᾶς ἔτεκον ἔμπαν πολεμίῳ πυρὶ πλαγεῖσαν, lines 28–31). The chorus' mother is the city of Abdera itself; their 'mother's mother' is therefore the city of Teos, and the lines must refer to a subsequent 'refounda-tion' of Teos itself by the Teian colonists at Abdera, shortly after a destruction of Teos (presumably by the Persians).[74] Strabo may be referring to this refoun-dation when he says, at the end of his brief account of the Teian foundation of Abdera, that 'some of them (sc. the Teians) returned back home at a later date'.[75] Unfortunately, the date of this refoundation remains uncertain. Teos was captured by the Persians at least twice, by Harpagos in the 540s BC and in the aftermath of the Ionian Revolt, after the battle of Lade in 494 BC (in which the Teians participated).[76] Teos was certainly burned by the Persians on the second occasion, and perhaps also on the first. Essentially we have two possi-bilities: either a group of Teian refugees returned to resettle Teos very shortly after their original colonization of Abdera in the 540s, or some of the descend-

---

[73]   Hence, also, the significance to the Abderites of their regaining of their ancestral territory around Toxotes in the second century AD: see below, Chapter 5.

[74]   Decisively argued by Radt 1958, 33–9, and by Graham 1991; see also Chryssanthaki 2001, 396–7; Rutherford 2001, 268–9.

[75]   Strabo 14.1.30.

[76]   Hdt. 1.168; 6.25.2, cf. 6.8.1 (Teian ships at Lade).

ants of the original Teian settlers were responsible for the reconstruction of Teos after the city was laid waste by the Persians in 494 BC. Most recent scholars have tentatively favoured the latter scenario, for good but not decisive reasons.[77] At any event, the refoundation of Teos from Abdera meant that the two cities enjoyed, by the late 490s at the latest, a relationship that was (to the best of our knowledge) wholly unique in the ancient Greek world:[78] each was mother-city to the other. As we will see, this 'reciprocal' colonial relationship between the two cities is of the first importance to their later relations with one another.

Abdera and Teos after the Persian Wars

In c.514–512 BC, coastal Thrace was conquered by Darius' general Megabazos, and Abdera presumably fell under Persian rule, although it remains unclear whether European Thrace was formally organized as a satrapy at this point.[79] Persian control of Thrace seems to have collapsed during the Ionian Revolt (499–493 BC), with the result that the Persian general Mardonios had to undertake a large-scale campaign of reconquest in the north Aegean in 492 BC.[80] There is good reason to believe that Abdera was one of the chief strongholds of Persian rule in Thrace after Mardonios' reconquest. When in 491 BC Darius was (falsely) informed that the island of Thasos was planning a revolt, he ordered the Thasians to tear down their walls and send their entire fleet to Abdera; we can therefore reasonably assume that Abdera was the main Persian naval base on the coast of Aegean Thrace.[81] It is likely that Abdera was under the control of one of the Persian governors (ὕπαρχοι) said by Herodotos to have been appointed throughout Thrace and the Hellespontine region at an uncertain date before Xerxes' invasion of 480 BC.[82] Abdera maintained her loyalty to the Persians throughout the period of the Persian Wars: during Xerxes' withdrawal from Greece in late 480 BC, he stopped in Abdera and made a treaty of friendship with them, giving them as gifts a golden dagger and a tiara embroidered with gold in recognition of the city's loyalty.[83] It is

---

[77] Graham 1991, 177; D'Alessio 1992; Rutherford 2001, 269.

[78] Graham 1992, 69–72, assembles some hypothetical parallels, speculating that both Miletos and Eretria might have been refounded by their colonies after their destruction by the Persians in 494 and 490 respectively; supporting evidence is lacking in both cases.

[79] Hdt. 5.2.2, 5.10. Vasilev 2015 is the most recent extended study.   [80] Hdt. 6.43–8.

[81] Hdt. 6.46.1, 6.47.2; Briant 2002, 157; Vasilev 2015, 159.

[82] Hdt. 7.106–7 (Maskames at Doriskos; Boges at Eion).

[83] Hdt. 8.120, with Lenfant 2002. Abdera had entertained Xerxes lavishly during his advance: 7.120.

worth noting that a coin-magistrate at Abdera whose tenure of office should date around 475 BC carried the name $A\Sigma\Pi A(-)$.[84] This is usually taken as an abbreviation of the Greek name Aspasios, but many Persian names begin with the element *aspa-* (e.g. Aspathines, Aspamitres), and it is conceivable that this man was in fact a Persian governor at Abdera (or a Greek with a Persian name) in the final years of Persian control of the city.

It was probably not until 476/5, when Kimon captured the Persian naval base at nearby Eion, that Abdera was brought into the (by now Athenian-led) Greek alliance.[85] Given the evidence for Abderite loyalty to Persia in the 490s and 480s, it is likely that this was a traumatic event, involving the execution or exile of the pre-existing pro-Persian faction at Abdera. We know from the ancient scholia to Pindar's second *Paean* that he discussed civil strife at Abdera in a lost part of the poem, and it is possible that the *stasis* alluded to by Pindar dates to the regime-change of 476/5.[86] We now have a remarkable further piece of evidence which may well reflect the situation at Abdera in the immediate aftermath of the city's entry into the Athenian alliance, in the form of a fragmentary inscribed law from Abdera which should date to the late 470s or 460s BC (Fig. 2.2):[87]

$[...-\acute{\epsilon}\tau]$-
1 $\epsilon o s \ v[\epsilon]$-
$\omega\tau\epsilon\rho[o]$-
$[s] \ \kappa\alpha\grave{\iota} \ [\gamma]$-
$\epsilon\rho\alpha\iota\underline{\tau}$-
5 $\epsilon\rho o s \ \pi$-
$\epsilon v\tau\epsilon\underline{\kappa}$-
$\alpha\iota\delta\epsilon\kappa$-
$\acute{\epsilon}\tau\epsilon o[s]\cdot$
$\ddot{o}\tau\iota \ \mathring{\alpha}v$
10 $\acute{\epsilon}\pi\alpha v\acute{\alpha}$-
$\underline{\sigma}\tau\alpha\sigma\iota$-
$\underline{s} \ \gamma\acute{\iota}v\eta$-
$\tau\alpha\iota \ \mathring{\eta} \ [\mathring{\kappa}]$

---

[84] May 1966, 96, Group XXX, 60, dated *c*.475 BC by Chryssanthaki-Nagle 2007, 107–10. May misread the legend as $A\Sigma\Gamma A$; for the correct reading, see Masson 1984, 49 ('sans doute $\mathcal{A}\sigma\pi\acute{\alpha}(\sigma\iota o s)$').

[85] Hdt. 7.107; Thuc. 1.98.1; Chryssanthaki 2001, 391.

[86] *Scholion* on Pind. *Pae*. 2, line 48, referring to *stasis* in the city ($\tau o\grave{u}s \ \grave{\epsilon}v \ \tau\hat{\eta} \ \pi\acute{o}\lambda\epsilon\iota \ \sigma\tau\alpha\sigma\iota\acute{\alpha}\zeta o v\tau\alpha s$) and a group of 'newcomers' ($\grave{\epsilon}\pi\acute{\eta}\lambda\upsilon\delta\alpha s$): Rutherford 2001, 260 (text), 270 (commentary).

[87] *IThrakAig* E1, re-edited by Thonemann 2020, 1–9. In line 9, the difficult $\ddot{o}\tau\iota \ \mathring{\alpha}v$ may be a mason's error for $\ddot{o}\tau\langle\epsilon\rangle \ \mathring{\alpha}v$, 'whenever'. In lines 1–5 it is unclear whether we should understand $v\epsilon\acute{\omega}\tau\epsilon\rho o s\dots\gamma\epsilon\rho\alpha\acute{\iota}\tau\epsilon\rho o s$ (nom. sing.) or $v\epsilon\omega\tau\acute{\epsilon}\rho o s\dots\gamma\epsilon\rho\alpha\iota\tau\acute{\epsilon}\rho o s$ (acc. pl.).

νεῶν ἀ-
15 πόβασ-
[ι]ς ΟΣ[.]
- - -

'...younger than [- -] years old and older than 15 years old. That if (or: whenever) an uprising occurs or a naval incursion....'

The first eight lines of the text appear to be fixing maximum and minimum ages of eligibility for military service of some kind. The lower age-limit (15) is exceptionally young by ordinary Greek standards, and strongly suggests that the Abderites were concerned to maximize available manpower in the face of a perceived crisis.[88]

Fig. 2.2. Fifth-century law from Abdera (MA 5524).

The copyright of the image belongs to the Greek Ministry of Culture and Sports; the monument is under the authority of the Greek Ministry of Culture and Sports/Ephorate of Antiquities of Xanthi.

[88] See Thonemann 2020, 3–5. Conscription of boys as young as 15 is attested in the Hellenistic world, but only under exceptional circumstances: Livy 26.25.11; Hatzopoulos 2001, 99–100, 109–11 (on the late Antigonid military *diagramma*: SEG 49, 722 and 855).

At Teos, meanwhile, little is known of the city's fortunes after the presumed Persian sack of 494 BC.[89] Earlier that year, the city had participated in the battle of Lade with seventeen warships—a substantial number, but considerably smaller than the fleets provided by Miletos (eighty), Chios (one hundred), and Samos (sixty).[90] When Teos appears in the Athenian tribute-lists in the late 450s, we find her regularly contributing six talents per annum, a similar sum to other middling Ionian cities (Ephesos, Erythrai) but considerably less than Abdera (normally fifteen talents). Teos' fifth-century silver coinage is far less abundant than that of Abdera, and the ongoing Turkish excavations have detected no building activity at Teos in the fifth or fourth centuries BC, confirming the picture of a city now greatly diminished in both population and resources. It is almost certainly to this period—the decades immediately after the Persian Wars, and the early years of Teian and Abderite membership of the Athenian-led Delian League—that we should date the sole surviving items of public epigraphy produced by Teos in the Classical period, the so-called Teian Dirae, the subject of the following chapter.

---

[89] Hdt. 6.25, 6.32.   [90] Hdt. 6.8.1.

3

The Teian 'Dirae' (Documents 2–3)

The two inscriptions known as the 'Teian Dirae' are our only extant examples of inscribed public curses from the Archaic or Classical period.[1] However, we know of several other cities which had a standard set of public curses regularly performed by civic magistrates on fixed occasions. At Athens in the fifth century BC, each meeting of the *ekklēsia* and *boulē* began with the ritualized performance of public curses by the herald, dictated to him by the under-secretary to the *ekklēsia* or the assistant to the *boulē*.[2] The text of the Athenian public curses does not survive, but their contents can be reconstructed from a variety of sources, the most important of which is the elaborate parody in Aristophanes' *Thesmophoriazousai*;[3] as we will see, they seem to have been very close in both form and content to the inscribed curses at Teos. At Chios in the fifth and fourth centuries BC, the *basileus* regularly performed a set of legally mandated public curses, whose contents can only be guessed at.[4] In the late fourth century BC, both Miletos and her colony Olbia had a set of formal public curses, apparently performed on the thirtieth day of each month; once again, we have no way of knowing what the content of these curses might have been.[5]

---

[1]   On public curses, see Ziebarth 1895; Latte 1920, 61–88; Lambrinudakis and Wörrle 1983, 310–13; Rubinstein 2007 (post-Classical). In purely formal terms, the closest analogy to the Teian *stēlai* (inscriptions carrying the wording of a set of curses to be performed by public magistrates) is *IG* XI 4, 1296 (Delos: III BC), a *stēlē* bearing a series of three curses to be performed by priests and priestesses against anyone who tries to abduct slaves from Delos: Rubinstein 2007, 272.

[2]   Dictation to herald: Dem. 19.70. The Athenian public curses are reconstructed by Rhodes 1972, 36–7 and by Sommerstein and Bayliss 2013, 48–50.

[3]   Ar. *Thesm.* 295–311.

[4]   Matthaiou 2011, 13–34 (Osborne and Rhodes 2017, no. 133: mid-fifth century BC), lines C7–9 (cf. A20–1): if anyone renders invalid a series of land-sales, 'let the *basileus* perform a curse against him when he performs the legally mandated curses' (ἐπαράσθω κατ᾽ αὐτ[ô] ὁ βασιλεὸς ἐπὴν τὰς νομ[α]ίας ἐπαρὰς ποιῆται). Similarly, in the fourth-century regulations of the Klytidai (Rhodes and Osborne 2003, no. 87, 330s BC), lines 35–6, anyone who uses the 'sacred building of the Klytidai' for illicit purposes has to pay a substantial fine, 'and let him be liable to the curses laid down by law' (καὶ ταῖς ἐκ [τῶν] νόμων ἀραῖς ἔνοχος ἔστω). In the Kaukaseis inscription (Koerner 1993, 238–40, no. 63, lines 14–15, with Matthaiou 2011, 18, *c.*450–425 BC), if anyone removes a *horos*, στατῆ[ρ᾽ ἀ]ποδότω [ἴ]θυναγ κἀν [τ]ῆπαρῆι ἐ[ν]εχέσθω.

[5]   *Milet* I 3, 136 (Rhodes and Osborne 2003, no. 93), lines 12–14, with Ehrhardt 1988, 237 (and *SEG* 37, 982). On this text, see further below.

Teos and Abdera: Two Cities in Peace and War. Mustafa Adak and Peter Thonemann, Oxford University Press.
© Mustafa Adak and Peter Thonemann, 2022. DOI: 10.1093/oso/9780192845429.003.0004

Specific curses associated with laws and other public and private documents are of course very widespread in the Greek world at all periods. Some of the most important analogies for the Teian public curses are found in the context of public oaths performed either by particular magistrates or by the entire citizen body, many of which include conditional curse-formulae which are basically similar in form and content to the inscribed curses at Teos.[6] As we will see, one of the two Teian inscriptions (Dirae II, **Document 3** below) is in fact a generically 'hybrid' text, incorporating both a set of curses ('if x does y, let him be destroyed') and a sequence of oaths ('I shall not do x'). A particularly close analogy is found in the early third-century citizen-oath of Cretan Itanos, which includes numerous clauses closely parallel to those found in the Teian curses.[7]

Nonetheless, the two sets of inscribed curses from Teos remain, thus far, generically isolated in the pre-Hellenistic epigraphic record. It is worth noting here the possible existence of a *third* set of fifth-century curses at Teos, or more precisely at the small neighbouring settlement of Airai, a coastal site around 10km west-north-west of the urban centre of Teos, which may or may not have been a Teian dependency in the early fifth century BC.[8] In 1912, Josef Keil published a tiny fragment of an inscription from the village of Aşağı Demircili (the site of ancient Airai).[9] Keil describes it as 'the lower part of a *stēlē* of red trachyte, broken above, H. 0.43m, W. 0.525m; huge letters of the first half of the fifth century BC, H. 0.10m'. The surviving text reads only [- -] | αὐτὸν | καὶ γέ|νος, '…him and his descendants'. Keil took this to be the end of an honorific decree, 'perhaps a proxeny decree', but the earliest proxeny decrees on stone do not start to appear until the late fifth century BC.[10] It is surely preferable to see this as the end of yet another early fifth-century series of Teian public curses ([τοῦτον ἀπόλλυσθαι καὶ] αὐτὸν | καὶ γέ|νος) inscribed and erected at Airai.

---

[6] For the close connection between public oaths and public curses (more precisely, for the latter as a subsidiary element of the former), see Sommerstein and Bayliss 2013, 3–4, 'an oath is a declaration whose credibility is fortified by a conditional self-curse'.

[7] *I.Cret.* III iv 8 (*Syll.*[3] 526), concluding with a comprehensive curse-formula; similarly in the citizen-oath associated with the mid-fourth-century synoikism of Orchomenos and Euaimon in Arkadia (Thür and Taeuber 1994, no. 15, lines 70–2, 88–90), the early third-century citizen-oath of Chersonesos (*IOSPE* I² 401 [*IOSPE*³ III 100], lines 53–7), the citizen-oath of Dreros around 200 BC (*I.Cret.* I ix 1, lines 75–89), and the citizen-oath in the Teian 'pirates inscription' (Hamon 2018, Decree II, lines 60–2: see further below).

[8] Robert and Robert 1976, 165–7; Hansen and Nielsen 2004, 1063 (L. Rubinstein). Airai was a substantial community in the mid-fifth century BC: between 454/3 and 447/6, it paid three talents a year to Athens, half the Teian tribute (six talents).

[9] Keil 1912, 75–6.

[10] Mack 2015, 82. Several second-century proxeny decrees from Crete do indeed end with the phrase αὐτὸν καὶ γένος (e.g. at Lappa: *I.Cret.* II xvi, nos. 5–8); but the phrase is equally common in curse-formulae.

The bulk of this chapter will be dedicated to a full re-edition and discussion of the two early fifth-century sets of inscribed curses at Teos (**Documents 2 and 3**). We designate the two texts as 'Dirae I' (a *stēlē* copied by William Sherard in the early eighteenth century, not seen since the mid-nineteenth century) and 'Dirae II' (a *stēlē* discovered in Sığacık in 1976 and first published by Peter Herrmann in 1981). This should not necessarily be taken as indicating the chronological priority of Dirae I; indeed, we will argue that the two *stēlai* are precisely contemporary (their dimensions were probably identical). Dirae II was—eventually—inscribed on all four faces of the stone; the transmitted text of the lost Dirae I was all inscribed on a single face of the stone, and we have no way of knowing for certain whether the stone was originally inscribed on more than one face. We reserve discussion of the historical background and significance of the two texts for the end of the chapter.

Document 2 (Dirae I): Public Curses at Teos

The stone carrying Dirae I has been lost since 1844. Our knowledge of the text is based on four independent sources:

(1) Transcript of lines 42–9 only: William Sherard, late May or early June 1709.
(2) Transcript of the entire text (lines 1–53): William Sherard, 20 June 1716.
(3) Transcript of the entire text (?): Samuel Lisle, 20 June 1716.
(4) Paper squeeze of lines 41–53: Philippe Le Bas 1844.

No previous edition of Dirae I has been based on a full collation of these four sources (with, as we will see, some unfortunate consequences for the constitution of the text), and hence their character needs to be laid out in some detail.

(1) In May–June 1709, William Sherard (1659–1728), consul of the Levant Company at Smyrna between 1703 and 1716, undertook an extensive journey in Karia and Ionia, in the course of which he copied a number of inscriptions in the region of Teos. His original transcripts of the stones recorded on this journey do not survive, but his 'fair copies', presumably written up shortly after his return to Smyrna, are preserved in the British Library.[11] Among the

---

[11] BL Add 10101 ff.81r–117v; a second fair copy of the same texts at ff.133r–173r. For a full description of the Sherard MSS in the British Library, see Crawford 2003.

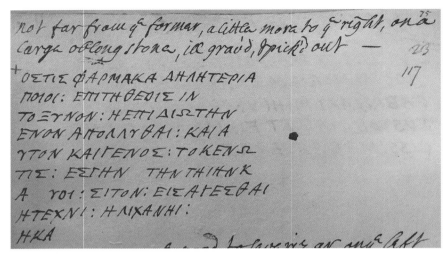

Fig. 3.1. William Sherard's fair copy of his 1709 transcript of Dirae I, lines 42–9.
© British Library Board (BL Add 10101 f.117r).

texts that he copied on this occasion were two inscriptions located 'in a
Turkish burying place 1/2 mile beyond Eraka, in the road (a little to the right
hand) to Sagagick'.[12] The first of these was the Roman recognition of Teian
asylia of 193 BC;[13] the second was Dirae I. Above his 1709 fair copy of Dirae I,
Sherard writes: 'Not far from the former [i.e. the Roman *asylia*-document], a
little more to the right, on a large oblong stone, ill grav'd, I pick'd out—', followed by a transcript of lines 42–9 (Fig. 3.1).[14] Sherard's 1709 copy is
extremely poor, apparently made in haste, with numerous misreadings and
incorrect line-divisions. At some later date (but certainly before 1716),
Sherard made a second fair copy of the stones recorded in 1709; below his
second fair copy of Dirae I lines 42–9, he appended the note 'I suspect
this above by the 2 points [i.e. the form of the interpuncts] to be very antient.
When I return I'll take better notice of it'.[15] One of Sherard's two fair copies
of his 1709 transcript was subsequently used (without acknowledgement)
as the basis of the edition of Dirae I lines 42–9 in Franz Hessel's 1731
*Antiquae inscriptiones quum Graecae tum Latinae olim a Marquardo Gudio
collectae*.[16]

---

[12] BL Add 10101 f.116r.
[13] Rigsby 1996, 314–16, no. 153; for the history of the various manuscript copies of this text, see
Famerie 2007.
[14] BL Add 10101 f.117r.   [15] BL Add 10101 f.173r.
[16] Hessel 1731, no. 2, in his 'Praefationis Appendix', with the same erroneous line-divisions and misreadings as Sherard's 1709 copy. Hence the Hessel publication cannot be used (as it is by

(2) In 1716, Sherard undertook two further short epigraphical journeys, the first of which, in mid-June (in company with Samuel Lisle), was dedicated solely to the area around Teos. He took a second, more complete transcript of Dirae I on 20 June 1716. Once again, the fair copy written up by Sherard on his return to Smyrna survives, this time including all fifty-three lines of the text, introduced with the following note: 'The inscription on the next side *HIΣΤΑΣ* etc. is in a Burial place on the right hand, 1/2 hour beyond Heraká, near that with the title *PΩMAIΩN*. The first 18 lines are not to be made out. We copied what was legible of these but by carelessness the paper was lost. <Afterwards 'twas found.> Besides the two points betwixt the words, there are other marks of its great Antiquity, such as these letters always so form'd [careful drawings of the *nu, pi, sigma*] & O instead of OY' (Figs 3.2–3.4).[17] A later fair copy of Sherard's 1716 transcript survives in a large compilation of inscriptions recorded by Sherard, later passed to the Earl of Oxford.[18]

(3) Samuel Lisle also made his own transcript of Dirae I on 20 June 1716. No copies of this transcript survive, but some idea of its character can be gained from the *editio princeps* of Dirae I, published by Edmund Chishull in his *Antiquitates Asiaticae* of 1728 (Fig. 3.5).[19] Chishull printed what was avowedly an 'eclectic' text, drawing on Sherard's 1709 and 1716 copies and on Lisle's 1716 transcript; hence where his text differs from Sherard's 1716 fair copy, we can assume that it reflects readings drawn from Lisle's lost copy.[20] Some of Lisle's presumed readings are evidently inferior to those of Sherard (e.g. at the start of line 6), but elsewhere he correctly reads sequences of letters miscopied by Sherard (e.g. at the end of line 8); it is therefore difficult to know whose readings to follow in cases where the true reading is uncertain (e.g. the start of line 17).

Herrmann 1981, 2 n. 7) as evidence that lines 42–53 were inscribed on a separate block from 1–41. Sherard's partial 1709 copy was also transcribed by Karl Otfried Müller in 1822 and transmitted to Boeckh, as Boeckh records in the lemma to *CIG* II 3044: 'adscripsit [Müllerus] simul vss. 42–49, qui soli sunt in Append. cod. Ask. II (ex cod. Chish. II, 75)'. The reference 'cod. Chish. II, 75' is to BL Add 10101 f.117r (see Crawford 2003, 99 for the alternative foliations).

[17] BL Add 10101 f.77v. Sherard's fair copies of inscriptions copied in his first 1716 journey are at ff.68r–78v; Dirae I is the final text in the sequence, with lines 1–20 squeezed in awkwardly on f.77v (= 'The first 18 lines [*sic*]', Sherard's copy of which was mislaid and later found, Fig. 3.2), lines 21–48 on f.78r (Fig. 3.3), and lines 49–53 on f.78v (Fig. 3.4).

[18] BL Harl. 7509 f.41r. On the character and history of this manuscript, see Crawford 2003, 90, 103–4.

[19] Chishull 1728, 96–101.

[20] Significant variants between Sherard's 1716 copy and Chishull's printed text are found in lines 3–8, 12–13, 17–20 (see the apparatus criticus below).

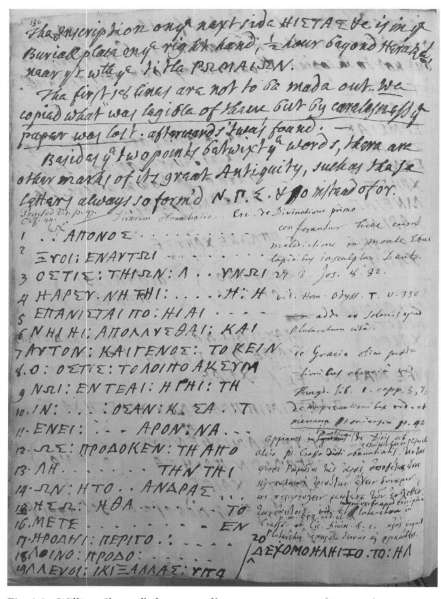

Fig. 3.2. William Sherard's fair copy of his 1716 transcript of Dirae I, lines 1–20.

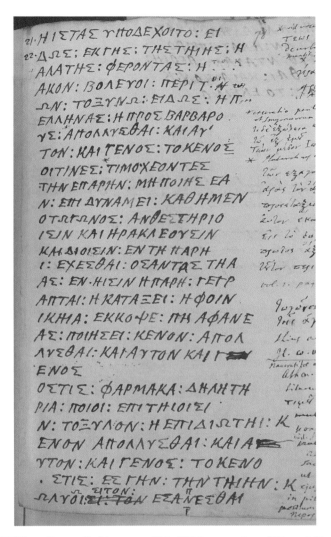

Fig. 3.3. William Sherard's fair copy of his 1716 transcript of Dirae I, lines 21–48.
© British Library Board (BL Add 10101 f.78r).

(4) The last scholar to see the stone was Philippe Le Bas, in 1844, whose copy underlies the text printed by William H. Waddington in *Inscriptions grecques et latines recueillies en Grèce et en Asie Mineure, Tome III* (1870).[21] Le Bas took a (rather poor) squeeze of the stone, today in the Fonds Louis Robert, including

---

[21] Le Bas and Waddington 1870, no. 59. Waddington's editions of the inscriptions recorded by Le Bas are often sloppy, and he seems not to have made consistent use of Le Bas's squeezes: Rigsby 1996, 292 n. 45 (noting that Sherard's copies of the Teian *asylia* decrees are occasionally superior to those published by Waddington).

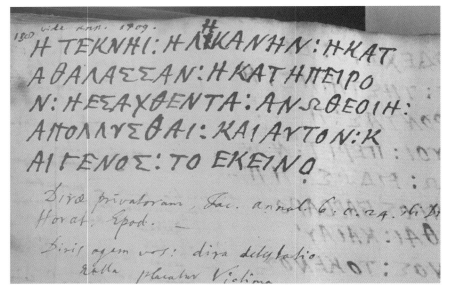

Fig. 3.4. William Sherard's fair copy of his 1716 transcript of Dirae I, lines 49–53.
© British Library Board (BL Add 10101 f.78v).

lines 41–53 (Fig. 3.6); only lines 41–6 are today clearly legible on the squeeze (a few scattered letters can be made out in lines 47–53).[22] The most important contributions of Le Bas's squeeze are (a) to provide us with our best evidence for the forms of the letters, and (b) to demonstrate with absolute certainty that lines 42–53 immediately followed lines 1–41 on the stone, since the four letters of line 41 are clearly visible on the squeeze above line 42.[23]

It seems extremely likely that lines 1–41 were inscribed *stoichedon*: in every passage where the text is reasonably secure (lines 6–9 and 19–41), each line has precisely eighteen letters.[24] However, as is clear from Le Bas's squeeze,

[22] We are indebted to Denis Rousset for providing us with photographs of the squeeze (Fonds Louis Robert Inv. No. 1874). For Le Bas's squeezes in the Fonds Louis Robert (including some seventy squeezes of inscriptions from Teos, many of which have since been lost), see Bresson, Rousset, and Carbon 2007, 655–6.

[23] Sherard's description and copy of the stone in BL Add 10101 ff.77v–78v also strongly suggest that he saw only a single stone, and the text was printed as such by Chishull and Boeckh. Waddington seems not to have noticed the remains of line 41 at the top of the squeeze, and printed lines 42–53 alone. As a result, Kirchhoff wrongly concluded that Dirae I in fact consisted of two separate inscribed stones (lines 1–41, lines 42–53), and that lines 42–53 were the earlier of the two (cf. Herrmann 1981, 2). All editors from Roehl onwards have printed lines 42–53 before lines 1–41, usually with lines 42–53 labelled 'A' and 1–41 labelled 'B'. This is corrected in the present edition.

[24] First noted by Herrmann 1981, 5. Herrmann (1981, 5 n. 2) suggests easy corrections to Sherard's copy at lines 7 and 26–8 to achieve lines of precisely eighteen letters.

3. ΟΣΤΙΣ : ΤΗΙΩΝ : Ε .. ΥΝΩΙ
4. ΗΑΙΣΥ. ΝΗΤΗΙ : .... ΗΙ : Η
5. ΕΠΑΝΙΣΤΑΙΤΟ : ΗΔΙ ...
6. ΧΗΤΑΙ : ΑΠΟΔΛΥΣΘΑΙ : ΚΑΙ
7. ΑΥΤΟΝ : ΚΑΙΓΕΝΟΣ : ΤΟΚΕΙΝ
8. Ο : ΟΣΤΙΣ : ΤΟΛΟΙΠΟ : ΑΙΣΥΜ
9. ΝΩΙ : ΕΝΤΕΩΙ : ΗΓΗΙΤΗΙΤΗ
10. ΙΗΙ : .... ΟΣΑΝ : Κ. ΣΑ .. Τ
11. ΕΝΕΙ : ... ΑΡΟΝ : ΝΑ ...
12. ΩΣ : ΠΡΟΔΟ ..... ΤΗ.ΠΟ
13. Λ .... ΤΗΝΤΗΙ
14. ΩΝ : ΗΤΟ.. ΑΝΔΡΑΣ ...
15. ΗΣΩΙ : ΗΘΑ .... ΤΟ
16. ΜΕΤΕ .... ΕΝ
17. ΑΡΟ. ΗΙ : ΠΕΡΙΓ ....
18. ... ΝΟ : ΠΡΟΔΟ ....
19. ΛΛΕΥΟΙ : ΗΚΙΞΑΛΛΑΣ : ΥΠΟ
20. ΔΕΧΟΙΤΟ : ΗΛΗΙΞΟΙΤΟ : ΗΛ
21. ΗΙΣΤΑΣ : ΥΠΟΔΕΧΟΙΤΟ : ΕΙ
22. ΔΩΣ : ΕΚΓΗΣ : ΤΗΣΤΗΙΗΣ ; Η*
23. ΛΛΛΤΗΣ : ΦΕΡΟΝΤΑΣ : Η***
24. ΑΚΟΝ : ΒΟΛΕΥΟΙ : ΠΕΡΙΤ**
25. ΩΝ : ΤΟΞΥΝΟ : ΕΙΔΩΣ : ΗΠ***
26. ΕΛΛΗΝΑΣ : ΗΠΡΟΣΒΑΡΒΑΡΟ
27. ΥΣ : ΑΠΟΔΛΥΣΘΑΙ : ΚΑΙΑΥ
28. ΤΟΝ : ΚΑΙΓΕΝΟΣ : ΤΟΚΕΝΟ
29. ΟΙΤΙΝΕΣ : ΤΙΜΟΧΕΟΝΤΕΣ :
30. ΤΗΝΕΠΑΡΗΝ : ΜΗΠΟΙΗΣΕΑ
31. Ν : ΕΠΙΔΥΝΑΜΕΙ : ΚΑΘΗΜΕΝ
32. Ο : ΤΩΓΩΝΟΣ : ΑΝΘΕΣΤΗΡΙΟ
33. ΙΣΙΝ : ΚΑΙΗΡΑΚΛΙΟΙΣΙΝ :
34. ΚΑΙΔΙΟΙΣΙΝ : ΕΝΤΗΠΑΡΗ
35. Ι : ΕΧΕΣΘΑΙ : ΟΣΑΝΤΑΣ*ΤΗΛ
36. ΑΣ : ΕΝΗΙΣΙΝ : ΗΠΑΡΗ : ΓΕΓΡ
37. ΑΠΤΑΙ : ΗΚΑΤΑΞΕΙ : ΗΦΟΙΝ
38. ΙΚΗΙΑ : ΕΚΚΟΨΕ : ΠΗΑΦΑΝΕ
39. ΑΣ : ΠΟΙΗΣΕΙ : ΚΕΝΟΝ : ΑΠΟΛ
40. ΛΥΣΘΑΙ : ΚΑΙΑΥΤΟΝ : ΚΑΙΓ
    ΕΝΟΣ
41. ΟΣΤΙΣ : ΦΑΡΜΑΚΑ : ΔΗΛΗΤΗ
42. ΡΙΑ : ΠΟΙΟΙ : ΕΠΙΤΗΙΟΙΣΙ
43. Ν : ΤΟΞΥΝΟΝ : ΗΕΠΙΔΙΩΤΗΙ : Κ
44. ΕΝΟΝ : ΑΠΟΔΛΥΣΘΑΙ : ΚΑΙΑ
45. ΥΤΟΝ : ΚΑΙΓΕΝΟΣ : ΤΟΚΕΝΟ :
46. ΟΣΤΙΣ : ΕΣΓΗΝ : ΤΗΝΤΗΙΗΝ : Κ
47. ΩΛΥΟΙ : ΣΙΤΟΝ : ΕΣΑΓΕΣΘΑΙ :
48. ΗΤΕΧΝΗΙ : ΗΜΗΧΑΝΗΙ : ΗΚΑΤ
49. ΑΘΑΛΑΣΣΑΝ : ΗΚΑΤΗΠΕΙΡΟ
50. Ν : ΗΕΣΑΧΘΕΝΤΑ : ΑΝΩΘΕΟΙΗ :
51. ΑΠΟΔΛΥΣΘΑΙ : ΚΑΙΑΥΤΟΝ : Κ
52. ΑΙΓΕΝΟΣ : ΤΟΕΚΕΙΝΟ.

* sic

Fig. 3.5. Edmund Chishull, *editio*
princeps of Dirae I, lines 3–53
(Chishull 1728, 98).

lines 42–53 were inscribed non-*stoichedon*, with eighteen letters in lines 42–3
and 45–6, nineteen letters in lines 44 and 47–52, and thirteen letters in line 53
(presumably with a *vacat* at the end of the line).[25] Lines 35–41 contain a 'concluding' curse protecting the *stēlai* from damage, and line 41 contains only

[25] Osborne and Rhodes 2017, 4, incorrectly state that lines 42–53 are *stoichedon* twenty. In lines
51–2, Sherard read ἀνωθεοίη : | ἀπόλλυσθαι, giving nineteen letters in both lines 51 and 52; Waddington
printed ἀνωθεοίη : κέν|ον ἀπόλλυσθαι (with a different line division between lines 52 and 53), but this
is not supported by Le Bas's squeeze, and we suspect that κέν|ον was an inadvertent addition by
Waddington. For the line-division in 52–3, we similarly follow Sherard rather than Waddington.

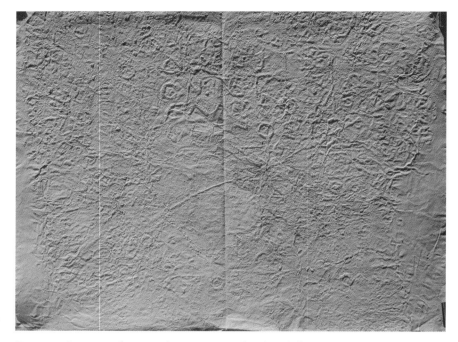

Fig. 3.6. Squeeze of Dirae I, lines 41–53, taken by Philippe Le Bas in 1844.
Image courtesy of the Fonds Louis Robert.

four letters, followed by a *vacat*, strongly suggesting that the text originally ended at line 41. The most economical explanation is that lines 42–53 should be seen as 'additional' curses, added to the stone at a slightly later date than lines 1–41.[26] This phenomenon—the 'accumulation' of additional clauses over time in an inscribed legal text—is also attested in the late sixth-century inscribed laws of Eretria; as we shall see, Dirae II (**Document 3** below) similarly consists of a gradual accumulation of curses on a single stone over a period of time (probably four different phases of inscribing).[27]

Our best guide to the date(s) of Dirae I is the form of the lettering, most clearly seen on Le Bas's squeeze of lines 41–53. We suspect that lines 42–53 were inscribed by a different stone-cutter from lines 1–41: aside from the abandonment of the *stoichedon* grid, the *omicron* in line 41 is distinctly smaller than the other preserved letters of line 41, while in lines 42–53 the *omicron* seems consistently to be the same height as the other letters. In

---

[26] In addition to the *vacat* in the second half of line 41 and the non-*stoichedon* arrangement of lines 42–53, note also that [θ]αλάτης is spelled with a *sampi* in lines 22–3, but with a double *sigma* in line 50 (θάλασσαν); the word may appear in line 15.

[27] *SEG* 41, 725 (Effenterre and Ruzé 1994–5, I 330–3, no. 91).

dating the text, we are hampered by the absence of closely dated parallels from northern Ionia (see also below, on Dirae II). The interpunct takes the form of two dots (:), and does not occupy its own letter-space.[28] The *upsilon* is consistently formed like a Latin V, as on faces A, D, and C of Dirae II. The *sigma* has quite widely splayed outer strokes, as does the *mu*. The left-hand stroke of the *nu* slants upwards to the right; the right-hand stroke of the *nu* is vertical, and does not descend to the bottom of the letter-space. The right-hand stroke of the *pi* is short. The Milesian inscription on political exiles, conventionally—we think correctly—dated to the mid-fifth century BC, looks to be somewhat later than Dirae I: in the Milesian text (which has no interpuncts), the *upsilon* is formed like a Latin Y, and the left and right bars of the *nu* are both vertical.[29] A somewhat closer parallel for the lettering of Dirae I is found in Aiakes' dedication from Samos, which may be as early as the 540s BC.[30] Dirae I is conventionally dated to the second quarter of the fifth century BC, and this seems likely to be correct; we favour a date towards the upper end of that period, perhaps in the 470s BC.

Document 2 (Dirae I): Text and Translation

A 'large oblong stone' (Sherard), discovered in a Turkish cemetery between Hereke and Sığacık (1709); last seen in 1844. H. *c.*1.2m; W. *c.*0.47–0.48m (inferred from dimensions of Le Bas's squeeze).[31] Letters 0.015–0.020m; interlinear spaces *c.*0.010–0.013m.

The text has been reprinted very many times, often in collections of inscriptions which went through several editions; our lemma is therefore selective.

Ed. Chishull 1728, 96–101; (*CIG* II 3044 [Boeckh, 1843]); Le Bas and Waddington 1870, no. 59 (lines 42–53 only, from a copy by Philippe Le Bas,

---

[28] For the heavy use of interpuncts, see Butz 2010, 61.

[29] *Milet* I 6, 187; Osborne and Rhodes 2017, no. 123. The re-dating of the Milesian inscription to the 490s BC by Slawisch 2011 is not convincing: note that her Abb. 1.b significantly misrepresents the form of the *nu*.

[30] *IG* XII 6, 2, 561. Note the interpuncts, the angled *nu*, the V-shaped *upsilon*, and the 'splayed' *sigma*. The Aiakes-inscription is clearly somewhat earlier than the Teos text: note the inconsistent use of the *stoichedon*-grid, the *epsilon* with downward-slanting horizontals, and the *rho* with loop descending to the bottom of the letter-space.

[31] The dimensions of the squeeze are H. 0.297, W. 0.5m. The squeeze covers the complete width of the stone, with around 0.010–0.015m of excess paper to left and right, and therefore the original width of the stone must have been *c.*0.47–0.48m. Thirteen lines of text are preserved on the squeeze, out of a total of fifty-three lines seen by Sherard; therefore the stone as seen by Sherard must have been around 1.2m high.

1844); (Roehl 1882, no. 497; Roberts 1887, 168–71, no. 142; Bechtel 1887, 96–8, no. 156; Hoffmann 1891–8, III 49–51, no. 105 [1898]; Michel 1900, no. 1318 [with restorations by B. Haussoullier]; Collitz 1884–1915, III/2, no. 5632 [F. Bechtel, 1905]; *Syll.*³ 37/38 [Hiller, 1915]; Schwyzer 1923, no. 710; Tod 1946, 27–30, no. 23; Buck 1955, 186–7, no. 3; Meiggs and Lewis 1969, 62–6, no. 30; Koerner 1993, 294–301, no. 78; Effenterre and Ruzé 1994–5, I 366–71, no. 104; Dössel 2003, 21–9; Colvin 2007, 113–15, no. 20; Osborne and Rhodes 2017, 4–15, no. 102A–B; Antonetti and De Vido 2017, 70–4, no. 15 [C. Vessella]).

Trans. Fornara 1977, 63–4, no. 63 (English); Brodersen, Günther, and Schmitt 1992, 26–7, no. 47A (German); Arnaoutoglou 1998, 84–5, no. 70 (English: unreliable).

See: Kirchhoff 1887, 13–15 (script and date); Ziebarth 1895 (public curses); Latte 1920, 68–70 (public curses); Bannier 1925, 285–8 (lines 1–6, 8–12); Pugliese Carratelli 1960 (lines 42–3); Gottlieb 1967, 18–24 (*timouchoi*); Ellsworth 1976, 231–2 (lines 31–2); Herrmann 1981, 1–4 (publication history), 9–10 (lines 29–41), 18–21 (lines 3–8: *SEG* 31, 984); Merkelbach 1982 (lines 3–8: *SEG* 31, 984); Paneris 1983 (lines 18–21 and Demokritos); Koerner 1987, 467–9 (magistrates); Jeffery 1990, 340 (date); Rubinstein 2007 (curses in Greek laws).

Lines 1–41 (Hand I?): *stoich.* 18
Lines 42–53 (Hand II?): non-*stoich.* (18–19 letters)

[. .]ΑΠΟΝΟΣ[. . . . . 10 . . . . .]
ΞΥΟΙ : ἐν αὐτῶι [. . . . 7 . . .]
ὅστις : Τηΐων : ⟨τ⟩[ῶι ξ]υνῶι
ἢ αἰσυ[μ]νήτη⟨ν⟩ : [ἱσται]η : ἢ
5 ἐπανισταῖτο : ⟨ἐπ⟩ αἰ[συμ]-
νηίηι : ἀπόλλυσθαι : καὶ
αὐτὸν : καὶ γένος : τὸ κέν-
ο : ὅστις : τὸ λοιπὸ : αἰσυμ-
νῶι : ἐν Τέωι : ἢ γῆι : τῆι Τη-
10 ίηι : [κένον] : ὃς ἂν : κ[α]⟨τ⟩α[κ]τ-
ε⟨ί⟩νει : [μὴ μι]αρὸν : ⟨εῖ⟩να[ι :]
[ὅσ]⟨τι⟩ς : προδο⟨ίη : ἢ⟩ τὴ⟨ν⟩ πό-
λ⟨ι⟩[ν : ἢ τὴν χώραν :] τὴν Τηΐων : ἢ τὸ[ς] ἄνδρας [: ἐν Μυον]-

15 ἤσωι : ἢ ΘΑ[..... 9 ....]ΤΟ
    ΜΕΤΕ[......12......]ΕΝ
    ΗΡΟΔΗΙ : ΠΕΡΙΓΟ [. . 4 . . : τ̑ο]
    λοι⟨π⟩ο̑ : ΠΡΟΔΟ[... : ἢ κιξα]-
    λλεύοι : ἢ κιξάλλας : ὑπο-
20 δέχοιτο : ἢ ληίζοιτο : ἢ λ-
    ηιστὰς : ὑποδέχοιτο : εἰ-
    δὼς : ἐκ γῆς : τῆς Τηΐης : ἢ [θ]-
    αλάΤης : φέροντας : ἢ [τι κ]-
    ακὸν : βολεύοι : περὶ Τ[ηΐ]-
25 ων : τ̑ο ξυν̑ο : εἰδὼς : ἢ π[ρὸς]
    Ἕλληνας : ἢ πρὸς βαρβάρ-
    ους : ἀπόλλυσθαι : καὶ αὐ-
    τὸν : καὶ γένος : τὸ κένο{Σ} :
    οἵτινες τιμοχέοντες :
30 τὴν ἐπαρὴν : μὴ ποιήσεα-
    ν : ἐπὶ δυνάμει : καθημέν-
    ο τὠγ̑ωνος : Ἀνθεστηρίο-
    ισιν : καὶ Ἡρακλέοισιν :
    καὶ Δίοισιν : ἐν τῆιπαρῆ-
35 ι ἔχεσθαι : ὃς ἂν ταστήλ-
    ας : ἐν ἧισιν : ἡπαρὴ : γέγρ-
    απται : ἢ κατάξει : ἢ φοιν-
    ικήια : ἐκκόψε⟨ι⟩ : ἢ ἀφανέ-
    ας ποιήσει : κ̑ενον ἀπόλ-
40 λυσθαι : καὶ αὐτὸν : καὶ γ-
    ένος vac.
(1) ὅστις : φάρμακα : δηλητή-
    ρια : ποιοῖ : ἐπὶ Τηΐοισι-
    ν : τὸ ξυνὸν : ἢ ἐπ᾽ἰδιώτηι : κ-
45 ̑ενον : ἀπόλλυσθαι : καὶ α-
(5) ὐτὸν : καὶ γένος : τὸ κένο :
    ὅστις : ἐς γῆν : τὴν Τηΐην : κ-
    ωλύοι : σῖτον : ἐσάγεσθαι :
    ἢ τέχνηι : ἢ μηχανῆι : ἢ κατ-
50 ὰ θάλασσαν : ἢ κατ᾽ἤπειρο-
(10) ν : ἢ ἐσαχθέντα : ἀνωθεοίη :
    ἀπόλλυσθαι : καὶ αὐτὸν : κ-
    αὶ γένος : τὸ κένο vac.

3: *ΤΗΙΩΝ:Λ* . . *ΥΝΩΙ* Sh(erard); *ΤΗΙΩΝ:Ε* . . *ΥΝΩΙ* L(isle);[32] Τηΐων : ⟨τ⟩[ῶι ξ]υνῶι H(errmann). 4: *ΗΑΡΣΥ.ΝΗΤΗΙ:* ..... *Η:Η* Sh.; *ΗΑΙΣΥ.ΝΗΤΗΙ:* ....
ΗΙ:Η L.; ἢ αἰσυ[μ]νήτη⟨ν⟩ : [ἰσταί]η : ἢ H. 5–6: *ΕΠΑΝΙΣΤΑΙΠΟ:ΗΙΑΙ* .... |
ΝΗΙΗΙ Sh.; *ΕΠΑΝΙΣΤΑΙΤΟ:ΗΔΙ* ... |*ΧΗΤΑΙ* L.; ἐπανισταῖτο : ⟨ἐπ⟩ αἰ[συμ]|νηίηι H. 7: *ΤΟΚΕΙΝ ad fin.* Sh.; τὸ κέν|ο coniecit H. 9: *ΝΩΙ:ΕΝ* Sh.; αἰσυμ|νῶ⟨ν⟩ Boe(ckh); αἰσυμ|νῶι Bannier. 10–11: *ΙΝ:* ...:*ΟΣΑΝ:Κ* . *ΣΑ* . . *Τ|ΕΝΕΙ:* ...*ΑΡΟΝ:ΝΑ* Sh.; [κ̄ενον] : ὃς ἂν : κ[α]⟨τ⟩α[κ]τ|ένει : [μὴ μι]αρὸν : ⟨εἶ⟩να[ι] A(dak)/Th(onemann). 12–13: *ΩΣ:ΠΡΟΔΟΚΕΝ:ΤΗΑΠΟ|ΔΗ*[- -] Sh.; *ΩΣ:ΠΡΟΔΟ* ..... *ΤΗ.ΠΟ|Λ*[- -] L.; [εἰδ]|ὼς προδο⟨ίη⟩ Blass *ap.* Bechtel 1887; τὴ⟨ν⟩ πό|λ⟨ι⟩[ν καὶ γῆν] τὴν Boe.; [καὶ τὴν γῆν] Haussoullier; [ὄσ]⟨τι⟩s : προδο⟨ίη : ἢ⟩ τὴ⟨ν⟩ πό|λ⟨ι⟩[ν : ἢ τὴν χώραν :] A./Th. 14: *ΩΝ:ΗΤΟ* . . *ΑΝΔΡΑΣ* ... Sh.; ἢ τὸ[s] ἄνδρας [: ἐν ν]ήσωι Boe.; [: ἐν Μυον]|ήσωι A./Th. 15: θα[λάσσηι : ἢ] τὸ Boe. 16: μετέ[πειτ᾿: ἢ τὸ] ἐν Hiller (μετέ[πειτα] *iam* Boe.). 17: *ΗΡΟΔΗΙ:ΠΕΡΙΓΟ* . : Sh.; *ΑΡΟ.ΗΙ:ΠΕΡΙΓ* L.; Ἀρο[ί]ηι : περι⟨π⟩ό[λιον] Hiller; περὶ ⟨τ⟩ὸ [ξυνὸ (?)] A./Th. 18: *ΛΟΙΝΟ:ΠΡΟΔΟ:* Sh.; λοι⟨μ⟩ὸ : προδο[ίη : ἢ κιξα]|λλεύοι Boe.; [τὸ]| λοι⟨π⟩ὸ Bechtel [1887]. 22–3: [θ]|αλά⟨σσ⟩ης Boe.; [θ]|αλάΤης Roehl. 26–7: *ΒΑΡΒΑΡΟ|ΥΣ* Sh.; βαρβάρ|ους coniecit H. 28: *ΚΕΝΟΣ ad fin.* Sh.; κένο : edd. 38: *ΕΚΚΟΨΕ:ΠΗ* Sh.; ἐκκόψε⟨ι⟩ : ἢ Chishull. 41: γ|ένος [τὸ κένο] add. Bechtel [1905]; del. H. 51–2: ἀνωθεοίη : | ἀπόλλυσθαι Sh.; ἀνωθεοίη : κ̄εν|ον ἀπόλλυσθαι W(addington). 52–3: αὐτὸν : κ|αὶ γένος Sh.; αὐτ|ὸν : καὶ γένος W. 53: τὸ ἐκείνο Sh.

(Text A) 'Whoever either sets up an *aisymnētēs* for the community of the Teians (5) or participates in a revolution aiming at establishing an *aisymnētēs*, let him perish, both him and his descendants. Whoever in future shall be *aisymnētēs* at Teos or in the land of Teos (10), whoever kills him shall not be polluted. Whoever betrays either the ci[ty or the territory] of the Teians, or the men in [Myon]esos, (15) or ... in future ... or engages in banditry or harbours (20) bandits, or engages in piracy or knowingly harbours pirates who are carrying things off from the land of Teos or the sea, or plots any evil concerning the community of (25) the Teians, with reference either to Greeks or barbarians, let him perish, both him and his descendants. Whoever, while serving as *timouchoi*, (30) do not perform the curse to the best of their ability when the festival-crowd is assembled at the Anthesteria and the Herakleia and the Dia, let them be subject (35) to the curse. Whoever destroys the *stēlai* on which the curse is inscribed, or knocks out the letters or makes them [the *stēlai*] invisible, let that man perish (40), both him and his descendants.'

---

[32] Sherard's readings are given from his 1716 fair copy in BL Add 10101 f.77v–f.78v; Lisle's readings are inferred from the text printed by Chishull 1728.

(Text B) 'Whoever makes harmful spells against the Teians as a community or against an individual, let that man (45) perish, both him and his descendants. Whoever prevents grain from being imported into the land of Teos by any device or means, either by (50) sea or by land, or pushes grain which has been imported away again, let that man perish, both him and his descendants.'

Document 2 (Dirae I): Commentary

Lines 3–8: These lines were first convincingly restored by Peter Herrmann on the basis of a parallel passage in Dirae II (**Document 3** below).[33] In Dirae II, lines A22–4, we read (as part of a series of oaths to be taken by civic magistrates at Teos and Abdera) αἰσυμνήτην οὐ στήσω [ο]ὔτε σὺμ πολλοῖσι[ν - -], 'I will not set up an *aisymnētēs*, nor with many men…'. In many Greek cities—notably Miletos—the *aisymnētēs* was a regular civic magistrate.[34] The oath in Dirae II demonstrates that this was not the case at Teos at the time that Dirae II was erected: here the term *aisymnētēs* is effectively equivalent to 'tyrant', a sense that is well known from Aristotle's discussion of the term (*Politics* 3, 1285a29–b1: αἱρετὴ τυραννίς, 'elective tyranny').[35] Herrmann therefore restored lines 3–8 of Dirae I as a curse against anyone who either sets up an *aisymnētēs* or participates in a revolution aiming at establishing an *aisymnētēs* (i.e. both successful and unsuccessful coup-attempts): it is likely enough that the oath in Dirae II similarly covered both successful and unsuccessful coups (restoring e.g. [ο]ὔτε : σὺμ πολλοῖσι[ν ἐπ' αἰσυμνηίηι ἐπαναστήσω], 'nor with many men [shall I participate in a revolution aiming at establishing an *aisymnētēs*]'). The possibility of revolution (ἐπανάστασις) is also a concern in an earlier passage of the oaths in Dirae II (lines A10–13), and it seems a reasonable assumption that both Dirae I and Dirae II date to a period when Teos (and Abdera) had a participatory regime in place, but were still concerned about the possibility of a return to one-man rule (as had certainly existed at Teos before the Ionian Revolt).[36] A contemporary law from

---

[33] Herrmann 1981, 18–21, expanding on a suggestion by Bannier 1925, 285–8.
[34] Sherk 1992, 229–32; Herda 2006, 58–61.
[35] Also 1286b38, 1295a12–14. See Faraguna 2005 (*SEG* 56, 2120).
[36] Herrmann 1981, 24; Graham 1991, 177; Graham 1992, 54: 'the ban against setting up an *aisymnetes* in both inscriptions makes it likely that they belong to the period after, but not too long after, the Ionian Revolt and Persian War period'. Note, though, that the Athenians continued to pass anti-tyrant legislation many decades (and indeed centuries) after the fall of the Peisistratid tyranny; the inference that the Teian curses must date 'not too long after' the fall of the pro-Persian tyranny is therefore questionable.

Abdera, discussed in Chapter 2 above, likewise seems to be concerned with putting measures in place to protect Abdera from revolution (ἐπανάστασις) or a 'landing from ships' (ἐκ νεῶν ἀπόβασις).[37]

The wording of the two clauses here (covering both successful and unsuccessful coup-attempts) finds very close parallels in Athenian anti-tyrant legislation: cf. e.g. *Ath. Pol.* 16.10 (a 'traditional law', perhaps going back to Drako or Solon), ἐάν τινες ἐπανιστῶνται ἐπὶ τυραννίδι ἢ συγκαθιστῇ τὴν τυραννίδα, ἄτιμον εἶναι καὶ αὐτὸν καὶ γένος, 'If anyone participates in a revolution aiming at tyranny or joins in setting up the tyranny, let him be without citizen rights, both him and his descendants'; *IG* II/III³ 1,2, 320 (Athenian law against tyranny, 337/6 BC), lines 7–8, ἐάν τις ἐπαναστῇ τῶι δήμωι ἐπὶ τυραννίδι ἢ τὴν τυραννίδα συνκαταστήσηι, 'if anyone participates in a revolution against the *dēmos* aiming at tyranny or joins in setting up the tyranny, etc.'[38]

The form of the curse found here (ὅστις + optative, ἀπόλλυσθαι καὶ αὐτὸν καὶ γένος τὸ κένο) is standard throughout Dirae I and Dirae II (usually κένον ἀπόλλυσθαι); we also occasionally find the alternative form ὃς ἄν + subjunctive (thus lines 35–41, and cf. lines 10–11). These two different forms are both widely attested in 'conditional' or 'automatic' curses from the early Archaic period onwards, with little obvious distinction in sense.[39]

Lines 8–11: In lines 8–9, Sherard read *ΑΚΣΥΜΝ|ΩΙ*, Lisle apparently *ΑΙΣΥΜΝ|ΩΙ*. Virtually all modern editors have accepted Boeckh's emendation αἰσυμ|νῶ⟨ν⟩ (present participle), but αἰσυμ|νῶι is a perfectly acceptable optative form, and should be retained in the text.[40] Lines 3–8 have already laid down a perfectly comprehensive curse against anyone who attempts to set up an *aisymnētēs* at Teos, and it would be curiously redundant to have a further curse here against any 'future' *aisymnētēs*. Hence we prefer to understand this passage as securing immunity from pollution for anyone who slays a potential future *aisymnētēs*: 'Whoever in future shall be *aisymnētēs* at Teos or in the land of Teos, whoever slays him shall not be polluted'.[41] For the phraseology (ὅστις αἰσυμνῶι...ὃς ἄν κατακτείνει), we might compare again the Athenian anti-tyranny law of 337/6 BC, *IG* II/III³ 1,2, 320, lines 7–11, ἐάν τις ἐπαναστῇ τῶι δήμωι ἐπὶ τυραννίδι...ὃς ἄν τὸν τούτων τι ποιήσαντα ἀποκτείνηι ὅσιος ἔστω, 'if anyone participates in a revolution against the

---

[37] *IThrakAig* E1, with Thonemann 2020, 1–9.
[38] On Athenian anti-tyrant legislation, see Ostwald 1955; Rhodes 1981, 220–3.
[39] Early epigraphic examples collected and discussed by Faraone 1996, 80–1.
[40] Thus, correctly, Bannier 1925, 286 n. 4; cf. also Herrmann 1981, 19 n. 55.
[41] Reading [κένον] : ὃς ἄν : κ[α]⟨τ⟩α[κ]τ|ένει in lines 10–11; ἀ[ποκ]τένει[ε] already suggested by Latte 1920, 69 n. 19.

dēmos aiming at tyranny... whoever slays the person doing any of these things is to be undefiled'.[42] A rather similar phrase (although in this case laying down material rewards for the killer, rather than immunity from pollution) is found in a mid-fifth-century law from Miletos prescribing exile under blood-guilt for certain individuals (perhaps the leaders of an oligarchic faction): καὶ ὃς ἄν τινα τούτωγ κατ[ακτείνε]ι, ἑκατὸν [στ]ατῆρας αὐτῶι γενέσθαι ἀπὸ τῶν [χρημά]των τῶν Νυμ[φαρή]το, 'and whoever slays any of these people, let him receive 100 staters from the property of Nympharetos'.[43] In lines 10–11, we have restored the short-vowel subjunctive ὃς ἄν κ[α]⟨τ⟩α[κ]τε⟨ί⟩νει; cf. the short-vowel subjunctives after ὃς ἄν in lines 37–9 below; and for the verb, cf. Dirae II A15–16, κατ[ακ]τε[ν]έω.

The restoration of the adjective [μι]αρόν in line 11 seems guaranteed by a very similar provision in an early Hellenistic inscription from Teos concerning a *sympoliteia* with the small town of Kyrbissos (discussed further below): any phrourarch at Kyrbissos who does not withdraw from his office after four months is to be exiled under a curse from both Teos and Abdera, καὶ ὃς ἄν ἀποκτείνηι αὐτὸν μ[ὴ] μιαρὸς ἔστω, 'and may whoever kills him not be polluted'.[44] In the middle of line 11, Sherard read [-]APON:NA[-]; we have tentatively assumed a lacuna (not indicated by Sherard) after the interpunct and before the letters NA, giving [μὴ μι]αρὸν : ⟨εἶ⟩να[ι].

Lines 12–18: Sherard evidently found this segment of text very difficult to read, and we are unable to propose a completely convincing reconstruction of the syntax or content. In line 12, Sherard read ΩΣ:ΠΡΟΔΟΚΕΝ:ΤΗΑΠΟ (fifteen letters only). If a new clause begins at the start of line 12, then Sherard's ΩΣ: ought to be a misreading for the last three letters of [ὅσ]⟨τι⟩ς. It is likely enough that Sherard's ΠΡΟΔΟΚΕΝ represents a verb or noun from προδίδωμι, 'betray' (cf. ΠΡΟΔΟ[- -] in line 18), and we would need an optative after ὅστις; Blass proposed προδο⟨ίη⟩, which gives the correct sense. In lines 12–13, Boeckh wondered whether Sherard's ΤΗΑΠΟ|ΛΗ[- -] might represent τὴ⟨ν⟩ πό|λ⟨ι⟩[ν], and we suspect that this is right; [ὅσ]⟨τι⟩ς : προδο⟨ίη : ἢ⟩ τὴ⟨ν⟩ πό|λ⟨ι⟩[ν] gives the correct line-length.[45] In lines 13–14,

---

[42] Similarly in the lost decree of Demophantos (probably *c*.403), summarized by Lyc. *Leocr.* 124–7, ἐάν τις τυραννίδι ἐπιτιθῆται ἢ τὴν πόλιν προδιδῷ ἢ τὸν δῆμον καταλύῃ, τὸν αἰσθανόμενον καθαρὸν εἶναι ἀποκτείναντα, and cf. Dem. 20.159; on the alleged text of this decree preserved in Andocides 1.96–8 (not authentic), see Canevaro and Harris 2012, 119–25; Harris 2013–14; Roisman and Edwards 2019, 204–8. For laws conferring honours on tyrannicides, cf. *SEG* 51, 1105 (Eretria, *c*.340 BC); *I.Ilion* 25 (early third century BC), and for the non-polluting character of justified killing, Harris 2015.

[43] *Milet* I 6, 187; Osborne and Rhodes 2017, no. 123, lines 3–5.

[44] Robert and Robert 1976 (*SEG* 26, 1306), lines 25–6.

[45] For the phraseology, compare e.g. Rhodes and Osborne 2003, no. 84 (Chios, *c*.334 BC), A10–11, τῶν δὲ προδόντων τοῖς βαρβάροις τὴν πόλιν.

the words τὴν Τηΐ|ων seem certain, but Boeckh's [γῆν] τὴν Τηΐ|ων is unlikely to be correct, since elsewhere in Dirae I the noun γῆ is always qualified with the adjective Τηΐη, not the genitive Τηΐων (lines 9–10, 22, 47). We have therefore tentatively restored ⟨ἢ⟩ τὴ⟨ν⟩ πό|λ⟨ι⟩[ν : ἢ τὴν χώραν :] τὴν Τηΐ|ων. In line 14, the noun ἄνδρας seems clear, but the restoration of the whole phrase in lines 14–15 is very uncertain. As Boeckh plausibly suggested, ΗΣΩΙ at the start of line 15 could be the dative of [ν]|ήσωι, but it would be surprising not to have the identity of the island specified, and we therefore wonder whether we might have here ἢ τὸ[ς] ἄνδρας [: ἐν Μυον]|ήσωι, referring to the island fortress of Myonesos (modern Çifit Kalesi), which we know to have belonged to Teos in the fifth century BC.[46] If this reconstruction is correct, the whole clause would be concerned with a person who betrays either the city (*polis*) of Teos, or its territory (*chōra*), or the garrison at Myonesos; a very similar sequence is found in the civic oath of Cretan Itanos (early third century BC), where we read πόλιν τὰν Ἰτανίων οὐ πρ[οδ]ωσέω οὐδὲ χώραν οὐδὲ νά[σ]ου[ς] τὰς τῶν [Ἰ]τανίων, 'I shall not betray the city of the Itanians or the territory or the islands of the Itanians'.[47]

In the middle of line 15, the word beginning ΘΑ is most likely to be θα[λάΤηι] or part of the verb θανατοῦν. In lines 16–17, Hiller restored [τὸ] ἐν | Ἀρο[ί]ηι : περι⟨π⟩ό[λιον], but the supposed toponym Ἀρο[ί]ηι is not attested elsewhere, and Sherard read ΗΡΟΔΗΙ at the start of line 17. Hiller's περι⟨π⟩ό[λιον] is a possible restoration in the middle of line 17, but given the total uncertainty about the content of this segment of text, it is better to leave the line unrestored (we could equally well have e.g. περὶ ⟨τ⟩ὸ [ξυνὸ]). In lines 17–18, Boeckh's προδο[ίη : ἢ κιξα]|λλεύοι (preceded by Bechtel's [τὸ]| λοι⟨π⟩ὸ) gives good sense, but leaves line 18 one letter too short.

Lines 18–28: The first part of this segment of text (lines 18–22) is concerned with anyone who engages in banditry or piracy, or who knowingly harbours bandits or pirates (the participle εἰδώς in lines 21–2 should presumably be taken with both 'harbouring bandits' and 'harbouring pirates'). The verb κιξαλλεύω is otherwise unattested; the noun κιξάλλης, 'bandit, highwayman', is only otherwise known from a fragment of Demokritos of Abdera, writing in the late fifth or early fourth century BC: κιξάλλην καὶ ληιστὴν πάντα κτείνων τις ἀθῶιος ἂν εἴη καὶ αὐτοχειρίηι καὶ κελεύων καὶ ψήφωι, 'anyone

---

[46] Thuc. 3.32.1; Hansen and Nielsen 2004, 1088 (L. Rubinstein), with references for the varying orthography Μυόν(ν)ησος; Adak 2021, 236.

[47] *I.Cret.* III iv 8 (*Syll.*³ 526), lines 9–11.

killing any bandit or pirate should be immune from punishment, whether he does so by his own hand, by ordering another to do so, or by vote'.[48] This fragment is strikingly close to Dirae I in both language and content, not only in the combination κιξάλλην καὶ ληιστὴν (bandit and pirate), but also in Demokritos' recommendation of immunity for any person who kills the malefactor (compare lines 8–11 above).[49] Demokritos is said both to have held public office at Abdera and to have composed laws for the city, and it is highly tempting to see the Demokritean fragment as an authentic piece of Abderite public law, elaborating and expanding on the provisions of Dirae I—or, more precisely, on a putative Abderite equivalent to Dirae I (see further below).[50] The clause at lines 22–3 (those who carry things off from the land of Teos or from the sea) presumably picks up on this distinction between bandits and pirates: bandits 'carry things off' by land, pirates carry things off by sea. Piracy was a serious concern for both Teos and Abdera, both in the fifth century BC and later: the concerns about a 'landing from ships' (ἐκ νεῶν ἀπόβασις) in the early fifth-century inscribed law from Abdera (discussed in Chapter 2 above) may well reflect fear of pirates, and an important and lengthy Teian inscription of the late fourth or early third century BC records a major pirate raid on Teos and its consequences.[51]

In lines 22–3, note the form [θ]αλάΤης with Τ (sampi), and contrast θάλασσαν in line 50 below (inscribed later); sampi for double sigma is also used (inconsistently) in a near-contemporary Erythraian inscription.[52] The clause in lines 23–5 is closely paralleled in the third-century civic oath of Itanos (early third century BC): οὐδὲ βουλεύσεω περὶ τᾶ[ς πόλ]ιος κακὸν οὐδέν, 'I shall not plot any evil concerning the city'.[53] In lines 25–7, the phrase ἢ π[ρὸς] Ἕλληνας ἢ πρὸς βαρβάρους, 'with reference to (LSJ s.v. πρός C.III.1) either Greeks or barbarians', is a way of stipulating that harmful collaboration with external powers of any ethnicity (either Greek or Persian) will lead to the perpetrator falling under a curse. The term βάρβαρος here surely refers to the

---

[48] Fr. B 260 Diels–Kranz = Stob. 4.2.18, with Paneris 1983; Procopé 1990, 27.

[49] Demokritos' specification of killing καὶ αὐτοχειρίηι καὶ κελεύων καὶ ψήφωι, 'by his own hand, by ordering another, or by vote', finds close parallels in the Athenian decree of Demophantos against persons who undermine the democracy, summarized by Lyc. Leocr. 127, διομωμόκατε . . . κτενεῖν τὸν τὴν πατρίδα προδίδοντα καὶ λόγῳ καὶ ἔργῳ καὶ χειρὶ καὶ ψήφῳ.

[50] Thus Paneris 1983, 302, citing Fr. B 259 Diels–Kranz (law-writing), A 2 (office-holding at Abdera).

[51] SEG 44, 949, with Meier 2017 and Hamon 2018, and the new fragment in Adak and Thonemann 2020, 9–12; on this text, see further below.

[52] I.Erythrai 2 (Osborne and Rhodes 2017, no. 122): ἐλάΤονος in A16–17, ἐλά[σ]σονας in A23–4.

[53] I.Cret. III iv 8 (Syll.³ 526), lines 27–8.

Persians in particular.[54] At the end of line 28, Sherard read $KENO\Sigma$ (giving the correct line-length, eighteen letters) when the sense requires κένο; Herrmann suggests reading κε⟨ί⟩νο or κένο ν., but it is equally possible that the mason inscribed the *sigma* in error (i.e. κένο{Σ}).[55]

Lines 29–35: In Dirae II, it is both the *timouchoi* and the treasurers who are responsible for reading out the things written on the *stēlē* (D11–17); here it is the *timouchoi* alone who do so. The *timouchoi* were evidently the chief civic magistrates at Teos in the early fifth century BC, and it is probably holders of this specific magistracy (rather than 'office-holders' more generally) who are referred to in Dirae II, A5–8 (ὃς ἂν τιμὴν ἔχων...τὸμ πλησί[ο]ν δολ[ῶ]ται). A board of *timouchoi* is independently attested in later periods at both Teos and Abdera.[56] Some earlier interpreters wrongly assumed that the phrase ἐπὶ δυνάμει in line 31 might signify 'by a statue/altar of Dynamis', but it must certainly mean 'to the best of their ability', as is shown by the parallel phrase in Dirae II, D17–19, ἐπὶ μνήμηι καὶ δυνάμει, 'to the best of their memory and ability'.[57] In lines 31–2, the phrase καθημένο τὠγῶνος (literally 'when the *agōn* sits') apparently has the sense 'when the people have assembled for the *agōn* at the named festival'.[58] There is no reason to doubt that ἀγών here refers to athletic contests: presumably these were the three major annual occasions when the entire Teian citizen body was gathered together in the early fifth century BC, therefore making them suitable occasions for the performance of public curses.[59] The three festivals named here also appear in Dirae II, D1–5. It is not clear whether the phrase in lines 34–5, ἐν τῆπαρῆι ἔχεσθαι, 'let him be subject to the curse', has a substantively different sense to the normal curse-formula ἀπόλλυσθαι καὶ αὐτὸν καὶ γένος τὸ κένο. The phrase is closely paralleled in two

---

[54] Though note the caution of Herrmann 1981, 25. The use of βάρβαροι = Persians is common in fourth-century public epigraphy: cf. e.g. Rhodes and Osborne 2003, nos. 17 (Erythrai, c.390–386 BC) and 84 (Chios, c.334 BC).

[55] Herrmann 1981, 5 n. 12.

[56] Teos: Gottlieb 1967, 18–24; Rhodes with Lewis 1997, 394; Adak and Stauner 2018, 20. Abdera: Gottlieb 1967, 24–8; *IThrakAig* E4, c.246/5 BC, and see further our note on **Document 1**, lines **B73–6**.

[57] See further on Dirae II (**Document 3**), D17–19 below. For the older interpretation of the phrase as ἐπὶ Δυνάμει, see Vollgraff 1918, 423; Schwyzer 1921, 76–7. Hamon 2018, 341 compares the phrase δυνατὸς ὤν in the curse against magistrates in the early Hellenistic 'pirates inscription' (Decree I, line 11); for this interpretation of ἐπὶ δυνάμει as concessive, cf. already Herrmann 1981, 12 n. 29. Compare also the common κατὰ τὸ δυνατόν in oath-formulae: Harris 2013–14, 145 n. 57.

[58] Thus already Boeckh; see further Ellsworth 1976, 231–2; Herrmann 1981, 9 n. 20.

[59] Around 300 BC, when the Teians swore collectively not to purchase luxury goods during a period of financial crisis, a curse against oath-breakers was performed at the Dionysia and Thesmophoria, in order to encompass both men and women: Hamon 2018, 361–2, Decree II, lines 60–2 (see further below). Similarly, at Gambreion in the third century BC, an imprecation associated with a funerary law was performed by the *gynaikonomos* before the Thesmophoria: Sokolowski 1965, no. 16 (*CGRN* 108).

fifth-century Chian inscriptions, the so-called 'Kaukaseis' inscription, κἂν [τ]ῆπαρῆι ἐ[ν]εχέσθω, 'and let him be subject to the curse', and the 'Dophitis' inscription, ἢν δὲ μὴ πρήξοισιν, ἐν ἐπαρῆι ἔστων, 'if they do not exact (the penalty), let them be subject to a curse'.[60]

Lines 35–41: The final passage of the original inscription is concerned with protecting the *stēlai* (plural) on which the curse is inscribed from deliberate damage; similar clauses are found in an inscribed treaty between Elis and Heraia of around 500 BC and in a fifth-century law from Argos.[61] The term φοινικήια (lines 37–8) simply means 'letters', with an echo of the Phoenician origin of the Greek alphabet; compare the term [φ]οινικογραφέων 'scribes', in Dirae II, D19–21. The phrase ἀφανέας ποιήσει ('makes them invisible', lines 38–9) also appears in the contemporary 'Dophitis' inscription from Chios, as part of a sequence of clauses protecting a series of boundary stones: ἢν τίς τινα τῶν ὅρων τούτων ἢ ἐξέληι ἢ μεθέληι ἢ ἀφανέα ποιήσει ἐπ' ἀδικίηι τῆς πόλεως, 'if anyone either tears up or moves or makes invisible any of these boundary-stones to the detriment of the city'.[62] In both instances, it is unclear whether the phrase signifies the physical removal of the stones ('invisible' = physically absent) or the defacement of the writing on them ('invisible' = illegible). In line 41, the words [τὸ κένο] were added by Bechtel, in order to produce the same phrasing as that used elsewhere; this is unnecessary, and is not supported by Le Bas's squeeze.[63]

Lines 42–53: The 'additional' curses in lines 42–53 were added to the stone at some later date (cf. on Dirae II below), and unlike lines 1–41, were inscribed non-*stoichedon*. The first curse bears against anyone who makes 'harmful spells' (φάρμακα δηλητήρια) against the Teians as a community or against an individual;[64] the second is directed against anyone who prevents grain from being imported (lines 47–8), or who 'pushes away again' grain which has been imported (line 51); the aim of the latter clause must be to prevent wealthy grain-producers at Teos from forcing potential grain-importers to depart with their cargo without selling it at Teos, in order to keep local grain-prices

---

[60] Kaukaseis: Koerner 1993, 238–40, no. 63, lines 14–15, with Matthaiou 2011, 18; Dophytis: Matthaiou 2011, 13–34 (Osborne and Rhodes 2017, no. 133), lines A20–1. A very similar phrase is found in the treaty between Elis and Heraia of c.500 BC, ἐν τἐπιάροι κ' ἐνέχοιτο τοῖ ʾνταῦτ' ἐγραμένοι (Minon 2007, no. 10), where ἐπιάροι = 'sacred fine'.

[61] Minon 2007, no. 10 (αἰ δέ τιρ τὰ γράφεα ταῖ καδαλέοιτο); SEG 33, 275 (αἴ τ[ις] ἀτελὲ τιθείε τὰ γράθματα τὰ [ἐ]ν τᾶι στάλα[ι] γεγραθμένα).

[62] Matthaiou 2011, 13–34 (Osborne and Rhodes 2017, no. 133), lines A9–13.

[63] Herrmann 1981, 9 n. 19.

[64] For the likely sense of φάρμακα, see Pugliese Carratelli 1960.

high and maximize their own profits.[65] The territory of Teos is relatively short on arable land (see above, Chapter 2), and the procurement of sufficient grain was a perpetual problem for the city: in the last years of the fourth century BC, at the time of the synoikism of Teos and Lebedos by Antigonos the One-Eyed, the Teians and Lebedians were particularly concerned about how to secure a sufficient supply of grain, since they were unable to produce enough from their own territory.[66]

Document 3 (Dirae II): Public Curses at Teos and Abdera

Dirae II describes itself as a *stēlē*, in the singular (D17). Hence we should assume that the text of Dirae II was contained in its entirety on this single stone, in contrast to Dirae I, inscribed on at least two *stēlai* (Dirae I, lines 35–7).[67] So far as we know, the extant part of Dirae I was inscribed on only a single face of the stone; by contrast, Dirae II is inscribed on all four faces of the surviving *stēlē* (Figs 3.7–3.11), and therefore the first thing that needs to be established is the sequence in which the four faces are to be read. Herrmann assumed that the text of Dirae II began with one of the two broader faces (Face A), followed by the shorter face on the viewer's left (Face B), and so on, so that the reader moves around the stone in a 'leftwards' direction (A–B–C–D, front–left–back–right), i.e. 'clockwise' (as viewed from above).[68] That the text began on one of the broad faces is surely correct; however, the sequence of faces assumed by Herrmann is almost certainly wrong. Aside from anything else, if one compares other sixth- and fifth-century BC *stēlai* inscribed on four faces, the universal practice (whenever the sequence of the four faces can be determined with certainty) seems to be for the reader to travel round the stone in a 'rightwards' direction, i.e. 'anticlockwise' (as viewed from above).[69] Our default assumption should be that this is also the

---

[65] Thus Bravo 1983, 22–3 (cf. Moreno 2007, 334), comparing the Solonian legislation against exporting any goods other than oil outside Attica (Plut. *Sol.* 24).

[66] Welles, *RC* 3 (*c*.302 BC), lines 72–101, esp. line 78, οὐ γὰρ ποεῖν ὑμᾶς ἱκανόν; for Antigonos' response, Briant 1994. See now also Adak 2021, 237–41.

[67] Cf. *I.Erythrai* 2 (Osborne and Rhodes 2017, no. 122), B2–3 (also a single, multi-face *stēlē*).

[68] Herrmann 1981, 6. Osborne and Rhodes 2017, 6–11, no. 102, print the text in the sequence A–C–B–D, without explanation; confusingly, they still number the faces *a-b-c-d* (so their *b* = Herrmann's C).

[69] Thus e.g. the sixth-century constitutional law from Chios (Jeffery 1956, 159–62); the mid-fifth-century 'Dophytis' inscription from Chios (Matthaiou 2011, 13–34, esp. 23); Eleusinian regulations of the early fifth century BC (*IG* I³ 6; *I.Eleusis* 19); *thesmia* of the Athenian deme Skambonidai, *c*.475–450 BC (*IG* I³ 244; for the correct order of the sides, see now Lambert 2019, 21–31); a fragmentary Athenian sacrificial calendar, *c*.475–450 (*IG* I³ 246; Lambert 2019, 18–19). Later on, the inscribed pillar at Xanthos (Osborne and Rhodes 2017, no. 193, late fifth century BC) follows the same 'rightwards'

case here—although, as we shall see, things are in fact a little more complex than that.

As Herrmann noted, the text of Dirae II (like Dirae I) is inscribed by more than one hand. The lettering on Face C is visibly different from the lettering on the other faces (Fig. 3.11): the letters are distinctly smaller (c.0.014m, compared to c.0.018–0.022m on Faces A, B, and D), with the result that the mason managed to fit twenty-three *stoichoi* across the face of the stone (contrast the sixteen *stoichoi* on the other broad face, Face A).[70] The interlinear spaces are also significantly narrower than on the other three faces. It is, moreover, quite certain that Face C should be read as the 'last' of the four faces: there is a *vacat* in the second half of line C4 (no *vacats* anywhere on Faces A, B, D), followed by (apparently) eleven carefully erased lines, with a large blank space below the erasure.[71] On Faces A, B, and D, the text continues all the way down to the bottom right-hand corner of the stone, and on Faces A and D the text breaks off mid-way through a clause (Face B is too fragmentary to judge for certain). We can therefore be confident that Herrmann's sequencing of the faces—with Face D as the 'last' face—cannot be right: on any hypothesis, Face C must come last.

Furthermore, although Herrmann does not note any differences between the lettering of Faces A, B, and D, it is in fact quite certain that the extant part of Face B was inscribed in a *third* hand, differing both from the hand of Faces A and D and the hand of the concluding Face C. Faces A and D were clearly inscribed by a single letter-cutter, who employed rather tall and elegant shallow-cut lettering, with narrow interlinear spaces (Figs 3.7–3.8). On Faces A and D, the *upsilon* is consistently inscribed like a Latin V, with no 'tail' at the bottom (as on Dirae I), and the left stroke of the *nu* is consistently vertical. The lines of Face A and Face D are also precisely horizontally aligned with one other on the stone (i.e. line D1 of Face D is situated at precisely the same height as line A2, and so on consistently down to D23 and A24), indicating that the *stoichedon* patterns on Faces A and D were planned out at one and the same time. The hand of Face B is different; the letters are both smaller and

pattern, as does the *lapis primus* of the Athenian Tribute Lists (inscribed piecemeal year-by-year). A possible exception to this rule is *SEG* 25, 358, a *lex sacra* from Kleonai, c.575–550 BC; but since the writing is vertical boustrophedon and the stone does not taper, it is, we think, not clear which way up the stone originally stood (i.e. whether we have the upper or lower part of the stone), which makes it impossible to tell whether the faces were to be read 'rightwards' or 'leftwards'. The 'rule' may only have applied when the lettering ran from left to right, as P. J. Rhodes points out to us. For a catalogue of Athenian documents inscribed on multiple faces of a single block in the early Classical period, see E. A. Meyer 2016, 359–60.

[70] Herrmann 1981, 5 ('feiner und entsprechend kleiner').

[71] Cf. the rationale of Jeffery 1956, 162 (*vacat* at the end of Face D of the Chios law).

Fig. 3.7. Dirae II, Face A.
Photo: Teos excavation archive.

Fig. 3.8. Dirae II, Face D.

Photo: Teos excavation archive.

Fig. 3.9. Dirae II, Face B.

Photo: Teos excavation archive.

Fig. 3.10. Dirae II, Face C.

Photo: Teos excavation archive.

Fig. 3.11. Dirae II, Face C, upper part.
Photo: Teos excavation archive.

more deeply cut, and the interlinear spaces and the spaces between adjacent letters are significantly broader than on Faces A and D (Fig. 3.9). The *upsilon* on Face B has a vertical 'tail' at the bottom, like the English *Y* (the sixth *stoichoi* of B5 and B6), and the left stroke of the *nu* sometimes slants sharply upwards to the right (note especially the *nu* in the fourth *stoichos* of B11). Furthermore, the lines of Face B are not horizontally aligned with those on Faces A and D.

It therefore seems clear that the text was inscribed in at least three, if not four phases. Since it is highly likely that the original inscription began on one of the broad faces, and it clearly cannot have begun on Face C, Face A must come first, as Herrmann rightly saw. Next comes Face D, the narrow face to the right, inscribed in the same hand as Face A (following the usual default 'rightwards' rule for the sequence of multi-face inscriptions). Since Face D breaks off mid-way through a clause, presumably the original text continued onto the lost upper part of Face B (the narrow face to the left): this sequence of faces for a three-face inscription (broad face, narrow face to the right, narrow face to the left) is also attested for a near-contemporary set of inscribed regulations from the neighbouring city of Erythrai.[72] A further series of

---

[72] *I.Erythrai* 2 (Rhodes and Osborne 2017, 118–23, no. 122): broad face, right-hand narrow face, left-hand narrow face.

curses was then added in a second hand, lower down on Face B (the extant text on Face B), perhaps continuing onto the back of the *stēlē* (Face C); a yet further series of curses was then added in a third hand on Face C (C1–4), perhaps with a *fourth* text inscribed below (the erasure below C4). As we have seen, this kind of 'accumulation' of clauses is also found in Dirae I (the 'additional' curses of Dirae I, lines 42–53).

We reconstruct the entire text of Dirae II as follows:

(I) Original text, hand I (Face A, continuing onto Face D, finishing in the lost upper part of Face B). Curses against magistrates (A1–11); oath to be taken by magistrates (A10–24); stipulation of the occasions when the oath is to be taken (D1–11); curses against magistrates who do not read out the curses and oath correctly (D11–23).

(II) Second text, hand II (Face B, lower part). Additional curses, of uncertain character (B1–26), perhaps continuing onto the upper part of Face C.

(III) Third text, hand III (Face C). Additional curses, concerned with 'handing over' or 'handing back' (C1–4).

(IV) Fourth text (?) (Face C). Unknown content, *c.*11 lines; carefully erased.

As with Dirae I, the only guide to the date of the texts of Dirae II is the style(s) of lettering. Herrmann compared the lettering of *I.Erythrai* 2 (Osborne and Rhodes 2017, no. 122), which does indeed look fairly similar to the lettering of 'hand II' (*upsilon* with 'tail'); the Erythrai text is usually dated to the 450s BC, suggesting that we should be looking for a date in the second quarter of the fifth century BC for the Teos text, probably in the earlier part of that period.[73] We see no way of telling whether Dirae I precedes Dirae II (see further below).

Document 3 (Dirae II): Text and Translation

Block of grey limestone, with several darker veins, broken above, complete below. Inscribed on all four faces. At the bottom of each face, a slightly

---

[73] Herrmann 1981, 5. Note the similar disposition on the stone of Dirae II and the Erythrai inscription (see above).

projecting margin, separated from the inscribed area by a lightly incised line.[74] The surface of Face B badly pitted; Faces A, C, and D well preserved. Discovered in a building in Sığacık (1976); subsequently in the Basmane Museum in İzmir, where it was copied in 1977 and 1979 by Peter Herrmann. Today in the garden of the Archaeological Museum in İzmir.

H. 0.83m; W. 0.46–0.47m; Th. 0.280–0.285m. Letters: 0.018–0.022m (Faces A, B, D); 0.014m (Face C). *Stoichedon* 16 (Face A), 9 (Face B), 23 (Face C), 9 (Face D). For the correct sequence of the four faces (A–D–B–C), see the commentary below.

Ed. Herrmann 1981; (*SEG* 31, 985; Koerner 1993, 301–7, no. 79; Effenterre and Ruzé 1994–5, I 370–5, no. 105; Dössel 2003, 30–40; Osborne and Rhodes 2017, 4–15, no. 102C).

Trans. Brodersen, Günther, and Schmitt 1992, 27–8, no. 47B (German); Arnaoutoglou 1998, 85–6, no. 71 (English: unreliable).

See: Merkelbach 1982 (A6–7, A13, A16–17, A21–2); Lewis 1982 (A16–17); Gauthier 1990, 85–6 (A16–17); Santiago Álvarez 1990–1 (lines A2, A6–7); Graham 1991 (A6–7); D'Alessio 1992 (A6–7); Graham 1992, 53–9 (relationship between Teos and Abdera); Faraguna 2005, 329–31 (the *aisymnētēs*); Hagedorn 2005, 137–41 (comparison with Deuteronomy); Reiche 2006, 187–206 (the *phoinikographos*); Youni 2007; Robinson 2011, 140–5 (democratic elements); Hamon 2018, 339–41 (afterlife).

Face A: *Stoich.* 16

[..... 10 .....]$\varLambda E$[.. 4 ..]
[.. 4 ..]$O\varSigma\underline{I}HN$: $\pi οι όμε[ν]$-
$ος$, $τοῦτον$: $\dot{\alpha}πόλλυ[σθ]$-
$αι$: $καὶ αὐτὸν$: $καὶ γέ[ν]$-
5   $ος$: $τὸ$ $[κ]\acute{ε}νο$: $ὃς$ $\mathring{α}ν$ $τιμὴ$-
$ν$: $\acute{ε}χων$: $[\xi]υνθέτοισιν$
$[T]ηΐ[ο]ι[σ]ιν$: $τὸμ$ $πλησί$-
$[ο]ν$: $δολ[\hat{ω}]ται$: $τοῦτον$: $\dot{α}$-

---

[74] An identical feature is found on the contemporary Eleusinian regulations from Athens, similarly inscribed on a four-sided pillar (*IG* I³ 6; *I.Eleusis* 19; Osborne and Rhodes 2017, no. 106); see the photos published by Meritt 1945, 64 (describing the incised line as a 'set-line').

[π]ὀλλυσθαι : καὶ αὐτὸ-
10   [ν κα]ὶ γένος : τὸ κένο : ἐ-
πανάστα[σ]ιν : οὐ βολε-
ύσω : οὐδὲ ποιήσω : οὐδ-
ὲ λυ[ή]σω : ο[ὐ]δὲ διώξω : ο-
[ὐ]δὲ [χρ]ήμ[α]τα : δημιώσ-
15   [ω : οὐ]δὲ δήσω : οὐδὲ κατ-
[ακ]τε[ν]έω : ἄμ μὴ σ[ὺ]ν δι-
[ακοσ]ί[ο]ισιν : ἐγ Τέωι
[ἢ] πλέοσ[ι]ν : [κ]αὶ ἄμ μὴ ὑ-
π[ὸ] πόλεω[ς] : ν[ό]μο : κατα-
20   λαφθέν[τ]α : ἐν δὲ Ἀβδή-
[ρ]οισιν : [σ]ὺμ πεντακο-
[σ]ίοισιν : ἢ πλ[έο]σιν : α-
ἰσυμνήτην : οὐ στήσω
24   [ο]ὔτε : σὺμ πολλοῖσι[ν]

A2: [-]ΟΣΙ̣ΗΝ H(errmann); [ἀν]οσίην S(antiago) Á(lvarez); [δημ]οσίην
A(dak)/Th(onemann). **A6–7**: [σ]ὺν θετοῖσιν [T]ηΐ[ο]ι[σ]ιν H. *dubitanter*;
[σ]υνθέτοισιν S. Á.; Effenterre and Ruzé; [ξ]υνθέτοισιν A./Th. **A13**: λυ[ή]σω
H.; λυ[μ]έω M. **A15**: δήσω. οὐδὲ H. *per lapsum*; δήσω : οὐδὲ *lapis*. **A16–17**:
σ[ὺ]ν . . ‖[. . . .]Ι . Ι̣ΣΙΝ H.; σ[ὺ]ν [ἐξ|ακοσ]ί[ο]ισιν G(schnitzer) *ap.*
M(erkelbach); σ[ὺ]ν δι̣|[ακοσ]ί[ο]ισιν Lewis (*dubitante* Gauthier). **A21–2**:
[σ]ύμπαντα κο̣|[ι]νοῖσιν H.; [σ]ὺμ πεντακο̣|[σ]ίοισιν G. *ap.* M.

Face D: *Stoich.* 9
Ἀνθ[εστη]ρ[ί]-
οισιν : καὶ Ἡ-
ρακλέοισι-
ν : καὶ {ι} Δίοι-
5   σιν : ἐν Ἀβδ[ή]-
ρο[ι]σιν : Ἀν[θ]-
εστηρίοι[σ]-
ιν : καὶ Ἡρα[κ]-
λέοισιν : κα̣-
10   ὶ Ζηνὸς : ἑορ-
τῆι : ὅστις δ-
ὲ τιμοχέων

ἢ ταμιεύων
μὴ ’ναλέξεε-
15 ν : τὰ γεγραθ-
μένα : ἐν τῆι
ϲτήληι : ἐπὶ
μνήμηι : καὶ
δυνάμει : ἢ [φ]-
20 οινικογρα-
φέων : κελευ-
[ό]ντων τιμό-
χων : κεῖνον

Face B: *Stoich*. 9
[.]Ι[...7....]
[.]ΙΔΣΟΕ[...]
[.]ΔΕ[...]Ε[.]Ν
[..]Μ[...6...]
5 [...] : τοῦτον
[ἀ]πόλλυσθα-
ι : ἐκ Τέω : κ[α]ὶ
Ἀβδήρων : [κ]α-
ὶ γῆς : Τ[ηΐ]ης
10 καὶ α[ὐ]τὸν : κ-
αὶ γένο[ς :] τὸ
κεῖνο : [..]ΝΤ
[.]ΠΑΡΑ[.]ΘΕ : [.]
[.]ΙΟ[...]Ι[..]
15 [.]Α[...7....]
[.]Ν[...7....]
5 lines illegible
22 [....8....]Δ
[...]ΟΝ[..]Η[.]
Ω[.]ΠΙ[.....]
25 ΕΙΟΥ[...]Ε[.]
ΙΟ[.]Τ[....]Ι

B10–11: α[ὐ]τὸν κ|αὶ γένο[ς] τὸ Η.; α[ὐ]τὸν : κ|αὶ *lapis.*; γένο[ς :] A./Th.

Face C: *Stoich*. 23
[...5..Ἀβ]δηριτέων : ἀ[π]αιτέο[ν]-

[τος τô ξ]υνô : μὴ 'ποδιδοίη : κεῖ[ν]-
[ον ἀπ]όλλυσθαι : καὶ αὐτὸν : κ[αὶ]
[γ]ένος τὸ κένο. *vacat*
c.11 lines deliberately erased

C2: μὴ 'π[ο]διδ[ο]ίη H.

Translation

A '...making ((?) public), let him perish, both him and his descendants. Anyone who holds public office for the Teian collectivity (?) who deceives the assembly (?), let him perish, both him and his descendants. I will not plot a revolution or take part in one, nor will I engage in civil strife, nor will I prosecute or confiscate property or bind (i.e. imprison?) or execute, unless with (the consent of) two hundred men or more at Teos and unless he is convicted by the law of the city, and at Abdera with (the consent of) five hundred men or more; I will not set up an *aisymnētēs*, nor with many men...'

D '...at the Anthesteria and the Herakleia and the Dia, in Abdera at the Anthesteria and the Herakleia and the festival of Zeus. Whoever holds the office of *timouchos* or treasurer and does not read out the things inscribed on the *stēlē* to the best of his memory and power, or whichever scribe (does not read them out) when the *timouchoi* instruct, let him...'

B '...let this man perish from Teos and Abdera and the land of Teos, both him and his descendants...'

C '...of the Abderites, [if] he does not return [it] when the community demands it back, let him perish, both him and his descendants.'

Document 3 (Dirae II): Commentary

A1–5: Herrmann prints ποιομε[ν]ος without an accent, apparently hesitating whether to understand ποιούμενος or ποιουμένους. The former is surely more likely to be correct, with the participle standing at the end of the clause describing the actions for which the individual will be cursed. Herrmann offers no suggestions for the sequence [- -]ΟΣΙΗΝ in line A2;[75] this is surely most likely to be the adjective [δημ]οσίην, and one wonders if the curse bears

---

[75] Santiago Álvarez 1990–1, 330 suggests [ἀν]οσίην, 'cometiendo un sacrilegio'.

on a magistrate who illegitimately confiscates another's property (e.g. [τὴν οὐσίην…δημ]οσίην ποιόμε[ν]ος vel sim.).[76]

A5–8: It is not clear whether the phrase (ὁ) τιμὴν ἔχων designates only the magistrate with the title of τιμοῦχος (Dirae I, line 29; Dirae II, lines D12, D22–3), or more generally anyone holding a civic magistracy at Teos or Abdera; our translation assumes the latter.[77] These lines pose three separate problems of interpretation: (a) the meaning of [σ]ὺν θετοῖσιν or [σ]υνθέτοισιν or [ξ]υνθέτοισιν [T]ηΐ[ο]ι[σ]ιν in A6–7, (b) the meaning of τὸμ πλησί[ο]ν in A7–8, and (c) whether δολ[ῶ]ται in A8 derives from δολόω, 'deceive, ensnare' or δουλόω, 'enslave'.

(a) In lines A5–6, Herrmann tentatively suggested [σ]ὺν θετοῖσιν [T]ηΐ[ο]ι[σ]ιν, noting the difficulty of extracting a satisfactory sense from the words.[78] This word-division has been accepted by most subsequent scholars, but (in our view) without a satisfactory explanation of their sense.[79] Graham thought that the θετοὶ Τήϊοι ('adopted Teians') were a subgroup of the civic body at Teos, identifying them with the returning colonists from Abdera who re-founded Teos at an unknown date (see above); by contrast, D'Alessio and Osborne and Rhodes supposed that they were a subgroup of the civic body at Abdera, either the original mid-sixth-century Teian colonists (Osborne and Rhodes) or a later, second wave of Teian settlers at Abdera (D'Alessio).[80] But on any interpretation, the preposition σύν is extremely difficult: one does not hold a magistracy 'with' a subset of the citizen body, 'adopted' or otherwise.

---

[76] Cf. lines A13–15 below, ο[ὐ]δὲ [χρ]ήμ[α]τα δημιώσ[ω]. For (legitimate) confiscation of property, cf. e.g. *I.Mylasa* 2 (361/0 BC), lines 10–11, ἐζημίωσαν δημεύσει τῆς οὐσίης καὶ ἐπώ⟨λη⟩σαν τὰ κτήματα αὐτῶν δημοσίηι; Rhodes and Osborne 2003, no. 39 (Athens and Ioulis, 363/2 BC), lines 41–2, φεύγειν αὐτὸς Κέω καὶ Ἀθήνας καὶ τὴν οὐσίαν αὐτῶν δημοσίαν εἶναι.

[77] Thus Herrmann 1981, 14.

[78] Herrmann 1981, 14: 'Sprachlich sehe ich nur die Möglichkeit, in [σ]ὺν θετοῖσιν zu trennen, aber was heisst das sachlich? θετός ist m. W. nur in der Bedeutung ‹angenommen, adoptiert› bezeugt, u. U. könnte man an Personen denken, die nicht γνήσιοι sind. Die Schwierigkeit des Verständnisses wird noch dadurch erhöht, dass m. E. nicht sicher zu sagen ist, ob die Klausel für Teos und Abdera gemeinsam gilt oder sich eventuell nur auf Abdera bezieht'. Similar caution in Koerner 1993, 304; Dössel 2003, 32–3.

[79] Merkelbach 1982: 'Wer als Magistrat mit adoptierten (= neueingebürgerten) Teiern den Nachbarn unterjocht'; Graham 1991: 'the newcomers from Abdera who refounded their mother city'; Osborne and Rhodes 2017, 6–9, 13: 'There seems to have been enough suspicion between the Abderans and the "adopted Teans" to occasion a specific undertaking not to side with the newcomers against the rump of Abderans'.

[80] D'Alessio 1992 connects the phrase to the ancient *scholion* on Pindar's second *Paean* (Σ on line 48), referring to stasis and a group of 'newcomers' or 'immigrants' (ἐπήλυδας) at Abdera (see further above), but the hypothesis that the 'newcomers' are a 'seconda ondata di coloni' is plucked out of the air (cf. Rutherford 2001, 270).

A smaller group of scholars have therefore preferred to read [σ]υνθέτοισιν [Τ]ηί[ο]ι[σ]ιν.[81] Effenterre and Ruzé take the whole clause to mean 'whoever, in the exercise of a magistracy for the "reunited Teians", harms his neighbour'; they consider the phrase σύνθετοι Τήϊοι as a kind of proper name for the 'reunited' collective of Teians who had stayed at Teos and Teians who had recently returned from Abdera.[82] We think a simpler explanation is both possible and preferable. In Dirae I, the collective citizen body of the Teians is three times designated as τὸ ξυνόν, and the Abderite citizen body is similarly designated on Face C of our text.[83] We suggest that τὸ ξυνὸν τῶν Τηίων and οἱ [σ]ύνθετοι (or perhaps better [ξ]ύνθετοι) Τήϊοι are semantically identical, and that both phrases signify simply 'the collectivity of the Teians', 'the Teians as a collective'. The phrase ὃς ἂν τιμὴν ἔχων [ξ]υνθέτοισιν [Τ]ηί[ο]ι[σ]ιν would mean 'whoever holds public office for the Teian collectivity'.[84]

(b) What is the meaning of τὸμ πλησί[ο]ν? The word has generally been taken to mean 'neighbour',[85] but this sense is severely problematic. Why would deceiving (or enslaving) one's neighbour be worse than deceiving or enslaving any other member of the community?[86] And if deception/enslavement was in itself an undesirable act, why is the curse only said to apply to office-holders—were non-office-holders permitted to deceive/enslave their neighbours with impunity? Most importantly of all, the whole text (so far as we can tell) is concerned not with regulating private behaviour, but with protecting the body politic and the democratic (or at least participatory) constitution at both Abdera and Teos, perhaps of recent creation: we would expect this clause to be concerned with regulating the behaviour of magistrates *in their capacity as magistrates*.[87] It is noteworthy that the term (ὁ) πλησίος also appears in an equally puzzling context in a near-contemporary set of judicial

---

[81] Santiago Álvarez 1990–1, 330 (*SEG* 45, 1628) and (independently) Effenterre and Ruzé 1994–5, 370–5.

[82] Effenterre and Ruzé 1994–5, 374: 'Cette fois, les Abdéritains sont accolés aux Téiens, avec lesquels ils forment sans doute ce que le document appelle *Synthetoi Teioi*, «les Téiens dans leur ensemble» les «Téiens réunis». Nous ne croyons pas qu'il faille faire de *syn* une préposition: nous comprenons l'expression (au datif) comme une sorte de nom propre, d'où l'absence de l'article'.

[83] Dirae I, lines 43–4, ὅστις φάρμακα δηλητήρια ποιοῖ ἐπὶ Τηίοισιν τὸ ξυνόν; Dirae I, lines 3–4, ὅστις Τηίων ⟨τ⟩[ῶι ξ]υνῶι ἢ αἰσυ[μ]νήτη⟨ν⟩ [ἰσταί]η (as reconstructed by Herrmann 1981, 20–1); Dirae I, lines 23–5, ἢ [τι κ]ακὸν βολεύοι περὶ Τ[ηί]ων τὸ ξυνὸ; cf. Dirae II, lines C1–2 below, [Ἀβδ]ηριτέων ἀ[π]αιτέο[ν][τος τὸ ξ]υνῶ.

[84] An alternative (in our view less plausible) solution would be to assume that [ξ]υνθέτοισιν is not an adjective but a noun: τὰ ξύνθετα = 'agreement' is attested in *CID* I 13 (Sokolowski 1962, no. 41, fourth century BC). The phrase could then mean 'by Teian agreement', 'by agreement of the Teians'.

[85] Herrmann 1981, 6 ('seinen Nächsten'); cf. Matthaiou 2006, 126 (commenting on *SEG* 56, 995, from Chios).

[86] Cf. the use of ἰδιώτης in Dirae I, line 44, to signify an individual Teian.

[87] Robinson 2011, 144: 'The fifth-century documents from Teos...show a strong emphasis on magistrates properly carrying out their functions or facing punishment'.

regulations from Erythrai.[88] In lines A22–6 of the Erythrai text, we read: πληρὸν δὲ τ[ὸ δ]ικαστήριον μὴ ἐλά[σ]σονας ἢ ἐξήκο[ντ]α ϙαὶ ἔνα· δικάζεν [δὲ π]λησίον τιθέντα κατὰ τὸν νόμον. The first clause means 'no fewer than sixty-one men are to fill the court', i.e. a quorum of sixty-one is required for the court to convene. The second clause is usually understood to signify 'they shall judge in accordance with the law (which) one has set up nearby', but the word-order renders this awkward or impossible.[89]

It is therefore worth wondering whether (ὁ) πλησίος (or πλήσιος) might have had a special meaning in northern Ionia in the early fifth century BC. We tentatively suggest that πλήσιος could be a substantivized adjective derived from πίμπλημι (aor. πλησ-), signifying 'full, quorate (assembly)'. Compounds in πλησι- are well-attested in Greek, as in the Homeric adjective πλησίστιος (transitive: 'filling the sails') and the personal names Πλησικράτης (intransitive: 'full of might').[90] The present participles of the verbs πλήθω and πληθύω are attested in precisely this sense (although always with an accompanying noun) in fifth- and fourth-century inscriptions: cf. e.g. Syll.[3] 257 (Delphi, 340/39 BC), πληθο[ύ]σης ἀγορᾶ⟨ς⟩, 'the assembly being full'; similarly IG I[3] 105 (409 BC?), ἄνευ τὸ δήμο τὸ Ἀθεναίον πλεθύοντος.[91] The nouns τὸ πλῆθος and ἁ πλήθα are of course very widely used to mean 'the mass', 'the people'.[92] A putative sense 'full/quorate (assembly)' would provide an excellent sense for A5–8 in the Teian text: 'Anyone who holds public office for the Teian collectivity who deceives the full assembly, let him perish'. This curse would then be precisely and pleasingly analogous to the Athenian curse performed at each assembly against orators who deceive the council, people, or law courts.[93] This

---

[88] I.Erythrai 2; Koerner 1993, 281–8, no. 75; Osborne and Rhodes 2017, no. 122 (probably of the late 450s BC).

[89] Thus Engelmann and Merkelbach in I.Erythrai 2 (cf. p.26): 'Sie sollen nach dem Gesetz richten, und man soll das Gesetz in der Nähe aufstellen'; Koerner 1993, 282: '(die Richter) sollen nach dem Gesetz richten, das man in der Nähe aufstellt' (with doubts at 286); Osborne and Rhodes 2017, 121: 'They shall judge having placed the law nearby, in accordance with the law'. Moroo 2014, 99 n. 10 understands [π]λησίον τιθέντα to denote the payment of a court fee.

[90] Πλησικράτης: IG XII Suppl. 429 (Thasos). On the office of πλατίϝοινος at Tiryns (SEG 30, 380), see Dubois 1980 (arguing for a derivation from πίμπλημι).

[91] Similarly in two late sixth- or early fifth-century texts from Olympia (Minon 2007, no. 4, line 4, σὺν...δάμοι πλεθύοντι; no. 13, line 8, ἄνευς βολὰν καὶ ζᾶμον πλαθύοντα). Cf. Robert, OMS I, 90; Herrmann 1981, 17 n. 47; Minon 2007, II 514–15. For the Delphi text, Rhodes with Lewis 1997, 135–6; for the meaning of ἄνευ τὸ δήμο τὸ Ἀθεναίον πλεθύοντος in IG I[3] 105, Rhodes 1972, 195–8 ('the people in assembly').

[92] ἁ πλήθα = 'assembly' or 'majority': Effenterre and Ruzé 1994–5, I no. 43, lines 39–40 (Hypoknemidian Lokris and Naupaktos, mid-V BC); ἁ πλεῖθα = 'assembly': SEG 22, 407, line 19 (Thisbe, III BC). πλῆθος = 'people': numerous examples; e.g. Osborne and Rhodes 2017, no. 121 (Athenian treaty with Erythrai, late 450s BC, contemporary with I.Erythrai 2), lines 21–3, βολεύσο hος ἂν [δύ]νομαι ἄριστα[– –] Ἐρυθραίον τὸ πλήθει καὶ Ἀθεναίον καὶ τὸν [χσυ]νμά[χ]ον.

[93] Dem. 23.97: διόπερ καταρᾶται καθ᾽ ἑκάστην ἐκκλησίαν ὁ κῆρυξ, οὐκ εἴ τινες ἐξηπατήθησαν, ἀλλ᾽ εἴ τις ἐξαπατᾷ λέγων ἢ βουλὴν ἢ δῆμον ἢ τὴν ἡλιαίαν. The precise wording of this curse is not known, but

interpretation of ὁ πλήσιος would also provide a plausible sense for the Erythrai text, assuming that the second clause is closely connected to the first: 'No fewer than sixty-one men are to fill the court; they are to judge, once one has convened a quorate (court), according to the law'.[94] However, in the absence of further supporting evidence, this must for the time being remain no more than a hypothesis.

(c) The verb δολ[ῶ]ται in A8 could derive either from δολόω, 'deceive, ensnare' or from δουλόω, 'enslave'. Herrmann favoured the former, Merkelbach the latter.[95] If we are right to suppose that *plēsios* signifies 'assembly', then clearly the former must be correct; if *plēsios* means neighbour, then we see no way of deciding for certain between the two.

A10–13: At the end of line A10, the grammatical structure of the text abruptly shifts from a series of normative statements, the 'curses' proper ('if *x* behaves in such-and-such a way, let him perish'), to a series of oaths in the first-person singular ('I shall not do *x*').[96] This series of oaths occupies the remainder of Face A, and must have continued on the upper part of Face D (see above, on the sequence of the four faces). The surviving lower part of Face D stipulates where these oaths are to be performed (D1–11), as must have been clarified in the lines immediately above D1 (see our note on D1–11).

The sequence of oaths begins with a promise not to plot or participate in a revolution (ἐπανάστασις, A10–11), here apparently an oligarchic or tyrannical plot against the participatory regimes of Teos and Abdera: see the commentary on Dirae I, lines 3–8. The contemporary law from Abdera (Chapter 2 above) is similarly concerned with the possibility of revolution (ἐπανάστασις) or naval assault (ἐκ νεῶν ἀπόβασις). A reasonably close comparison, as Herrmann recognized, can be found in a late fifth-century Thasian law (probably passed under the oligarchy of 411–407 BC) stipulating rewards for informers who provide information about revolution (ἐπανάστασις); in the Thasian law, the 'first plotter' (i.e. instigator) of the revolution (τὸ πρῶτο

---

it certainly included the verb ἐξαπατᾶν, as is clear from the paraphrases in Dem. 18.282 (ὁ τὴν πόλιν ἐξαπατῶν) and Ar. *Thesm.* 343 (εἴ τις ἐξαπατᾷ ψευδῆ λέγων); cf. Dem. 19.70 (ἐψευσμένον). See Rhodes 1972, 36–7; Sommerstein and Bayliss 2013, 48–50, and further below.

[94] For τίθημι in the sense 'convene', cf. H. *Od.* 9.171, καὶ τότ᾽ἐγὼν ἀγορὴν θέμενος μετὰ πᾶσιν ἔειπον; perhaps *SEG* 56, 995, C3–5 (Chios).

[95] Herrmann 1981, 14–15; Merkelbach 1982, 212. Herrmann compares a passage from the Gortyn code, where the verb δολόσασθαι is now generally considered to mean 'be tricked/deceived': *I.Cret.* IV 72, col. ii, lines 36–7 and 44–5 (Gagarin and Perlman 2016, 346).

[96] On this generic shift, cf. Herrmann 1981, 13–14; Koerner 1993, 303.

βολεύσαντος) is subject to a curse (ἐν τῆι ἐπαρῆι ἔστω).[97] Much later, in the late fourth or early third century BC, the Abderites inscribed a similar law laying down rewards for informers who denounce a planned revolution at Abdera.[98] In A13, as Herrmann saw, the verb λυ[ή]σω is the future of the rare verb λυάω = στασιάζω, 'engage in civil strife'.[99]

A13–22: This passage sets a quorum for the courts or assemblies at both Teos and Abdera which are required for the imposition of penalties on individuals (two hundred and five hundred respectively): presumably this stipulation applies to all four of the activities listed in A13–16 (prosecution, confiscation of property, imprisonment—literally 'binding'—or execution).[100] This passage provides our clearest evidence that the regimes in place at both cities were democratic—or at least participatory—at the time the text was inscribed.[101] The size of the quorum at Teos (A16–17) depends on the reading at the end of line A16: Gschnitzer suggested [ἑξ|ακοσ]ί[ο]ισιν (six hundred), but Lewis believed that he could read δι̣|[α κοσ]ί[ο]ισιν (two hundred) on the photograph published by Herrmann, and this reading is confirmed by our autopsy of the stone.[102] Lewis noted that the relative sizes of the quora at Teos and Abdera (2:5) are identical to the proportions of the two cities' normal tribute-payments to Athens in the mid-fifth century BC (Teos normally six talents, Abdera normally fifteen talents), but this may be no more than a coincidence; for relatively large cities like Teos and Abdera, Athenian tribute was assessed on the basis of resources, not population.[103] In lines A18–20, the clause [κ]αὶ ἂμ μὴ ὑπ[ὸ] πόλεω[ς] ν[ό]μο καταλαφθέν[τ]α ('and unless he is convicted by the law of the city') strictly only applies to trials at Teos, but we ought perhaps not to push this too hard: the phrase can easily be taken as applying to trials at both cities.[104]

---

[97] Herrmann 1981, 15 n. 41; Osborne and Rhodes 2017, no. 176.

[98] *IThrakAig* E2: [ὃς ἂν ἐπανάστασιν] ἐπιβουλευομέν[ην] ἐπὶ Ἄβδηρα κατείπηι κτλ. On informers, see further Rubinstein 2016.

[99] Herrmann 1981, 15–16; Koerner 1993, 304; Dössel 2003, 33; unnecessarily doubted by Merkelbach 1982. The verb appears in Callimachus' *Aetia*, Fr. 43.74 (with Harder 2012, II 350–1).

[100] Parallels for the four punishments are assembled by Herrmann 1981, 16, to which add now the oath in the Pistiros inscription (*IGBulg* V 5557 ter, with *SEG* 63, 492: mid-fourth century BC), οὐ δήσω οὐδὲ ἀποκτ[ενέ]ω οὐδὲ ἀφαιρήσομαι χρήμα[τα]. In line A15, Herrmann prints a full stop rather than an interpunct after δήσω (followed by *SEG* and Osborne and Rhodes 2017, no. 102), but this is simply a typographical error: the interpunct is clearly legible on the stone.

[101] Lewis 1982, 72; Gauthier 1990, 86; Robinson 2011, 140–5.

[102] Gschnitzer *ap.* Merkelbach 1982; Lewis 1982.

[103] Gauthier 1990, 85–6 (questioning Lewis's reading). Nixon and Price 1990, 160 n. 38, note that Thasos normally paid a tribute of thirty talents, and that fifth-century Thasian courts consisted of three hundred men (Osborne and Rhodes 2017, nos. 103, 176, 177); hence a voting quorum evidently cannot bear a direct relationship to levels of tribute-assessment. Three hundred was also the quorum for courts on Chios in the mid-fifth century BC (Osborne and Rhodes 2017, no. 133).

[104] Graham 1992, 56; contrast Herrmann 1981, 28.

A22–4: As Herrmann showed, this passage enables us to restore a difficult passage in Dirae I (lines 3–10) as a curse against anyone who either sets up an *aisymnētēs* or initiates a revolution with the aim of establishing an *aisymnētēs*: see the commentary on Dirae I above.[105] The clause that begins at A24 was presumably a second oath on a similar theme, perhaps to the effect: 'nor with many men [shall I participate in a revolution aiming at establishing an *aisymnētēs*]' ([ο]ὔτε : σὺμ πολλοῖσι[ν ἐπ᾽αἰσυμνηίηι ἐπαναστήσω] vel sim.).[106]

D1–11: The sequence of oaths must have concluded in the lost upper part of Face D. The text begins at D1 mid-way through what must be a list of the festivals at Teos at which the oaths are to be sworn each year (the list of Abderite festivals begins at line D5); the general sense must be something like [τὸς ὅρκος τούτος ὀμόσαι τὸς τιμὴν ἔχοντας καθημένο τὠγῶνος ἐν Τέωι] Ἀνθ[εστη]ρ[ί]οισιν κτλ., '[the office-holders are to swear these oaths when the crowd is assembled for the contest at Teos] at the Anthesteria, etc.'[107] The list of festivals is the same at Teos and Abdera, aside from the fact that the festival of Zeus is designated the *Dia* at Teos and the Ζηνὸς ἑορτή at Abdera; we have no explanation for this (was the drafter of the text unsure of the name of the Abderite festival?). The Anthesteria festival at Abdera is now directly attested for the first time in **Document 1** above, line **B62**.

D11–23: There then follows the beginning of a curse against office-holders who do not read out correctly 'the things inscribed on the *stēlē*' (τὰ γεγραθμένα ἐν τῆι [σ]τήληι, D15–17). Presumably the curse proper begins with the final word on Face D and continued at the top of Face B (D23: κεῖνον [ἀπόλλυσθαι καὶ αὐτὸν καὶ γένος τὸ κεῖνο]); this may perhaps have been the end of the original text. The 'things inscribed on the *stēlē*' probably encompasses both the curses (A1–10) and the oaths (A10–24).

The reciting of the curses and oaths is performed by two groups of magistrates, the *timouchoi* and the treasurers (D11–13).[108] The magistrates are to read out the curses and oaths inscribed on the *stēlē* ἐπὶ μνήμηι καὶ δυνάμει (D17–19; ἐπὶ δυνάμει alone in Dirae I, line 31), a phrase which has led to

---

[105] Herrmann 1981, 18–21 (*SEG* 31, 984).
[106] Compare the pair of clauses in Dirae I, lines 3–6, as restored by Herrmann: ὅστις ... ἢ αἰσυ[μ]νήτη⟨ν⟩ [ἱσταί]η ἢ ἐπανισταῖτο ⟨ἐπ᾽⟩ αἰ[συμ]νηίηι.
[107] Cf. Dirae I, lines 29–32, οἵτινες τιμοχέοντες τὴν ἀπαρὴν μὴ ποιήσεαν ἐπὶ δυνάμει καθημένο τὠγῶνος Ἀνθεστηρίοισιν κτλ.
[108] In the third-century Teian inscription on the union with Kyrbissos, the *tamiai* are involved in public oath-taking to the extent that they provide the sacrificial victims (τὰ ὅρκια): *SEG* 26, 1306, line 57.

much inconclusive discussion; the words would most naturally mean something like 'to the best of their memory and ability'.[109] At any event, it seems
clear that the crucial point is that the magistrates are required to read out the
curses and the oaths word-for-word, not providing a rough-and-ready summary of their content. Herrmann understood the clause at D19–23 to mean
that the *timouchoi* (but not the treasurers?) could 'delegate' the reading-out of
the curses and oaths to a professional scribe (φοινικογράφος); if the task was
so delegated, then the scribe was subject to the same penalties as a *timouchos*
or a treasurer for failing to read out the text accurately.[110] However, a simpler
explanation is possible. We know that at Athens, the curses performed before
each meeting of the *ekklēsia* and *boulē* were pronounced by the herald, but
that the curses were read out to the herald (probably one clause at a time) by
the under-secretary to the *ekklēsia* and the assistant (*hypēretēs*) to the *boulē*.[111]
The same is presumably also the case here. It is possible that this process (dictation to the *timouchoi* and treasurers by the scribe) underlies the otherwise
puzzling specification that the magistrates are to read out the curses and oaths
'to the best of their memory': the magistrates have to 'remember' the precise
wording given to them by their scribal prompter.

B1–26: As a result of our reordering of the faces of the stone (A–D–B–C) and
our attribution of the text on Face B to a different hand from Faces A and D,
the curious structure of the text as a whole envisaged by Herrmann (a second
series of curses on Face B, resuming after the oath in A10–24) can now be
abandoned.[112] It is now clear that what we have on Face B is a completely new
set of curses, appended after the end of the original text on the lost upper part
of Face B. Unfortunately, the stone is so worn that it is impossible to establish
exactly what these 'additional' curses might have been concerned with.
Everywhere else in both Dirae I and Dirae II the standard curse-formula
(with minor variants) is simply τοῦτον ἀπόλλυσθαι καὶ αὐτὸν καὶ γένος τὸ
κένο, 'let him perish, both him and his descendants'; only here (B6–9) do we
find the more expansive formula ἀπόλλυσθαι ἐκ Τέω καὶ Ἀβδήρων καὶ γῆς

---

[109] Herrmann 1981, 11–12; Koerner 1993, 307; Dössel 2003, 36–7; Reiche 2006, 199–203.
Thomas 1996, 22–3 thinks that the phrase 'might be envisaging reciting from memory'.
[110] Herrmann 1981, 12. On the function of the *phoinikographoi*, see especially Reiche 2006,
187–206.
[111] Dem. 19.70: after quoting the curse performed by the herald at each assembly-meeting,
Demosthenes says that it is impossible that Aeschines could be unaware of the contents of the curse,
'since when he was *hypogrammateus* to you (the *dēmos*) and *hypēretēs* to the *boulē*, he himself used to
read out (ἐξηγεῖτο) this law to the herald'. On these Athenian public curses, see Rhodes 1972, 36–7;
Sommerstein and Bayliss 2013, 48–50.
[112] Cf. Dössel 2003, 35.

Τηΐης, 'let him perish from Teos and Abdera and the land of Teos'.[113] The sense of this—to judge from the similar but more expansive clause in the third-century law on the *sympoliteia* between Teos and Kyrbissos (see below)—is that the infringer will be exiled under a curse from Teos, Abdera, and Teian territory, his property will be confiscated, and the person who slays him will not be polluted.[114] We see no way of knowing why the drafter of this additional series of curses chose to include this more comprehensive phraseology. Nor is it clear whether there is any significance to the fact that the phrasing here only refers to exile from the land (i.e. territory) of Teos, not from the land of Abdera also.[115] It is at any event hard to believe that the cursed individual could have been exiled from Teos, Teian territory, and the city of Abdera, but could remain on Abderite territory with impunity.

C1–4: The surviving text on Face C is inscribed in a hand that differs substantially from the hands of Faces A+D and Face B. The individual *stoichoi* are considerably smaller, with the result that the mason managed to fit twenty-three *stoichoi* to a line, compared with sixteen *stoichoi* to a line on the other broad face, Face A; the interlinear spaces are also notably smaller. The verbs *ἀπαιτεῖν* and *ἀποδιδόναι* are often used together in contexts where an individual or a community is required to pay back a loan, but that can hardly be the sense here.[116] It is more likely that we are dealing with a requirement on magistrates at Abdera (perhaps specifically the 'treasurers', the *tamiai* of line D13?) to return the funds under their management at the end of their term of office. A close parallel is found in the near-contemporary *thesmia* of the Athenian deme Skambonidai (*c*.475–450 BC), in which deme-officials swear an oath to the effect that they will preserve the common funds of the deme and 'hand back what is proper' (*ἀποδιδόναι τὸ καθῆκον*) in the presence of an auditor; a penalty-clause follows, apparently laying down punishments for

---

[113] Herrmann 1981, 22–3.
[114] SEG 26, 1306, lines 23–6: φ[ε]ύγειν τε αὐτὸν ἀραῖον ἐκ Τέω καὶ ἐξ Ἀβδήρων καὶ ἐκ τῆς χώρας καὶ τῆς Τηΐων καὶ τῆς Ἀβδηρ[ι]τῶν καὶ τὰ ὄντα αὐτοῦ δη[μό]σια ε[ἶ]ναι καὶ ὃς ἂν ἀποκτείνηι αὐτὸν μ[ὴ] μιαρὸς ἔστω; see further below.
[115] Herrmann 1981, 28 with n. 85 (highly speculative); Graham 1992, 56–7 ('[the] document was simply abbreviating').
[116] e.g. *I.Knidos* 221 (*c*.300 BC), lines B24–7, ἀπαιτεύντων δὲ ἁμῶν τὰ ὑπόλοιπα τῶν χρημάτων τούτων ἃ γίνεται σὺν τ[ό]κωι, τὰ μέρη τὰ ἁμὰ οὐκ ἀποδίδοντι Καλύμνιος φάμενοι ἀποδεδώκεν αὐτά κτλ.; *Sardis* VII 1, 1 (III BC), lines I.2–3, οἱ νεωποῖαι τὸ χρυσίον τῆς [παρακαταθή]κης τὸ τῆς Ἀρτέμιδος ἀπαιτοῦσιν παρ᾽ ἐμοῦ, ἐγὼ δὲ οὐκ ἔχω πόθεν ἀποδώσω αὐτοῖς; *IG* XII 7, 67 (Amorgos, II BC), lines 52–3, τὸ δὲ ἀρχαῖον ἀργύριον ἀποδώσουσιν ἐν ἓξ μησὶν ἀφ᾽ οὗ ἄν ἀπαιτήσῃ[ι] Πρα[ξι]κλῆ[ς]. In *IG* I³ 34 (Osborne and Rhodes 2017, no. 154), the Kleinias decree of *c*.425/4 BC, the terms are used of demands for tribute by Athenian officials: lines 22–5, [Ἀθ]εναίοις δὲ hελομένος ἄνδρας τέττ[αρας ἀποστέλλεν ἐς] τὰς πόλες ἀντιγραφσομένος τ[ὸμ φόρον τὸν ἀποδοθέντα κα]ὶ ἀπαιτέσοντας τὸμ μὲ [ἀποδοθέντα].

magistrates who do not do so.[117] As it stands, the text only refers to Abdera (line C1), but it is likely enough that the same requirement was made of magistrates at Teos: the general sense of the clause is presumably something like [ὅστις δὲ ταμιεύων τὰ κοινὰ χρήματα Τήϊων ἢ Ἀβ]δηριτέων ἀ[π]αιτέο[ν|τος τὸ ξ]υνὸ μὴ 'ποδιδοίη, 'whichever treasurer does not return the public funds of the Teians or the Abderites when the community demands them back, let him perish'.[118]

There is a *vacat* at the end of line C4, marking the end of this segment of additional text. Below C4, as Herrmann noted, around eleven lines of text have been very comprehensively erased; these lines presumably included a further additional curse or curses which the Teians and Abderites later decided to revoke, for unknown reasons.[119]

The Relationship Between Dirae I and Dirae II

The relationship between Dirae I and Dirae II has hitherto been profoundly unclear: does Dirae II supersede Dirae I, or provide a supplement to it, or are the two sets of curses in some way independent of one another? Scholars have tended to assume that Dirae I precedes Dirae II, but there is nothing that clearly proves this. The two texts (at least the two 'original' texts) seem in fact to be very close to one another in date: the lettering of the two texts is similar in both size and style, as are the general layout of the two inscriptions (*stoichedon*, interpuncts) and their vocabulary and syntax.[120] It is likely that the original dimensions of the stones were identical: the width of Dirae I seems to have been *c*.0.47–0.48m, while the width of Dirae II is 0.46–0.47m. Furthermore, both texts were subject to an accumulation of additional clauses over time: one additional pair of clauses in the case of Dirae I (lines 42–53), and apparently three additional groups of clauses in the case of Dirae II (Faces B and C).

The most obvious difference between Dirae I and Dirae II is of course that Dirae I is concerned with Teos alone, while Dirae II is concerned with both

---

[117] *IG* I³ 244 (Osborne and Rhodes 2017, no. 107; Lambert 2019, 21–31), B3–12: καὶ τὰ κοιν[ὰ] τὰ Σκαμβονιδῶν σοô καὶ ἀποδόσο παρὰ τὸν εὔθυνον τὸ καθῆκον; B15–21, hό τι ἂν τὸν κοινὸν μὲ ἀποδιδôσιν παρὰ τὸν εὔθυνο[ν π]ρὸ [- -].

[118] Herrmann 1981, 8 takes the genitive [Ἀβ]δηριτέων closely with [τὸ ξ]υνô, 'wenn die Gemeinde der Abderiten es zurückfordert'; we prefer to take the genitive [Ἀβ]δηριτέων as dependent on a lost noun preceding (note the position of the participle ἀ[π]αιτέο[ν|τος]).

[119] Herrmann 1981, 8, 23.

[120] Herrmann 1981, 4–5, 23–5.

Teos and Abdera. But there is a further difference of the first importance between the two texts. As far as we can tell, every single one of the curses inscribed on Dirae II is directed at serving magistrates alone: this is certain for the curse in Dirae II, lines A5–10 (ὃς ἂν τιμὴν ἔχων, A5–6), and is highly likely for the curses in A1–5 (if we are correct to see this passage as concerned with the public confiscation of private property) and in C1–4 (return of public funds at the end of a magistrate's term of office). Similarly, the majority of the oaths recorded on Dirae II (A10–24) seem only to make sense if directed at serving magistrates (especially A13–16: public confiscation of property, imprisonment, execution; by definition, a private citizen could not confiscate another's property). It is therefore worth seriously considering the possibility that Dirae II is not in fact a document intended to be binding on the entire citizen bodies of Teos and Abdera, but only on their leading magistrates— that is to say, the oaths in Dirae II, lines A10–24, are not a 'Bürgereid' (Herrmann) but an 'Amtseid' or oath of office. It is noteworthy that some of the closest parallels for these oaths are found in the Athenian bouleutic oath (i.e. an oath taken by magistrates).[121]

In stark contrast to Dirae II, not a single one of the curses in Dirae I is explicitly directed against serving magistrates, and many of them are clearly intended to bear upon the entire citizen body of Teos—most obviously Dirae I, lines 42–53, the 'additional' curses against anyone who makes harmful drugs or who prevents grain-imports.[122] Furthermore, as indicated in our commentary to Dirae I, some of the closest parallels for the content of Dirae I are to be found in the early third-century citizen-oath of the Cretan city of Itanos, sworn by the entire citizen body, where we find oaths not to betray the city, territory or islands of Itanos (lines 9–11, cf. Dirae I, 12–15), not to initiate or participate in revolutionary activity (lines 16–19, cf. Dirae I, 3–8), and not to plot any evil concerning the city (lines 27–8, cf. Dirae I, 23–5); those who do any of these things are subject to a curse (lines 44–9).[123] But the closest and most striking parallels come from the curse known to have been performed by the herald before each meeting of the Athenian *ekklēsia* and *boulē* in the

---

[121] Herrmann 1981, 16–17; cf. Rhodes 1972, 189, 194; Sommerstein and Bayliss 2013, 40–3. We have argued above that the clause in Dirae II, lines A5–10, is closely parallel to a clause in the Athenian assembly-curses against orators who deceive Athenian democratic bodies.

[122] The curse in Dirae I, lines 8–10, is the exception that proves the rule: the curse is not directed against a serving magistrate, but against anyone who might *in future* set himself up as an *aisymnētēs*— and the main force of the clause is in fact to protect whichever private individual might slay this potential future *aisymnētēs* (lines 10–11).

[123] *I.Cret.* III iv 8 (*Syll.*[3] 526).

Classical period.[124] Categories of person known to have featured in the Athenian 'assembly-curse' include the following:

(1) those who plot any evil against the city: εἴ τις ἐπιβουλεύει τι τῷ δήμῳ κακόν (Ar. *Thesm.* 335); cf. Dirae I, 23–5, ὅστις...[τι κ]ακὸν βολεύοι περὶ Τ[ηΐ]ων τὸ ξυνὸ;

(2) those who make overtures to the Persians (Isoc. 4.157, Ar. *Thesm.* 336–7), cf. Dirae I, 26–7;

(3) those who attempt to become tyrant or join in restoring a tyrant: εἴ τις...ἢ τυραννεῖν ἐπινοεῖ ἢ τὸν τύραννον συνκατάγειν (Ar. *Thesm.* 338–9); cf. Dirae I, 3–6, ὅστις ἢ αἰσυ[μ]νήτη⟨ν⟩ [ἰσται]η ἢ ἐπανισταῖτο ⟨ἐπ'⟩ αἰ[συμ]νηίηι;

(4) those who betray the city: εἴ τις εἰδὼς ἐκείνους προδέδωκεν (Dem. 23.97, cf. Lyc. *Leocr.* 29–31, προδότης τῆς πατρίδος; Ar. *Thesm.* 346, προδιδοῦσα); cf. Dirae I, 12–14, [ὅσ]⟨τι⟩ς προδο⟨ίη ἢ⟩ τὴ⟨ν⟩ πόλ⟨ι⟩[ν ἢ τὴν χώραν] τὴν Τηΐων.

These analogies are far too close to be coincidental. We think that Dirae I must be, in essence, an assembly-curse, very closely comparable in both form and content to the assembly-curse performed at Athens at the beginning of each meeting of the *ekklēsia*. 'In essence' an assembly-curse, since we are told that the curse in Dirae I is in fact only to be performed three times a year, at the festivals of the Anthesteria, Herakleia, and Dieia. Then again, we have no way of knowing how active the assembly was at Teos in the early fifth century BC: it is theoretically possible that the Teian popular assembly only met to vote on measures three times a year; or perhaps the Teians did not perform the curse before each assembly-meeting.[125]

We therefore suggest that we should see Dirae I and Dirae II as precisely contemporary and complementary texts, directed at different subsets of the citizen body. Dirae II is a set of curses directed specifically and solely at serving magistrates at both Teos and Abdera (the *timouchoi* and treasurers), incorporating the wording of a magistrates' oath (the 'Amtseid', A10–24).[126]

---

[124] Rhodes 1972, 36–7; Sommerstein and Bayliss 2013, 48–50. The curse seems to have concluded with a very similar curse-formula to that found in Dirae I, to judge from the paraphrases in Dem. 19.71 (εὔχεσθ' ἐξώλη ποιεῖν αὐτὸν καὶ γένος καὶ οἰκίαν) and Ar. *Thesm.* 349–50 (κακῶς ἀπολέσθαι τοῦτον αὐτὸν κᾠκίαν ἀρᾶσθε). Both *ekklēsia* and *boulē*: Dem. 19.70.

[125] The norm in the wider Greek world seems to have been monthly assembly-meetings: Rhodes with Lewis 1997, 503–6.

[126] Hitherto, scholars have generally assumed that the curses and oaths of Dirae II are binding on the entire citizen bodies of Teos and Abdera, and that it is only their oral proclamation that is delegated to the magistrates: thus implicitly Herrmann 1981, 13–14, 28 (calling the oaths a 'Bürgereid', 'citizen-oath'); more explicitly, Hawke 2011, 122–3; Sommerstein and Bayliss 2013, 10 ('citizenship oath' sworn by 'Teian youths'). Rubinstein 2007, 283 is more cautious: 'it is not absolutely clear whether the oath was to be sworn by all citizens of Teos or specifically by incoming officials only'.

Dirae I, by contrast, is an assembly-curse, incorporating at least one promise of immunity for public benefactors (lines 10–11), bearing on the citizen body of the city of Teos alone, and performed on their behalf by the Teian *timouchoi*. Presumably the two stones were set up side by side, to be read out one after the other at the three relevant festivals.

It is, finally, worth asking the question whether the Teian 'assembly-curse' (Dirae I) and the Teian/Abderite 'magistrates' oath and curse' (Dirae II) might have been directly influenced by contemporary Athenian practice. Here, unfortunately, we are reduced to speculation, since we have no other evidence for the form and content of assembly-curses or magistrates' oaths elsewhere in the Greek world in the fifth century BC: we have no way of knowing whether Teian or Athenian oaths and curses were in any way atypical of wider Greek civic practices. There is some reason to think that the Athenians occasionally interfered in the constitutions of allied cities, particularly after revolt: the most famous example is the decree for Erythrai, perhaps of the late 450s BC, in which some of the arrangements for the *boulē* at Erythrai mirror Athenian practice. There are also signs that cities within the Athenian sphere of influence began to imitate Athenian decree-formulae in the later fifth century (Miletos and Kyzikos are the clearest examples).[127] But the date of the Teian Dirae (probably the 470s BC) seems too early for direct Athenian influence; it is therefore preferable to assume a parallel but independent development.

Dirae II again: the relationship between Teos and Abdera

We can now return to the critical and delicate question as to what precisely Dirae II indicates about the relationship between Teos and Abdera in (probably) the 470s BC. Opinions have here varied widely, sometimes resting heavily on what we have argued to be incorrect interpretations of Dirae II, lines A6–7.[128] Strictly speaking, we only know for certain that Teos and Abdera followed common practice in the sphere of office-holding and the control of magistrates: as we have seen, Dirae II is solely directed at serving magistrates (*timouchoi* and treasurers), and Dirae I (the Teian 'assembly-curses') makes no mention of Abdera. But it would be perilous to assume that Abdera did not have its own set of assembly-curses closely modelled on—or precisely

---

[127] Erythrai: Osborne and Rhodes 2017, no. 121. Miletos and Kyzikos: Lewis 1984; Rhodes with Lewis 1997, 552. On Athenian 'promotion' of democratic institutions, Brock 2009.

[128] Graham 1991 ('adopted Teians' at Teos); D'Alessio 1992, Osborne and Rhodes 2017, 13 ('adopted Teians' at Abdera); Effenterre and Ruzé 1994–5, 374 ('reunited Teians' at Teos).

reproducing—the Teian assembly-curses. As we have seen, there is good reason to think that at least one of the curses of Dirae I (directed against bandits and pirates) had a very close analogy at Abdera, employing identical (rare) vocabulary.[129] Our default assumption ought surely to be that the two cities used identical—or at least closely aligned—sets of curses and oaths for both magistrates (Dirae II) and the wider citizen body (Dirae I and its putative Abderite 'sister'-inscription).

By what agency was the text of Dirae II generated? There are, formally speaking, four possibilities: that the Teians were able to legislate unilaterally for both cities; that the Abderites were able to legislate unilaterally for both cities; that the two communities developed the legislation consensually; or that an external power imposed common legislation on the two cities. The last possibility can surely be ruled out: although Athens was certainly in a position to impose constitutional arrangements on both Teos and Abdera, it is hard to see why they might have wished to introduce political practices bearing on these two cities alone (exile from Teos and Abdera alone, rather than from all allied cities). The phraseological 'asymmetry' of Dirae II may point towards Teian agency: in clauses where both cities are mentioned, Teos always appears first (A16–22, D1–11, B5–11, apparently C1); Teos once appears alone (A5–7: magistrates for the 'Teian collectivity', with no mention of Abdera); and in two places the phraseology is more comprehensive for Teos than for Abdera (A18–20, an additional legal clause concerning Teian trials; B7–9, 'Teos and Abdera and the land of Teos').[130] However, it is risky to place too much weight on this, since we only have the 'Teian copy' of Dirae II: it is quite possible that a putative Abderite copy of Dirae II would have reversed this asymmetry of wording.

Nonetheless, if one of the two cities was in a position to legislate for the other, it is surely more likely that Teos, as the 'senior' (albeit significantly smaller) city of the two, was legislating for Abdera rather than vice versa. Perhaps the most economical hypothesis is that Dirae II is an expansion or elaboration of a piece of joint-legislation established at the time of the original Teian (re-)foundation of Abdera in the mid-sixth century BC. It is reasonable to assume that when the Teians re-founded Abdera in the mid-540s BC, they brought with them the Teian festival calendar (the shared festivals of Dirae II: Anthesteria, Herakleia, Dia) and the Teian structure of civic magistracies (*timouchoi* and *tamiai*), and it is plausible enough that they would also have

---

[129] See above, on Dirae I, lines 18–22, and its relationship to Demokritos Fr. B 260 Diels–Kranz.
[130] On this asymmetry, Herrmann 1981, 28; Graham 1992, 56.

transplanted any pre-existing system of controls on magistrates (a magistrates' oath and associated curses).[131] On this hypothesis, links between mother-city and colony would have continued to be sufficiently close in the late sixth and early fifth century that subsequent additions to the repertoire of curses (e.g. curses against a potential *aisymnētēs*) would have been automatically added to the constitutions of both cities.

How, therefore, should we conceive the political relationship between the two cities at the time of the erection of Dirae I and II?[132] We see no reason to think that Teos exercised any kind of ongoing political hegemony over Abdera, nor that the two cities formed a single political entity (a *sympoliteia*). As Graham noted—following a hint by Jeanne and Louis Robert—a reasonably close analogy is found in the case of Paros and her colony Thasos. By the fifth century BC at the latest, Thasos (like Abdera) was a considerably larger and more powerful city than her erstwhile mother-city, and there is no reason to think that either city enjoyed any kind of hegemony over the other. But in the mid-sixth century BC, a single individual (a certain Akeratos) could serve as magistrate in both cities, and in the mid-fourth century, the Parians could honour an Athenian general as a benefactor of both the Parians and the Thasians.[133] This kind of relationship, where 'the legal division between the two states was slightly blurred' (Graham's phrase), seems to bring us reasonably close to the situation at Teos and Abdera.

However, by far the closest parallel is the relationship between Miletos and her Pontic colony Olbia. In the late fourth century BC, perhaps between 325 and 311 BC, the Milesians erected a *stēlē* reaffirming the ancestral links between Miletos and her Pontic colony Olbia.[134] The two cities enjoyed a relationship of *isopoliteia*, such that Milesians who settled in Olbia enjoyed full citizen rights there (and vice versa); citizens of one city were permitted to act as office-holders in the other. The inscription includes a clause to the effect that Milesians in Olbia 'are to participate in the curses on the thirtieth days (*triakades*), just as they participate in the curses at Miletos' (ἐπαρᾶσθαι ταῖς τριακάσιγ, καθάσσα καὶ ἐμ Μιλήτωι ἐπαρῶνται).[135] The precise institutional context is obscure: in

---

[131] It is perfectly possible that Teos already had some kind of democratic or participatory constitution in the mid-sixth century BC: Chios certainly did (Robinson 1997, 90–101).

[132] The fullest and most helpful discussion is that of Graham 1992, 56–9, drawing on Herrmann 1981, 26–30; see further Koerner 1993, 303 (agnostic); Reiche 2006, 188 n. 10; Youni 2007, 734–5.

[133] Graham 1992, 59 (following Robert and Robert 1976, 213), on *IG* XII Suppl. 412 and *IG* XII 5, 114; see also Pouilloux 1989; Osborne 2009, 108–10.

[134] *Milet* I 3, 136 (Rhodes and Osborne 2003, no. 93); for the date, *SEG* 37, 982.

[135] The clause is convincingly thus interpreted by Ehrhardt 1988, 237 and 542 (cf. *SEG* 37, 982), after a suggestion by Peter Herrmann; followed by J. Vinogradov, *BE* 1990, 499, and by Herrmann in *Milet* VI 1, p. 170.

particular, it is very unclear what the 'thirtieth days' (*triakades*) might be (assembly-meetings on the thirtieth day of every month, or a single annual event?).[136] For our purposes, the crucial thing is that both Miletos and her colony Olbia employed *parallel* sets of public curses, such that participation in the Olbian public curses at the *triakades* could be conceived as precisely analogous to participation in public curses at Miletos. Although we have no evidence for the content of the Milesian/Olbian curses, it is likely enough that we are dealing with a situation broadly similar to that attested in Dirae I and II: a set of public oaths and curses that are shared between colony and mother-city, perhaps going back to the original colonial foundation, which remained in force at both cities— perhaps in the same institutional or festival context (if the *triakades* were held at both Olbia and Miletos)—many years later.

Further than this our evidence does not allow us to go. But there is no good reason to think that the close institutional, legal, and religious relationship between Teos and Abdera attested in the Teian Dirae was in any way unusual. As we have seen, the Teian curses themselves find close analogies in the public curses in force at Athens in the same period, and the existence of 'shared' curses at Teos and Abdera may well find a close analogy in the public curses of Miletos and her colony Olbia.

The 'afterlife' of the Teian Dirae

The performance of public curses at Teos continued well into the Hellenistic period, as we learn from three Teian inscriptions of the third and second centuries BC. The precise relationship between these Hellenistic curses and the inscribed fifth-century documents is not entirely clear, and hence the evidence needs to be laid out in some detail.

The earliest Hellenistic evidence for an ongoing tradition of public curses at Teos is a lengthy and difficult inscription, apparently dating to either *c.*302 or 287/6 BC, recording a major pirate raid on Teos and its consequences.[137] The pirates—perhaps acting in the interests of either Demetrios Poliorketes or his rival Lysimachos—have carried off a large number of Teian hostages, for whom the city needs to pay a substantial ransom. The Teians have decided

---

[136] We have no particular reason to think that Day 30 was a standard day for assembly-meetings at Miletos or Olbia, although a third-century proxeny decree of Olbia was passed on the thirtieth day of an unstated month (*SEG* 31, 710).

[137] *SEG* 44, 949; re-edited by Meier 2017 (for the date, 167–72), and again (with important new readings and restorations) by Hamon 2018. We refer to Hamon's revised text throughout.

to raise the money through loans from private citizens, raised by subscription, to be paid back by the city in future at 10 per cent interest. The stone carries two separate decrees, followed by a list of those who have lent money to the city. Only the end of the first decree survives, with an account of future honours to be conferred on those civic magistrates (*stratēgoi* and *timouchoi*) who show particular energy on the city's behalf in the crisis, and curses against both magistrates and private citizens who do not follow the stipulations of the decree. The relevant passage for our purposes reads as follows (Decree I, lines 9–13):[138]

$$[\dot{a}\rho\hat{a}\sigma\theta\alpha\iota\ \delta\dot{\epsilon}]$$

10 [τὸν] κήρυκα [πρὸς] ταῖς ἄλλαις ἀραῖς καθ᾽ ἕκαστον [ἔτος ὤιτι]-
[νι? ἄ]ρχων μὴ ἐ[κτε]λ[ο]ίη δυνατὸς ὢν τὰ ἐψηφισμένα τ[ῆι πόλει? ἢ]
[ἄρχ]ων ἢ ἰδι[ώτης μὴ] αὐτὸς ποιοῖ τὰ τῆς ἀποδόσεως [τὰ ἐν? τοῖ]-
[ς ψη]φίσμα[σι? ἃ ἐψηφί]σατο ἡ πόλις ἐπὶ πρυτάνεως Μέ[ντορος?]

'Each [year, in addition to] the other curses, [let the] herald [curse anyone who] as magistrate does not [execute] the things decreed by [the city] if he is able to do so, [or any magistr]ate or private citizen who does not himself perform the things concerning the repayment (of the loans) [as stipulated in the] decrees [which] the city voted on when Me[ntor] was prytane.'

This clause shows that in the early Hellenistic period, a series of public curses was performed each year at Teos, apparently by the city's herald. (There is no mention of the herald in the fifth-century curses from Teos.) The decree adds a further pair of public curses to the traditional repertoire: a curse against any magistrate who does not carry out the actions required of him in the present decree if he is capable of doing so, and a curse against any magistrate or private citizen who does not assist in the process of reimbursing the city's creditors. Presumably both curses are only to be performed until such time as all of the creditors have been paid back in full. The likely wording of the curse is indicated by a passage in the second decree of the 'pirates' dossier. All inhabitants of Teos, both citizens and resident foreigners, are to swear a collective oath not to seek to acquire luxury goods of certain specified kinds, presumably until the city's debts have been repaid.[139] The herald is to perform a

---

[138] Following the text and interpretation of Hamon 2018, 339–44.
[139] Hamon 2018, 361–2.

public prayer at the Dionysia and the Thesmophoria, invoking curses on anyone who breaks the oath (Decree II, lines 60–2):

60   [εὔξασ]-
[θαι δὲ τὸν κήρυ]κα τοῖς Διονυσίοις καὶ τοῖς Θεσμοφορίοις τῶι ἐμμένοντι [τῶι ὅρκωι]
[ἄμεινον εἶναι, τ]ὸν δὲ μὴ ἐξώλη εἶναι καὶ αὐτ[ὸ]ν καὶ γένος τὸ ἐκείνου.

'[Let the hera]ld [pray] at the Dionysia and the Thesmophoria [that it should be
for the better] for the one who observes [the oath], and that he who does not
should be destroyed, both him and his descendants.'

The curse-formula in line 62 is very similar to that found in Dirae I and II
(normally κένον or τοῦτον ἀπόλλυσθαι καὶ αὐτὸν καὶ γένος τὸ κένο, 'may he be
destroyed, both him and his descendants'), and we are clearly dealing with a
conventional Teian procedure for cursing malefactors. The two festivals listed
here (the Dionysia and the Thesmophoria) are different from those listed in
Dirae I and II (Anthesteria, Herakleia, and Dia), but there is no reason to suppose that this reflects a change in the Teian festival calendar.[140] Unlike the
curse in Decree I of the 'pirates inscription', this prayer is not an addition to
the city's standard repertoire of public curses. Since the oath that it under-
writes was to be performed by both citizens and resident foreigners, it is
understandable that the Teians should have chosen to have this prayer performed at the city's largest annual festival, the Dionysia, at which resident
foreigners could be expected to be present; similarly, since the oath also limits
luxurious expenditure on female dress (Decree II, lines 47–9), it is natural
enough that the prayer should also be performed at the chief women's festival
at Teos, the Thesmophoria.[141]

At an uncertain date in the early Hellenistic period, but at any event not too
distant in time from the 'pirates inscription', the city of Teos absorbed a neighbouring community, the small town of Kyrbissos, in a political union
(*sympoliteia*).[142] As we learn from a long inscription detailing arrangements
for the future administration of Kyrbissos, the town lost its autonomy, and
was henceforth treated as a 'fort' or 'stronghold' (χωρίον) of Teos, under the

---

[140] As postulated by Meier 2017, 154.
[141] On the Thesmophoria in Ionia, see Schipporeit 2013, 277–311.
[142] Date: Hamon 2018, 374 (early third century); Adak 2021, 237–9 (end of fourth century, under
Antigonos). On *sympoliteiai* in Hellenistic Asia Minor, see Reger 2004; Walser 2009; Schuler 2010.

authority of a Teian garrison-commander (φρούραρχος).[143] Much of the extant inscription is concerned with the appointment and duties of the Teian phrourarch, who holds office for only four months, and may not then serve again for a five-year period. The text includes a set of penalties against any phrourarch who refuses to hand over the fort of Kyrbissos at the end of his term of office (lines 21–7):

ὃς δ' ἂν παραλαβὼν
τὸ χωρίον μὴ παραδῶ[ι τ]ῶι φρουράρχω[ι] τῶ[ι] ὑπὸ τῆς πόλεως ἀποστ[ελ]-
λομένωι ἀεὶ καθ' ἑκάστην τετράμη[νο]ν, φ[ε]ύγειν τε αὐτὸν ἀραῖον
ἐκ Τέω καὶ ἐξ Ἀβδήρων καὶ ἐκ τῆς χώρας καὶ τῆς Τηΐων καὶ τῆς Ἀβδηρ[ι]-
25   τῶν καὶ τὰ ὄντα αὐτοῦ δη[μό]σια ε[ἶ]ναι, καὶ ὃς ἂν ἀποκτείνηι αὐτὸν μ[ὴ]
μιαρὸς ἔστω· ἐὰν δὲ μαχόμενος [ἀποθάνηι, ὑπάρχ]ε[ι]ν αὐτοῦ δημόσια τὰ ὄντα.

'Whoever, having taken over the stronghold, does not hand it over to the phrourarch sent out on each occasion by the *polis* for each four-month period, let him be exiled under a curse from Teos and from Abdera and from the territories of both the Teians and the Abderites, and let his property be made public, and may whoever kills him not be polluted; and if such a man dies in battle, let his property be made public.'

The stipulation of exile from both Teos and Abdera is startling, and it is obviously tempting to assume that the early fifth-century legal and institutional 'contract' between the two cities (whatever its precise character might have been: see above) was still in place unchanged in the early Hellenistic period. However, some caution is in order. As Herrmann already saw, the comprehensive curse-formula here is essentially an expansion and clarification of a curse-formula already found in Dirae II, lines B5–12: τοῦτον [ἀ]πόλλυσθαι : ἐκ Τέω : κ[α]ὶ Ἀβδήρ[ω]ν : [κ]αὶ γῆς : [Τηΐ]η[ς] καὶ α[ὐ]τὸν : καὶ γένο[ς :] τὸ κεῖνο, 'let this man perish from Teos and Abdera and the land of Teos, both him and his descendants'.[144] The rather allusive wording of Dirae II, ἀπόλλυσθαι ἐκ Τέω, 'perish from Teos', is expanded in the Teos–Kyrbissos text into the more explicit φεύγειν … ἀραῖον ἐκ Τέω, 'be exiled from Teos under a curse', with the further specifications that the individual's

---

[143] Robert and Robert 1976 (*SEG* 26, 1306); see further Gray 2015, 146–9. On the term χωρίον in this context, Schuler 1998, 50–1. The site of Kyrbissos has now been plausibly identified with a small fortified settlement at Kocadömen Tepe, 18km north-east of Teos: Koparal 2013.

[144] Herrmann 1981, 22–3.

property be confiscated and anyone be permitted to kill him without incurring pollution. Likewise, the phraseology of lines 25–6 (ὃς ἂν ἀποκτείνηι αὐτὸν μ[ὴ] μιαρὸς ἔστω) is suggestively close to the wording of our new restoration in Dirae I, lines 8–11 ([κεῖνον] ὃς ἂν κ[α]⟨τ⟩α[κ]τε⟨ί⟩νει [μὴ μι]αρὸν ⟨εἶ⟩να[ι]). As we have seen, the idea of cursing a magistrate who does not relinquish his office at the end of his normal term is already found in Dirae II, lines C1–4, which is best understood as a curse against magistrates who do not return public funds at the end of their term of office (see above). The use of curses as a deterrent to impel civic magistrates to leave office after a fixed term is also attested at Erythrai in the early fifth century BC, but as Lene Rubinstein has noted, the Teos–Kyrbissos text is in fact the sole surviving example of such a curse from any part of the Greek world in the late Classical or Hellenistic periods.[145]

We should therefore take seriously the idea that the inclusion of exile from Abdera in the curse against rogue phrourarchs in the Teos–Kyrbissos text is essentially *conventional* in character. That is not to say that it does not mean exactly what it says: we have to assume that the early Hellenistic Abderites were quite content for the Teians to legislate in this way on their behalf (and perhaps vice versa).[146] Rather, the curse in the Teos–Kyrbissos text reflects a long-standing Teian and Abderite process for dealing with civic magistrates who fail to withdraw from office at the end of their normal term: exile under a curse from both cities. In the early fifth century, as we learn from Dirae II, the two cities shared a single process for dealing with magistrates who overstepped their powers; the Teos–Kyrbissos text suggests that this process was still operational, in (so far as we can tell) an effectively unchanged form, around the turn of the fourth to third century BC. But the persistence of a conventional legal institution need not necessarily mean that the exceptionally close fifth-century ties between the two cities in the social and religious sphere also persisted down into the early Hellenistic period. The convention that exiles from one city are also exiled from the other could, in theory, be a 'fossilized' institution, no longer reflecting the real social character of the relationship between the two cities.

There is one final piece of evidence to suggest that not only the general tradition of public cursing, but the specific public curses recorded in Dirae I

---

[145] Rubinstein 2007, 273–4, citing *I.Erythrai* 1 (Koerner 1993, 277–81, no. 74).

[146] Robert and Robert 1976, 213: 'le décret de Téos légifère en banissant le phrourarque rebelle du territoire d'Abdère, comme de celui de Téos; il n'y a pas à négocier avec la colonie pour cela; il y a en ce cas un accord préalable et fundamental; c'est le domaine du droit criminel, exactement dans le cas d'un crime contre l'État'.

and Dirae II, continued to be in force at Teos throughout the Hellenistic period. At some point in the early second century BC, a certain Polythrous son of Onesimos gifted a large sum of money (34,000 drachms) for the establishment of a school at Teos, for the benefit of all free children at Teos, both boys and girls (Fig. 1.9 above).[147] Towards the end of the decree, we read the following (lines B60–4):

60   ἀναγγελλέτωσαν δὲ οἱ ἑκάστοτε γινόμενοι τιμοῦχοι πρὸς τῆι ἀρᾶι, ὅστις τὸ
ἀργύριον τὸ ἐπιδοθὲν ὑπὸ Πολυθροῦ τοῦ Ὀνησίμου εἰς τὴν παιδείαν τῶν ἐλευθέ-
ρων παίδων ⟨κ⟩ι⟨ν⟩ήσειεν τρόπωι τινὶ ἢ παρευρέσει ἡιοῦν ἢ ἄλληι που καταχωρίσειεν
καὶ μὴ εἰς ἃ ἐν τῶι νόμωι διατέτακτα⟨ι⟩ ἢ μὴ συντελοίη τὰ συντεταγμένα ἐν τῶι
νόμωι, ἐξώλης εἴηι καὶ αὐτὸς καὶ γένος τὸ ἐκείνου.

'May the *timouchoi* in office each year announce, in addition to the curse, that whoever diverts the money granted by Polythrous son of Onesimos for the education of free children in any manner or on any pretext, or who allocates it in any other manner than for the purposes laid down in the law, or who fails to fulfil the instructions in the law, that he should be destroyed, both him and his descendants.'

The natural interpretation of the phrase ἀναγγελλέτωσαν…πρὸς τῆι ἀρᾶι (B60) is that the Teian *timouchoi* are to add this new curse (against anyone who misuses Polythrous' endowment) to an existing series of curses pronounced each year by the *timouchoi*.[148] The form of the curse itself (ἐξώλης εἴηι καὶ αὐτὸς καὶ γένος τὸ ἐκείνου, 'may he be destroyed, both him and his descendants') is once again very similar to that found in both Dirae I and Dirae II (τοῦτον ἀπόλλυσθαι καὶ αὐτὸν καὶ γένος τὸ κένο, 'may he be destroyed, both him and his descendants'). It is hard not to suppose that we are dealing here with a formulaic 'addition' to the standard set of curses performed each year by the Teian *timouchoi*—not, in fact, fundamentally different in kind from the 'additional' curses inscribed on Faces B and C of Dirae II (and at the bottom of Dirae I) at some point fairly soon after the erection of the original *stēlai*. Once again, as Rubinstein has shown, the curse in the Polythrous

[147] *Syll.*³ 578.
[148] One might have expected the plural πρὸς ταῖς ἀραῖς, as in the 'pirates inscription' (Decree I, line 10, [πρὸς] ταῖς ἄλλαις ἀραῖς) but note that Dirae I uses the singular ἡ ἐπαρή to refer to the whole sequence of public curses inscribed across more than one *stēlē* (Dirae I, lines 30, 34–5, 36).

inscription has no parallels anywhere else in the Greek world in the late
Classical or Hellenistic periods.[149]

As will be clear, we believe that the close connections between the curses in
these three later Teian texts (the 'pirates inscription' of c.300 BC, the early
Hellenistic Teos–Kyrbissos *sympoliteia*, and the second-century school-
foundation of Polythrous) and the curses inscribed on Dirae I and II are not
accidental. Instead, they reflect not only a continued 'tradition of public cursing' at Teos, but the continuing validity and use, right down into the later
Hellenistic period, of the very inscribed fifth-century Teian curses that we can
still read today.[150] There is nothing problematic about very old inscribed laws
continuing to be used and consulted in much later periods—one need only
think of the ongoing use of Solon's *axones* and *kyrbeis* in Classical Athens, or
of the Twelve Tables in late Republican and early imperial Rome. That our
evidence for public curses in Hellenistic Teos might reflect continued use specifically of the inscribed Dirae, rather than a more general ongoing 'tradition
of cursing', is supported both by the fact that the Hellenistic curses at Teos
have so few parallels anywhere else in the Greek world (as Rubinstein has correctly highlighted), and by the close verbal similarities between the Hellenistic
curses (particularly the curse against phrourarchs in the Teos–Kyrbissos *sympoliteia*) and the wording of Dirae I and II.

In this chapter, we have argued that the 'Teian Dirae' themselves may in fact
be rather less idiosyncratic documents than they appear at first sight, and
that the kind of relationship they imply between Teos and Abdera in the
early fifth century BC (and in later periods) might not have been radically
atypical of colony–mother-city relations in the Greek world. But as the new
decree of the Abderites for Teos makes abundantly clear, the events of the
160s BC make it very difficult to sustain the position that Teos and Abdera
were bound by no closer ties than those linking any other mother-city to
its colony.

With the questionable exception of the Teos–Kyrbissos text (discussed
above), we have no direct evidence for diplomatic or other relations between
Teos and Abdera at any point between the early fifth and early second centuries BC.[151] As we have seen, the tribute paid by the two cities to Athens in the
mid-fifth century BC (Teos normally six talents, Abdera normally fifteen

---

[149] Rubinstein 2007, 274–5.   [150] Thus already Lambrinudakis and Wörrle 1983, 310–11.
[151] The Athenian comic poet Eupolis, in his *Kolakes* of 421 BC, referred to the philosopher
Protagoras of Abdera as 'Protagoras the Teian' (Fr. 157 Kassel–Austin, from Diog. Laert. 9.50); it is
conceivable that Protagoras had citizenship in both cities (but note the caution of Graham 1992, 57).

talents) strongly suggests that Abdera was a considerably more prosperous and populous place than her mother-city, but that relationship seems to have been reversed in the course of the fourth and third centuries BC. In the fourth century BC, Abdera suffered a series of major exogenous shocks, the first and perhaps most significant of which was a massive military defeat by the Triballi in 375 BC, in which the Abderites 'are said to have lost the most men in the shortest time of any city of comparable size'.[152] In the second half of the fourth century BC, the entire urban centre of Abdera was relocated to the south: the Archaic settlement (the 'North Enclosure': Chapter 2 above) was abandoned, and a new 'South Enclosure' was laid out on a grid-plan immediately to the south.[153] The new urban centre, covering an area of around 1.125km^2, was ringed on three sides by an impressive new fortification wall, around 4,965m in length, large parts of which are preserved today; to the south, the new city was open to the sea.[154] The precise chronology and motivations for this relocation remain somewhat unclear. The embayment to the west of the North Enclosure seems to have been entirely silted up by the mid-fourth century BC, but there is also a massive destruction level across the North Enclosure, apparently dating to the late fourth century BC.[155] It is tempting to wonder whether the destruction of the North Enclosure and the subsequent reloca-tion of the city to the South Enclosure might be associated with the conquest of Abdera by Philip II (probably dating to 347 BC), but coin-finds from the North Enclosure (including numerous Abderite bronzes of c.346–336 BC) seem to indicate that the destruction should be dated somewhat later in the fourth century.[156] Our knowledge of the history of Abdera in the early Hellenistic period is wretchedly poor, but to judge from the coinage struck by the city in the third and second centuries, the city seems never to have recovered anything like its fifth-century prosperity.[157] As we will see in the next chapter, the fate of Teos in the Hellenistic period was quite different.

[152] Aen. Tact. 15.8–10 (quotation); Diod. Sic. 15.36.1–4; Isaac 1986, 106; Graham 1992, 64–5; Veligianni 1995, 158–70; K. Kallintzi 2012, 134–6.

[153] Chryssanthaki 2001, 397–402; Triandaphyllos 2004; K. Kallintzi 2018, 23–5.

[154] K. Kallintzi 2012, 136–9.

[155] Destruction level: Chryssanthaki 2001, 397–8; cf. Koukouli-Chrysanthaki 2004, 247.

[156] Chryssanthaki 2001, 398–400; note also *IG* II³ I, 302 (pro-Athenian Abderite refugees in Athens, 345 BC). The Classical city at Cape Molyvoti, between Abdera and Maroneia, also seems to have been destroyed around the middle of the fourth century BC: Arrington et al. 2016, 24; and see Chapter 5 below.

[157] Chryssanthaki-Nagle 2007, 141–8 (silver: nothing after the early third century), 201–324 (bronze).

4

Teos in the Second Century BC
(Documents 4–5)

The history, institutions, and culture of Teos between the late fourth and the late second century BC are known to us in unusually rich and circumstantial detail, thanks above all to the city's abundant and varied Hellenistic epigraphic record.[1] Space forbids a full analysis of the city's internal history in this period (much of which is anyway of only marginal significance for relations between Teos and Abdera), and in this chapter we focus on two aspects of Hellenistic Teos of particular relevance to the new Abderite decree for the Teians: the Hellenistic temple and cult of Dionysos at Teos, and the political status and economic condition of Teos in the mid-second century BC.

The Temple and Cult of Dionysos at Teos

The new decree of Abdera for Teos specifies that the Abderite ambassadors to Teos are to request permission to erect a copy of the decree at Teos, either 'in the sanctuary of Dionysos or [(?) in the agora]' (**Document 1**, lines **B80–1**). As is clear from the findspot of the two fragments, the Teians decided to grant permission to erect the decree in the Dionysos sanctuary: both parts of the decree were discovered near one another in the *temenos* of the temple of Dionysos at Teos, a few metres away from the south-west corner of the temple, not far from the findspot of the Antiochos III dossier and the unpublished letters of Ptolemy III and Berenike to the Teians (see below, n. 11). As we will

---

[1] A full corpus of the inscriptions of Teos is currently being prepared by Mustafa Adak. Landmark studies of the Hellenistic history and culture of Teos include Herrmann 1965 (Teos and Antiochos III: see also Ma 2002, esp. 308–21); Robert and Robert 1976 (*sympoliteiai* with Kyrbissos [not later than *c*.300 BC, on the basis of lettering] and an unknown community [Ulamış, late IV BC: see also Chandezon 2003, 205–12]); Rigsby 1996, 280–325 (Teian *asylia* decrees); Aneziri 2003, 71–109 (Teos and the Dionysiac Artists: see also Ma 2007b); Şahin 1994, Meier 2017, and Hamon 2018 (the 'pirates inscription' of *c*.300 BC); Adak and Stauner 2018 (lease of a heroic *temenos*: see also Jones 2019). For Teos in the late fourth and third century BC, see now Adak 2021; for second-century Teos, Boulay 2018.

Teos and Abdera: Two Cities in Peace and War. Mustafa Adak and Peter Thonemann, Oxford University Press.
© Mustafa Adak and Peter Thonemann, 2022. DOI: 10.1093/oso/9780192845429.003.0005

see in Chapter 6, the monumental bronze statue of the *Dēmos* of the Teians erected by the Abderites in the agora at Abdera was very closely modelled on the Hellenistic cult-statue of Dionysos at Teos.

The cult of Dionysos at Teos certainly goes back to at least the mid-sixth century BC, as shown by the mention of the Anthesteria in Dirae I and II (**Documents 2** and **3**, Chapter 3 above) as one of the three major civic festivals shared between Teos and her colony Abdera. It is likely enough that Dionysos was already the chief civic deity of Teos in the Archaic period, a position which he demonstrably occupied at both Teos and Abdera in later periods. Dionysiac motifs are common on the coinages of both Abdera and Teos from the Classical periods onwards, and the god is notably prominent in the poetry of Anakreon of Teos, who refers to the wearing of celery-wreaths at a festival (ἑορτή) of Dionysos (*PMG* F410), presumably at either Teos or Abdera.[2] The Teian Dionysia seems to have been the chief 'international' festival of Teos at least by the time of the 'pirates inscription' of either c.302 or 287/6 BC, in which the herald is required to perform a public prayer at the Dionysia and the Thesmophoria, the former festival apparently selected as one at which resident foreigners would be present.[3] A group of second- and first-century victor-lists from the Teian Dionysia show that in the later Hellenistic period the festival included contests of satyr-plays, tragedies, and comedies, as well as Pyrrhic and other choral dances of men and boys; in the early second century BC, foreign benefactors of Teos seem regularly to have had honorific crowns conferred on them at the Teian Dionysia, 'when we perform choruses to Dionysos'.[4] Similarly, honours for civic benefactors at Hellenistic Abdera were regularly proclaimed at the Abderite Dionysia, and honorific decrees for *proxenoi* and other benefactors seem always to have been inscribed in the sanctuary of Dionysos at Abdera; the priest of Dionysos served as the eponymous magistrate of Abdera in the Hellenistic period.[5]

---

[2] Isaac 1986, 82–4; Cole 1995, 313–16.

[3] Hamon 2018, Decree II, lines 60–2; further discussion in Chapter 3 above.

[4] Satyr-plays and tragedies: Le Guen 2001, no. 46B. Comedy, 'Pyrrhichē', and other choral dance: *CIG* 3089 (re-edited by Adak and Thonemann 2020, 21–5) and 3090. Ma 2007b, 220–32, shows that other second-century thymelic victor-lists from Teos (Le Guen 2001, nos. 46A, C–D; *SEG* 57, 1134–6) concern contests organized by the Dionysiac Artists. Crowns for foreign benefactors: *I.Magnesia* 97, lines 36–47; Glaukos of Magnesia receives *prohedria* at 'the contests held by the city', with proclamation of crowns each year at the Dionysia when choral-dances to Dionysos take place ([ὅταν] τοὺς χοροὺς συντελῶμεν τῶι Διονύσωι). It is not clear whether the Teian Dionysia ever achieved Panhellenic status: *IG* XII 4, 2, 938 (Kos: Augustan), lines A21–2 (a pentathlon victory in the age-class of *paides Pythikoi* at the Teian Dionysia) does not settle the matter. A penteteric Dionysia Kaisareia is attested at Teos in the Roman imperial period: Robert 1937, 34–5. For Dionysia-festivals as a context for public honours in the Hellenistic world, Ceccarelli 2010.

[5] Proclamation of honours at the Dionysia: *IThrakAig* E7, lines 22–5; E8, lines 20–3; E9, lines 19–22; **Document 6** below (Chapter 5), lines 29–31. Inscribing of honours in the sanctuary of

Fig. 4.1. Aerial photograph of the sanctuary of Dionysos at Teos.
Photo courtesy of Musa Kadıoğlu.

The ruins of the great Hellenistic temple of Dionysos are today among the most impressive remains to be seen at Teos (Fig. 4.1), although the temple itself was extensively reworked under Hadrian, somewhat obscuring its original form. The Dionysos-sanctuary was situated in the far western part of the urban centre of Teos, south-west of the acropolis, just within the Hellenistic wall-circuit. The temple itself, in the Ionic order, was the largest temple of Dionysos in the Aegean world, measuring 16.01m × 32.92m between the axes of the corner pillars (a ratio of 1:2.06); the *temenos* was trapezoidal in shape, and covered a vast area of 8,869m².[6] The cult-epithet (*epiklēsis*) under which Dionysos was worshipped at this sanctuary is not known with certainty, but may well have been (*pro*)*kathēgemōn*.[7]

Dionysos: *IThrakAig* E7, lines 28–31 (ἀναγραψάτωσαν οἱ νομοφύλακες εἰς τὸ ἱερὸν [τ]οῦ Διονύσου οὗ αἱ καὶ τῶν ἄλλων προξέ[ν]ων ἀναγεγραμμέναι τιμαί εἰσιν); E8, lines 31–3. Eponym: Sherk 1991, 225; Chryssanthaki 2001, 392; and see our note on **Document 1**, line **B85** (Chapter 1 above).

[6]   Dimensions based on outer edges of the surrounding *temenos*-walls: Kadıoğlu 2020, 176.

[7]   Four second-century *asylia*-decrees from Crete describe Dionysos as '*archēgetēs* of the city' (Rigsby 1996, nos. 154, 155, 159, 161), but this does not seem to be the official cultic *epiklēsis*. The epithet *Sētaneios* (*IGRR* IV 1567) is attested only for a private association of *mystai* in the Roman imperial period. In other imperial-period texts, including a public cult-regulation of the Tiberian period (Sokolowski 1965, no. 28), the god is described as (*pro*)*kathēgemōn*: Robert 1937, 22–7; Robert, *OMS* V, 341 n. 23; Adak and Kadıoğlu 2017, 13–14; Boulay 2018, 146–8.

The Hellenistic temple of Dionysos at Teos is said by Vitruvius to have been designed by the architect Hermogenes, to whom he also attributes the design of the Hellenistic temple of Artemis Leukophryene at Magnesia on the Maeander.[8] Modern scholarship on the chronology of Hermogenes' career is vast and (thus far) inconclusive: the dominant view now seems to be that his chief works should be dated to the period c.220–190 BC, although some scholars prefer to place him in the mid-second century BC.[9] The argument for a 'late' date for Hermogenes is largely based on the presumed second-century dating of the Artemis-temple at Magnesia; at Teos, by contrast, the arguments pointing towards a late third-century date of construction for the Dionysos-temple are very strong. It seems extremely likely that the temple was at least partly complete by c.203 BC, since in that year the Teians voted to erect marble cult-images of Antiochos III and Laodike 'beside the cult statue of Dionysos', and decreed that the royal couple should 'share in the temple and the other rituals/honours to Dionysos'. The second decree of the Teians for Antiochos and Laodike, probably dating to the same year, explicitly specifies that the decree is to be inscribed 'on the *parastas* of the temple of Dionysos'.[10] What exactly the '*parastas* of the temple' might be (not necessarily part of the temple-structure itself) need not concern us here; what matters is that the Antiochos-dossier clearly indicates that the temple-complex was already in existence, complete or incomplete, by c.203 BC.[11]

As the long history of the Dionysos-cult at Teos demonstrates, there must certainly have been a sanctuary to Dionysos at Teos before the construction of the Hermogenes temple.[12] As we will see in Chapter 6, there is some reason to think that an archaic cult-statue of Dionysos is depicted on second-century coins of Teos, no doubt associated with this hypothetical earlier temple of

---

[8] Vitr., *De arch.* 3.3.8; 4.3.1; 7.Pref.12.

[9] The bibliography is vast: see e.g. Davesnes 1987; Hoepfner and Schwandner 1990; Le Guen 2001, I 206–8; Aneziri 2003, 174–9; Bingöl 2012; Bingöl 2013 (with references to other recent work at Magnesia); Uz 2013; Kadıoğlu 2020.

[10] Cult-images: *SEG* 41, 1003 I, lines 44–7. Sharing temple: *SEG* 41, 1003 I, lines 50–1. Inscription on *parastas* of temple: *SEG* 41, 1003 II, lines 104–6 (εἰς τὴν παραστάδα τοῦ νεὼ τοῦ Διονύσου).

[11] Herrmann 1965, 31–3 and 89–93, for the inscription's findspot within the *temenos*, around 20m from the south-west corner of the temple. Herrmann was agnostic on the location of the *parastas*: the current excavators consider it to be a free-standing monument within the *temenos* rather than an integral part of the Dionysos-temple itself. Recent excavations have uncovered letters of Ptolemy III and Berenike II inscribed on a block with identical dimensions, which may therefore belong to the same monument (perhaps back to back with one of the blocks bearing the Antiochos texts). The letter of Berenike II grants autonomy and tax-exemption to the Teians (C 13–14: ὅπως ἐλεύθεροι ὄντε[ς - - -] καὶ ἀφορολόγητο[ι]); see Adak 2021, 258.

[12] It is possible that the sanctuary in which one of the two copies of the *sympoliteia*-agreement between Teos and Kyrbissos (*SEG* 26, 1306: c.300 BC) was to be erected was this hypothetical 'old' sanctuary of Dionysos at Teos; unfortunately, the text breaks off at the critical point (Robert and Robert 1976, 232).

Dionysos. However, repeated excavations in the area of the Hermogenes temple over the past 150 years have uncovered no traces of an earlier temple on the site; recent excavations in the interior of the Hermogenes temple have brought to light no ceramic material dating earlier than around 220–200 BC.[13] This putative pre-third-century temple of Dionysos must therefore have been located elsewhere in the city, and it is highly tempting to wonder whether it might be identified with the late archaic Ionic temple on the Teian acropolis, one of the most spectacular discoveries of the recent Turkish excavations at Teos.[14]

We might note, finally, that the hypothesis of a 'relocation' of the chief Teian sanctuary of Dionysos to a new site in the late third century BC is strongly supported by the curiously marginal location of the Hermogenes temple within the urban plan, squeezed in next to the western city-wall at some distance from the acropolis, the agora, and the other major public buildings of Teos. It is likely enough that, when the Teians decided to 'upgrade' their Dionysos-cult in the late third century, there was simply no space for a vast new temple in the city-centre. According to a tradition preserved by Diodoros, the Teians claimed (like a few other Greek cities: Elis, Naxos, Eleutherai) that Teos was the place of Dionysos' birth: 'and the Teians offer as a visible sign (*tekmērion*) that the god was born among them the fact that right up to the present day, at fixed times, a spring of exceptionally sweet-smelling wine appears of its own accord out of the earth in their city' (3.66.2). It is conceivable that the relatively marginal position of the Hermogenes-temple—perhaps originally outside the Teian wall-circuit?—was justified by its location on the site of this miraculous spring.[15]

At any event, it seems highly likely that construction of this lavish new temple of Dionysos began at some point during the decades when Teos lay within the orbit of Attalos I of Pergamon, to whom the city was probably subject and tributary *c*.229–223 BC and again *c*.218–206 BC.[16] In light of the central place of the cult of Dionysos Kathēgemōn in the self-representation of the

---

[13] Communication from M. Kadıoğlu, 06/02/20.

[14] Kadıoğlu, Özbil, Kerschner, and Mommsen 2015, 353–62 (dating the temple to the third quarter of the sixth century BC).

[15] The distinctive pose of the Hellenistic cult-statue of Dionysos at Teos, pouring wine from a *kantharos* (see Chapter 6 below), may well be intended to evoke the wine-miracle described by Diodoros. For analogous 'wine-miracles' associated with the cult of Dionysos, see Plin. *NH* 2.231 and 31.16 (Andros: also Paus. 6.26.2); Paus. 6.26.1 (Elis); Merkelbach 1988, 54–5. For the possibility that the Teian wine-miracle might be depicted on a relief of uncertain provenance in the İzmir Archaeological Museum (Inv. 241), see Fuchs 2018, 149 (with 157 fig. 2).

[16] Polyb. 5.77.4–6, with Ma 2002, 58 n. 25 (arguing against the vague 'protectorate' posited by R. E. Allen 1983, 45–57).

Attalid royal house, it is likely enough that Attalos I was in some way personally involved in the construction of the temple of Dionysos at Teos, though direct evidence is lacking.[17] Likewise, it is hard not to think that the decision of the Teians to 'upgrade' their Dionysos-cult so dramatically in the late third century BC was in some way connected to the presence at Teos at this period of the association (*koinon*) of Dionysiac Artists of Ionia and the Hellespont.

The early history of the Ionian and Hellespontine *koinon* of the Dionysiac Artists is deeply obscure. The *koinon* certainly existed by 237/6 BC (an honorific decree of the Aitolians), and it is likely enough that its physical home was Teos from the time of its original organization.[18] The Dionysiac Artists were, however, always institutionally independent from the city of Teos. In the late third century, when the city of Magnesia on the Maeander despatched several teams of *theōroi* to seek recognition from communities around the Greek world of the Leukophryeneia festival, the city of Teos and the *koinon* of the Dionysiac Artists were approached by different teams of *theōroi*.[19] The chief officials of the *koinon* were the eponymous priest (of Dionysos) and an annually appointed agonothete, with responsibility for the organization of *koinon*-festivals; from the 160s BC onwards, the office of agonothete was expanded into a joint office of 'agonothete and priest of Eumenes'.[20] The *koinon* seems to have organized a number of festivals, the most important of which was an annual *panegyris* for Dionysos, held in the theatre at Teos, but separate and independent from the civic Dionysia of Teos.[21] Financially, the *koinon* was also a separate body, which (remarkably) struck its own silver tetradrachm-coinage in the mid-second century BC; the *koinon*'s finances seem to have been managed by a board of *meristai* or 'distributors'.[22]

Our most important source for the early history of the Dionysiac Artists at Teos is a Teian decree of uncertain date (probably of the late third century BC), the extant part of which is largely concerned with the purchase by the

---

[17] Dionysos Kathēgemōn and Attalos I: Müller 1989.

[18] Aitolian decree: *IG* IX I² 175; Le Guen 2001, no. 38; Aneziri 2003, D1. Originally based at Teos: strongly implied, though not stated explicitly, by Strabo 14.1.29.

[19] Rigsby 1996, 242–7, nos. 102–3. In the first Teian decree in honour of Antiochos III (*SEG* 41, 1003 I; Ma 2002, 308–11, no. 17: *c*.203 BC), the *dēmos* of the Teians and the *koinon* of the Dionysiac Artists are clearly distinguished as independent bodies.

[20] Ma 2007b, 223–6.

[21] Multiple festivals: Le Guen 2001, no. 44, line 10. *Panegyris*: *IG* XI 4, 1061+1136 (Le Guen 2001, no. 45; Aneziri 2003, D10), lines 27–30, making it clear both that the *panegyris* took place in the theatre at Teos and that it was separate from the Teian Dionysia (Aneziri 2003, 89); also *I.Magnesia* 54 (Le Guen 2001, no. 40; Aneziri 2003, D8), lines 31–3; *RC* 53 (Le Guen 2001, no. 47; Aneziri 2003, D12), esp. II B (the *panegyris* not a joint responsibility of the *koinon* and Teos, but of the *koinon* alone).

[22] Coinage: Lorber and Hoover 2003; Psoma 2007, 239 (favouring an earlier date). *Meristai*: see below, on the new decree for Timogenes (**Document 4**), lines 23–5.

city of Teos of a property 'in the city or the territory' valued at 6,000 drachmas (Fig. 4.2).[23] This property is to be donated to the Artists, classified as 'sacred', and exempted in future from all civic taxes. The intended purpose of the property is not clear: the sum set aside by the Teians for the purchase is at the top end of the market value of lavish private houses in desirable urban locations, and suggests that we may be dealing with a large 'club-house' for the use of the Artists.[24] It is a natural, but not necessary assumption that this decree should be placed early in the period of residence of the Artists at Teos; it certainly dates to a period when Teos was dependent on the Attalids of Pergamon, implying a date either *c*.229–223 BC or *c*.218–206 BC.[25] The decree clearly indicates that the Hermogenes-temple was already in existence at this point, since the *stēlē* was to be set up 'by the temple of Dionysos' (lines 21–3); like many other inscriptions originally erected in the Dionysos-sanctuary, it was later removed from its original location and was discovered in the cemetery of nearby Seferihisar.[26]

New evidence for the early history of the *koinon* of the Dionysiac Artists at Teos derives from an honorific decree of the *koinon* in honour of a certain Timogenes (**Document 4**), uncovered in 2017 in secondary use in the Hermogenes-temple (Fig. 4.3); once again, the decree demonstrably postdates the construction of the temple (see lines 20–2).[27] The letters seem reasonably close to those of the Teian decree on the purchase of land for the *koinon* (note

---

[23] Demangel and Laumonier 1922, 312–19, no. 2 (with photograph of squeeze at 313); (*SEG* 2, 580; Bringmann and von Steuben 1995, I 302–3, no. 262; Le Guen 2001, no. 39; Aneziri 2003, D2, with 174–9; *GEI* 041); Meier 2012, 357–62, no. 51. See further Holleaux 1924, 24–7; Robert 1937, 39–44. The inscription is now in the Archaeological Museum of İzmir, inv. no. 3542. The lettering of the decree (*alpha* with straight cross-bar; *omicron* and *theta* small and slightly elevated; *pi* with short right *hasta*) implies a late third- or early second-century date (thus Holleaux; Ma 2007b, 235–7). The form of the *alpha* may imply a date earlier than the Antiochos III dossier, which typically uses an *alpha* with curved cross-bar (Herrmann 1965, 49), but this is not certain, since Block F of the Antiochos dossier uses an *alpha* with straight cross-bar. Robert and Robert 1976, 159, are agnostic ('loin d'être fixée').

[24] Nevett 2000, for house-prices at Olynthos.

[25] That Teos was under Attalid rule at this point is indicated by (a) the grant of exemption from 'the taxes imposed by the city' (line 9), indicating that Teos paid taxes to an external body at this point (which therefore cannot be the Seleukids: Herrmann 1965, 101–4), and (b) the part-funding of the purchase from the Teian slush-fund 'for the administration (*dioikēsis*) of the city', the capital for which comes from a royal treasury (*basilikon*) (lines 16–18). This appears to be a regular and predictable subvention by the king, not earmarked for any particular purpose (Schuler 2005, 401; Rhodes 2007, 360–1; Kaye, forthcoming); there is therefore no reason to think that the king was involved in the Teian decision to direct 3,000 drachms of these royal *dioikēsis*-funds to the purchase of land for the Artists.

[26] Since the inscription was not discovered *in situ*, it is theoretically possible that the 'temple of Dionysos' mentioned in the inscription was an 'old' temple of Dionysos at Teos, not the new Hermogenes-temple (Aneziri 2003, 178); but this is effectively ruled out by the new decree of the Dionysiac Artists for Timogenes, which almost certainly antedates the Teian decree on the purchase of land, and which was discovered *in situ* in the *temenos* of the Hermogenes-temple.

[27] The discovery is announced by Kadıoğlu et al. 2019, 60–1; Kadıoğlu 2020, 179.

Fig. 4.2. Teian decree on the purchase of land for the Dionysiac Artists (late third century BC).

Photo: Teos excavation archive.

Fig. 4.3. Document 4: Decree of the Dionysiac Artists in honour of Timogenes (probably late third century BC).

Photo: Teos excavation archive.

in particular the straight cross-bar of the *alpha*), suggesting a date in the last quarter of the third century BC; as we will see, the decree-formulae provide some support for this date.[28] The beginning of the decree is missing, and hence we do not know what specific services Timogenes performed for the Artists. It is very likely that he was a citizen of Teos, since there is no provision for the sending of a copy of the decree to another city (contrast e.g. the near-contemporary decree of the Dionysiac Artists for Epikles of Kos, *IG* XII 4, I, 120).[29]

---

[28] The new decree for Timogenes may in fact be the earlier of the two: the right- and left-hand strokes of the *mu* in the new decree are always vertical, not angled outwards as in the Teian decree on the purchase of land; the upper and lower bars of the *sigma* are horizontal, and the right-hand vertical of the *nu* extends to the bottom of the letter-space. The lettering is also broadly similar to that of a victory-list from Teos (*SEG* 57, 1137: almost certainly from a contest organized by the Dionysiac Artists), dated to the late third or very early second century by Ma 2007b, 232–44.

[29] The name 'Timogenes' is too banal to provide any assistance: seventy-four instances in *LGPN* (none, as it happens, from Ionia).

Document 4: The Dionysiac Artists Honour Timogenes

Stēlē of grey marble, broken above; tenon preserved below. The inscribed surface badly weathered at left; rear side unworked. Uncovered in 2017 in the southern *krepis* of the temple of Dionysos at Teos, where the *stēlē* was used as *spolia* in later renovations. H. +0.76m; W. 0.37m; Th. 0.13m; Letters: 0.005–0.008m.

Date: Late third century B C?

```
      [- - - - - - - - - - - - - - - - - - - - - -]Ο̣[. .]
      [- - τοῖς περὶ τὸν Διόνυσον] τεχνίταις·
      [δεδόχθαι τῶι κοινῶι] τ̣[ῶ]ν περὶ τὸν Διόνυ-
      [σον τεχνιτῶν· ἐπ]αινέσαι καὶ στεφα[ν]-
  5   [ῶσαι Τιμογέν]ην στεφάνωι τῶι ἐκ τοῦ
      [νόμου] ἀρετ[ῆ]ς ἕνεκεν καὶ εὐνοίας ἣν ἔ-
      [χων δ]ιατελε̣ῖ εἰς τὸ κοινὸν τῶν περ[ὶ]
      [τὸ]ν Διόνυσον τεχνιτῶν, ἵνα πᾶσιν ἦ̣[ι]
      [φα]νερὸν τοῖς βουλομένοις εὐεργετεῖν
 10   [τὸ κοι]ν̣ὸ̣ν [τῶ]ν τεχνιτῶν ὅτι ὑφ' ὧν ἂν εὖ π[ά]-
      [θηι ἐπίστ]αται καὶ δύναται χάριν ἀποδιδό-
      [ναι κατ' ἀξία]ν τῶν εὐεργετημάτων·
      [τῆς δὲ ἀναγ]γελίας τοῦ στεφάνου ἐπιμ[ε]-
      [ληθῆναι] τ̣[ὸ]ν̣ ἀγ̣[ω]νοθέτην Μενίτην· ὅπω[ς]
 15   [δὲ] κα̣[ὶ] ε̣ἰς τὸ[ν λοιπ]ὸ̣ν χρόνον διαμένωσιν
      [αὐ]τῶ̣[ι αἱ] δε[δ]ομ̣[ένα]ι̣ τιμαὶ ὑπὸ τῶν τεχνι̣-
      τῶν, τοὺς ἀγωνοθ[έ]τ̣ας τοὺς γι̣ν̣ομ̣έ̣νους
      [κ]ατ' ἐνιαυτὸν ἐπιμελεῖσθαι ὅπως γίνη-
      ται ἡ ἀναγγελία τοῦ στεφάνου Τιμογέ̣-
 20   νηι καθότι ἔδοξεν τοῖς τεχν[ί]τ̣αις· ἀνα-
      γράψαι δὲ τόδ[ε] τὸ [ψήφι]σ̣μα ἐν τῶι ἱερῶι
      τοῦ Διονύσου ἐν τῶ[ι ἐπιφαν]ε̣στάτωι τόπω[ι]·
      τὸ δὲ ἀνήλω[μα τὸ ἐ]σ̣όμενον εἰς ταῦτα
      δοῦναι τοὺς μ̣εριστὰς ἀπὸ τῶν κοινῶν
 25   προσόδων.
```

Translation

'[. . . for the] *technitai* [of Dionysos; be it resolved by the *koinon*] of the [*technitai*] of Diony[sos] to praise and cro[wn Timogen]es with the crown prescribed by the [law] for the sake of the virtue and goodwill which he persists in h[olding] towards the *koinon* of the *technitai* of Dionysos, so that it may be clear to all those wishing to confer benefactions on the *koinon* of the *technitai* that it knows how to return gratitude to those at whose hands it has benefited, and is capable of so doing, [in a manner wo]rthy of their benefactions; and let the agonothete Menites have respon[sibility for the procl]amation of the crown; and so that the honours conferred on him by the *technitai* might persist also in the future, let the agonothetes in office each year have responsibility for the proclamation of the crown for Timogenes, just as it has been resolved by the *technitai*. And write up this [decr]ee in the sanctuary of Dionysos in the most [promi]nent place; and let the *meristai* provide the future expense for this from the common revenues.'

Commentary

3–8: The decree-formulae are precisely paralleled in other extant late third-century decrees of the Dionysiac Artists of Ionia and the Hellespont: compare *IG* XII 4, I, 120 (Kos, probably late third century), lines 10–13, δεδόχθαι τῶι κοινῶι τῶν τεχνιτῶν· ἐπαινέσαι Ἐπικλῆν Θευδώ[ρ]ου Κῶιον καὶ στεφανῶσαι αὐτὸν στεφάνωι τῶι ἐκ τοῦ νόμου ἀρετῆς ἕνεκεν καὶ εὐνοίας τῆς εἰς τοὺς τεχνίτα[s]; *I.Magnesia* 54 (Rigsby 1996, 245–7, no. 103; Le Guen 2001, no. 40; Aneziri 2003, D8: *c.*207–205 BC), lines 22–30, δεδό[χθαι τῶι κοινῶι τῶν περὶ τὸν] Διόνυσον τεχνιτῶν... ἐπαινέσαι... καὶ στεφανῶσαι στεφάνωι τῶ[ι ἐκ] τοῦ νόμου] ε[ὐ]σ[ε]βείας ἕνεκεν.[30] The 'crown prescribed by law' is more fully described in a second-century decree of the Dionysiac Artists as 'the crown prescribed by law with which it is an ancestral custom for the *technitai* to crown their benefactors' (στεφάνωι τῶι ἐκ τοῦ νόμου ὧι πάτριόν ἐστι τοῖς τεχν[ίταις στεφανοῦν τοὺς αὐ]τῶν εὐεργέτας: *IG* XI 4, 1061+1136; Le Guen 2001, no. 45; Aneziri 2003, D10: *c.*171 BC). In second-century Iasian decrees for foreign judges, it is explicitly the *value* of the crown which is prescribed by law (χρυσῶι στεφάνωι ἀπὸ πλήθους τοῦ ἐκ τοῦ νόμου: *I.Iasos* 73–4 [*I.Priene*² 108–9], 78; *Milet* VI 3, 1036), and that may well also be the case here.

8–12: The closest parallels for this hortative clause are found in a late fourth-century honorific decree from Priene (*I.Priene*² 17), lines 24–7, ἵνα εἰδῶσιν

---

[30] Cf. also *I.Magnesia* 89 (Le Guen 2001, no. 41; Aneziri 2003, D9), lines 35–7, with reference to the earlier decree *I.Magnesia* 54.

ἅπ[αν]τες ὅτι ὁ δῆμος ὁ Πριηνέων ὑφ' ὧν [ἄν εὖ] πάθηι ἐπίσταται χάριτας ἀποδιδό[ναι ἀ]ξίας τῶν εὐ⟨ε⟩ργετημάτων, and in the well-known decree of Neonteichos and Kiddoukome (*I.Laodikeia* 1, 267 BC), lines 30–4, ὅπως ϵἰδ[ῶ]σι καὶ οἱ ἄλλοι ὅτι Νεοτ[ει]χεῖται καὶ Κι[δ]διοκωμῖται ὑφ' ὧ[ν] ἄν τι πάθωσι ἀγαθ[ὸ]ν ἐπίσταρται τιμὰς ἀντιδιδόναι. We know of no parallels for the combination of the verbs ἐπίστασθαι and δύνασθαι in line 11; ἐπίστασθαι alone is usual, but δύνασθαι is attested in this context at Priene in the late fourth and third centuries (*I.Priene*² 16, line 26; 32, line 16), in third-century decrees from Amyzon in Karia (Robert and Robert 1983, nos. 21 and 38), and elsewhere.

13–14: In other honorific decrees of the Dionysiac Artists, the agonothete is likewise responsible for the proclamation of crowns (Aneziri 2003, 152–4). The proclamation is elsewhere specified as taking place at the Artists' annual *panegyris*, an annual festival independent of the civic Dionysia at Teos: see *I.Magnesia* 54 (Le Guen 2001, no. 40; Aneziri 2003, D8), lines 31–3; *IG* XI 4, 1061+1136 (Le Guen 2001, no. 45; Aneziri 2003, D10), lines 23–4, 27–8. It is relatively unusual for the agonothete in office that year to be named, as here (see also *I.Erythrai* 115, lines 11–12; *I.Mylasa* 632, lines 28–30); the personal name Menites is in fact extremely rare (only four examples in *LGPN*, three from Athens, one from Lykia). The proclamation of the crown is to be repeated each year (lines **14–20**); the annual crowning of benefactors (Ma 2013, 34–6) is also attested in the second-century decree of the Dionysiac Artists for their prominent member Kraton of Chalcedon (Le Guen 2001, no. 45, lines 22–5; on Kraton, see Le Guen 2007).

23–5: The *meristai* ('distributors') are elsewhere attested as financial magistrates of the Dionysiac Artists only in the decree recognizing the stephanitic Leukophryeneia at Magnesia (*I.Magnesia* 54, lines 36–7; Aneziri 2003, 147), in which the *meristai* provide the funds for annual sacrifices to be performed by *theōroi* of the Artists at the Leukophryeneia. The term is seldom used of financial magistrates elsewhere (apparently only at Istros, where they appear alongside an *oikonomos* and *tamias*: *IScM* I, 6, 15, 16, 18, with Ehrhardt 1988, 219), but the verb μερίζειν is standard for financial disbursements by treasurers.

We take the opportunity to publish here another new text, a short metrical dedication from the sanctuary of Dionysos at Teos (**Document 5**; Fig. 4.4). The text is inscribed on a small marble base, uncovered in 2015 in the western part of the sanctuary of Dionysos, near the city wall. The form of the lettering—in particular the *sigma*, with upper and lower strokes splayed

Fig. 4.4.   Document 5: Dedication to Dionysos (perhaps second century BC).
Photo: Teos excavation archive.

outwards—suggests a date distinctly later than the Timogenes decree, probably in the first half of the second century BC, although a later date is also possible.

Document 5: Dedication to Dionysos

Small marble base, complete at left, above, and below; broken at right and behind. Above, a round recess for the attachment of a statuette. H. 0.05m; W. +0.21m; Th. +0.11m; Letters 0.007m.

Date: first half of the second century BC?

σῶιζε πόλιν, Διὸς υἱὲ Δ[ιώνυσ’(?) - - - - -]
στῆσε δέ σοι τόδε ἄγαλμα ΒΙΟ[- - -]

'Preserve the city, son of Zeus, D[ionysos…;]
Bi[- -] set up this cult-image to you.'

The inscription takes the form of two hexameter verses, a little more than half of each of which is preserved. In verse 1, the imperative request to the god to 'preserve the city' is very common in prayers and hymns: compare e.g. *Sardis* VII 1, 50, Ἄρτεμι, Σάρδεις σῶζε διηνε[κὲ]ς εἰς ὁμόν[οιαν]; *I.Ephesos* 1253 (hymn to Asklepios), σύν τε φίλῳ πατρὶ σῶζ[ε πόλιν], Παιηόνιες παῖ.[31] At the end of the first verse, the 'son of Zeus' is surely Dionysos, and the remains of a *delta* are clear after υἱέ; the vocative Δ[ιόνυσε] would be unmetrical, and

---

[31]   Further examples in Thonemann 2020, 19.

hence it is likely enough that the god's name was spelled Διώνυσος, as often in verse texts. It is conceivable that he was addressed as Δ[ιώνυσ᾽ εἰραφιῶτα], as in the fragmentary first *Homeric Hymn to Dionysos*.[32] In verse 2, the unelided τόδ(ε) ἄγαλμα is well-paralleled in metrical texts: e.g. *Milet* I 9, 365 (*SGO* I 01/20/10); *IG* XII 5, 216 (Paros). The *agalma* was presumably a small statuette of the god fixed in the recess on the upper part of the base. The letters *BIΟ*[- -] at the end of verse 2 (the third letter either an *omicron*, *omega*, or *theta*) are presumably the start of the dedicator's name: by some distance the most likely candidate is the common Greek name *Βίω*[ν], four times attested at Hellenistic Teos (*LGPN* V.1, s.v.), although other names are possible (e.g. *Βίθ*[υς], also attested at Teos).

Teos in the 160s BC

The new Abderite decree for the Teians (**Document 1** above) offers us only a few hints of local conditions at Teos in the 160s BC. There is no good reason to doubt that the Teians did indeed provide extraordinarily prompt and generous help to the Abderites in the years after the sack of 170 BC. Nonetheless, the decree includes various indications that the Teians were not in the best of financial health at this point (or at least could plausibly claim as much). In the immediate aftermath of the resettlement of Abdera, sometime in the early 160s, the Abderites requested financial assistance from the Teians in the urgent task of rebuilding the city-walls and temples. The Teians provided what help their present financial circumstances permitted, as the decree explains (**B18–22**) in a passage of notably tortured syntax (reflecting the awkwardness of the sentiment being expressed by the Abderites):

> προήκατο χρημάτων ἀναποδότων πλῆ-
> θος, ὅσο[ν] ἰσχύειν αὐτῶι τότε ἐδίδοσαν οἱ καιροί, δεικνὺς ὡς οὐ τῆ[ι]
> 20   πολυπληθίαι τῶν ὑπαρχόντων τὴν ἑτοιμότητα τῆς χορηγία[ς]
> ὑπομένειν, τῆι δὲ εὐνοίαι πρὸς πᾶν τὸ παρακαλούμενον ἀνέλλει- ν.
> πτον τὴν φιλο[τι]μίαν παρέχεται·

'(The Teian *dēmos*) handed over a large sum of money which did not need to be repaid, as much as the present (difficult) circumstances then permitted them to

---

[32] West 2001, Fr. D11: καὶ σὺ μὲν οὕτω χαῖρε, Διώνυσ᾽ εἰραφιῶτα. We owe this neat suggestion to Robert Parker. On the epithet εἰραφιώτης, Bernabé 2013.

be able to do, showing how they provide their generosity unfailingly, not through an abundance of property to sustain a ready supply of income (?), but rather through goodwill in the face of every request.'

The Abderites do not elaborate on the 'circumstances' (*kairoi*) which prevented the Teians from offering more money.[33] It is, though, very striking that the Abderites do not specify how much money the Teians in fact provided, and one wonders whether it might have been disappointingly small. Sometime later, when the Abderites again approached the Teians and requested a loan for the purchase of oxen, the Teians once again claimed to be in financial difficulties (**B28–31**):

$$T \acute{\eta} \ddot{\iota} o\iota \ \tau \hat{\omega}\iota \ \mu \grave{\epsilon}\nu \ \pi \lambda o\upsilon \tau \epsilon \hat{\iota}\nu \ \lambda \epsilon \iota \pi \acute{o}\mu \epsilon -$$
$$\nu o\iota, \ \tau \hat{\omega}\iota \ \delta \grave{\epsilon} \ \epsilon \grave{\upsilon}\nu o\epsilon \hat{\iota}\nu \ \pi \acute{\alpha}\nu \tau \alpha \varsigma \ \grave{\alpha}\nu \theta \rho \acute{\omega}\pi o\upsilon \varsigma \ \grave{\upsilon}\pi \epsilon \rho \acute{\alpha}\gamma o\nu \tau \epsilon \varsigma, \ \pi \rho o\acute{\epsilon}\chi \rho \eta \sigma \alpha \nu \ \ddot{\alpha}\tau o-$$
30    $$\kappa \alpha \ \tau \acute{\alpha}\lambda \alpha \nu \tau \alpha \ \pi \acute{\epsilon}\nu \tau \epsilon \ \epsilon \grave{\iota}\varsigma \ \ddot{\epsilon}\tau \eta \ \pi \acute{\epsilon}\nu \tau \epsilon, \ \beta o\upsilon \lambda \acute{o}\mu \epsilon \nu o\iota \ \kappa \alpha \tau \grave{\alpha} \ \mu \eta \theta \grave{\epsilon}\nu \ \grave{\epsilon}\lambda \lambda \iota \pi \hat{\eta} \ \tau \hat{\omega}\nu$$
$$\sigma \upsilon \mu \phi \epsilon \rho \acute{o}\nu \tau \omega \nu \ \tau \grave{o}\nu \ \delta \hat{\eta}\mu o\nu \ \grave{\eta}\mu \hat{\omega}\nu \ \gamma \epsilon \nu \acute{\epsilon}\sigma \theta \alpha \iota \cdot$$

'The Teians, although lacking in wealth, but outstripping all other men in goodwill, advanced us five talents without interest over five years, wishing that in no respect our *dēmos* should be lacking in what is beneficial.'

The sum of money loaned to Abdera is large, but not astronomically so; however, the five-year interest-free term is extraordinarily generous (and unparalleled elsewhere among inter-community loans), suggesting that the Teians were not trying to wriggle out of supporting Abdera, but were simply not in a position to lend more.

Despite the abundance of third- and second-century epigraphic evidence from Teos, it is impossible to construct anything like a continuous narrative of the city's fortunes during this period. The late third century BC does seem to have been a period of relative prosperity at Teos: the construction of the great Dionysos-temple, as we have seen, almost certainly dates to the last quarter of the third century, and it seems likely for various reasons that the Hellenistic city walls of Teos (around 4km in length) were also constructed in phases during this period.[34] By far the greater part of the city's Hellenistic

---

[33] The appeal to 'difficult financial circumstances' as a pretext for providing less monetary assistance than might be expected is well paralleled in other Hellenistic decrees: compare e.g. the similar responses of Xanthos to Kytenion in 206/5 BC (*SEG* 38, 1476, lines 52–7) and of Hyllarima to Theangela in the early second century (Robert 1936, 92–3).

[34] City walls: McNicoll 1997, 157–60; Taşdelen and Polat 2018.

silver coinage was also struck in the period *c.*220–190 BC (tetradrachms with Alexander-types, and silver hemidrachms with civic types), and it is even possible that this coinage was struck in order to fund the building of the city's wall-circuit.[35] It is true that in the first Teian decree in honour of Antiochos III and Laodike (probably dating to 203 BC) the Teians describe themselves as 'thoroughly weakened in both public and private affairs due to the continuous wars and the scale of the contributions (*syntaxeis*) that we used to pay', but this should clearly be taken with a pinch of salt: the rhetoric of the decree depends on drawing a sharp contrast between the Teians' miserable condition before Antiochos' reconquest of western Asia Minor and the benefits now flowing to Teos thanks to the king's generosity.[36]

There is, nonetheless, good reason to think that Teos did well out of the decade-and-a-half of revived Seleukid rule over western Asia Minor (203–189 BC). Shortly after his take-over of Teos, Antiochos III declared the city and territory of Teos to be inviolable (*asylos*), as well as free both from tribute (*phoroi*) and from the 'contributions' (*syntaxeis*) which they had previously paid to Attalos I of Pergamon.[37] Two fragmentary Seleukid royal letters to the Teians, probably of the 190s BC, refer to 'democracy', 'freedom' (*eleutheria*), and 'other privileges', all of which had presumably been granted, confirmed, or preserved by Antiochos.[38] Antiochos' recognition of the *asylia* of Teos was followed, between 203 and 201 BC, by a successful series of Teian embassies around the Greek world, soliciting similar recognitions of Teian inviolability from other Greek communities, including Delphi, the Delphic Amphiktyony, the Aitolian League, the Athamanian kings, and numerous Cretan cities.[39] Particularly noteworthy is the later recognition of Teian *asylia* by the praetor M. Valerius, the tribunes, and the senate of Rome, precisely dated to 193 BC. This extraordinary document closely echoes the language of the original grant

---

[35] Kinns 1980, 218–23, 519–20, AR series VI–VII; for the (hypothetical) link with the wall-circuit, Thonemann 2015, 56. The majority of Teos' Alexander tetradrachms (Price 1991, 2308–2312) were certainly struck under Antiochos III, since a specimen of Price 2312 appears in the Mektepini hoard of *c.*195 BC.

[36] *SEG* 41, 1003, I (Ma 2002, 308–11, no. 17), lines 12–14: ἐξησθενηκότας ἡμᾶς κα[ὶ] ἐν τοῖς κοινοῖς καὶ ἐν τοῖς ἰδίοις διά τε τοὺς συνεχεῖς πολέμου[ς] καὶ τὸ μέγεθος ὧν ἐφέρομεν συντάξεων; cf. Chrubasik 2016, 224–5.

[37] *SEG* 41, 1003, I (Ma 2002, 308–11, no. 17), lines 18–20, 33–4, 47–9; similarly in the second Teian decree for Antiochos and Laodike, *SEG* 41, 1003, II (Ma 2002, 311–17, no. 18), lines 50–3, where Antiochos is said to have 'lightened' the heavy and harsh taxes (*telē*) and released them from 'contributions' (*syntaxeis*). On the terminology, see Herrmann 1965, 138–43.

[38] Ma 2002, 317–21, no. 19, B line 9, C lines 5–6 (rightly rejecting the speculative restorations of F. Piejko reported in *SEG* 41, 1004).

[39] Rigsby 1996, 280–314, nos. 132–52. The chronology remains in some doubt, and the priority of Antiochos' recognition of Teian *asylia* is not universally accepted: see Herrmann 1965, 121–38; Ma 2002, 260–5; Knäpper 2018, 137–8.

by Antiochos, right down to confirming the Teians' 'immunity from tribute'; the Romans also pledge that if the Teians persist in their attitude of goodwill towards them, then they too will likewise endeavour to increase the Teians' privileges in future.[40] As we will see, the Teians' early establishment of good diplomatic relations with Rome would stand them in good stead on more than one occasion later in the century.

In autumn 190 BC, at the height of the naval war between Rome and Antiochos, Teos was faced with a sudden and dramatic choice between preserving their loyalty to Antiochos and throwing in their lot with Rome.[41] The Roman praetor L. Aemilius Regillus, on the point of sailing north from Samos, learned that the Teians had recently furnished liberal supplies to Antiochos' fleet and had promised him a further 5,000 jars of wine. Aemilius immediately sailed for Teos, 'intending either, if the Teians were willing, to take over the supplies prepared for the enemy, or to treat them as enemies'. On his arrival at Teos, Aemilius decided to focus the Teians' minds by immediately sending his men out to ravage Teian territory. Livy's narrative continues as follows:

> When this devastation was taking place before their eyes, the Teians sent spokesmen to the Roman admiral bearing olive-branches wound with woollen fillets. When they tried to absolve their city of any hostile action or word against the Romans, he charged them with having aided the enemy fleet with all manner of provisions, and also with the quantity of wine they had promised to Polyxenidas. He said that if they gave the same to the Roman fleet, he would recall his soldiers from their ravaging; but if not, he would treat them as enemies. When the ambassadors brought this stern response back with them, the magistrates called the people together in assembly, so that they could take counsel on what to do.

In this stark crisis, the Teians (no doubt after much agonized weighing-up of the odds of Roman victory) decided to abandon the king and submit to

---

[40] Rigsby 1996, 314–16, no. 153, with 285–6; Ma 2002, 356–8, no. 38, with 100–2; Bloy 2012, 198; Isayev 2017, 247; Knäpper 2018, 144–5. We ought not to lay too much weight on the Romans' recognition of the Teians as 'immune from tribute as regards the Roman people' (ἀφορολόγητον ἀπὸ τοῦ δήμου τοῦ Ῥωμαίων, lines 20–1). The same recognition is found in the letter of the Athamanian kings (Rigsby 1996, 296–7, no. 135, lines 7–8), and Rigsby plausibly argues that both the Romans and the Athamanian kings, as 'powers that could in principle subject cities to tribute', were simply echoing the wording of Antiochos' original grant (Rigsby 1996, 283 with n. 19). Note, however, Livy's remark at 34.57.10 (Rome acting *ultra vires* in stipulating which cities in Asia were to be non-tributary).
[41] The following narrative summarizes Livy 37.27.3–29.6; the extended quotation is 37.28.1–3. On the events, see also Grainger 2002, 303–4; Boulay 2018, 135–6.

Aemilius' demands. The Roman fleet moved into the main harbour of Teos, and started loading up the wine and other provisions previously promised to Antiochos. A single Teian peasant then offered a practical demonstration of the city's goodwill, by reporting to Aemilius that the Seleukid war-fleet was lying at anchor a few miles to the east, just off the promontory of Myonnesos, and that a short time previously some of the Seleukid war-ships had appeared to be on the move. Aemilius scrambled his fleet, and the crushing Roman victory at the battle of Myonnesos followed later that same day.

The Teians seem to have been amply rewarded for their eleventh-hour transfer of loyalty to Rome. It now seems very likely that the Teians retained their status as a free city after the treaty of Apameia in 188 BC.[42] This is as we should expect, given their prompt submission to Aemilius in 190, and their pre-existing diplomatic relations with Rome as attested in the *asylia*-recognition of 193. At an uncertain date, the Teians established a joint cult of 'Roma and Good Faith (*Pistis*)' (Fig. 4.5), and it is tempting to think that this cult owes its origins precisely to the Romans' 'good faith' in preserving Teos' privileged status in 188 BC.[43]

At present, the archaeology of Teos does not allow us to say much about the city's prosperity or otherwise in the years after Apameia. The theatre, which already existed in the third century BC, seems to have been renovated at some point during the second century, and the *bouleuterion* was also rebuilt; the current excavator of Teos believes that the large altar in front of the Dionysos-temple was only completed around 170 BC, and some of the structures around the outer edge of the *temenos* of Dionysos seem also to date to the mid-second century.[44] The small Ionic temple in the agora has also been tentatively dated to the mid-second century BC.[45] The Teians also struck a further sequence of

---

[42] It was long believed that Teos was assigned to the Attalids after 188: thus e.g. Bikerman 1937, 221; Mellor 1975, 55–6; R. E. Allen 1983, 103–5; Graf 1985, 158; Le Guen 2007, 250; Strang 2007, 86. But the grounds for this belief were already questioned by Magie 1950, II 958–9, Walbank 1979, 167–8, and Lehmann 1998, 21, and have now been systematically challenged by Boulay 2018. A further argument that Teos was free after 188 is now furnished by the emergence of a Teian civic tetradrachm-issue which must date to the mid-second century BC (*Roma* Auction XVII (28/03/19), Lot 451, discussed further in Chapter 6 below). Meadows 2013, 188–91, argues that Attalid subject-cities may have minted their own Attic-weight coinage after 188; but his only parallel for Attic-weight tetradrachms being struck by an alleged subject-city (Temnos) cannot stand, since Temnos too was almost certainly free after 188 (Le Rider 2001, 41; Boulay 2018, 143).

[43] Dragoumis 1895, with Mellor 1975, 56; Robert and Robert 1976, 212–13 n. 237: ἱερεὺς ἀπε|δείχθη Ῥώμη|ς καὶ Πίστεως | Στράτων Ἑσ|τιαίου. The inscription was rediscovered in 2015 among thorn-bushes, some 125m south-west of the theatre; the lettering is difficult to date with any precision (first century BC?). The date of *CIG* 3074, an altar for Zeus Ktesios, Zeus Kapitolios, Roma, and Agathos Daimon, is uncertain (Mellor 1975, 219).

[44] Theatre and *bouleuterion*: Tuna 1997, 222–4. Altar and stoas: Kadıoğlu 2020, 182–7.

[45] Tuna 1998, 323–5. New evidence suggests the temple may have been dedicated to Roma.

Fig. 4.5. Appointment of a priest of Roma and Pistis (first century BC?).
Photo: Teos excavation archive.

silver tetradrachms with Alexander-types at some point in this period, perhaps in the 170s BC.[46]

The Teians certainly cultivated good relations with other free cities of western Asia Minor and beyond. A decree of the Aiolian city of Temnos, discovered in the Dionysos-sanctuary at Teos, records a Temnian grant of *isopoliteia* to the Teians; the decree cannot be precisely dated, but the first editor plausibly located it in the post-Apameian period.[47] An inscribed dossier from Magnesia on the Maeander, recording Teian honours for a certain Glaukos son of Admetos of Magnesia, may well also date to this period, or

[46] Price 1991, 2313–14; two further issues of Alexanders (Price 2474 and *CH* 10.301.333), previously attributed to Euromos, almost certainly also belong to this post-188 Teian group (we are grateful to Philip Kinns for advice on this point).

[47] *SEG* 29, 1149; for the date, Herrmann 1979, 245–6. The lettering is closely comparable to that of the new Abderite decree for Teos. That Temnos had a cult of 'the kings' at this point (line 10, perhaps Attalos I and Eumenes II) certainly does not show that Temnos was subject to the Attalids (Boulay 2018, 139).

perhaps a little earlier.[48] At an uncertain date, perhaps in the 160s BC, the Teians undertook a somewhat mysterious diplomatic initiative to have some of the recognitions of *asylia* gained in the last years of the third century 'renewed'; the motives for this second round of embassies are wholly obscure, and the Teians seems to have restricted themselves to cities on Crete and (perhaps) the city of Knidos.[49]

We are particularly well informed about Teos' relationship with the Attalid kings of Pergamon, the dominant power in western Asia Minor after Apameia. Several members of the Attalid royal house were the recipients of public cult at Teos, as had been the case for the Seleukids in earlier periods.[50] A Teian cultic regulation, apparently dating to the mid-second century, refers to the performance of sacrifices by two Teian cultic officials, 'the priest of Aphrodite and of Thea Apollonis Eusebes, and the priestess of her and of Queen Stratonike', and further provides for the establishment of an altar of Thea Apollonis Eusebes *Apobatēria* ('the alighter') at an uncertain location, perhaps in the agora.[51] To all appearances, the Teian cult of Aphrodite was served by both a male priest and a female priestess.[52] At some point, perhaps (but not necessarily) after Apollonis' death, each cultic official was also given responsibility for the cult of a female member of the Attalid royal house: the priest of Aphrodite also presided over the cult the 'queen mother' Apollonis, and the priestess of Aphrodite did the same for the reigning queen Stratonike

---

[48] *I.Magnesia* 97; the *alpha* has a horizontal cross-bar. The Teians describe the Magnesians as 'ancestral kinsmen and friends of the *dēmos*' (lines 12–13).

[49] Rigsby 1996, 316–25, nos. 154–61; see further Chaniotis 1988a, 348–9, E71; Chaniotis 1988b; Knäpper 2018, 138, 145.

[50] Third-century ruler-cult at Teos: Adak 2021. The cult of Seleukid kings appears to have continued at Teos down through the second century BC, to judge from the mysterious inscribed list of deified Seleukid and Ptolemaic monarchs from Teos (*OGIS* 246), on which see Herrmann 1965, 149–52; Boulay 2018, 142.

[51] *OGIS* 309; improved text in Robert 1937, 9–20; see also Kotsidu 2000, 355–6, KNr. 240; Theotikou 2013, 291–3. The inscription (now very worn) was re-discovered in 2010, out of context near the south-west corner of the agora, built into a late antique wall; it is now in the excavation house at Teos (inv. 2010/26). The date of the text cannot be determined with any precision. It clearly falls after the death of Apollonis, sometime between 183 and 159 BC (Robert 1962, 260 n. 1), and before the death of Stratonike, firmly dated to 135 BC (R. E. Allen 1983, 203); a date relatively early within this period seems likely. The cult of Apollonis *Apobatēria* evidently commemorates a personal visit of Apollonis to Teos, the date and context of which is quite unknown.

[52] The phraseology is ambiguous: τὸν ἱερέα τ[ῆς Ἀφρο]δίτης καὶ θεᾶς Ἀπολλωνίδος Εὐσεβοῦς καὶ τὴν ἱέρειαν αὐτῆς κα[ὶ βα]σιλίσσης Στρατονίκης (lines 4–6). Robert 1937, 15, assumed that αὐτῆς refers back to Apollonis, but it is surely easier to assume that it refers back to Aphrodite—i.e. Aphrodite served by a pair of priestly officials, each of whom is also responsible for the cult of one of the two royal women. For male/female priestly 'pairs' (sometimes, but not always, husband and wife), see van Bremen 1996, 133–6 (all from later periods); for an example from fourth-century BC Attica, see now *SEG* 54, 214, lines 23–8 (a priest and priestess of 'Hagne Theos'). We are grateful to Robert Parker for advice on this point. Priestesses of Dionysos are attested at Teos in the late Hellenistic and early imperial period: *SEG* 4, 598 (Hediste); Robert 1937, 24–5 (Claudia Tryphaina).

(wife of Eumenes II since *c.*175 BC). Both Apollonis and Stratonike were thus associated with an existing Teian cult of Aphrodite as 'temple-sharers' (*synnaoi*), just as Antiochos III and Laodike had previously been associated with the Teian cult of Dionysos.[53]

The cult of Apollonis and Stratonike at Teos continued at least down to the end of the Attalid period, and quite probably beyond, as we learn from an unpublished inscription from Teos (inv. 2014/01). This stone is a large marble pilaster carrying a small inset relief altar at the base, on which there appear (in the genitive) the names of Antiochis Aphrodite Nikephoros (Stratonike's mother), Thea Apollonis Eusebes, and Thea Stratonike. The designation of both Apollonis and Stratonike as *thea*, 'goddess', indicates that the text must post-date the death of Stratonike in 135 BC.[54] We have as yet no clear evidence for a Teian cult of any male members of the Attalid house: references to a priesthood of King Eumenes/Eumenes the god in second-century agonistic victor-lists from Teos have now been conclusively shown to refer to an official of the Dionysiac Artists, not the *polis* of Teos.[55]

Our most important piece of evidence for relations between Teos and the Attalid royal house is a fragmentary and difficult royal letter of Eumenes II to the *koinon* of Dionysiac Artists of Ionia and the Hellespont, probably dating late in Eumenes' reign.[56] The letter is primarily concerned with a dispute between the Artists and their host city of Teos over the management of the *koinon*'s annual *panegyris* for Dionysos. The chief bone of contention seems to have been the scope of authority of the *koinon*-officials responsible for managing the *panegyris* (the 'panegyriarchs'). Both parties agreed that the panegyriarchs should have sole responsibility for the conduct of the festival itself; but the Teians argued that the *koinon*'s panegyriarchs had illegitimately extended their authority over the 'surrounding harbours where those arriving for the *panegyris* put in' and the 'outlying territory' of the city, and were thereby depriving the city of revenues which properly belonged to it.[57] Such disputes seem normally to have been managed by a joint tribunal (*koinodikion*), presumably composed of representatives of both the Teians

---

[53] *SEG* 41, 1003, I (Ma 2002, 308–11, no. 17), lines 44–52. It is likely enough that the cult of Apollonis and Stratonike was modelled on the earlier Teian cult of Antiochos and Laodike: Herrmann 1965, 55; Ma 2002, 250; Mirón 2018, 35–6.

[54] For similar texts from Teos, with lists of deceased and living monarchs in the genitive, see *OGIS* 246 (above, n. 50); Jones 2011 and Jones 2020 (Ptolemies).

[55] Ma 2007b, 223–31; Adak and Thonemann 2020, 21.

[56] *I.Pergamon* 163; Welles, *RC* 53; Le Guen 2001, no. 47; Aneziri 2003, D12, with 97–104 (with a new sequencing of the fragments).

[57] II C, lines 9–15, as restored and interpreted by Thonemann 2011, 119.

and the Artists, which was evidently unable to resolve the present dispute; the two parties therefore appealed to Eumenes to arbitrate (he seems to have decided in favour of the Teians).[58] As has recently been pointed out, the fact of Eumenes' arbitration does not require us to assume that the Attalids exercised any *de iure* authority over the city of Teos: the king has been brought in to break a deadlock.[59] It is nonetheless striking that it was to Eumenes II that the appeal was directed, rather than to a neutral *polis*; if the Artists hoped that their close relationship with the Attalid royal house would lead to a decision in their favour, they were clearly disappointed.[60] A difficult passage of Eumenes' letter to the *koinon* refers to a 'synoikism' between the Teians and the Artists, but there is no sign that this was ever put into effect.[61]

Of far greater significance for our understanding of the services that the Teians were able to render to Abdera in the years after 170 BC were their ongoing close relations with the Romans. As we have seen, the Romans had recognized Teian *asylia* already in 193 BC, and it is likely that the Teians' prompt defection from Antiochos in autumn 190 was recognized in the treaty of Apameia with confirmation of Teos' status as a free city. At some point after 146 BC, relations between Teos and the Artists broke down altogether, and the Artists left Teos for (briefly) Ephesos. According to Strabo, when the Artists were resettled at Myonnesos (a small island town on the coast between Teos and Lebedos) by Attalos II or III, apparently in the 140s or 130s BC, 'the Teians sent an embassy asking the Romans not to permit Myonnesos to become a fortified outpost against them, and they (the Romans) relocated the Artists to Lebedos'.[62] Although Strabo does not give any further details, the Teians' ability to mobilize Roman support to overturn a decision of the Attalid king is truly startling, and it is hard not to think that the Teians were able to call on influential supporters and patrons at Rome.

The most impressive item of evidence for Teos' relations with Rome in the mid-second century BC is the well-known Abderite decree in honour of Amymon and Megathymos, almost certainly dating to 166 BC (or perhaps

---

[58] II A, lines 3–9, with Ager 1994, 10–11; Aneziri 2003, 99–100. Members of the tribunal swore an oath to judge 'according to the laws, the letters of the kings, and the decrees of the *dēmos*' (III B, lines 5–9).

[59] Boulay 2018, 137–8.   [60] On the Artists and the Attalids, see Aneziri 2003, 104–9.

[61] Synoikism: III A, lines 7–8, with Aneziri 2003, 100–4.

[62] Strabo 14.1.29: Ἀττάλου δ᾽ εἰς Μυόννησον αὐτοὺς καταστήσαντος μεταξὺ Τέω καὶ Λεβέδου, πρεσβεύονται Τήιοι δεόμενοι Ῥωμαίων μὴ περιιδεῖν ἐπιτειχιζομένην σφίσι τὴν Μυόννησον, οἱ δὲ μετέστησαν εἰς Λέβεδον. The acropolis of Myonnesos was located on the small offshore island of Çıfıt Kalesi, connected to the mainland by a causeway: Hansen and Nielsen 2004, 1088 (L. Rubinstein). The town seems to have been a Teian dependency in earlier periods; we have tentatively restored its name in Dirae I, lines 14–15 (**Document 2**, Chapter 3 above).

shortly afterwards). Along with the new honorific decree of Abdera for the Teians (**Document 1** above), the Abderite decree for Amymon and Megathymos also constitutes our chief contemporary source for the situation at Abdera in the immediate aftermath of the sack of 170 BC, and we therefore re-edit it in full in the chapter that follows.

5

Abdera, Kotys, and Maroneia in the 160s BC (Document 6)

As the new Abderite decree for the Teians makes clear (**Document 1**, lines **B31–52**), one of the major issues facing the Abderites after the sack of 170 BC was the loss of a large stretch of her territory to the neighbouring city of Maroneia. It is all too easy to imagine how the destruction of Abdera and enslavement of her population by Hortensius might have emboldened her immediate neighbours to seize parts of Abderite territory for themselves: the destruction of cities in the ancient Greek world was often followed by large-scale territorial annexations of this kind.[1] With the subsequent restoration of Abdera—legally, by senatorial decree in late summer 170 BC, and practically, with Teian help over the following years—the status of these 'lost' territories naturally became a bone of contention between Abdera and her neighbours.

The new decree mentions only a single territorial dispute of this kind, between Abdera and Maroneia (of which more shortly). But we have good reason to think that the Maroneians were not the only neighbouring power to seize parts of Abderite territory in 170 BC. Another lengthy Abderite decree from Teos, known since the nineteenth century, records a dispute between Abdera and a Thracian king by the name of Kotys, who had similarly laid claim to a stretch of Abdera's 'ancestral territory'. The date and historical context of this decree have been a matter of lively debate in the modern scholarship, with some scholars associating it with the period of the Third Macedonian War, and others dating it to *c*.90 BC. As will swiftly become clear, we are firmly of the view that the 'Kotys' decree must date to 166 or perhaps 165 BC, and that the Abderite dispute with Kotys unrolled precisely in parallel to the territorial dispute with Maroneia—although perhaps, as we will suggest, with a somewhat less satisfactory outcome for Abdera.

---

[1] The most famous example is the division of the territory of Thebes between her Boiotian neighbours in 335 BC (Hyp. *Epitaph.* 17; Diod. Sic. 18.11.3–4; Arr. *Anab.* 1.9.9); for the many examples from Hellenistic Crete, see Chaniotis 2005a, 11.

Teos and Abdera: Two Cities in Peace and War. Mustafa Adak and Peter Thonemann, Oxford University Press.
© Mustafa Adak and Peter Thonemann, 2022. DOI: 10.1093/oso/9780192845429.003.0006

Fig. 5.1. Document 6: Honours for Amymon and Megathymos, Fragment A.
Photo: Teos excavation archive.

Fig. 5.2. Document 6: Honours for Amymon and Megathymos, Fragment B.

Photo: Teos excavation archive.

Fig. 5.3. Document 6: Honours for Amymon and Megathymos, Fragments A+B.
Photo: Teos excavation archive.

Document 6: Abdera Honours Two Teian
Ambassadors to Rome

Teos, inv. No. 2010/31. Stele of bluish marble, cut vertically down the centre into two halves; broken above. Until 2012, both parts built separately into a fountain-house (Ballıkuyu) in the SE of Seferihisar, where they were copied by E. Pottier and A. Hauvette-Besnault in 1880 (Pottier and Hauvette-Besnault

1880), and by Peter Herrmann in 1966 and 1969 (Herrmann 1971). Now in the garden of the depot at Teos.

Fr. A (left: Fig. 5.1): H. 1.59m; W. 0.28m (above), 0.26m (below); Th. 0.285m (above), 0.315m (below). Fr. B (right: Fig. 5.2): H. 1.66m; W. 0.235m (above), 0.305m (below); Th. 0.285m (above), 0.315m (below). Combined W. (after restoration: Fig. 5.3): 0.44m (above), 0.618m (below). Letters: 0.014m (lines 2–4); 0.009–0.011m (lines 5–50). Interlinear space: 0.006–0.009m.

Ed. Pottier and Hauvette-Besnault 1880; (*Syll.*[1] 228 [Dittenberger, 1883]; Dumont and Homolle 1892, 442–4, no. 110b4; *Syll.*[2] 303 [Dittenberger, 1898], with II p. 816 [restorations by M. Holleaux]; Michel 1900, no. 325; *Syll.*[3] 656 [Hiller, 1917]; *IGRR* IV 1558 [Lafaye, 1927]); Herrmann 1971 [no text: cf. *BE* 1971, 564]; (Ager 1996, 493–6, no. 169; Canali de Rossi 1997, 291–4, no. 337; Canali de Rossi 2001, 191–2, no. 139 [lines 19–27 only]; Eilers 2002, 238–9, C101 [lines 1–27 only]; Manov 2002; *IThrakAig* 191–7, E5 [Loukopoulou et al., 2005]; *ISE* III[2] no. 183 [Canali de Rossi, 2006]).

Trans. Sherk 1984, no. 26 (English: lines 1–34 only); Eilers 2002, 238–9 (English: lines 1–27 only); Manov 2002, 29–30 (Bulgarian); Canali de Rossi, *ISE* III[2] no. 183 (Italian),

See: Wilhelm 1898, 226–7 (lines 19–20, 44–8); Haussoulier 1900, 27 (P. Foucart: lines 24–7); Holleaux 1901, 130 n. 1 (lines 25–6, 40); Gelzer 1912, 72–3 (line 21; patronage); Wilhelm 1914a, 186 (line 37); Wilhelm 1921a, 33 (line 46); Wilhelm 1925, 55 (line 12); Robert 1935, 507–13 (*OMS* I, 320–6: lines 12, 17–18, 21, 23–7, 47); Robert 1960, 327 n. 2 (*OMS* II, 843: line 22: cf. *SEG* 19, 687, *BE* 1961, 389); Robert, *Hellenica* XI–XII [1960], 103–4 (lines 6–7); Seibert 1963, 178 (line 10); Bogaert 1968, 118–19 (lines 44–8: public banks); Condurachi 1970 (diplomatic context; 'ancestral territory'); Robert and Robert 1976, 212–13 n. 237 (*OMS* VII, 356–7: line 10); Chiranky 1982, 470–81 (date: cf. *SEG* 32, 1206); Hatzopoulos and Loukopoulou 1987, 64–7 (Kotys' claims); Touloumakos 1988, 307–9 (patronage); Robert and Robert 1989, 35–6 (date); Erskine 1994 (patronage); Linderski 1995, 474–6 (embassy; date); Kallet-Marx 1995, 166–7 (patronage); Ferrary 1997a, 209 (date); Ferrary 1997b, 106–7 (date); Marek 1997, 173–7 (date); Lehmann 1998, 25–7 (patronage); Eilers 2002, 114–19 (date; patronage); *BE* 2002, 7 (pp. 625–6: lines 17–18, 22); Manov 2002 (date); Daubner 2006, 37–9 (success of embassy); Chryssanthaki-Nagle 2007, 314–16 (financial situation); Camia 2009, 160–3 (date); Goldbeck 2010, 196–201 (date; *salutatio*); Bloy 2012, 192–200 (lines 7–8; date; patronage and *salutatio*); Savalli-Lestrade 2012, 175 (embassy); Meier 2017, 132 (financing of *stēlē*).

Date: *c.*166 BC.

ὁ δῆμος ὁ Ἀβ[δηριτῶν]

(*in wreath*)   (*in wreath*)
Ἀμύμο-   Μεγάθυ-
να Ἐπι-   μον Ἀθη-
κούρου.   ναίου.

5   ἐπειδὴ χρείας τῶι δήμ[ωι γενο]μένης πρεσβείας εἰς
     Ῥώμην ὑπὲρ τῆς πατρίου [χώρας], περὶ ἧς ἐπιδοὺς ἀξίω-
     μα βασιλεὺς Θραικῶν Κότ[υς τῆι συ]γκλήτωι διά τε τοῦ υἱοῦ
     αὐτοῦ καὶ τῶν ἅμ᾽ ἐκείν[ωι συνεξ]απισταλέντων ὑπ᾽[αὐ]-
     τοῦ πρεσβευτῶν ἠιτεῖτ[ο τὴν π]άτριον ἡμῶν χώραν, ο[ἱ]
10   αἱρεθέντες πρεσβευτα[ὶ ὑπὸ το]ῦ δήμου τοῦ Τηΐων, Ἀμύ-
     μων τε Ἐπικούρου καὶ Μ[εγάθυμ]ος Ἀθηναίου, ἄνδρες
     καλοὶ καὶ ἀγαθοὶ καὶ ἄξ[ιοι τῆς ἰδ]ίας πατρίδος καὶ εὖνοι
     τῶι ἡμετέρωι δήμωι, οἵτ[ινες τὴ]ν πᾶσαν σπουδήν τε καὶ
     φιλοτιμίαν εἰσηνέγκαν[το προθ]υμίας οὐδὲν ἐλλείπον-
15   τες, ἔν τε γὰρ ταῖς συνεδ[ρίαις τ]αῖς γενομέναις ὑπὲρ τῆς
     χώρας πᾶσαν ἐπίνοιαν π[αρέσχ]οντο χάριν τοῦ μηθὲν π[α]-
     ραλειφθῆναι τῶν δυναμ[ένων ἐπα]νορθῶσαι τὰ πράγματα, ἀ-
     ρί<σ>την ἅμα καὶ σωτήριον ὑ[πὲρ τῶ]ν ἀπορουμένων ἀεὶ προ[σ]-
     τιθέντες γνώμην, εἴς τε [Ῥώμην π]ρεσβεύσαντες ὑπὲρ τοῦ
20   δήμου ψυχικὴν ἅμα καὶ σω[ματικὴν] ὑπέμειναν κ[α]κοπαθίαν,
     ἐντυγχάνοντες μὲν τοῖ[ς πρώτοι]ς Ῥωμαίων καὶ ἐξομηρευ-
     όμενοι διὰ τῆς καθ᾽ἡμέρα[ν προσκαρ]τερήσεως, παραστησάμε-
     νοι δὲ τοὺς πάτρωνας τῆς [ἰδίας πόλ]εως εἰς τὴν ὑπὲρ τοῦ ἡμε-
     τέρου δήμου βοήθειαν, τ[ινάς τε προ]νοουμένους τοῦ ἀντιδίκου
25   ἡμῶν καὶ προστατοῦντα[ς διὰ τῆς τ]ῶν πραγμάτων παραθέσε{ι}-
     ώς τε καὶ τῆς καθ᾽ἡμέρα[ν γενομέν]ης ἐφοδείας ἐπὶ τῶν ἀτρί-
     ων ἐφιλοποιοῦντο· περὶ δ[ὴ τούτων ἔ]δοξεν τῆι βουλῆι καὶ τῶι δή-
     μωι τῶι Ἀβδηριτῶν ἐπαιν[έσαι τε το]ὺς προγεγραμμένους ἄν-
     δρας καὶ καλεῖσθαι εἰς προ[εδρίαν κατ᾽] ἐνιαυτὸν Διονυσίων τῶι ἀ-
30   γῶνι, ἕως ἂν ζῶσιν, καὶ σ[τεφανοῦσ]θαι χρυσῶι στεφάνωι ἐς ἀεί,
     τὴν ἀναγγελίαν ποιουμέν[ου τοῦ ἱερο]κήρυκος διότι ὁ δῆμος στε-
     φανοῖ χρυσῶι στεφάνωι Ἀ[μύμονα Ἐ]πικούρου Τήϊον ἀρετῆς ἕνε-
     κεν καὶ εὐνοίας τῆς εἰς ἑα[υτὸν καὶ Με]γάθυμον Ἀθηναίου Τήϊον χρυ-
     σῶι στεφάνωι ἀρετῆς ἕνε[κεν καὶ εὐν]οίας τῆς εἰς ἑαυτόν· οἱ δὲ νο-

35   μοφύλακες οἱ ἐπὶ ἱερέως Ἥρα[- c.7 - ἀν]αγραψάτωσαν τόδε τὸ ψήφισ-
     μα εἰς στήλην λευκοῦ λίθ[ου καὶ στησά]τωσαν ἐν τῶι ἐπιφανεστάτωι
     τόπωι τῆς ἀγορᾶς· ἵνα [δὲ καὶ Τήϊοι γ]ινώσκωσιν τὴν τοῦ δήμου
     προθυμίαν, ἣν ἔχει πρὸς τ[οὺς καλοὺς] καὶ ἀγαθοὺς τῶν ἀνδρῶν, ἑ-
     <λ>έσθωσαν οἱ νομοφύλακ[ες πρεσβε]υτὰς δύο πρὸς Τηΐους, οἵτ[ιν]ες
40   ἀποδημήσαντες εἰς Τέ[ων καὶ ἀποδό]ντες τόδε τὸ ψήφισμα παρακα-
     λέσουσιν Τηΐους προσαγγ[εῖλαι τὰς ἐ]ψηφισμένας ὑπὸ τοῦ δήμου ἡ-
     μῶν τοῖς πολίταις αὐτῶν [τιμὰς καὶ σ]υγχωρῆσαι τοῖς πρεσβευταῖς
     στῆσαι στήλην λευκοῦ λίθ[ου ἐν τῶι ἐ]πιφανεστάτωι τόπωι, ἐν ἧι καὶ
     ἀναγραφήσεται τόδε τὸ ψή[φισμα· τὸ δ]ὲ γενόμενον ἀνάλωμα εἴς
45   τε τὴν στήλην καὶ τὴν ἀναγ[ραφὴν τοῦδε] τοῦ ψηφίσματος ἀπογραψά-
     μενοι τῆι πόλει οἱ πρεσβε[υταί, ὅπως δ]ιαμείβωνται, κομισά[σ]θωσαν
     ἀπὸ τῆς τραπέζης, θεμέν[ων - - c.7 - -] τὸ διπλάσιον τῶν νομοφυλά-
     κων ἀπὸ τῶν εἰς τὰς πρεσβ[είας· τὸ δὲ] ψήφισμα τόδε εἶναι εἰς εὐχα-
     ριστίαν τοῦ δήμου· ἐ[ἱρέθησα]ν πρεσβευταὶ Ἡρακλεί-
50   δης Ἀλκίφρονος, Ἀλκ[ίφρων Δη]μητρίου.

Critical Notes

6 πατρίο[υ] P(ottier)/H(auvette)-B(esnault). **8** ἐκείν[ωι ἐξ]αποσταλέντων
P./H.-B. **9** ᾐτεῖτ[ο τὴν π]άτριον P./H.-B.; ᾐτεῖ τ[ὴν π]άτριον D(ittenberger)[1]. *ad
fin.* χώραν| P./H.-B. **12** ἄξ[ιοι σφετέρ?]ας πατρίδος P./H.-B.; ἄξ[ιοι τῆς ἰδί]ας
πατρίδος Wilhelm 1925, 55; [ἰδ]ίας *legit* H(errmann). **13** οἷ[ς προσῆκε?]ν
πᾶσαν P./H.-B.; ὄ[ντες τὴ]ν πᾶσαν D.[1]; οἵτ[ινες τὴ]ν πᾶσαν H. **14** εἰσήνεγκαν
[προθυμ]ίας P./H.-B.; εἰσήνεγκαν [προθ]υμίας H. **17–18** ἀ|ρατὴν P./H.-B.;
ἀ|ρίστην *coniecit* Robert 1935, 509 (*OMS* I, 322); Α|ΙΙΑΤΗΝ *lapis*. **18**
[πραγμάτω]ν P./H.-B.; [περὶ τῶ]ν D.[1]; ὑ[πὲρ τῶ]ν H. **18–19** π[ρο]|τιθέντες
P./H.-B.; προ[σ]|τιθέντες H. **19** εἰς Τη[ΐους καὶ π]ρεσβεύσαντες P./H.-B.; εἴς τε
῾Ρ[ώμην π]ρεσβεύσαντες *coniecit* Wilhelm 1898, 227; *ΕΙΣΤΙ*[- -] *legit* H. **20**
σω[τήριον] ὑπέμειναν ἰδιοπάθιαν P./H.-B.; σω[ματικὴν] D.[1]; κακοπαθίαν
coniecit Wilhelm 1898, 227; κ[α]κοπαθίαν *legit* H. **21** τοῖ[ς πρώτοι]ς ῾Ρωμαίων
P./H.-B.; τοῖ[ς ἡγουμένοι]ς Holleaux, *Syll.*[2] II p.816. **22** καθ᾽ ἡμέρα[ν
προσκυν]ήσεως P./H.-B.; [ἀπαντ]ήσεως Robert 1960, 327 n. 2 (*OMS* II, 843);
[καρ]τερήσεως H.; [προσκαρ]τερήσεως Canali de Rossi 2001, 192 *post* H. **22–3**
καταστησάμε|νοι P./H.-B.; παραστησάμε|νοι H. **23** [πατρί]δος P./H.-B.;
[πόλ]εως H.; [αὐτῶν πόλ]εως Canali de Rossi 2001, 192. **24** τ[ε καὶ
προ]νοουμένους P./H.-B.; τ[οὺς προ]νοουμένους D.[1]; τ[οὺς δὲ προ]νοουμένους
Foucart *ap.* Haussoulier 1900, 27; τ[ινάς τε προ]νοουμένους Robert 1935, 513

(*OMS* I, 326). **25–6** προστατοῦντα[ς ἡμετέρ?]ων πραγμάτων παραθέσει, | ὥστε P./H.-B.; [διὰ τῆς τ]ῶν πραγμάτων παραθέσει|ώς τε Holleaux, *Syll.*[2] II p.816, Foucart *ap.* Haussoulier 1900, 27; παραθέσε{ι}|ώς Eilers 2002, 239. **26–7** ἀτρε[ί]|ων P./H.-B.; ἀτρί|ων *legit* Foucart *ap.* Haussoulier 1900, 27, H. **27** περὶ δ[έ] P./H.-B.; περὶ δ[ή] D.[1]. **28** ἐπαιν[έσαι το]ὺς P./H.-B. **30** στεφάνωι ἐν ἀγ[ῶνι] P./H.-B.; στεφάνωι ἐς ἀεί H. **31** ποιουμέν[ου τοῦ] κήρυκος P./H.-B. **35** ἐπὶ ἱερέως H[- -] P./H.-B.; HPA[- -] H. **36** [καὶ ἀναθέ]τωσαν P./H.-B.; [καὶ στησά]τωσαν D.[1]. **37** ἵνα [πάντες κο]ινῶς ἴδωσιν P./H.-B.; ἵνα [πάντες γ]ινώσκωσιν *coniecit* Wilhelm 1914a, 186; ἵνα [δὲ Τήιοι γ]ινώσκωσιν *legit* H. **37–8** ἀγαθοὺς ... αν [καὶ σπευ?]|δέσθωσαν P./H.-B.; ἀγαθοὺς [τῶν] ἄν[δρων καὶ ἐ]|<λ>έσθωσαν *coniecit* D.[1]; ἀγαθοὺς τῶν ἄνδρων, ἐ|<λ>έσθωσαν *legit* H. **40** εἰς Τέ[ων καὶ δό]ντες P./H.-B.; [ἀποδό]ντες Holleaux 1901, 130 n. 1. **41** προσαγγ[εῖλαι ἐ]ψηφισμένας P./H.-B.; [τὰς] *addidit* D.[1]. **42–3** πρεσβε[ῦσιν ἀνα]|στῆσαι P./H.-B.; πρεσβε[υταῖς] | στῆσαι *coniecit* D.[1], *legit* H. **43** ἐν [ἧι]| P./H.-B.; ἐν ἧι καὶ | H. **44** *fin.* ἐπί P./H.-B.; εἴς H. **45** ἐπὶ ἀναγ[γελίαν τὴν] τοῦ P./H.-B.; ἐπὶ ἀναγ[ραφὴν] τοῦ D.[1]; τὴν ἀναγ[ραφὴν] τοῦ H. **45–6** ἀπο[- -]|μενοι τῆι πόλει, οἱ πρεσβε[υταὶ Τηίου?]ς ἀμείβωνται κομι[ζόμενοι] P./H.-B.; ἀπο[λογισά]|μενοι τῆι πόλει οἱ πρεσβε[υταί, ὅπω]ς ἀμείβωνται, κομι[ζόντων] Wilhelm 1898, 227 ([ὅπω]ς *iam* D.[1]); κομι[σάσθων] Wilhelm 1921a, 33; ἀπογραψά|μενοι *et* κομισά[σ]θωσαν *legit* H. **47** θεμέν[ων - - -] τὸ διπλάσιον P./H.-B.; [αὐτοῖς] Wilhelm 1898, 227; [ἐφόδιον] Robert 1935, 509 n. 2. **47–8** νομοφυλάκ|ων P./H.-B.; νομοφυλά|κων H. **49–50** *suppl.* D.[1].

Translation

'The *dēmos* of the Abderitai (honoured) Amymon son of Epikouros, Megathymos son of Athenaios. (5) Since—when the *dēm*[os had] need of an embassy to Rome concerning the ancestral [territory], about which Kotys, king of the Thracians, submitting a written petition to the senate through his son and the ambassadors that he (Kotys) sent along with him (his son), had laid claim to our ancestral territory—(10) the ambassadors selected by the *dēmos* of the Teians, Amymon son of Epikouros and Megathymos son of Athenaios, fine and good men, worthy of their own homeland and well disposed to our *dēmos*, who brought to bear all eagerness and ambition, lacking nothing by way of enthusiasm (15)—for in the meetings that took place concerning the territory they exercised all their intelligence so that nothing might be omitted that could rectify the situation, always putting forward the best and most salutary proposals concerning the problem; and going on an embassy to [Rome] on behalf of the (20) *dēmos*, they endured both mental and ph[ysical] suffering, and met with the [leading] Romans and won them over through their daily perseverance, and induced the patrons of [their] city to the assistance of our *dēmos*; and they secured the friendship of [some] of those who had care for our (25) opponent and were acting on his behalf, through their presentation of the business and daily attendance at their *atria*; and so, concerning [these things], it is resolved by the *boulē* and the *dēmos* of the Abderites [both] to praise the afore-written men, and for them to be invited annually to a front seat at the contest of the Dionysia, (30), as long as they live, and for them to be c[rown]ed with a gold crown in perpetuity, with the sacred herald making the proclamation that "The *dēmos* crowns with a gold crown Amymon son of Epikouros of Teos, for the sake of his virtue and goodwill towards them, [and] Megathymos son of Athenaios of Teos, for the sake of his virtue and goodwill towards them". And let the (35) *nomophylakes* in office during the priesthood of Hera[- -] write up this decree on a *stēlē* of white marble and erect it in the most prominent spot on the agora; and in order that [the Teians too] might know the enthusiasm which the *dēmos* bears towards [fine] and good man, let the *nomophylakes* elect two ambassadors to the Teians, who will (40) go to Teos, hand over this decree, and call on the Teians to proclaim the [honours] voted by our *dēmos* for their citizens, and to permit the ambassadors to erect a *stēlē* of white marble in the most prominent spot, on which this decree will be written up; and as for the expense incurred for (45) the *stēlē* and the inscription of [this] decree, let the ambassadors invoice it to the city, so that they might be reimbursed, and let them draw it from the public bank, with the *nomophylakes* providing double/two-fold [- -] from the (fund) reserved for embassies; and let this decree be for the purpose of (showing) the gratitude of the *dēmos*. The elected ambassadors were Herakleides (50) son of Alkiphron and Alkiphron son of Demetrios.'

Commentary

This inscription has a long and complex publication history; Louis Robert described it as 'un texte comme privilégié pour l'enseignement de la critique'.[2] The two fragments of the inscription were first copied at Seferihisar by Edmond Pottier and Amédée Hauvette-Besnault, who published the *editio princeps* in 1880. A greatly improved edition was provided by Wilhelm

---

[2] Robert, *OMS* IV, 306.

Dittenberger in the first edition of the *Sylloge Inscriptionum Graecarum* in 1883; a series of further corrections to the text were made around the turn of the century by Adolf Wilhelm, Maurice Holleaux and Paul Foucart (who had access to a squeeze made by Pottier and Hauvette-Besnault), and subsequently by Louis Robert. The two fragments were seen again at Seferihisar by Peter Herrmann in 1966 and 1969, who published his readings (without a new text) in 1971; it is noteworthy how many of Wilhelm's conjectures in the text were subsequently confirmed by Herrmann's new readings (lines 12, 19–20, 45–6). The inscription has been fairly often reprinted over the past twenty-five years, most notably in the major 2005 corpus of the inscriptions of Aegean Thrace by Louisa Loukopoulou and others (with very full lemma and apparatus), but little further progress has been made on the constitution of the text. Pottier and Hauvette-Besnault's *editio princeps* remains the only full edition to have been based on autopsy of the stone.

The present edition is based on a fresh reading of the stone in the Teos archaeological depot, where the two fragments of the inscription have now been mortared together. The top part of the left-hand fragment was already broken off when Herrmann saw the stone in the late 1960s, and hence the readings of line 1 and the left-hand part of lines 2–3 can no longer be verified.[3] The reunification of the two fragments has made it clear that in restoring the central part of each line, earlier editors did not take sufficient account of the breadth of the lacuna created by the sawing of the *stēlē* in half for re-use. The lacuna in the middle of the *stēlē* is very slightly broader at the bottom than at the top (largely as a result of greater damage to the left-hand edge of the right-hand fragment); since the letters also diminish in size as we travel down the stone (with the exception of lines 49–50, inscribed in larger letters), the size of the lacuna gets gradually longer as the text proceeds. In lines 5–20, the lacuna is fairly constant at 5–7 letters (8 letters in line 12, with three *iotas*); in lines 21–35, it broadens out to 7–9 letters; in lines 36–48 it broadens still further to 8–10 letters (11 letters in line 37, with three *iotas*), before dropping back to 7 letters in lines 49–50. We have accordingly suggested longer restorations in the middle part of lines 8, 9, 14, 22 (following Herrmann and Canali de Rossi), 23, 28, 31, 37, 40 (following Holleaux), 45, and 46, and have reverted to a shorter restoration in line 21.

---

[3] This is not stated by Herrmann 1971, but is clear from Herrmann's contemporary notes and photographs, kindly passed to Mustafa Adak by Norbert Ehrhardt.

5–6: For the construction, cf. *IG* XII 7, 388 (Amorgos: *c*.200–150 BC), lines 6–8, χρείας τε γενομένης ἀναγκαίας τῶι δήμωι διαφόρου διὰ τοὺς περιστάντας καιρούς; *I.Mylasa* 105 (second century BC), line 6, χρημάτων τε χρείας γενομένης τῶι δήμωι; *I.Priene*² 64 (after 129 BC), lines 31–2, γενομένης τε χρείας ... τῶι δήμωι διαφόρων εἰς τὰ συμφέροντα.

6–9: The construction περὶ ἧς (sc. χώρας) ... ἠτεῖτ[ο τὴν π]άτριον ἡμῶν χώραν is awkward. ἀξίωμα (lines 6–7) is a rather rare technical term for a written petition or request (Robert, *Hellenica* XI–XII, 103–4). The term is later used for petitions to Roman authorities, apparently as an equivalent of the Latin *libellus* (e.g. *IAph2007* 8.32, line 1: Samian petition to Octavian, 38 BC), but was already in use in the Hellenistic period, as in the treaty of Eumenes I with the mercenaries at Philetaireia in the 260s BC (*OGIS* 266, line 1: [ἀξ]ιώματα ἃ ἐπε[χώρησ]εν Εὐμένης). A similar phrase appears in Welles, *RC* 69, line 3 (Hiera Kome: [ἐπέ]δωκεν or [ἀνέ]δωκεν ἀξίωμα), but the date of this document is uncertain (Boulay 2017, 262–71). In line 8, ἐκείν[ωι ἐξ]αποσταλέντων is too short for the lacuna, and hence we prefer [συνεξ]αποσταλέντων, a well-attested compound form (e.g. *I.Priene*² 108, lines 23 and 51; *I.Priene*² 122, line 13; *I.Kaunos* 18, line 49; *I.Kaunos* 19, line 77).[4] In line 9, Pottier and Hauvette-Besnault restored the imperfect middle ἠτεῖτ[ο τὴν π]άτριον ἡμῶν χώραν; Dittenberger and later editors preferred the imperfect active ἤτει τ[ὴν π]άτριον, which is certainly too short for the lacuna. At the end of line 9, earlier editors printed only χώραν, but we think we can make out the first *omicron* of the definite article ο[ἷ] on the stone.

10–15: In line 14, earlier editors restored εἰσήνεγκαν [προθ]υμίας, but this is once again too short for the lacuna, and we hence prefer to restore the middle εἰσήνεγκαν[το], as in *IAph2007* 2.503 (first century BC), line 26, ἐφ' ᾗ εἰσηνέγκαντο ἀνδρῄα τε καὶ σπουδῇ.

15–19: The sequence of thought surely implies that the ambassadors have not yet travelled to Rome (their journey is described in lines 19–20); presumably the 'meetings' (συνεδρίαι) at which the Teian ambassadors provided encouraging ideas took place at Abdera. In **Document 1**, lines **B38–41**, the Teians similarly provide a group of σύνεδροι who assist in the preparation of the Abderite case against Maroneia; presumably in both cases we are dealing with an *ad hoc* legal team who put together a suitable dossier of evidence in

---

[4] This new restoration undermines the tentative argument of Bloy 2012, 196 that Kotys' son might already have been in Rome at the time Kotys sent his ambassadors.

advance of the hearing. At the start of line 18, the letters *ATHN* are clear on the stone, preceded by (apparently) two vertical strokes, which could be either a *pi*, a *nu*, or the letters *rho* and *iota* squeezed rather close together. The first editors' ἀρατήν (< ἀρατός, 'prayed for', 'desirable') has no epigraphic parallels, and the best solution is probably to read *A|PIATHN*, and to assume that this was a mason's error for ἀρί⟨σ⟩την, as suggested by Robert 1935, 509 (*OMS* I, 322). The phrase ὑ[πὲρ τῶ]ν ἀπορουμένων has no epigraphic parallels, and presumably derives from the philosophical usage τὸ ἀπορούμενον, 'the problem before us' (e.g. Arist. *Ph.* 202a13).

19–22: In line 21, Holleaux's suggested restoration τοῖ[ς ἡγουμένοι]ς Ῥωμαίων met with the approval of Robert 1935, 509 (*OMS* I, 322, citing the parallels collected by Wilhelm 1914b, 46), and has been accepted by most subsequent editors;[5] however, it seems too long for the lacuna, and we should probably retain the original editors' shorter restoration τοῖ[ς πρώτοι]ς Ῥωμαίων.[6] The verb ἐξομηρεύεσθαι in lines 21–2 is otherwise unattested epigraphically; here it must bear the metaphorical sense 'to win over to one's side', as in Diod. Sic. 27.7 and in a gloss preserved in the Suda (s.v. ἐξομηρευσάμενοι· ὁμογνώμονας ποιήσαντες). In line 22, Herrmann (1971, 74–5) restored τῆς καθ᾽ ἡμέρα[ν καρ]τερήσεως, remarking that the compound προσκαρτέρησις (*IG* XII Suppl. 249, line 8: Andros) would be too long for the lacuna; in fact, the compound (also favoured by Canali de Rossi 2001, 192) fits the lacuna perfectly (eight letters).

22–4: In line 23, Herrmann (1971, 75) restored simply τοὺς πάτρωνας τῆς [πόλ]εως, but this is far too short for the lacuna, and leaves it ambiguous which *polis* is meant. Canali de Rossi (2001, 192) suggested restoring τῆς [αὐτῶν πόλεως]; we would prefer τῆς [ἰδίας πόλ]εως, implicitly contrasted with τοῦ ἡμετέρου δήμου in lines 23–4; cf. lines 12–13 above for an identical contrast (ἄξ[ιοι τῆς ἰδ]ίας πατρίδος καὶ εὖνοι τῶι ἡμετέρωι δήμωι).

24–7: The verb προνοοῦμαι usually signifies to 'have care over' or to 'provide for'; here it must mean something like 'favour the cause of'. In line 24, we prefer Robert's restoration τ[ινάς τε προ]νοουμένους (Robert 1935, 513) to Foucart's τ[οὺς δὲ προ]νοουμένους (Haussoulier 1900, 27), since it is unlikely that the Teian ambassadors won over all of Kotys' supporters. For the term παράθεσις (lines 24–5), 'presentation', see Robert 1945, 37. The extraordinary

---

[5] See now also the decree for Polemaios, Robert and Robert 1989, 13, col. II lines 24–5: ἐνέτυχεν μὲν τοῖς ἡγουμένοις Ῥωμαίοις.

[6] Gelzer 1912, 73, citing Plut. *Cat. Min.* 8.5.

description of the ambassadors' 'daily attendance at the *atria*' of Kotys' Roman supporters (lines 26–7) is—depending on the date of the inscription (see below)—the earliest description of the morning *salutatio*, apparently also referred to by Polyb. 31.29.8 (χαιρετισμός).

27–34: In line 28, the restoration ἐπαιν[έσαι το]ὺς seems short for the lacuna, and hence we have added the particle τε (picked up by καὶ καλεῖσθαι in line 29). In line 31, previous editors have restored ποιουμέν[ου τοῦ] κήρυκος, but the restoration is certainly too short for the lacuna, and other Abderite decrees show that such proclamations were made by the 'sacred herald', the ἱεροκῆρυξ (*IThrakAig* E7, line 25; E8, line 23; E9, line 22; **Document 1** above, lines B71–2).

34–7: The name of the eponymous priest of Dionysos in line 35 is most likely to be Ἡρα[κλείτου] or Ἡρα[κλείδου] (cf. the ambassador Ἡρακλείδης in lines 49–50); similar formulae in *IThrakAig* E8, lines 31–2, ἀναγραψάτωσαν δὲ οἱ νομοφύλακες οἱ ἐπὶ ἱερέως Διονύσου τόδε τὸ ψήφισμα, and in **Document 1** above, lines B84–5. In line 36, there is no way of telling whether the stone carried [ἀναθέ]τωσαν or [στησά]τωσαν.

37–44: In line 37, Herrmann (1971, 75) restored ἵνα [δὲ Τήϊοι γ]ινώσκωσιν, but the restoration (with two *iotas*) is on the short side, and the sense requires 'in order that the Teians *too* might know', as in *IThrakAig* E7, lines 33–4, ἵνα δὲ καὶ ὁ δῆμος ὁ Ἀκανθίων ἐπιγνῷ, and in **Document 1**, line B73 (ἵνα δὲ καὶ ἐν Τέῳ) and line B84 ([ἵνα δὲ] καὶ Τήϊοι παρακολουθῶσιν); hence we prefer ἵνα [δὲ καὶ Τήϊοι γ]ινώσκωσιν. In line 40, the restoration accepted by most editors (εἰς Τέ[ων καὶ δό]ντες) seems too short, and the normal verb in this context is ἀποδοῦναι (e.g. *I.Priene*² 110, lines 22–3, οἵτινες ἀφικόμενοι εἰς Πριήνην καὶ ἀποδόντες τόδε τὸ ψήφισμα παρακαλέσουσιν κτλ.; similarly *IG* XII 4.1, 178; cf. *IThrakAig* E7, line 36, τὴν ἀποίσουσαν τὸ ψήφισμα); hence we prefer Holleaux's suggested restoration (1901, 130 n. 1), εἰς Τέ[ων καὶ ἀποδό]ντες.

44–8: In line 45, earlier editors restored τὴν ἀναγ[ραφὴν] τοῦ ψηφίσματος, which is clearly too short; we prefer τὴν ἀναγ[ραφὴν τοῦδε] τοῦ ψηφίσματος. In line 46, after the lacuna in the centre of the stone, where Pottier and Hauvette-Besnault read a *sigma*, in fact we clearly have a vertical stroke (probably an *iota*; conceivably a *tau* or *rho*), and hence we should presumably restore a compound form of ἀμείβεσθαι; we suggest [δ]ιαμείβωνται. The general sense of lines 44–8 seems to be that the ambassadors will pay the expenses of the erection of the *stēlē* at Teos from their own pockets; they will then invoice the city for these expenses (ἀπογραψάμενοι τῆι πόλει, lines 45–6), and will be reimbursed ([δ]ιαμείβωνται, line 46) from the public bank at Abdera. A very similar phrase appears in **Document 1** above, lines **B69–70**: [τὸ] δὲ ἐσόμενον ἀνάλωμα εἰς τὴν θυσίαν καὶ τὸν ἀγῶνα ἀπο[γραψάμενος ὁ γυμνα]σίαρχος λαβέτω ἀπὸ τῆς τραπέζης, 'let the gymnasiarch in[voice] the future expenses for the sacrifice and the contest and draw them from the public bank'. The clause in lines 47–8 is highly problematic, and it is not clear how closely it should be connected to the financial arrangements in lines 44–7. The *nomophylakes* are instructed to furnish 'double' or 'two-fold', from the fund reserved for embassies' (ἀπὸ τῶν εἰς τὰς πρεσβείας). For dedicated funds of this kind at Abdera, compare the Abderite decree for Philon of Akanthos, where the *nomophylakes* are to draw the expenses for the inscribing of the decree at Abdera 'from the fund reserved for sacrifices' (ἀπὸ τῶν εἰς τὰς θυσίας, *IThrakAig* E7, lines 32–3); a similar clause may have stood in line **B84** of **Document 1** above, where we have tentatively restored χορηγείτωσαν οἱ νομ[οφύλακ|ες ἀπὸ τῶν εἰς τὰς πρεσβείας]. However, it is not at all clear what this 'double' payment might be, and we hence leave the lacuna in line 47 unrestored. It seems very unlikely that the ambassadors would have been reimbursed twice the expense of the *stēlē* (restoring, with Wilhelm 1898, 227, θεμέν[ων αὐτοῖς] τὸ διπλάσιον). Robert suggested, more plausibly, that they might have received double their travel expenses (Robert 1935, 509 n. 2 [*OMS* I, 322], θεμέν[ων ἐφόδιον] τὸ διπλάσιον),[7] but this would be a curious pendant to the account of the financing of the *stēlē* at Teos in lines 44–7, and it is not clear why the Abderites might particularly want to reward their ambassadors in this way.[8] Since the *nomophylakes* were also responsible for the erection of the original *stēlē* at Abdera (lines 34–7), and nothing is said there about funding for the Abdera inscription, it is conceivable the *nomophylakes* are here being instructed to draw down and set aside from the public bank 'double' the cost of the Abdera *stēlē*, in order to have funds to hand to pay for both copies; but it would be surprising for the funding for both *stēlai* to come from the fund for embassies. We leave the problem unresolved.

48–50: For the concluding phrase τὸ δὲ ψήφισμα τόδε εἶναι εἰς εὐχαριστίαν τοῦ δήμου (lines 48–9), cf. *IThrakAig* E7, lines 40–1; E9, line 44; **Document 1** above, line **B89**.

---

[7] Cf. *IThrakAig* E4, line 9, where the travel expenses of *theōroi* are designated as πορεῖον, not ἐφόδιον.

[8] Charles Crowther suggests that θεμέν[ων ἐφόδιον] τὸ διπλάσιον could mean simply 'providing two sets of travel expenses (i.e. one to each of the two ambassadors)'; but it is hard to see why the decree would need to specify this.

As noted above, uncertainty has long surrounded the date and historical context of this inscription. Until the early 1980s, it was generally assumed that the inscription should be placed in the immediate aftermath of the Third Macedonian War, on the basis of an identification of 'Kotys, king of the Thracians' (line 7) with an Odrysian king Kotys known from literary sources. Polybios and Livy tell us that one of the chief allies of Perseus during the Third Macedonian War was an Odrysian king by the name of Kotys.[9] After the battle of Pydna, Kotys' son Bithys (along with some other Thracian nobles) was captured by the Romans in the company of Perseus at Samothrace and taken to Carseoli as a hostage. In late 167 BC, Kotys sent an embassy to Rome to ransom his son and the other Thracians, claiming (not very plausibly) that he had fought with Perseus not of his own free will, but only because he had previously been compelled to provide hostages to Perseus. The senate, bearing in mind 'the friendship which Rome had previously had with Kotys, his ancestors and the Thracian people' ([*amicitia*] *quae cum Cotye maioribusque eius et gente Thracum fuisset*, Livy 45.42.8), decided not to pursue their dispute (διαφορά) with Kotys, but to bind him to them through favourable treatment (ἀναδούμενοι διὰ τῆς τοιαύτης χάριτος, Polyb. 30.17); they accordingly released Bithys and the other hostages, with a substantial financial gift to the Thracian envoys (Livy 45.42.11).[10]

This round of diplomatic negotiations between Kotys and Rome in late 167 BC seems at first sight to fit rather well with the contents of the present decree. In our decree, we find a 'Kotys, king of the Thracians' laying claim to a stretch of the 'ancestral territory' of Abdera, and appealing to the senate for confirmation of his claim (lines 6–9).[11] The Abderites accordingly resolved to send their own embassy to Rome to affirm their ancestral possession of this stretch of territory (lines 5–6). They decided to make use of two Teian ambassadors, Amymon and Megathymos, apparently because Teos (unlike Abdera) had city-patrons at Rome who could be persuaded to represent Abdera's claims in the senate (lines 22–4). Our decree clearly indicates that the Roman decision over whether or not to support Kotys' claim to this territory was finely balanced (lines 21–7)—indeed, the decree does not in fact make clear whether

---

[9] Polyb. 27.12.1–3 (his character); Livy 42.29.12, 42.51.10, 42.57.6, 42.58.6, 42.59.2, 42.60.2, 42.67.3–5, 44.42.2, 45.6.2.

[10] Condurachi 1970, 581–90; Walbank 1979, 440; Chiranky 1982, 461–70; Touloumakos 1988, 309; J. Allen 2006, 80–1.

[11] As Louis Robert showed, the dispute was not over the freedom of Abdera (as earlier scholars had assumed), but over possession of part of her territory, no doubt contiguous to Kotys' kingdom: Robert 1935, 510–13 (*OMS* I, 323–6); Robert, *Hellenica* V, 57–8; Robert, *OMS* IV, 306; *OMS* V, 562; Condurachi 1970, 583–5.

the Teian ambassadors were ultimately successful or not (see further below).[12] This situation slots rather neatly into the general diplomatic context of Kotys' own embassy to Rome of late 167 BC, as reported by Polybios and Livy. Polybios and Livy make it clear that the Roman senate had to weigh up carefully whether to punish Kotys for his support of Perseus or conciliate him as a potentially useful future ally; it is quite possible that one of the issues under consideration (as well as the fate of the king's son Bithys) was whether or not Kotys should be permitted to retain a stretch of Abderite territory that he had annexed during the war.

This 'early' dating of the decree for Amymon and Megathymos to the aftermath of the Third Macedonian War was challenged at length by Gary Chiranky in 1982, and his arguments were subsequently developed further by Claude Eilers and Fabian Goldbeck.[13] After listing various alleged problems with the early dating, Chiranky proposed to down-date the decree to the early first century BC, reviving a tentative suggestion of Lenk and Rostovtzeff that the Kotys of the inscription could instead be identified with an obscure later Thracian king by the name of Kotys.[14] This later Kotys is mentioned by Diodoros as having put down a rebellion in Macedonia at some point between 93 and 87 BC; Chiranky suggested that he might therefore have been emboldened to claim part of Abdera's territory as a reward for his services.[15]

The case against an 'early' dating has various different elements. First, Chiranky and Eilers argued that the 'Kotys, king of the Odrysians' who supported Perseus in the Third Macedonian War could not conceivably have had any kind of claim on Abderite territory, since the second-century Odrysian kingdom was not contiguous with Abdera, but lay far to the north-east in the upper Hebros valley.[16] However, this argument runs up against the complete absence of hard evidence for the extent of the Odrysian kingdom in the later Hellenistic period: we simply have no idea where the south-western limits of the Odrysian kingdom might have been located during this period. In the fifth century BC, Thucydides describes the Odrysian kingdom as extending precisely from 'the city of Abdera to the Black Sea' (Thuc. 2.97.1), and it is

---

[12] Robert 1935, 513 (*OMS* I, 326); Condurachi 1970, 585–6; Touloumakos 1988, 309 n. 22; Kallet-Marx 1995, 167 n. 29; Daubner 2006, 37–9; Savalli-Lestrade 2012, 175.

[13] Chiranky 1982; Eilers 2002, 114–19; Goldbeck 2010, 196–201. For strong counter-arguments in favour of the early date, Marek 1997, 173–7; Bloy 2012, 192–200.

[14] B. Lenk, *RE* VI (1937), s.v. Thrake (Geschichte), col. 438; Rostovtzeff 1941, II 766.

[15] Diod. Sic. 37.5a: Chiranky 1982, 480; Eilers 2002, 119; Goldbeck 2010, 197–8. For this Kotys, see Sullivan 1990, 29–30; Kallet-Marx 1995, 36–7.

[16] Chiranky 1982, 473; Eilers 2002, 115–16, citing Polyb. 23.8.4–7 for Odrysian territory in the upper Hebros around Philippopolis.

perfectly possible that in the early second century BC a Thracian ruler with the centre of his territory in the upper Hebros valley could still plausibly have laid claim to lands south of the Rhodope mountain range.[17] Eilers further claims that the territory of the Thracian Sapaioi lay between the Odrysians and Abdera in the second century BC, but this seems to be a straightforward misunderstanding: the Sapaioi controlled the mountainous region on the right bank of the river Nestos, west and north-west of Abdera (where they are rightly placed in the *Barrington Atlas*), while the 'core' of Odrysian territory lay to the north-east of Abdera.[18]

Peter Delev has recently added a fascinating new element to this argument.[19] Although Polybios describes Kotys as 'king of the Odrysians', there are some signs that Polybios may have used 'Odrysian' as a generic term for 'Thracian': he describes Dromichaites, ruler of the Getai, as an 'Odrysian king'.[20] Delev has argued that there is nothing in the ancient accounts of the Third Macedonian War to tie Perseus' ally Kotys firmly to the Upper Hebros region—where there may indeed have been no united 'Odrysian kingdom' of any kind in the second century BC—and has therefore suggested that the Kotys known from Polybios and Livy is more likely to have ruled over a Thracian kingdom somewhere closer to the Aegean coast, perhaps even over the Sapaioi to the west of the river Nestos (directly contiguous with Abderite territory).[21] Be that as it may, and wherever the centre of Kotys' kingdom might have been situated, it is certainly perilous to conclude that Polybios' Kotys could not have plausibly laid claim to part of Abderite territory in the early 160s BC, whether from the north-east (the Hebros valley) or north-west (the territory of the Sapaioi).[22] (It is worth remarking that we have no idea where the kingdom of the early first-century Kotys was located either.)

---

[17] Marek 1997, 175; Bloy 2012, 194–5.

[18] Eilers 2002, 116, rightly criticized by Bloy 2012, 195. Eilers's claim that 'in Strabo's time' the territory of the Sapaioi lay between Abdera and the Odrysians seems to be based on a misunderstanding of the phrase περὶ Ἄβδηρα in Strabo 12.3.20, which does not mean 'on all sides of Abdera' but simply 'near Abdera'.

[19] Delev 2018.

[20] Kotys as 'king of the Odrysians': Polyb. 30.17.1; Livy 42.29.12, 42.51.10 (cf. 44.42.2). Dromichaites: Polyb. fr. 102.

[21] This argument runs up against the objection that in 171 BC, a Thracian dynast by the name of Autlesbis, with the help of the Attalid general Korrhagos, had attacked the borders of Kotys' territory and captured a region called 'Marene' (Livy 42.67.4–5, and see the Prologue); this region is most naturally placed east of the Hebros, close to the European territories of Eumenes II (Hatzopoulos and Loukopoulou 1987, 65).

[22] It is equally possible that the core of Kotys' kingdom lay in the Upper Hebros, but that he had recently expanded his influence into the territory of the Sapaioi, immediately north-west of Abdera: Hatzopoulos and Loukopoulou 1987, 66; Delev 2015, 67.

Second, proponents of a late date for the decree lay great weight on what they see as the unlikelihood (for both linguistic and institutional reasons) that a Greek civic decree of the 160s BC could already have employed the Latin loan-words *patronus* (πάτρων, line 23) and *atrium* (ἄτριον, lines 26–7).[23] There is a certain circularity in this argument (the earliest attestation of a phenomenon must be down-dated because there are no earlier examples of the phenomenon), and the argument is hardly decisive for the term ἄτριον, since this particular loan-word is in fact attested only here.[24] It is true that πάτρων is not otherwise attested in Greek inscriptions until the 120s BC.[25] However, as Dylan Bloy has shown, it requires extreme special pleading to deny the existence of relationships of patronage (albeit not otherwise denoted with this particular loan-word) between individual Romans and Greek cities in the early second century BC; in the words of Jean-Louis Ferrary, 'cities had patrons before the word *patron* was used in Greek inscriptions'.[26] To take only a single example, in 191/190 BC, M'. Acilius Glabrio wrote to the Delphians: 'Concerning the affairs of the sanctuary, if the Thessalians or any others send embassies, I will try [in Rome (?), as far] as I am able, to see to it that the ancestral rights which you have possessed from the outset are preserved, with the autonomy of both the city and the sanctuary [maintained]'.[27] Although he happens not to use the word *patronus*, Glabrio's promise of future assistance in the event of embassies to Rome from other Greek states threatening Delphic autonomy looks functionally identical to the services provided by Teos' Roman *patroni* in the decree for Amymon and Megathymos. On the specific question of linguistic usage, we might also note that the decree for Amymon and Megathymos is (like **Document 1** above) particularly rich in highly unusual and specialized vocabulary: this is the only Greek inscription in which we find τὸ ἀπορούμενον used in the sense of 'a present problem' (line 18: a philosophical usage), and ἐξομηρεύεσθαι in the metaphorical sense 'to win someone over' (lines 21–2: scarcely paralleled anywhere in Greek literature).

---

[23] Chiranky 1982, 474–8; Eilers 2002, 117–18; Goldbeck 2010, 198 n. 5.

[24] See Tybout 1993, 46–8.

[25] Eilers 2002, 109–44 (Goldbeck 2010, 198 n. 5); the earliest dated example is *IG* XII 6, 1, 351 (Samos, *c.*120 BC).

[26] Ferrary 1997b, 108; Marek 1997, 175; Bloy 2012, 168–91. Cf. e.g. Polyb. 21.29.12; Livy 42.14.7 (Rhodes, 172 BC), and M'. Acilius Glabrio to Delphi (below). Bloy neatly points out that Eilers's definition of patronage is circular: 'for him, patronage is that relationship defined by the use of the Greek title *patron*; if it happened before the adoption of that title, then it cannot be patronage, even if what is known of the relationship otherwise fits his definition' (Bloy 2012, 175).

[27] Jacquemin, Mulliez and Rougemont 2012, no. 144, lines 8–10.

Goldbeck has further argued that the Roman social institution of the morning *salutatio* which appears to be described in lines 26–7 only came into being in the Gracchan period, but his case for a Gracchan 'revolution' or formalization of the *salutatio* pertains specifically to its use in Roman electoral politics, and there does appear to be a clear mid-second-century reference to the *salutatio* in Polybios (31.29.8: χαιρετισμός).[28] There is certainly no good reason to think that repeated visits by Greek ambassadors to the *atria* of influential senators would have been in any way socially peculiar in the 160s BC. Indeed, Andrew Erskine (who favours an early date for our inscription) has nicely argued that the remarkable detail provided in our decree about the round of calls at the *atria* reflects 'curiosity about Roman practice and institutions with interest in their language'; our decree would thus reflect, among other things, the knowledge-gathering process by which Hellenistic cities came to understand how to deal with Rome in the earlier second century BC.[29]

Third, Chiranky argues that there would have been no need or reason for Abdera to have had recourse to envoys from Teos in the 160s BC, since Abdera was a *civitas libera* that enjoyed good relations with Rome. Teos, by contrast, was a subject city within the Attalid kingdom (or so he assumes); the Teians had, moreover, backed Antiochos III in 190 BC, and hence would not have been in Rome's good graces.[30] By the 90s BC, the situation had changed: Teos was part of the Roman province of Asia, and hence would have had better access to patrons at Rome than the free city of Abdera. But this argument is not persuasive, not least because it seems highly likely that Teos was *not* in fact subject to the Attalids after 188 BC.[31] Crucially, Abdera's appeal to Teos for assistance in the embassy need not imply anything at all about the legal status of the two cities vis-à-vis Rome; it could simply reflect the fact that Teos happened to have influential Roman patrons while Abdera did not.[32] It clearly made sense for the Abderites to use all possible diplomatic channels to turn the senate in their favour, and they could well have turned to Teos purely and solely because they knew that the Teians enjoyed privileged access to influential senators.[33] There is nothing intrinsically problematic about a city not formally subject to Rome having Roman patrons: one need only think of the cases of M'. Acilius Glabrio and Delphi in 181/180 BC (see above), Kolophon

---

[28] 'Gracchan revolution': Goldbeck 2010, 217–24. Goldbeck's claim (193–5) that the χαιρετισμοί of Polybios 31.29.8 took place in the *forum* rather than the *domus* is not convincing: Bloy 2012, 192 n. 125.

[29] Erskine 1994, 49.

[30] Chiranky 1982, 473–4, 477–9; Kallet-Marx 1995, 167 n. 27; Linderski 1995, 475.

[31] Boulay 2018, and see above, Chapter 4, for more detailed discussion.

[32] Gelzer 1912, 73; Bloy 2012, 198.   [33] Marek 1997, 176.

in the late second or early first century BC, or Q. Oppius and Aphrodisias in the mid-80s BC.[34] We might also recall, as discussed in Chapter 4 above, that Teos had enjoyed diplomatic relations with Rome since 193 BC (Roman recognition of Teian *asylia*), and at some point in the late 140s or early 130s BC, the Teians sent a successful embassy to Rome to persuade the senate not to permit the *koinon* of Dionysiac Artists, recently expelled from Teos, to settle at the neighbouring city of Myonnesos; this latter event shows clearly that Teos had access to powerful patrons at Rome well before the creation of the Roman province of Asia.[35] Conversely, it is very hard to imagine that Abdera could still have been lacking her own Roman patrons by the 90s BC, not least in the light of the three fulsome second- or early first-century BC Abderite honorific decrees for Roman benefactors.[36]

It is frustrating that the new Abderite decree for Teos (**Document 1**) does not decisively settle the date of the decree for Amymon and Megathymos. The new decree makes no allusion to the territorial dispute with Kotys or the embassy of Amymon and Megathymos to Rome. Conversely, the decree for Amymon and Megathymos makes no allusion either to the kinship between the Teos and Abdera (so prominent in the new decree), or to the extensive and varied assistance provided by the Teians to Abdera in the difficult times during and following the Third Macedonian War. If we stick with a date in the early 160s BC for the territorial dispute between Abdera and Kotys, it is more than a little surprising that the Abderites did not choose to mention this dispute expressly in the longer decree honouring the Teians for their various services over the years. Then again, as we have seen, we do not know whether the dispute with Kotys in fact ended in success for Abdera. If the Abderites did not in the end succeed in recovering this stretch of 'ancestral territory', they could well have decided to quietly omit this unsuccessful Teian embassy to Rome from the later, longer honorific decree.

However, the new Abderite decree for Teos does in other respects provide strong circumstantial support for dating the decree for Amymon and Megathymos to 166 BC or shortly thereafter. We now know that the sack of Abdera in 170 BC was followed by a long period of severe population shortage and agrarian impoverishment at Abdera; we also know that another of Abdera's neighbours, the city of Maroneia, took the opportunity of Abderite

---

[34] Delphi: see above, n. 26. Kolophon: Lehmann 1998, 22–7; Lehmann 2000, 227–8; Eilers 2002, 124–37. Aphrodisias: Reynolds 1982, no. 3; Eilers 2002, 23–5.

[35] Teian *asylia*: Rigsby 1996, 314–16, no. 153. Dionysiac Artists: Strabo 14.1.29. Further discussion above, Chapter 4.

[36] *IThrakAig* E8–E10.

weakness to annex part of her territory. If it is the case—as seems all but certain—that large parts of Abderite territory were temporarily abandoned in the immediate aftermath of the sack of 170 BC, it is easy to imagine that Kotys, like the Maroneians, could have seized the chance to expand his territory at Abderaʾs expense.[37] Whether the son of Kotys mentioned in the decree for Amymon and Megathymos (lines 7–8) is identical to the Bithys who was a Roman hostage in 167 BC is harder to judge. If the dispute between Abdera and Kotys was heard in late 167 BC as part of the wider senatorial deliberations on Kotysʾ future, then obviously we must be dealing with two different sons of Kotys, since Bithys was already in Italy in 167, and hence could not have been sent as Kotysʾ envoy.[38] But it is possible that the dispute was not heard until 166 or even later, in which case Bithys could easily have been sent back to Rome by his father to represent the Thracian position on the matter; after all, Bithys had spent some time in Italy, and knew the ropes.

As will be clear, our view is that the decree for Amymon and Megathymos ought to be placed in 166 BC or shortly afterwards. The situation so vividly described in the decree for Amymon and Megathymos—encroachment on Abderite territory by Kotys of Thrace, a pending senatorial hearing, an appeal by Abdera to her mother-city for assistance, and an enthusiastic and generous Teian response backed up by the full force of Teian diplomatic capital—fits beautifully into what we now know of relations between Teos and Abdera in the years immediately following the sack of 170 BC. Just as the Teians called in a favour from Miletos at a key moment during the dispute with Maroneia (**Document 1**, lines B44–8), so they called in favours from their patrons at Rome at the key moment of the dispute with Kotys: in both cases we see the Teians enthusiastically mobilizing their networks of international connections in support of their struggling daughter-city.

We return, finally, to the question of what the actual outcome of the Teian embassy to Rome in late 167 or 166 BC might have been. As we have seen, the decree for Amymon and Megathymos does not specify whether or not the embassy succeeded in its aim of persuading the senate to eject Kotys from the stretch of Abderite ʿancestral territoryʾ that he had occupied; the absence of any such specification has led most scholars to assume that the embassy

---

[37] No chronological indications can be derived from the fact that the territorial dispute with Maroneia was settled by foreign judges from Erythrai, while the dispute with Kotys was (apparently) settled by the senate; Maroneia and Abdera were both free cities, while Kotysʾ kingdom fell into a quite different category.

[38] Bloy 2012, 196 ingeniously interprets lines 7–8 of the decree for Amymon and Megathymos as indicating that the anonymous son of Kotys was already in Rome and the envoys were sent to join him; but this is now ruled out by our new restoration in line 8 (see above).

was ultimately unsuccessful, and that Kotys was left in possession of the relevant stretch of land. The apparent absence of any mention of this embassy in the new Abderite decree for Teos may point in the same direction (although it is just conceivable that it could have been mentioned in the lost central part of the new decree). However, as Gabriella Parissaki has pointed out to us, there is in fact a highly tempting third possibility, namely that the senate neither accepted Kotys' claim nor restored the land to Abdera, but instead annexed it to the Macedonian first *meris*, one of the four Macedonian 'districts' into which the former Antigonid kingdom was divided under the settlement of Aemilius Paullus in spring 167 BC.[39] Under the settlement of 167, the first *meris* was to include the villages, forts, and towns along the Aegean coast east of the Nestos, with the exception of Ainos, Maroneia, and Abdera, which retained their status as free cities.[40] But since the territory of Abdera probably originally extended as far as the foothills of Mt Rhodope in the north (Chapter 2 above), the restoration to Abdera of *all* of her ancestral territory would have created a physical discontinuity in the first *meris*. Rome might therefore have seen the attractions of shaving off a northern strip of Abderite territory in 167 and assigning it to the first Macedonian *meris* (the strip along which, somewhat later, the *via Egnatia* would run).[41] If so, the embassy of Amymon and Megathymos would have been only a qualified success: Kotys expelled, but without the full restoration to Abdera of their 'ancestral territory'.

If this ingenious hypothesis is correct, then something else may fall into place. In the early second century AD, perhaps in AD 131/2, the emperor Hadrian restored to Abdera a stretch of territory which the city had lost at some point in the past, on the left bank of the Nestos around the modern village of Toxotes, 23km north-west of Abdera.[42] Scholars have long wondered whether the land restored to Abdera at this point might be identical with the territory seized by Kotys at the time of the Third Macedonian War.[43] Certainty is impossible, but it is striking that the territory restored to Abdera by Hadrian

---

[39] It now seems certain that the four *merides* already existed in some form in the late Antigonid period: Hatzopoulos 1996, I 231–60; Ferrary 2018, 301; Kremydi 2018, 282–5 (with important new evidence from Gitana in Thesprotia).

[40] Livy 45.29.6; Diod. Sic. 31.8.8. The fullest study remains that of L. Loukopoulou in Hatzopoulos and Loukopoulou 1987, 61–110.

[41] The date of construction of the *via Egnatia* remains uncertain, but certainly cannot be as early as 167 BC: Walbank 1985; Kallet-Marx 1995, 347–9. Bloy 2012, 196, likewise suggests that the territory of the first *meris* east of the Nestos might in practice have been confined to settlements along the route of the later *via Egnatia* (which presumably followed the course of the main Antigonid road through the region, for which see Livy 39.27.10).

[42] *I.ThrakAig* E78 and E79.   [43] e.g. Robert 1938, 192 n. 3; Condurachi 1970, 586, 591–4.

seems to have been located precisely at the point where the *via Egnatia* crossed the river Nestos, opposite the town of Topeiros on the right bank of the river.[44] It is clearly tempting to suppose that the land restored to Abdera by Hadrian might have been a 'strip' along the *via Egnatia* (and the road's putative royal predecessor) east of the Nestos, assigned to the first Macedonian *meris* in 167 BC precisely in order to link up the Macedonian territories west and east of the Nestos.

Abdera and Maroneia

The Hellenistic and Roman urban centre of Maroneia lies some 40km to the east of Abdera (see Map 2). The Hellenistic city of Maroneia occupied a coastal site on the bay of Agios Charalambos, below the heights of Mt Ismaros, famous in antiquity for its vines.[45] The territorial dispute between the two cities described so vividly in the new inscription strongly suggests that the territories of Abdera and Maroneia were contiguous in the early second century BC. Exactly where the frontier between their territories might have been is another matter.

In the Archaic and Classical periods, at least one, and perhaps two independent Greek communities lay on the Thracian coast between the territories of Abdera and Maroneia. The one about which we can be quite certain is the small *polis* of Dikaia, plausibly located on the hill of Katsamakia near the modern village of Fanari, on the coast immediately south-east of Lake Bistonis.[46] The boundary between the territories of Dikaia and Abdera is said by pseudo-Skylax to have been the river 'Koudetos', plausibly (if conjecturally) identified with the river Kompsatos, said by Herodotos to flow into Lake Bistonis from the north-east; the territory of Dikaia must therefore have stretched along the east shore of Late Bistonis, roughly between the modern villages of Fanari in the south and Salpi in the north.[47] Dikaia was certainly an independent city in the late Archaic and early Classical periods, as is clear from its substantial silver coinage of the late sixth and early fifth centuries

---

[44] Adams 1986.

[45] Already in H. *Od.* 9.196–201; Archilochos, fr. 2 West; Plin. *HN* 14.53–4.

[46] Isaac 1986, 109–11; Hansen and Nielsen 2004, 877–8 (L. Loukopoulou); *IThrakAig* pp. 129–30; Loukopoulou and Psoma 2008, 56–7, 60; Tiverios 2008, 104–5.

[47] Pseudo-Skylax, *Periplous* §67 (cf. Hdt. 7.109), with Loukopoulou and Psoma 2008, 56–7; Shipley 2019, 150. The Kompsatos today preserves its ancient name.

BC.[48] However, the city may already have been within the political orbit of
Abdera by the mid-fifth century BC: in the Athenian Tribute Lists, the city is
referred to as 'Dikaia by Abdera' (normally paying 3,000 drachms, compared
to 15 talents for Abdera), and the two cities were apparently assessed as a single unit in the Athenian tribute-reassessment decree of 425/4 BC (for the
astronomical sum of 75 talents).[49] Dikaia struck no coinage after the Classical
period, and the city is seldom mentioned in Hellenistic and Roman literary
sources, suggesting that its territory may have been incorporated into that of
either Abdera or Maroneia at some point in the later Classical period.[50]

Whether or not there was a *second* coastal settlement between the territories of Abdera and Maroneia in the Archaic and Classical periods is a long-
standing problem which cannot be treated in detail here. On the Thracian
coast, roughly 12km south-east of the presumed urban centre of Dikaia and
21km north-west of the Hellenistic city of Maroneia, lies the peninsula of
Molyvoti, with the remains of a substantial urban settlement of the Archaic to
Classical periods; the city was apparently destroyed *c.*350–340 BC, although
with some limited reoccupation in the later fourth and early third century.[51]
The identity of this settlement remains hotly disputed. The first excavator of
the site, Georgios Bakalakis, identified the site on Cape Molyvoti with the
Thasian coastal *emporion* of Stryme, but this identification runs into a host of
problems (incompatibility with Herodotos' account of Xerxes' march through
Aegean Thrace; the absence of the Paro-Thasian alphabet from the numerous
inscriptions from the site).[52] More recently, Louisa Loukopoulou and Selene
Psoma have made a strong case for identifying the site as the Archaic and
Classical urban centre of Maroneia, which would have relocated to its later
site at Agios Charalambos (where virtually no pre-Hellenistic material is
known) only in the late fourth century BC; they suggest that Stryme was
located further to the east, along the rocky coastal strip south of Mt Ismaros.[53]

---

[48] May 1965; Schönert-Geiss 1975, 15–29; Psoma 2015, 179–82. The coins carry a bust of Herakles
on the obverse, no doubt alluding to the story (Strabo 7.44) that it was Herakles who dug the channel
immediately below the site of Dikaia which connects Lake Bistonis to the sea: Isaac 1986, 109–10;
Tiverios 2008, 104–5.

[49] *IG* I³ 71, III lines 153–4.

[50] Note that Strabo 7.44 and 7.47 still refers to Dikaia as a *polis*.

[51] Arrington et al. 2016 (for the destruction level, 24; the date confirmed by N. Arrington, *per litt.*),
and for the numerous fifth- and fourth-century epitaphs from the site, *IThrakAig* E109–66.

[52] Bakalakis 1967, esp. 143–5; cf. Tuplin 2003, 387–8; Hansen and Nielsen 2004, 880–1
[L. Loukopoulou]; Loukopoulou and Psoma 2008, 62–3; Arrington et al. 2016, 4–5.

[53] Loukopoulou and Psoma 2008; Psoma, Karadima, and Terzopoulou 2008, xlix–liv, 123–30,
243–54; Archibald 2013, 71; for doubts about the identification, Saba 2018. The Maroneians had a
long-running dispute with Thasos over control of Stryme, dating back as far as the seventh century
BC: Archilochos fr. 291 West (from Philochoros, *BNJ* 328 F 43); Dem. 12.17, 50.20–3.

For our own purposes, all that matters is that the urban centre on Cape Molyvoti seems no longer to have been inhabited to any significant extent after the mid-third century.[54]

None of this directly illuminates the question of where the stretch of territory disputed between Abdera and Maroneia in the early 160s BC might have been located, but it does at least allow us to propose a working hypothesis. It is very difficult to believe that Maroneia could have laid claim to land anywhere to the west of Lake Bistonis: the distance from the urban centre of Maroneia is just too great. But as we have seen, the city of Dikaia, on the south-east shore of Lake Bistonis, seems to have ceased to exist as an independent *polis* at some point in the fifth or fourth century BC. If—and it is a big if—the territory of Dikaia was in fact annexed by Abdera at this point, then this would have created an Abderite 'enclave' east of Lake Bistonis, between Fanari in the south and the river Kompsatos in the north. It is very easy to see why the Maroneians would have wished to seize this putative enclave for themselves, thereby gaining access to the rich fisheries of Lake Bistonis (previously monopolized by Abdera?), in addition to a prime stretch of agricultural land.[55]

This can be nothing more than a hypothesis, but it would neatly explain why the dispute with Maroneia ended up proving so remarkably complex and document-heavy (**Document 1**, lines **B38–44**). The Abderites claimed that the land seized by Maroneia belonged to their own 'ancestral territory' (πάτριος χώρα, line **B32**), and the Teians evidently took the same view, 'considering as their own possessions the lands conquered and settled by their own ancestors' (ἴδια νομίσαντες ἑαυτῶν εἶναι τὰ διὰ τῶν ἰδίων προγόνων κρατηθέντα καὶ κατοικισθέντα, lines **B35–7**). Taken at face value, this would imply that the land under dispute was evidently and unproblematically part of the territory originally conquered by the first Teian settlers at Abdera in the mid-sixth century BC. But the Maroneians were clearly able to muster strong arguments to the contrary, suggesting that the status of the land as Abderite 'ancestral territory' was in fact open to question—as it would indeed have been, had the relevant stretch of land originally belonged to a third *polis* which had since ceased to exist!

This speculative chain of reasoning may be pushed one stage further. We have no way of knowing what arguments eventually persuaded the Erythraian

---

[54] Arrington et al. 2016, 54–5. Note in particular the near-total absence of Hellenistic coins from the site: Psoma, Karadima, and Terzopoulou 2008, 243–54; Arrington et al. 2016, 44–53.

[55] Fisheries: Arist. *Hist. an.* 8.13 (598a).

judges to award the disputed territory to Abdera (**Document 1**, lines **B49–50**). It is possible that they were instructed to employ the simple criterion often used by the Roman senate in arbitrating territorial disputes, awarding the land to whichever party was in possession at the point when the litigants became allies of the Roman people.[56] Possible, but in our view unlikely, since it is hard to imagine that this straightforward factual question could have given rise to the knotty arguments and multiple depositions evoked in the Abderite decree for Teos (lines **B38–44**). It is more likely that the dispute was resolved according to the legal principle regularly employed by Greek international arbitrators: the land would belong to whichever side had first acquired it by legitimate means, whether that be by inheritance, purchase, donation, or conquest.[57] As a result, land disputes often involved fantastically complex controversies over historical, historiographic, or even mythical traditions. Most famously, in the 190s BC, when a Rhodian commission arbitrated a long-running dispute between the cities of Priene and Samos over a stretch of land on the north flank of Mt Mykale around the fortress of Karion, the judgement turned on which of the two cities had been allotted Karion at the end of the semi-mythical Meliac War in the eighth century BC—a 'fact' eventually established by reference to no fewer than eight works of local historiography (one of which was judged by the commission to be fraudulent in some way).[58] It is easy to see how the dispute between Abdera and Maroneia, if it did (hypothetically) concern the question of legitimate title to the former territory of Dikaia, could have ended up requiring some formidably time-consuming research into the local historiography of the region in the sixth to fourth centuries BC: when was Dikaia founded, and by whom? When did it cease to exist as a *polis*? When did the Abderites first lay claim to its former territory, and by what right? It is, indeed, tempting to wonder whether the language used by the Abderites in lines **B35–7**—'[the Teians] considering as their own possessions the lands conquered and settled by their own ancestors' (ἴδια νομίσαντες ἑαυτῶν εἶναι τὰ διὰ τῶν ἰδίων προγόνων κρατηθέντα καὶ κατοικισθέντα)—is a kind of 'executive summary' of the argument eventually

---

[56] Chaniotis 2004, 193–4; Camia 2009, 199–202. See e.g. Sherk 1969, no. 7 (dispute between Magnesia and Priene, c.175–160 BC), lines 53–5 (Ager 1996, 321–7, no. 120; Camia 2009, 71–85, no. 7, II lines 20–2); Sherk 1969, no. 9 (Ager 1996, 425–9, no. 156; Camia 2009, 51–64, no. 5: dispute between Melitaia and Narthekion, c.140 BC).

[57] Chaniotis 2004, citing (186) the Magnesian arbitration between Itanos and Hierapytna (c.111 BC), *I.Cret.* III iv 9 (Ager 1996, no. 158 *II*; Camia 2009, no. 10 II), lines 133–4, for these four forms of legitimate acquisition (ἢ παρὰ προγόνων π[αραλαβόν]τες αὐτοὶ [ἢ πριάμενοι κατ'] ἀργυρίου δόσιν ἢ δόρατι κρατήσαντες ἢ παρά τινος τῶν κρεισσόν[ων σχόντες]).

[58] *I.Priene*² 132, with Magnetto 2008; on the use and critical assessment of historiographic texts to settle the dispute, see now Thomas 2019, 240–3, 283–6.

made by the Milesian advocate on Abdera's behalf at the final hearing: it was the *Teians* (or so the Abderites argued) who were responsible for the original conquest and settlement of the lands east of Lake Bistonis. For all we know, the argument may even have been true.[59] At any event, there is no doubt about the outcome of the dispute: the Erythraians were persuaded of the justice of the Abderite case, and restored the disputed territory to Abdera.

The two territorial disputes of the early 160s BC—both, in our view, to be dated in or around 166 BC—thus make for a striking counterpoint with one another. The immediate origins of the two disputes were, we assume, identical: in each case, a hostile neighbour of Abdera took advantage of the sack of 170 BC to annex a stretch of Abderite territory. But Rome chose to settle these two land-disputes in very different ways. The conflict between Abdera and Kotys impinged directly on Roman geopolitical interests in the region: at stake were Rome's future relations with a potentially useful client-king, and perhaps (as suggested above) the territorial integrity of the Macedonian first *meris*. Hence the arbitration was performed by the senate; as we argued above, the outcome was almost certainly defeat for Abdera, and quite probably for Kotys too. The dispute between the free cities of Abdera and Maroneia, by contrast, was of no particular significance to Rome, and so the arbitration was delegated to an independent third party; this time, Abdera was victorious.

In both instances, the Teians provided energetic and concrete support to the Abderite cause, mediated through specific individual Teian citizens: ambassadors to Rome to lobby on Abdera's behalf in the dispute with Kotys, and a team of legal specialists to prepare and present the Abderites' brief in the dispute with Maroneia. But the Abderites chose to commemorate these two episodes of Teian support in strikingly different ways.[60] After the conclusion of the dispute with Kotys, the Abderites voted to honour the two Teian ambassadors to Rome—not the Teian *dēmos*—in fulsome terms *qua* individuals; the emphasis throughout the decree for Amymon and Megathymos is on their extraordinary personal qualities (enthusiasm, intelligence, endurance, perseverance: **Document 6**, lines 11–27), and the only agency exercised by the Teian *dēmos* in the decree lies in their original selection of the ambassadors (lines 9–10). It is quite clear that the Abderites' victory in the Maroneia

---

[59] We do not know who founded Dikaia or when; Samos and Thasos have been suggested, on very fragile grounds (Tiverios 2008, 104–5).

[60] It is our strong suspicion that the two decrees were in fact drafted by the same individual. Both decrees, as we have seen, are unusually rhetorically and syntactically elaborate, and both show a marked enthusiasm for rare philosophically tinged vocabulary. See our commentaries on both inscriptions, *passim*.

dispute was likewise due to the labours of individual Teians, the 'commission-ers' (*synedroi*) selected to prepare the Abderites' dossier of evidence, and the individual advocate appointed to present their case at the tribunal (**Document 1**, lines **B38–43**). Yet the emphasis in the new Abderite decree is quite differ-ent: the individual Teian legal specialists are left unnamed, and the decree focuses not on their personal qualities, but on the agency of the Teian *dēmos* as a whole (the Teians 'dedicated themselves worthily and magnificently to the lawsuit over this stretch of land', lines **B37–8**, and 'completely took on in all respects the care of the lawsuit', lines **B42–3**).

It is possible, of course, that this apparent contrast is an illusion created by accidents of survival: the Abderites may well also have voted fulsome *ad hominem* honorific decrees for the commissioners and advocate in the Maroneia dispute, which just happen not to have survived. But it is nonethe-less striking how concerned the Abderites were, in the new decree in honour of the Teian *dēmos*, to present the Teians as a single anonymous collective acting with a single will (no Teian is mentioned by name at any point in the 120 surviving lines of text). And as we will see in Chapter 6, the thorough-going personification of the Teian *dēmos* in the new decree is not merely a rhetorical idiosyncrasy, but is in fact absolutely integral to the honours con-ferred on the Teian *dēmos* by the grateful people of Abdera.

6

The Statue of the *Dēmos* of the Teians

One of the most remarkable parts of the new decree of Abdera for the Teians (**Document 1**) is the description of the honorific statue of the *Dēmos* of the Teians, erected by the grateful Abderites in the most prominent place on the agora at Abdera (lines **B56–61**):

στῆσαι δὲ καὶ εἰκόνα χαλκῆν κολοσσικὴν τοῦ Δήμου τοῦ
[Τηΐων ἐπὶ τῆς] ἀγορᾶς ἐν τῶι ἐπιφανεστάτωι τόπωι, τῆι μὲν δεξιᾶι σπέν-
[δοντα κανθάρω]ι, τῆι δὲ ἀριστερᾶι ἀπηρεισμένον ἐπὶ τὴν στήλην ἐν ἧι γε-
[γράψεται τόδ]ε τὸ ψήφισμα, ἔστω δὲ καὶ κιόνιον παρεστηκὸς ἐκ τῶν εὐωνύ-
60   [μων, ἐφ᾽ οὗ ἐπ]έστω Νίκη στεφανοῦσα τὸν Τηΐων Δῆμον κισσοῦ στε-
[φάνωι·

'(Be it resolved) also to erect a colossal bronze statue of the *Dēmos* of the [Teians], on the agora in the most prominent spot, pouring a libation [with a kantharos] with the right hand, and with the left hand/arm leaning on the *stēlē* on which this decree shall be inscribed; and let there be a small column standing by on the left-hand side, [on which] let there be placed a Nike crowning the *Dēmos* of the Teians with an ivy-wreath.'

This is by some distance our longest surviving description of a Hellenistic honorific statue. The fact that the Abderites felt the need to describe the projected monument at such length strongly suggests that the statue-type was not a standard one; as we shall see, the statue is in fact idiosyncratic in almost every conceivable way.

To start with scale: the statue is described as 'colossal' (κολοσσικήν, line **B56**). Thanks to a number of recent studies, we can now be confident that the adjectives κολοσσικός and κολοσσιαῖος in Hellenistic epigraphy signify simply 'oversize', rather than (as previously thought) denoting a particular type of statue (with clasped legs).[1] The conventional height for an honorific statue

---

[1] Dickie 1996; Badoud 2011; Bresson 2012, 211–12, 216–17 (on *SEG* 61, 1140); Ma 2013, 250–1.

Teos and Abdera: Two Cities in Peace and War. Mustafa Adak and Peter Thonemann, Oxford University Press.
© Mustafa Adak and Peter Thonemann, 2022. DOI: 10.1093/oso/9780192845429.003.0007

was 4 cubits, slightly over life-size (*c*.1.80–2.20m).[2] A range of heights above 4 cubits are specified in epigraphic and literary sources for Hellenistic honorific statues. A late third-century bronze statue of the *Dēmos* of the Mylasians was 5 cubits high, the same size as a later cult-statue of Attalos III at the Pergamene Asklepieion.[3] Honorific bronze statues of the *Dēmos* of the Antiocheians (Alabanda) and Antiochos III at Delphi were 8 cubits high; according to Polybios, there was a 10-cubit statue of Attalos I in the agora at Sikyon.[4] The Colossus of Rhodes—an order of magnitude bigger—falls into a category of its own.[5] Polybios claims that the Rhodians erected a 30-cubit statue (*c*.13.5–14.0m) of the *Dēmos* of the Romans in their sanctuary of Athena in 164 BC.[6] This is suspiciously out of line with any other Hellenistic honorific statues known to us (none larger than 10 cubits),[7] and one wonders whether Polybios is in fact describing the total height of the Rhodian monument, not the statue alone; the early second-century pillar-monument erected on Samos in honour of the *Dēmos* of the Romans was a minimum of 7.38m tall, not including the base and the statue itself (so perhaps 10–11m in total).[8]

A very rough indication of the likely height of the statue of the *Dēmos* of the Teians is provided by the fact that it had its left hand or arm resting on top of the *stēlē* on which the decree is to be inscribed (more on this pose later). The total height of the Teian *stēlē* seems to have been *c*.2.75m, depending on the amount of uninscribed space at the base of the *stēlē*.[9] We have no way of knowing whether the Abderite copy of the decree was taller or shorter than the Teian copy (did it have a pediment?); note, though, that the lettering of the Teian copy is already extremely small by the standards of Hellenistic decrees (8–9mm), and it is hard to imagine that the Abderite copy could have been inscribed in still smaller letters.[10] The 'hand/arm resting on the *stēlē*' is compatible with the top of the *stēlē* being anywhere between the statue's waist

---

[2] R. R. R. Smith 2006, 29–30; Keesling 2017, 46.
[3] *Dēmos* of the Mylasians: *SEG* 58, 1220, and see further below. Attalos III: *OGIS* 332, line 7, with Robert 1987, 463.
[4] Delphi: *FD* III.4, 163, line 26. Sikyon: Polyb. 18.16.2.
[5] Supposedly 70 cubits: Badoud 2011, 118–21. Cult statues of gods could of course reach enormous proportions: e.g. the statue of Apollo Iatros at Apollonia Pontica, allegedly 30 cubits high (Plin. *HN* 34.17).
[6] Polyb. 31.4.4.
[7] Though note the fictitious fourth-century decree of 'Byzantion and Perinthos' preserved in the manuscripts of Dem. 18.90–1, a forgery of (perhaps) the later Hellenistic period (Canevaro 2013, 261–5; Russell 2017, 36 n. 52), which envisages the erection at Byzantion of three 16-cubit statues, depicting the *Dēmos* of the Athenians being crowned by the *Dēmos* of the Byzantines and Perinthians.
[8] Tiede 1990, 234–7, with Abb. 12.   [9] See above, Chapter 1, n. 3.
[10] The lettering of the contemporary decree for Amymon and Megathymos (**Document 6** above, Chapter 5) is 9–11mm in height; roughly contemporary inscribed decrees at Abdera have lettering between 10mm (*IThrakAig* E11, E12) and 16–18mm (*IThrakAig* E9).

and its chest. Nonetheless, if we assume a 2.50–2.75m *stēlē* at Abdera, and a comfortable pose with the left hand (or elbow) a little above waist-height, then the statue could hardly be much less than 4m or much more than 5m in height.[11] As we have seen, we have secure attestations in this period of other honorific bronze statues between 8 and 10 cubits in height (*c*.3.6–4.5m); our best guess is that we are dealing with a 10-cubit statue (*c*.4.5m).

Honorific (and other) statues of the *Dēmos*: a short history

The Abderite statue of the *Dēmos* of the Teians is an important addition to a large and complex dossier of epigraphic and visual evidence for honorific statues of personified *Dēmoi*. The material is abundant but scattered, and seems never to have been systematically brought together.[12] We here collect together all the examples known to us.

The earliest surviving visual depictions of the personified *Dēmos* appear on Athenian document reliefs of the fourth century BC. On these reliefs, the Athenian *Dēmos* is generally depicted as a mature bearded male, with medium-length hair (often bound by a fillet), wearing a himation over the left shoulder but otherwise nude to the waist; he sometimes carries or leans on a staff.[13] No Classical statues of the Athenian *Dēmos* survive, but Pausanias mentions a statue of the *Dēmos* by the fourth-century sculptor Leochares which was still visible in the Peiraieus in the second century AD.[14]

Very many of the extant fourth-century Athenian document reliefs are associated with honorific decrees for individuals, and depict the personified *Dēmos* crowning the human honorand.[15] On such honorific reliefs, the *Dēmos* is usually depicted as considerably taller than the person being crowned, on a

[11]   Another variable is of course the form of the base. If the *stēlē* was set into the floor of the agora at ground-level, but the statue stood on an independent base, then the statue could be significantly shorter than these calculations would suggest.

[12]   The largest collection of material is that of Messerschmidt 2003, 10–47, with catalogue 168–80, 209–30.

[13]   Lawton 1995, 55–8; Glowacki 2003, with tabulation of extant reliefs; A. C. Smith 2011, 96–102; Martin 2013, I 10–13.

[14]   Paus. 1.1.3. He also records seeing a statue of the Athenian *Dēmos* in the Bouleuterion (1.3.5), sculpted by Lyson (date uncertain), and a monumental statue (ἀνδριὰς μεγέθει μέγας) of the *Dēmos* of the Spartans in the *agora* at Sparta (3.11.10), of unknown date. Fifth- and fourth-century paintings featuring depictions of the Athenian *Dēmos* are attested in literary sources: Habicht 1990, 259–60; Glowacki 2003, 450–1; Messerschmidt 2003, 209–10.

[15]   Exceptional in many ways is the document relief associated with the anti-tyranny law of Eukrates in 336 BC (*IG* II/III³ I,2, 320: standing *Dēmokratia* crowning seated *Dēmos*), on which see Blanshard 2004.

similar scale to Athena in cases where she also appears in the relief.[16] This motif of the *Dēmos* crowning (or passing a crown to) a human honorand is also occasionally found on reliefs outside Athens, as on a document relief from Samos of the late fourth century BC.[17]

We know of four Hellenistic examples of honorific monuments for individual humans which take this general form (a statue-group depicting a personification of the *Dēmos* crowning the human honorand).[18] The earliest is described in a decree of Mylasa dating to the second half of the third century BC (although not inscribed until the later second century BC): the Mylasans vote to erect a bronze statue of the dynast Olympichos, probably in the agora at Mylasa, 'and also to erect a bronze statue of the *Dēmos*, 5 cubits high, crowning the statue of Olympichos'.[19] A century later, in (perhaps) the mid-second century BC, the city of Kyme voted extraordinary honours for the civic benefactor Archippe, including a bronze statue of Archippe to be erected in front of the *bouleuterion*, 'and let there be erected on the same base also a colossal bronze statue of the *Dēmos* crowning her'; the base also carried a bronze statue of her father Dikaiogenes.[20] In the late second or early first century BC, a citizen of (apparently) Mesembria was posthumously honoured at Mesembria and Tomis with statue-groups described in identical language: 'a bronze statue and an accompanying statue of the *Dēmos* crowning his statue'.[21] Finally, the honours voted for Diodoros Pasparos at Pergamon in the mid-first century BC included several statues, among them 'a colossal bronze statue being crowned by the *Dēmos*', to be erected wherever Diodoros might choose.[22]

In the first two of these four cases (Olympichos and Archippe), it is notable that the size of the statue of the *Dēmos* is explicitly indicated as above life-size

---

[16] Lawton 1995, 57–8; Glowacki 2003, 459; Blanshard 2004, 11.

[17] *IG* XII 6, 20 (illustrated e.g. *LIMC* III 2, 276, Demos 64), an honorific decree for a Kardian, thanking him for assistance in the return of the Samians from exile: a large seated *Dēmos* passes a crown to a much smaller mortal. Comparable too is the monument of C. Iulius Zoilos at Aphrodisias (late first century BC), on which *Dēmos* is depicted clasping the hand of Zoilos, who is meanwhile being crowned by the personified *Polis* of Aphrodisias: R. R. R. Smith 1993, 32–41.

[18] For this statue-type, cf. Wilhelm 1921b, 78–80.

[19] *SEG* 58, 1220 (Isager and Karlsson 2008; *CGRN* 150), lines 5–6: στῆσαι δὲ καὶ τοῦ Δήμ[ου εἰκόνα χαλκῆν πήχε]ων πέντε στεφανοῦσαν τὴν Ὀλυμ[πίχου εἰκόνα]; see further Marek and Zingg 2018, 120–6.

[20] *SEG* 33, 1035, lines 2–4: παρ[στᾶ]σαι δ[ὲ αὐ]τᾶ ἐπὶ τῶ αὐτῶ βάματος καὶ εἰκόνα χαλκέαν τῶ Δά[μω κ]ολοσσιαίαν στεφάνοισαν αὐτάν; similarly *SEG* 33, 1037, lines 12–14. For the date, see van Bremen 2008.

[21] *SEG* 50, 687 bis: εἰκόνι χαλκῆι καὶ παραστέματι Δήμου στεφανοῦντι αὐτοῦ τὴν εἰκόνα. At Mesembria the 'accompanying statue' (παράστεμα) can only be the *Dēmos* of Mesembria; at Tomis it was presumably the *Dēmos* of Tomis, although the inscription does not make this clear.

[22] *IGRR* IV 292, lines 24–6: στεφανῶσαι αὐτὸν ... καὶ ἄλλῃ χαλκῆι κολοσσικῆι στεφανου[μένηι ὑπὸ] τοῦ δήμου.

('5 cubits' in the Olympichos group, 'colossal' in the Archippe group), while that of the statue of the honorand is not. We may therefore reasonably assume that in each instance the statue of the *Dēmos* was distinctly taller than the (life-size?) human honorand, a pattern which, as we have seen, is also standard on Classical Athenian document reliefs.[23]

In each of these cases, the statue-image depicts the personified *Dēmos* honouring a human individual. Literary sources also inform us of the existence of Hellenistic statue-groups which featured one *Dēmos* crowning another *Dēmos*: Polybios informs us that in the wake of the Rhodian earthquake of *c.*226 BC, Hieron II of Syracuse erected a pair of statues at Rhodes depicting the *Dēmos* of the Syracusans crowning the *Dēmos* of the Rhodians.[24]

A somewhat different group of Hellenistic *Dēmos*-statues (like our new example at Abdera) consists of honorific statues for the *Dēmos* itself, sometimes in association with honoured individuals. Such statues were typically set up in contexts of international diplomacy: community *x* erects a statue of the *Dēmos* of community *y*, usually (but not always) in the city of the community *x* rather than that of community *y*. The earliest example known to us dates to 201 BC, when the Delphians passed a decree recognizing the *asylia* of Chrysaorian Antiocheia (Alabanda), and 'crowned' both the *Dēmos* of the Antiocheians and Antiochos III with bronze statues 8 cubits high, to be erected in the sanctuary of Pythian Apollo.[25] The physical relationship between the two statues is not clear: the fact that the decree was to be inscribed 'on the base of King Antiochos' suggests that the two statues were separate monuments.

Examples of honorific statues for the *Dēmoi* of foreign cities proliferate in the second and first centuries BC. In 182 BC, the Aitolian League recognized the *asylia* of Athena Nikephoros at Pergamon and the Panhellenic status of the Pergamene Nikephoria; among the honours voted by the Aitolians were gilt statues of Eumenes II (equestrian), his three brothers, his mother Apollonis, and the *Dēmos* of the Pergamenes (all 'on foot').[26] At some point in the second century BC, a Hellenistic monarch (perhaps Orophernes of Kappadokia) decided to erect a bronze statue of the *Dēmos* of the Prieneans at Priene, for

---

[23] Bresson 2012, 212.

[24] Polyb. 5.88.8. The statues were erected at the Rhodian *deigma*, apparently part of the harbour-market: Bresson 2016, 309–13.

[25] *CID* IV 99 (Rigsby 1996, 332–4, no. 163; Ma 2002, 305–8, no. 16; Messerschmidt 2003, 174–5, D16), line 26, στεφανοῖ ἑκάτερον εἰκόνι χαλκέαι ὀκταπάχει; 'base of King Antiochos', line 33. Cf. also Biard 2010.

[26] *FD* III 3, 240 (Rigsby 1996, 371–4, no. 178), lines 11–14, [στεφανῶ]σαι ἕκαστον αὐτῶν εἰκόνι χρυσέαι, τὸμ μὲν βασιλέα ἐφ' ἵππου, τοὺς δὲ ἄ[λλους πεζικᾶι].

unknown reasons. This statue cost a minimum of 3,000 drachms, and perhaps considerably more; comparison with other attested costs for honorific statues in the Hellenistic period suggests that this must have been an especially lavish monument.[27] On Delos, in either 122/121 or 110/109 BC, the *koinon* of the Poseidoniasts of Berytos dedicated a bronze statue of the *Dēmos* of the Athenians to Apollo,[28] and in the aftermath of the first Mithradatic War (*c.*85 BC), the Lykian *koinon* honoured the *Dēmos* of the Xanthians with a gold crown and a 'colossal bronze statue' (probably at Xanthos) in recognition of its exemplary behaviour during the war.[29]

Particularly numerous (and apparently all dating to the second half of the second century BC) are honorific statues of foreign *Dēmoi* erected in gratitude for the despatch of foreign judges; in each case the statue seems to have been set up in the city conferring the honours.[30] Honorific bronze statues of the foreign *Dēmos* alone, without accompanying statues of the judges, were set up by the city of Tanagra in honour of the *Dēmos* of the Megarians;[31] by the city of Peparethos for the *Dēmos* of the Larisaians, and perhaps also for the *Dēmos* of the Lakedaimonians (the relevant clause is restored from the decree for Larisa);[32] and by the city of Demetrias for the *Dēmos* of the Magnesians on the Maeander.[33] In other instances, the bronze statue of the foreign *Dēmos* was set up alongside statues of the judges themselves: so the Larbenoi erected a bronze statue of the *Dēmos* of the Magnesians, 'as beautiful as possible, in the most prominent place in the city', along with bronze statues of the three Magnesian judges and their *grammateus*;[34] the city of Akraiphia set up a bronze statue of the *Dēmos* of the Larisaians, along with bronze statues of the three individual judges;[35] the small city of Peltai in Phrygia honoured the *Dēmos* of the Antandrians with a bronze statue, along with a bronze statue of the single Antandrian judge;[36] and the city of Peparethos honoured the *Dēmos* of the Andrians with a bronze statue, accompanied by bronze

---

[27] *I.Priene*² 10, lines 9–10, εἰς τὴν εἰκόνα τοῦ Δήμου ἣν ἐποι[ησάμ]εθα ὑ[π]αναλώσαντας Ἀλεξανδρείας δραχμὰς τρισχιλίας. See Martin 2013, I 14 n. 74; Ma 2013, 264–5 (cost); as Ma notes, there is no reason to think that this was part of a larger statue-group.

[28] *I.Délos* 1777 (Messerschmidt 2003, 173–4, D15); for the date, Cohen 2006, 208.

[29] *SEG* 55, 1503: εἰκόνι χαλκῇ κολοσσικῇ.   [30] Ma 2007a, 91–3.

[31] *IG* VII, 20, lines 3–4.   [32] *SEG* 26, 677, lines 51–3 (Larisa); *SEG* 47, 357, line 9 (Sparta).

[33] *I.Magnesia* 104, with Robert, *OMS* II, 1073; Helly 1971, 553–4. It is not clear whether the five Magnesian judges also received individual statues.

[34] *I.Magnesia* 101, lines 22–3, στῆσαι δὲ αὐτοῦ καὶ εἰκόνα χαλκῆν ὡς καλλίστην ἐν τῶι ἐπι[φα]νεστάτωι τόπωι τῆς πόλεως. On the identity of the Larbenoi (probably in Karia), Robert 1962, 142–9.

[35] *IG* VII, 4130, lines 30–2; 4131, lines 3–5. The judges' statues are specified as '4 cubits high'; the size of the statue of the *Dēmos* of the Larisaians is not specified (was it larger?).

[36] Michel 1900, no. 542, lines 32–4.

statues of the three Andrian judges.[37] A further decree for Andrian judges seems also to have involved the erection of a bronze statue of the *Dēmos* of the Andrians along with bronze statues of the judges, although the relevant clauses are restored.[38] In the mid-second century BC, the city of Eretria honoured no fewer than five different cities for sending foreign judges (Miletos, Sparta, Oropos, Messene, Kos). In the first three instances, we are told that the Eretrians erected honorific bronze statues (at Eretria) of the relevant *Dēmos* (the Milesians, Lakedaimonians, and Oropians); only the Lakedaimonian judges also receive individual statues. The *Dēmoi* of the Messenians and Koans may also have received statues, but the relevant parts of the decrees are missing.[39]

An especially interesting case comes from the city of Istros (perhaps second century BC). A decree in honour of a civic benefactor, Dionysios son of Strouthion, specifies that his bronze statue is to be erected 'in the agora, next to the *Dēmos* and the statues standing beside it'.[40] We have no way of knowing in what context this personification of the *Dēmos* of Istros was originally erected, but it seems to have served as the focal point for the erection of honorific statues for citizens of Istros (the other statues standing beside it are presumably civic honorifics like the statue voted for Dionysios). The sanctuary of the *Dēmos* and Charites at Athens (see further below) similarly served as a location for the erection of Athenian honorific monuments in the later Hellenistic period.[41]

The second century BC also saw a proliferation of honorific bronze statues of the *Dēmos* of the Romans (the *populus Romanus*), erected by Greek communities both in their home cities and at Rome.[42] Few of these can be precisely dated. Perhaps the earliest example is a pillar monument carrying a statue of the *Dēmos* of the Romans erected by the Samians and dedicated to Hera, tentatively dated to *c*.188 BC.[43] A fragmentary inscription from Delos,

---

[37] *SEG* 51, 1073 (Andros), lines 5–6 (restored); for the attribution of the latter decree (Peparethos or Gyaros?), *SEG* 56, 989.

[38] *IG* XII Suppl. 258, lines 13–16.

[39] Miletos: *Milet* I 3, 154, lines 8–13. Sparta: *IG* XII Suppl. p. 201, lines 1–3 (*Dēmos*) and 5–6 (judges). Oropos: *I.Oropos* 330, lines 13–17, and 331, lines 8–11, with *SEG* 57, 449 (to be erected 'in the most beautiful spot of the city [sc. of Eretria]'). Messene: *SEG* 41, 330. Kos: *IG* XII 4, 1, 169. See further Gauthier 1993; Knoepfler 2001, 409–20; Ma 2007a, 91–3.

[40] *IScM* I, 19, lines 13–15: [ἐν τῆι ἀγο]ρᾶι παρὰ τὸν Δῆμον καὶ τὰς εἰκόν[ας τὰς παρεστώ]σα[ς αὐ]τῶ[ι]; Robert, *OMS* V, 50–1 n. 2.

[41] Habicht 1982, 85; Mikalson 1998, 173; Messerschmidt 2003, 212–14.

[42] Martin 2013, I 95–7.

[43] Tiede 1990; inscription, *IG* XII 6, 1, 350 (Habicht 1990). The monument may reflect Samian gratitude for Manlius Vulso's overturning in 188 BC of the Rhodians' settlement (in Priene's favour) of the long-standing land dispute between Samos and Priene a few years earlier (Ager 1996, no. 99).

dating around 170 BC, refers to 'crowns' for the *Dēmos* of the Romans and the senate, but it is not clear whether a statue (or indeed a cult) was involved.[44] Another monumental pillar carrying a bronze statue of the *Dēmos* of the Romans was erected at Kaunos, probably in gratitude for the liberation of Karia from Rhodes in 167 BC.[45] Polybios tells us that a statue of the *Dēmos* of the Romans was set up in the sanctuary of Athena at Rhodes in 164 BC; this too may have been a pillar monument of a similar kind, if the height reported by Polybios (30 cubits) refers to the total height of the monument rather than the statue alone.[46] On the Capitoline at Rome, probably in the mid-second century BC, honorific statues of the *Dēmos* of the Romans were set up by the city of Laodikeia on the Lykos and Mithradates IV of Pontos, and apparently also by Ephesos and the Lykian *koinon*;[47] at Kos, a statue of the *Dēmos* of the Romans was erected at some point in the first century BC.[48] A statue of the *Dēmos* of the Romans is also known from Termessos, but the date is wholly uncertain (perhaps first century BC?).[49]

The erection of honorific statues of the personified *Dēmos* continued in the Roman imperial period, both as 'external' honorific practice (city *x* erects a statue of the *Dēmos* of city *y*, at either city *x* or city *y*) and in its less common 'internal' form (a statue of the *Dēmos* of city *x* erected by city *x* within city *x*).[50] At some point in the first century BC, the Koans erected a bronze statue of the *Dāmos* of the Myndians in the Asklepieion at Kos.[51] At Athens, around the turn of the era, honorific statues of the *Dēmos* of the Lakedaimonians, the *Dēmos* of the Delphians, the *Dēmos* of the Romans, and the *Dēmos* of the Andrians were erected on the Acropolis, perhaps near the Propylaia; an unidentified *koinon* also erected a statue of the *Dēmos* of the Athenians on the Acropolis, perhaps around the same date.[52] Also dating around the turn of

---

[44] *I.Délos* 465 c, line 20, with Habicht 1990, 262.
[45] *I.Kaunos* 89; cf. Errington 1987 on the emergence of cults of Roma in Karia after 167.
[46] Polyb. 31.4.4; see further above, on 'colossal' statues.
[47] *IGUR* I 6 (Laodikeia); *IGUR* I 9 (Mithradates); *CIL* I² 727 (Ephesos); *CIL* I² 726 (Lykian *koinon*); for the date, Habicht 1990, 264; cf. also Messerschmidt 2003, 35–47, 177–9.
[48] *IG* XII 4, 2, 856.   [49] *SEG* 57, 1433.
[50] 'Internal' honorific statues of the personified *Dēmos* are attested e.g. at Amastris (Marek 1993, 163 no. 18, III AD), Ephesos (*I.Ephesos* 2052: II AD), Aphrodisias (*IAph2007* 8.52 [I AD], 2.111 [II AD], 14.12 [II/III AD], 12.922 [III AD], Stratonikeia (*I.Strat.* 1026: I AD), Hierapolis (*SEG* 41, 1199: c. AD 100), Eumeneia (*SEG* 28, 1115: II AD), Apameia (*IGRR* IV 792: I AD), Balboura (*SEG* 38, 1445: III AD), Kremna (*I.Pisid.Cen.* 10 and 37, II and III AD respectively), Termessos (*TAM* III 1, 48 and 49, III AD), Side (*I.Side* 29: III AD). In the mid-first century AD, the Lindians set up a statue of the *Dēmos* of the Rhodians (*Lindos* II, 438), the *polis* of which Lindos formed a part. See Martin 2013, I 253–79 (catalogue).
[51] *IG* XII 4 2, 873, I, with Höghammar 1993, 51–2 (apparently an over-life-size statue).
[52] *IG* II² 3446 (Delphians), 3447 (Romans), 3452 (Andrians); *SEG* 30, 139 (Lakedaimonians); *IG* II² 2964 (Athenians); cf. Schmalz 2009, 127–8.

the era is a base at Oropos that carried a bronze statue of the *Dēmos* of the Athenians.[53] Between AD 17 and AD 50, the Sardians set up at Sardeis a statue of the *Dēmos* of the Athenians, 'their kinsmen'.[54] Under Domitian, the Philadelphians set up a statue of the *Dēmos* of the Ephesians at Ephesos, and in the early third century AD, the Ephesians erected statues at Ephesos of the *Dēmoi* of the Knidians and Koans.[55] Around AD 200, the Lakedaimonians set up a statue of the *Dēmos* of the Selgeis at Selge.[56] In the third century AD, the Aphrodisians erected statues of the *Dēmoi* of at least seven neighbouring cities (including Keretapa, Hierapolis, Kibyra, Apollonia and Herakleia under Salbake, and Tabai) on the occasion of the grant to Aphrodisias of a new sacred contest.[57] At an uncertain date, the people of Ioulis on Keos erected (at Ioulis) an honorific monument for the *Dēmos* of the Athenians, perhaps including a statue.[58] Also undatable are a statue of the *Dēmos* of the Pergamenes erected by the Athenians at Pergamon, and a statue of the *Dēmos* of the Eleians erected by the Lakedaimonians at Olympia.[59]

The *Dēmos* of the Teians: iconography

There is virtually no direct evidence for the appearance of these various Hellenistic statues of personified *Dēmoi*. Classical Athenian depictions of the personified *Dēmos* in document reliefs always depict him as a mature bearded male (see above); extant Roman-period marble statues of the personified *Dēmos* and depictions on provincial bronze coinage show that by the Augustan period at the latest, he could also be represented as a youthful male figure.[60] It has been plausibly argued that the late Hellenistic statues of the *Dēmos* of the Romans may have adopted the characteristic iconography of the *Genius populi Romani*, a mature bearded male holding a cornucopiae.[61] In

---

[53] *I.Oropos* 460, with the simple label Δῆμος Ἀθηναίων.
[54] *Sardis* VII 1, 40.
[55] *I.Ephesos* 236, 2054, 2055.   [56] *I.Selge* 6.
[57] Rouché 1993, 182–7, nos. 58–64; now *IAph 2007* 12.924–12.930.
[58] *IG* XII 5, 626; dated to the second century BC, on unclear grounds, by Messerschmidt 2003, 176 D17.
[59] *I.Pergamon* II, 452; *IvO* 316.   [60] *LIMC* 3.1, 375–82, s.v. Demos; Martin 2013, I 34–50.
[61] Fears 1978, 279–80 (refuting the argument of Mellor 1975, 25–6, 152–3, that depictions of Roma and the *Dēmos* of the Romans were indistinguishable); Martin 2013, I 93–101. For example, coins of Alexandria struck under Nero (*RPC* I 5204, 5214, 5224, 5234, 5254) depict the '*Dēmos* of the Romans' with the cornucopiae of the *Genius populi Romani*. But on first- or second-century bronzes of Synnada (*BMC Phrygia* 394, no. 15; Martin 2013, II 234; *RPC* III 2620A) the '*Dēmos* of the Romans' is depicted holding a *phialē* in his outstretched right hand, with a scroll (?) in his left hand; clearly there was variety.

the context of Hellenistic honorific statues for *Dēmoi* who had despatched foreign judges, John Ma speculates that 'The representation of the people of foreign communities might have taken the form of a male, citizen-like figure, in the standard garb of himation and chiton, embodying civic values: this would have been particularly appropriate in the transaction of foreign judges, where a city asked another for good men to help with intra-civic disputes'.[62]

The new Abdera decree is thus particularly valuable in providing a detailed description of the oversize statue of the *Dēmos* of the Teians erected in the agora at Abdera. The *Dēmos* is described as 'pouring a libation with the right hand' (τῆι μὲν δεξιᾶι σπέν[δοντα], **B57–8**), almost certainly from a kantharos ([κανθάρω]ι, **B58**; for the restoration, see below). With its left hand or arm, the *Dēmos* is 'leaning on the *stēlē* on which this decree shall be inscribed' (τῆι δὲ ἀριστερᾶι ἀπηρεισμένον ἐπὶ τὴν στήλην ἐν ἧι γε[γράψεται τόδ]ε τὸ ψήφισμα, **B58–9**). Although *stēlai* carrying honorific decrees conferring statue-honours are often set up next to the relevant statues,[63] we know of no real parallels for this wholesale incorporation of the inscription into the statue-monument. The closest analogy is found on an Augustan statue-base from Oropos, which apparently carried a personification of the Athenian Areiopagos. The cuttings on the top of the base show that the statue-group took the form of a life-size bronze statue, with (apparently) a bronze or marble *stēlē* (W. *c.*0.40m, Th. 0.065m) standing immediately to the right of the statue on top of the base (Fig. 6.1). John Ma attractively suggests that 'the stele might have represented the laws, and the Areiopagos would thus have been represented in its traditional role as "guardian of the laws"'.[64]

What is the precise position of the *Dēmos*' left arm in the statue at Abdera? The Greek term ἡ ἀριστερά could equally well refer to the statue's left hand, or its left arm more generally; hence the statue could in principle either be standing upright, with the left hand resting lightly on the (flat?) top of the *stēlē*, or leaning on the *stēlē* with its left elbow or forearm, with part of the statue's weight being carried by the *stēlē*. The choice of verb seems to indicate that the latter is intended, since (ἀπ)ερείδεσθαι typically means to 'lean' or 'support oneself' on something. Homer uses the phrase ἔγχει ἐρειδόμενος to indicate supporting one's weight on a spear, and Pausanias describes a statue at Elis of

---

[62] Ma 2007a, 93. For speculation on the appearance of the colossal statue of the *Dēmos* of the Antiocheians at Delphi, Biard 2010, 147–51.

[63] e.g. *I.Délos* 1517, lines 40–1, and *SEG* 33, 682 (Paros), lines 27–8 (honours for Aglaos of Kos, *c.*154 BC); *SEG* 39, 1244 (Klaros: decree for Menippos), Col. III, lines 47–8; *I.Priene*² 16 (honours for Megabyxos), lines 19–22, with Blümel's commentary.

[64] *I.Oropos* 461, with Ma 2007a, 95–6. For other idiosyncratic cuttings on Hellenistic statue-bases (none closely parallel to the present case), Ma 2018.

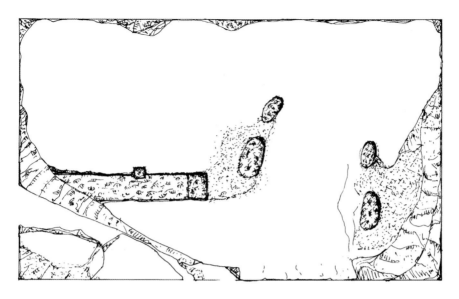

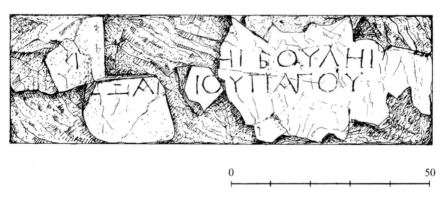

0   50

Fig. 6.1. Statue-base of the Athenian Areiopagos (?), from Oropos, with cutting for bronze or marble *stēlē. I.Oropos* 461.

Reproduced from V. Petrakos, *Οἱ ἐπιγραφὲς τοῦ Ὠρωποῦ* (Athens 1997), no. 461, p. 379, fig. 68, courtesy of The Archaeological Society at Athens.

a beardless youth with his legs crossed, 'leaning on a spear with both hands' (ταῖς χερσὶν ἀμφοτέραις ἐπὶ δόρατι ἠρεισμένος).[65] One of the fourth-century BC healing miracles from Epidauros concerns a lame man who arrived at the

---

[65] H. *Il.* 14.38, 19.49; *Od.* 10.170; similarly *Il.* 2.109 (Agamemnon leans on his sceptre) and 8.496 (Hector leans on his spear). Statue at Elis: Paus. 6.25.5. Cf. Dio Cass. 65.13, ἑστηκότας καὶ ἐπὶ τὰ δόρατα ἐπερηρεισμένους, 'standing and leaning on their spears', and Ov. *Fast.* 1.177 (Janus leans on his staff, *incumbens baculo*).

sanctuary 'leaning on a crutch' ([ἐπὶ βακτηρίας] ἀπερειδόμενος).⁶⁶ Herodotos similarly uses the verb to describe statues 'resting on their knees' (τοῖσι γούνασι ἐρηρεισμένους), and Diodoros describes a person 'supported on two feet' as τῷ δυσὶν ἠρεισμένῳ σκέλεσι.⁶⁷ The Delian inventory-lists include references to a stone statuette of Aphrodite in a niche, 'leaning on a rudder' (ἀφροδίσιον ἐν ναιδίῳ ἀπηρεισμένον ἐπὶ πηδαλίου).⁶⁸ In Callimachus' *Aetia*, Klio begins a speech while 'resting her hand on her sister's shoulder'; most probably she is being physically supported by her sister, rather than simply touching her affectionately.⁶⁹ The only similar example known to us which seems not to involve weight-transfer comes in Plutarch's *Life of Sulla*, where Sulla's future wife Valeria briefly rests her hand on Sulla's garment to pluck off a thread (*Sull.* 35, τήν τε χεῖρα πρὸς αὐτὸν ἀπηρείσατο); the Greek most naturally describes Valeria simply resting her hand lightly on Sulla's shoulder, rather than leaning on him. However, given the other passages cited here, the balance of probability seems to us to be in favour of the *Dēmos* of the Teians leaning on the top of the *stēlē* with its left elbow or forearm.

On the left-hand side of the statue (presumably behind the statue's left shoulder), a small column (*kionion*), is to be erected, presumably of marble, with a (bronze?) Nike perched on top, crowning the Teian *Dēmos* with an ivy-wreath (ἔστω δὲ καὶ κιόνιον παρεστηκὸς ἐκ τῶν εὐωνύ[μων], ἐφ' οὗ ἐπ]έστω Νίκη στεφανοῦσα τὸν Τηΐων Δῆμον κισσοῦ στε[φάνωι], B59–61). Nike does not seem a particularly appropriate deity to appear in this statue group (no 'victory' has been won by either the Teians or Abderites), and one might have instead expected a personification of the *Dēmos* of the Abderites to be conferring this ivy-crown.⁷⁰ However, the motif of a Nike crowning a human, a deity, or a personification is widespread in Hellenistic art, and not only in contexts of military or athletic victory. Hellenistic royal coinages often depict a small Nike (held by Zeus or Athena) crowning the name of a ruler (Lysimachos, Philetairos, Flamininus, Antiochos IV), or (less often) the name of a city or private individual.⁷¹ In his *Life of Sulla*, Plutarch describes a real-life spectacle laid on in the

---

⁶⁶ *IG* IV² 1, 123, line 125. The lame Hephaistos rests the weight of his shoulder on his hammer in Ap. Rhod. *Argon.* 4.957: ἐπὶ στελεῇ τυπίδος βαρὺν ὦμον ἐρείσας.

⁶⁷ Hdt. 4.152; Diod. Sic. 4.12.6. Cf. e.g. Pl. *Symp.* 190a; Arist. *Hist. an.* 567a.

⁶⁸ *I.Délos* 1416, A.1 line 16; 1417, B.1 line 13; 1452, line A16; see Bruneau 1980, 170.

⁶⁹ Callim. *Aet.* Fr. 43.57, χεῖρ' ἐπ' ἀδελφειῆς ὦμον ἐρεισαμένη, taken by Harder 2012, II 335–6 as indicating physical support (as apparently also in Nonnus, *Dion.* 39.254–5).

⁷⁰ Cf. the statue-group erected at Rhodes by Hieron II of Syracuse *c.*226 BC, depicting the *Dēmos* of the Syracusans crowning the *Dēmos* of the Rhodians: Polyb. 5.88.8. It seems unlikely that the Nike in the Abderite statue-group is intended to allude to the 'victory' in the lawsuit against the Maroneians: the decree uses the verb κατώρθωσεν (B49), not ἐνίκησεν.

⁷¹ Cities: e.g. bronze trichalka of Thessalian Pelinna (early second century BC), *SNG Cop.* 192; *CNG Triton* XV, 525–6, 535; also bronzes of the Syrian Tetrapolis (149–147 BC), Martin 2013, I 22–6. Individuals: Athenopolis at Priene, Thonemann 2015, 64.

theatre at Pergamon in 88 BC, when a statue of Nike holding a wreath was winched down from on high towards Mithradates, as if descending from the heavens to crown him.[72] We know of no other examples of a Nike crowning a personified *Dēmos*, but the image of a small Nike crowning the seated Tyche of Antiocheia is a common motif on gems of the early imperial period.[73]

The earliest visual representation of a small Nike on a column crowning a larger figure is found on autonomous bronze coins of Karne in Phoenicia, precisely dated to 221/220 BC (Fig. 6.2).[74] These coins depict a standing Asklepios (or a local deity identified with Asklepios, e.g. Ešmun) with a small column to his left, on which perches a small Nike placing a crown on the god's head. In the Roman imperial period, images of Nike on a column crowning a deity proliferate on the coinages of Phoenicia; numerous coin-issues of Berytos depict the city-goddess Tyche within a tetrastyle temple, being crowned by a Nike on a column, and the same basic type (with variants) appears on the coins of some thirteen other cities of the region (Fig. 6.3).[75] The presence of the column renders it effectively certain that all these coins depict real-life statue-groups at Karne, Berytos, and elsewhere: as Andreas Kropp has put it, 'The two-dimensional surface of the coin renders such a

Fig. 6.2. Karne (AE), 221/0 BC. Obv.: bust of Tyche r. Rev.: Asklepios standing r., leaning on serpent staff; at r., small column surmounted by Nike, crowning Asklepios. *CNG* E-Auction 421 (30/05/18), Lot 366 (20mm, 5.04g).

Classical Numismatic Group, LLC (www.cngcoins.com).

---

[72] Plut. *Sull.* 11. There is a very similar description in Plutarch's *Life of Sertorius* (22.2) of honours paid to Metellus 'in the cities' after a victory over Sertorius: mechanical Nikai were suspended over Metellus' head at banquets, and descended bearing 'golden trophies and wreaths'.

[73] M. Meyer 2006, 186–92, 209–10.   [74] Duyrat 2002, 38, Karne Series 3; Fleischer 1983, 258.

[75] Fleischer 1983, 254–8; Kropp 2011, 389–98. The earliest coins were struck under Trajan, but Tyche crowned by Nike on a column already appears on countermarks applied at Berytos under Claudius: Howgego 1985, 150, nos. 242–3.

Fig. 6.3. Berytos (AE), AD 217. Obv.: bust of Macrinus r. Rev.: Tyche standing facing within tetrastyle temple; at r., small column surmounted by Nike, crowning Tyche. *CNG* 93 (22/05/13), Lot 991 (24mm, 12.05g).
Classical Numismatic Group, LLC (www.cngcoins.com).

support obsolete—the Nike could simply be shown fluttering in mid-air—but the depiction of the column prop shows that a three-dimensional model (for which the support was indispensable) lies at the root of this image'.[76]

Returning to the statue of the *Dēmos* of the Teians, we might ask ourselves why the Abderites selected these particular, highly unusual attributes and pose for the statue, and why they bothered to describe them at such length in the decree—a description which, in its length and detail, is completely unparalleled in honorific epigraphy.[77] Evidently the pose and attributes were carefully selected and agreed by the Abderite *dēmos* (rather than being left to the sculptor's discretion), in order to maximize the honour to the Teians; this was no ordinary personification of the *Dēmos*, but one which was in some way intended to express the extraordinary gratitude of the Abderites for the Teians' equally extraordinary benefactions.

As it happens, a second-century coin-type from Teos, which emerged only in 2019, provides the answer. A single specimen is known of a Teian tetradrachm-issue, struck sometime around the middle of the second

---

[76] Kropp 2011, 398.
[77] When decrees offer any specifications at all about the form of an honorific statue, they tend to be highly tailored to the individual honorand: cf. e.g. the cult-statue of Lysimachos erected at Priene, which appears to have been flanked by a bronze lion (*I.Priene*² 2, lines 15–16, [καὶ π]αραστήσει ἐξ δεξιᾶς λ[έ]ο[ντα]), reflecting the prominence of Lysimachos' status as a 'lion-slayer' in his royal ideology (Lund 1992, 6–8, 160–1).

Fig. 6.4. Teos (AR), *c.*165–140 BC. Obv.: bust of youthful Dionysos r., wearing ivy-wreath. Rev.: Dionysos standing l., pouring libation from kantharos with r. hand, holding thyrsus in l.; left elbow resting on pedestal at r., surmounted by small figure. At r., *THIΩN*; at l., *Λ–Κ* monogram. *Roma* XVII (28/03/19), Lot 451 (36mm, 16.67g).

Roma Numismatics Ltd (www.RomaNumismatics.com).

century BC (Fig. 6.4).[78] The obverse type carries a beardless bust of the youthful Dionysos, with a curling lock of hair falling onto his shoulder; he wears a wreath of ivy-leaves and flowers high on the head above the hairline, and a headband on the brow just below the hairline.[79] The reverse carries a full-length depiction of the youthful Dionysos, with his head turned to his right; his body is shown in an *S*-shaped posture, with the right hip thrust outwards, and the left leg slightly bent. His torso is nude to the genitals; below the genitals, he has a cloak draped around his hips and hooked over his left elbow. His extended right hand holds a kantharos, from which the god appears to be pouring a libation; the left hand grasps a long thyrsus. The bent left elbow rests on the top corner of a rectangular pedestal with upper and lower mouldings, which bears part of the god's weight.[80] On top of the pedestal, facing away from Dionysos, stands a small figure, apparently bearded (see further below).[81]

---

[78] *Roma* Auction XVII (28/03/19), Lot 451; *Roma* Auction XX (29/10/20), Lot 187: 16.67g, 36mm, 1h.

[79] On this characteristically 'Dionysiac' headband, see K. M. Meyer 2012; R. R. R. Smith 2019, 75–7.

[80] For the emergence of external supports for leaning bodies in Greek bronze and marble sculpture (fourth century BC onwards), see Anguissola 2018, 46–51.

[81] Identified by the cataloguer for Roma Numismatics as Marsyas holding a wineskin; for an alternative possibility, see below.

Fig. 6.5. 'Jacobsen' Dionysos, second century AD. Ny Carlsberg Glyptotek,
I.N. 526 (H. 1.61m including plinth).
Image courtesy of the Ny Carlsberg Glyptotek.

The depiction of Dionysos on the new tetradrachm of Teos is very similar to
the well-known 'Jacobsen' statue-type of Dionysos, best known through a
Roman copy in the Copenhagen Ny Carlsberg Glyptotek (Fig. 6.5).[82] As on the
Teian tetradrachm, this statue-type depicts a youthful Dionysos with long hair,
wearing a wreath of ivy-leaves and flowers, with the head turned to his right.
The body is in an S-shaped posture, with the right hip thrust outwards, and the
left leg slightly bent; the body's weight rests on the left elbow, supported on a
tree-stump. The torso is nude; below the genitals, there is a cloak draped
around the hips, and wound around the left elbow. The arms are missing, but
parallel 'leaning Dionysos' statues suggest that the right hand originally held a
kantharos, as on the Teian tetradrachm. The similarities between the 'Jacobsen'
statue-type and the image on the new Teian tetradrachm are sufficiently close

---

[82] I.N. 526; Poulsen 1951, Cat. 155; Moltesen 2002, 176–9, no. 48. On the statue-type, see further
Pochmarski 1974, 73–8; *LIMC* III 1, 436 no. **126**.

as to make it highly likely that the 'Jacobsen' type (and perhaps all the extant 'leaning Dionysos' statues) are copies of a lost Teian original.[83]

The new tetradrachm was struck during a period when many cities in western Asia Minor and neighbouring regions were producing large-denomination coins which depicted their chief civic patron deity. Many of these coins demonstrably depict the civic cult-statue of the god, and that is surely also the case here, as shown by the presence of the rectangular pedestal on which the god is resting his left elbow (a physical 'support' which must derive from a real-life statue).[84] That the image of Dionysos on the reverse of the new Teian tetradrachm is indeed a representation of the chief cult-statue of Dionysos at Teos receives decisive confirmation from Teian bronze coins struck in the Roman imperial period.[85] Teian imperial bronzes frequently depict on the reverse a beardless Dionysos, standing in this same pose with the same attributes (*S*-shaped posture, kantharos in right hand, thyrsus in left, nude torso with cloak draped around hips and slung over left arm or shoulder); on issues struck under Nero and (perhaps) in the Flavian period, the figure is placed within a tetrastyle temple.[86] Most striking of all, Teian bronzes struck under

Fig. 6.6.   Teos (AE), *c.* A D 128–38. Obv.: bust of Hadrian r. Rev.: Dionysos standing l., pouring libation from kantharos with r. hand, holding thyrsus in l.; left elbow resting on decorated pedestal at right. 31mm, 18.73g. *RPC* III 1998.

Münzkabinett, Staatliche Museen zu Berlin, 18276617. Photograph by Bernhard Weisser.

---

[83] 'Leaning Dionysos': *LIMC* III 1, 434–7, nos. **117–28**.

[84] Meadows 2018, 304–5 (Knidos, Samos, Mytilene, Apollonia Pontica); Thonemann 2015, 62–3 (Ephesos).

[85] This is sufficient to dispose of the speculative attempt by Megow 1994 (tentatively followed by Kadıoğlu 2020, 181–2) to identify a monumental marble Dionysos-bust in Leiden as a copy of the Teian cult-statue of Dionysos.

[86] Standing Dionysos alone: *RPC* I 2511–12, 2515–16, 2519–20; *RPC* II 1040, 1042; *RPC* IV.2 1007, 2769 (temp.); *RPC* VI 4725 (temp.); *RPC* IX 577. In tetrastyle temple: *RPC* I 2517, *RPC* II 1043.

Hadrian and Antoninus Pius show a beardless Dionysos in this same pose, but with his left elbow resting on a rectangular pedestal with upper and lower mouldings, exactly as on the reverse of the new Teian tetradrachm (Fig. 6.6).[87]

The small bearded figure standing on the pedestal on the new Teian tetradrachm is an unsolved puzzle; he is not depicted in enough detail on the tetradrachm to make his identity certain, and he is absent from the later imperial period bronzes that depict the pedestal. However, in both coin-art and sculpture of the Hellenistic and Roman periods, 'new-style' dynamic and realistic images of deities are often depicted alongside older 'archaic' cult-images of the same deity, as for example on second-century tetradrachms of Knidos (Artemis Hyakinthotrophos: Fig. 6.7).[88] It is therefore worth wondering whether the small figure on the pedestal might be an older Teian cult-statue (a *xoanon*?) of a bearded Dionysos, anachronistically incorporated into the image of the 'new-style' youthful Dionysos-statue.[89]

When we turn back to the description of the Abderite honorific bronze statue of the *Dēmos* of the Teians, the similarities with the 'new-style' Teian cult-statue of Dionysos are, we think, overwhelming. The statue of the *Dēmos* of the Teians is described as 'pouring a libation ... with the right hand', from a vessel which can be comfortably restored as a kantharos (τῆι μὲν δεξιᾶι σπέν[δοντα κανθάρω]ι, B57–8). The statue of the *Dēmos* is described as 'resting' or 'leaning' with its left hand/arm on a stone support (here the inscribed *stēlē*), just as the left elbow of the cult-statue of Dionysos at Teos was supported on a pedestal (τῆι δὲ ἀριστερᾶι ἀπηρεισμένον ἐπὶ τὴν στήλην ἐν ἧι γε[γράψεται τόδ]ε τὸ ψήφισμα, B58–9). To the left of the statue of the *Dēmos* is a further small column (κιόνιον, B59) bearing a Nike, which crowns the Teian *Dēmos* with an ivy-wreath (B60–1); in the Teian cult-statue, Dionysos was also depicted wearing an elaborate ivy-wreath. The conclusion is inescapable: the statue of the personified *Dēmos* of the Teians at Abdera was deliberately designed in order to evoke the cult-statue of Dionysos at Teos, both in its pose

---

[87] *RPC* III 1998; *RPC* IV.2 1004 (temp.).

[88] Meadows 2018, 302; on the coinage, Le Rider 1979. For similar motifs in statuary, see R. R. R. Smith 2013, 170, with n. 136.

[89] This putative older Teian cult-image of a bearded Dionysos may perhaps appear as a symbol on a small issue of Teian Alexanders struck *c.*204–190 BC (Price 1991, no. 2312; cf. Kinns 1980, 220–1, 519, no. 125; Thonemann 2015, 56). The symbol depicts a bearded Dionysos standing facing to his right, wearing a cloak slung over his left shoulder; he pours a libation from a kantharos in his right hand, and holds a sceptre in his left hand. A similar image of Dionysos also appears on coins of Abdera struck between 415 and 395 BC (May 1966, 163, no. 204; for the date, Chryssanthaki-Nagle 2007, 117–19): a bearded Dionysos, apparently fully clothed, facing to his right, with an upright kantharos in his right hand and a thyrsus in his left hand.

Fig. 6.7. Knidos (AR), *c.*175–150 BC. Obv.: bust of Apollo r., wearing laurel wreath. Rev.: Artemis standing l. holding plant-sprig (?) in extended r. hand, with forepart of stag below; l. elbow resting on *polos* of archaic female cult-statue. At r., *KNIΔION* (with reversed *nus*). *Roma* XIII (23/03/17), Lot 335 (30mm, 16.61g).
Roma Numismatics Ltd (www.RomaNumismatics.com).

(leaning on a support with its left elbow, right hand outstretched) and its attributes (kantharos, ivy-wreath).

Unfortunately, we have no way of knowing how far the physiognomy and clothing of the Abderite statue of the *Dēmos* of the Teians were assimilated to Dionysos. It seems very unlikely that the statue was nude from the genitals upwards, like the Teian Dionysos-statue: for the Abderite statue to be identifiable as an image of the *Dēmos*, it must surely have been clothed in the traditional civic garb of himation (perhaps with chiton beneath) and sandals.[90] Whether the statue was bearded, like earlier Greek personifications of *Dēmoi*, or beardless, like the Teian Dionysos (and some later Greek *Dēmos*-statues), is impossible to tell.

At any event, the statue of the *Dēmos* of the Teians was evidently not a simple copy or replica of the cult-statue of Dionysos at Teos. It was, instead, carefully planned in order to *evoke* the Teian Dionysos through the use of a distinctive pose and distinctive attributes. This kind of symbolic evocation of deities in statue-portraits of non-Olympians may well have been a standard feature of divinizing Hellenistic ruler-portraiture, but the relative lack of extant full-length ruler images makes it difficult to judge how common it

---

[90] Dillon 2006, 110–12. But for an apparently nude figure of the Athenian *Dēmos* on Hellenistic lead tokens from Athens, see Martin 2013, I 16–17.

Fig. 6.8. Statuette of Demetrios Poliorketes (?), Herculaneum, first century BC. Naples NAM 5026 (H. 0.30m). D-DAI-ROM-59.763.

Photo: Hartwig Koppermann.

was.[91] A close parallel is furnished by a bronze statuette of (probably) Demetrios Poliorketes from the Villa of the Papyri at Herculaneum (Fig. 6.8). The king is depicted wearing a diadem and royal chlamys, but in a pose that was clearly intended to recall images of the god Poseidon. Demetrios stands with his right leg raised on a rock, his body bent forward, and his right elbow resting on his knee, precisely the same pose as that struck by the god Poseidon in images on the reverse of Demetrios' tetradrachm coinage (Fig. 6.9). The statuette is unambiguously an image of a human king, but his pose has been carefully selected in order to evoke the god Poseidon (whose son Demetrios claimed to be).[92]

The enjoyment that Hellenistic viewers took in the ambiguities that resulted from these kinds of 'transferrals' of attributes and poses is nicely illustrated by two Hellenistic epigrams on portraits of Hellenistic monarchs.[93] In the first,

---

[91] On coin-portraiture, the bibliography is huge: see most recently Iossif 2018.

[92] Masséglia 2015, 26–8, with figs I.3 and I.4. Demetrios as 'son of Poseidon': Chaniotis 2011 (on the ithyphallic hymn of 291 BC, Duris of Samos, *BNJ* 76 F 13).

[93] Gutzwiller 2002, 93–4; Dillon 2010, 122; Brecoulaki 2019, 53. We are grateful to Hariclia Brecoulaki for drawing our attention to these epigrams. The Herakles/Lysimachos epigram may have a real-life analogy in an early third-century monumental marble portrait bust from Ephesos, depicting

Fig. 6.9. AR Tetradrachm of Demetrios Poliorketes, *c.*292–287 BC. Obv.: bust of Demetrios r., wearing diadem and bull's horn. Rev.: Poseidon standing l., r. leg raised on a rock, r. elbow resting on knee, trident in l. hand. ANS 1967.152.208 (30mm, 16.97g).
Courtesy of the American Numismatic Society.

attributed to either Asklepiades or Poseidippos, a viewer hesitates over whether to identify a statue as Aphrodite or Berenike I (*AP* 16.68):

Κύπριδος ἅδ' εἰκών· φέρ' ἰδώμεθα μὴ Βερενίκας·
  διστάζω ποτέρᾳ φῇ τις ὁμοιοτέραν.

'This is a statue of Kypris—but wait, I wonder if it's not Berenike;
  I hesitate to say which it more closely resembles.'

In the second, the poet gives instructions as to how to tell the difference between portraits of Herakles and Lysimachos (*AP* 16.100):

Χαίτην καὶ ῥόπαλον καὶ ἐν ὀφθαλμοῖσιν ἀταρβῆ
  θυμὸν ὁρῶν, βλοσυρόν τ' ἀνδρὸς ἐπισκύνιον,
ζήτει δέρμα λέοντος ἐπ' εἰκόνι· κἢν μὲν ἐφεύρῃς,
  Ἡρακλέης, εἰ δ' οὔ, Λυσιμάχοιο πίναξ.

'When you see long hair and a club, and a fearless spirit
  In the eyes, and a fierce frown on the man's brow,
Look for a lion's skin in the portrait; and if you find it,
  It's Herakles; if not, it's an image of Lysimachos.'

a youthful long-haired male figure with furrowed brow and olive-wreath, plausibly identified as Lysimachos with attributes of Herakles: Atalay and Türkoğlu 1972–5; R. R. R. Smith 1988, 67–8.

The profoundly innovative character of our Abderite monument is perhaps most clearly seen in the wholesale incorporation of the honorific *stēlē* bearing the inscribed decree into the statue-group (lines **B58–9**). This has, so far as we know, no parallels in earlier Greek honorific practice; but it does have a close analogy in the pedestal with decorative mouldings on which rested the left elbow of the Teian cult-statue of Dionysos, as depicted on the new Teian tetradrachm and on imperial bronzes. We have no way of knowing whether this 'original' pedestal in the Teian statue-group was plain, decorated, or even inscribed;[94] what matters is the way in which the original statue-support is imaginatively transformed in the Abderite honorific monument into something completely new. The *Dēmos* of the Teians is symbolically depicted as having taken the people of Abdera under its wing.

Scholars have debated at length whether depictions of gods and goddesses on Classical and early Hellenistic document reliefs should be interpreted as metonymic representations of the political actors in the associated decrees. When (say) the goddesses Athena and Hera appear on a relief sculpture associated with an Athenian honorific decree for the Samians, ought we to read the goddesses as symbolically equivalent to the states mentioned in the decree—is the goddess Athena simply visual shorthand for the political collective of the Athenians, Hera likewise for the Samians?[95] The new Teian monument adds an unexpected layer of complexity, since we now know that a personification of a political collective (the *Dēmos* of Teians) could be depicted in a manner that deliberately *blurs* the distinction between the political community and the divine patron of that community.

However, we would once again insist on the significance of the complete lack of parallels for the extended description of the statue of the Teian *Dēmos* included in the Abderite honorific decree for the Teians. The Abderites' decision to include this lengthy 'design-plan' for the statue surely indicates that this was a radically unconventional way of depicting the *Dēmos*; its unconventionality may well reside precisely in its extraordinary blurring of the distinction between Teian *Dēmos* and Teian Dionysos. The reason why the Abderites were moved to create such a startling and innovative monument is not hard to find: it was, we suggest, a consequence of their no less radical

---

[94] On the Hadrianic bronzes discussed above (*RPC* III 1998), the pedestal has decorative mouldings at top and bottom (as on the second-century BC tetradrachm), and is decorated with a single wavy line, with pellets in the loops; the left and right faces of the pedestal are represented by lines of pellets.

[95] Blanshard 2007; Elsner 2015, 53–63; Mack 2018, 372–6, 391–4.

decision to initiate a form of sacrificial ritual in honour of the *Dēmos* of the Teians at both Abdera and Teos.

The *Dēmos* of the Teians: cult

Our decree does not explicitly state that the Abderites established a cult of the *Dēmos* of the Teians. But two separate passages of the decree do seem to indicate that the honours voted by the Abderites had a cultic character. Opposite the colossal bronze statue of the Teian *Dēmos* ([κατὰ πρ]όσωπον δὲ τῆς εἰκόνος, B61), the Abderites voted to set up an altar, on which an annual sacrifice was to be performed by the gymnasiarch during the Anthesteria festival (a festival of Dionysos), with an associated torch-race; the sacrifice was to be accompanied by a prayer offered by the sacred herald, apparently to the effect that 'the gods should give good things to the Teians and Abderites' (διδόναι τὰ ἀγαθὰ τοὺς [θεοὺς Τηΐοις καὶ] Ἀβδηρίταις, B63–4). To which god or gods was this altar dedicated, and to whom was the sacrifice performed? There are three possibilities: 'the gods' (to whom the prayer is directed); Dionysos (in whose honour the Anthesteria festival was celebrated), and the *Dēmos* of the Teians (with whose statue the altar is closely associated). In favour of the third possibility, we might compare the honours voted by the people of Mylasa for the dynast Olympichos in the late third century BC: '(be it resolved) to set up a bronze statue of him in the [?sacred agora] in the most prominent spot...and to dedicate to him, opposite the statue ([ἀπέναν]τι τῆς εἰκόνος), an altar of white marble, similar to that of Maussollos in the sanctuary of Zeus [Labraundos/Osogōllis], and perform for him a procession and sacrifice each year on the fourteenth day of the month [- -], on which day the *dēmos* obtained freedom and democracy'.[96] But the Mylasan text—unlike our decree—makes it absolutely clear that the altar opposite the statue is indeed dedicated to Olympichos, and that the sacrifice is performed to him.[97]

Less ambiguity surrounds the sacrifice performed each year by Abderite envoys at (almost certainly) the Teian Leukathea festival. Each year, Abderite ambassadors were to sacrifice a bull on behalf of the *dēmos* of the Abderites

---

[96] *SEG* 58, 1220 (*CGRN* 150), lines 3–14, esp. lines 8–9, ἱδρύσασθαι δὲ [καὶ αὐτῶι ἀπέναν]τι τῆς εἰκόνος βωμὸν, and lines 11–12, συντελεῖν αὐτῶι πομπὴν καὶ θυσί[αν]; the repeated αὐτῶι (restored in line 9) clearly indicates that the altar is dedicated to Olympichos. For the altar to Maussollos, Ameling 2013; see further Marek and Zingg 2018, 121–6.

[97] The agora was a standard location for the establishment of altars dedicated to Hellenistic rulers: *I.Ilion* 31, lines 5–6 (Seleukos I); *I.Priene*[2] 2, lines 17–19 (Lysimachos); Robert 1937, 9–20, lines 14–15 (Teos; Queen Apollonis); see Robert 1937, 174; Isager and Karlsson 2008, 46.

'as a thank-offering to the Teian *Dēmos*' (θύσοντας [ὑπὲρ τοῦ δήμου ἡμῶν βο]ῦν ἐμ μηνὶ Λευκαθιῶνι χαριστήρια τῶι Τηΐων Δήμωι, **B75–6**). Elsewhere, when a name in the dative is associated with sacrifices designated as *charistēria*, the name in the dative is always that of the deity to whom the sacrifices are offered.[98] The analogy of this sacrifice to the *Dēmos* of the Teians at Teos strongly suggests that the altar in the agora at Abdera was indeed dedicated to the *Dēmos* of the Teians, as its placement opposite the colossal bronze statue strongly suggests.

Cults of the personified *Dēmos* are relatively widespread in the Hellenistic period, albeit almost always in an 'internal' civic context (the *Dēmos* of city *x* worshipped within city *x*). Best known is the civic cult of the *Dēmos* and the Charites at Athens, introduced in the late third century B C.[99] We also know of Hellenistic or Julio-Claudian cults of the *Dēmos* at Chios,[100] Kos,[101] Erythrai,[102] Magnesia on the Maeander,[103] Miletos,[104] Iasos,[105] Aphrodisias,[106] Kyaneai,[107] Oinoanda,[108] Kition,[109] and much later at Synnada.[110] In all these instances, the *Dēmos* of city *x* seems to have been worshipped only within city *x*. Only superficially different is the joint-cult of Hestia, the *Dēmos* (of the Athenians) and Roma on second-century Delos, since this cult was surely established in the wake of the Athenian takeover of Delos by Roman grant in

---

[98] e.g. *SEG* 33, 1038 (Archippe at Kyme), lines 13–16, [ὁ δῆμος] καλῶς ἔχον ἡγεῖται καὶ οἰκεῖον τῆς οὔσης αὐτῷ πρὸς Ἀρχίππην εὐνοίας ἐπιτελέσαι τοῖς θεοῖς ἐπὶ τούτοις τὰ πρέποντα χαριστήρια (sacrifices to the gods expressing the people's goodwill towards Archippe); *Milet* I 3, 155 (II B C), lines 19–21, καλῶς ἔχον ἐστὶν καὶ τῶι ἡμετέρωι δήμωι τῶι τε Ἀπόλλωνι τῶι Διδυμεῖ ἀπονείμαι τὰ προσ[ή]κοντα χαριστήρια. But examples are legion.

[99] Habicht 1982, 84–93; Parker 1996, 272–3; Mikalson 1998, 172–9; Messerschmidt 2003, 21–3; Lawton 2017, 47–50. A fifth-century rock-cut inscription on the Hill of the Nymphs at Athens reads ἱιερὸν Νυμφ[ô]ν δέμο (*IG* I³ 1065), and this is sometimes taken as evidence for a cult of the personified *Dēmos* at Athens already in the Classical period; but the complete absence of other evidence for the cult of the *Dēmos* at Athens before the late third century urges caution, and the wording could equally well signify 'shrine of the Nymphs of the people' or 'the people's shrine of the Nymphs' (Parker 1996, 233 n. 56; Lawton 2017, 66 n. 205).

[100] *SEG* 39, 886 (Herakles and *Dēmos*: I B C).

[101] Paul 2013, 157–8; the earliest attestation *IG* XII 4, 1, 79 (early II B C: associated with Zeus).

[102] *I.Erythrai* 32–3, 102–4, 217; *SEG* 31, 971; *SEG* 37, 937. The earliest probably *I.Erythrai* 32 (III B C).

[103] *I.Magnesia* 208: a 'priest of the *Dēmos*', I B C; dedications to the *Dēmos*, *I.Magnesia* 205–7.

[104] *Milet* I 7, 299 and *Milet* II 3, 400 (both I B C).

[105] *I.Iasos* 252 (Homonoia and *Dēmos*, late III B C; for the date, Fabiani 2015, 266–7).

[106] A 'priest of the *Dēmos*' on first-century B C silver coinage: Macdonald 1992, 61, Type 7. Numerous dedications to Aphrodite, the emperors, and the *Dēmos* in the Roman imperial period: Chaniotis 2010, 238 n. 25. See Robert, *OMS* V, 49–56; Habicht 1990, 263.

[107] *SEG* 40, 1270 (Eleuthera and *Dēmos*, I B C/I A D).

[108] *OGIS* 555; improved text, Milner and Eilers 2006, 70 (Julius Caesar and *Dēmos*, late I B C).

[109] Yon 2004, no. 2009 (I B C/I A D, with Polis and Homonoia).

[110] *MAMA* VI 380 and 380a: priest of Boule and *Dēmos*, III A D.

167/6 BC: the Athenian *Dēmos* was in no sense an 'external' power to the Delians.[111]

Considerably more unusual is the scenario attested in our decree, where a cult of the *Dēmos* of city *x* was established in city *y* as part of a package of honours conferred by city *y* on city *x*. Indeed, to the best of our knowledge, the *Dēmos* of the Teians is only the third *Dēmos* known to have received worship outside its own *polis*-community. The other two examples are the *Dēmos* of the Rhodians and the *Dēmos* of the Romans (the *populus Romanus*).[112] Cults of the *Dēmos* of the Rhodians are twice attested outside Rhodes in the Hellenistic period. At Karian Hyllarima in 197 BC, the *Dēmos* of the Rhodians appears in a list of deities to whom sacrifices are performed by the local priest of 'all the gods'; Hyllarima was at this point under Rhodian control (the document is dated by the eponymous Rhodian priest of Helios).[113] At Priene, a fragmentary honorific inscription of the first century BC appears to refer to an annual sacrifice to the *Dēmos* of the Rhodians.[114] This is a somewhat different case to that of Hyllarima, since Priene was never under direct Rhodian control. We do not know when this sacrifice was introduced; one wonders whether it might have been established in gratitude for the Rhodian judges' settlement of the Prienean territorial dispute with Samos in Priene's favour in the 190s BC.

The cult of the *Dēmos* of the Romans is also very seldom attested, no doubt because of the wide popularity of the cult of the goddess Roma. The earliest evidence for sacrificial ritual comes from Athens, where in (perhaps) 160/159 BC the *prytaneis* seem to have performed sacrifice to the *Dēmos* of the Romans.[115] At Miletos, there was a joint priesthood and cult of the *Dēmos* of the Romans and Roma *c.*130 BC, and on Delos, we have a dedication to Athena

---

[111] Priest of Hestia, *Dēmos* and Roma: *I.Délos* 2605, line 9 (158/7 BC); *I.Délos* 1877 (129/8 BC); see also Williams 2004 (*SEG* 54, 717: dedication to Hestia and the *Dāmos*). The alleged dedication of an altar to the Charites and the *Dēmos* of the Athenians in the Thracian Chersonese *c.*340 BC (Dem. 18.92) is clearly anachronistic: Canevaro 2013, 265–7.

[112] As Louis Robert repeatedly insisted, the cult of the personified *Dēmos* of a city ('the *Dēmos* of the Rhodians', always masculine) should be firmly distinguished from the cult of the eponymous personification of the city itself ('Rhodos', generally feminine): Robert, *Hellenica* X, 263 n. 3; Robert, *OMS* V, 426 n. 1; Robert 1967, 7–14; Robert 1969, 316–23 (with discussion of cults of the personified Polis). For personifications of cities in Classical Athenian literature and art, A. C. Smith 2011, 102–6. At Kos, in the second century BC, there was both a cult of the eponymous Kos (and Rhodos) and a separate cult of the *Dāmos* of the Koans: Paul 2013, 156–8. For cults of Rhodos, see Mellor 1975, 24–5.

[113] Debord and Varinlioğlu 2018, 41–2, no. 9, with 124–5 (date) and 166–7 (cult).

[114] *I.Priene*² 77, line 4, [ὁμοίως δὲ καὶ ὑπὲρ τῆς] πόλεως κατ᾿ἐνιαυτὸν τῶι δήμωι τῶι Ῥοδίων ἐπ[ετέλεσεν], 'similarly, on behalf of the city he performed the annual [?sacrifice] to the *Dēmos* of the Rhodians'.

[115] *Agora* XV, 180; the date of the archon Pleistainos is not firmly fixed, but seems likely to have been 160/59 BC (John Morgan, *per litt.*); Tracy 1990, 141–2, dated him to a period shortly before 150 BC.

Nike and the *Dēmos* of the Romans dated to 125/4 B C.[116] Dedications to the emperor(s) and the senate and people of Rome are reasonably common in the Roman imperial period.[117]

Both of these cults are evidently very different from the cult of the Teian *Dēmos* at Abdera. In the second century BC, both Rhodes and Rome were imperial powers, to whom political loyalty could be expressed in a number of different ways, of which the cult of the *Dēmos* of the Rhodians/Romans was only one (and by no means the most significant). By contrast, the cult of the *Dēmos* of the Teians was in no way an expression of political dependence; for all the Abderites' overwhelming gratitude for the unparalleled benefactions of the Teians, the two cities remained within a fundamentally 'horizontal' peer-polity relationship, not a 'vertical' relationship of dominance and subordination.

The whole package of honours for the Teians—a colossal statue of the *Dēmos* of the Teians modelled on the Teian cult-statue of Dionysos, with an associated altar, and sacrificial rituals to the Teian *Dēmos* at both Abdera and Teos—has no real parallels anywhere else in the Hellenistic Greek world. But then again, perhaps that is what we ought to expect. We might recall the wording of the two phrases which frame the long narrative of the Teians' benefactions towards Abdera: the Teians wish 'to leave no opportunity for exceeding them in benefactions to any of those *dēmoi* that have dedicated themselves to comparable ends' (**A9–10**), and the decree commemorates their success in 'having set up through their actions an eternal memorial for all men of their goodwill towards their kin, and leaving space for no one else to surpass them in benefaction' (**B50–2**: see the Epilogue below). Just as the benefactions performed by the Teians had visibly outstripped those ever previously undertaken by any other Greek city, so too the honours conferred by the Abderites were—quite consciously and deliberately—like nothing anyone had ever seen before.

---

[116] *Milet* I 7, 203; *I.Délos* 1807. A cult of the *Dēmos* of the Romans may have existed on Delos already *c.*170 B C: *I.Délos* 465 c, line 20 (crowns for the *Dēmos* of the Romans and the senate). *Pace* Messerschmidt 2003, 142 n. 811, 217–18, *FD* III 1, 152 (Delphi, 150/49 B C), line 13, does not attest a cult of the *Dēmos* of the Romans at Delphi (the reference is to the Romaia festival).

[117] e.g. *IAph2007* 12.305 (I A D); *TAM* V, 2, 1335 (Dareioukome); *OGIS* 479 (Dorylaion); *SEG* 36, 1094 (Sardeis); *I.Iznik* 31.

Epilogue
Two Greek Cities in Peace and War

In 219 BC, half a century before the Roman sack of Abdera, the Roman con-
sul L. Aemilius Paullus stormed the Dalmatian island-city of Pharos (modern
Stari Grad, on the Croatian island of Hvar) and razed the city to the ground.[1]
The Romans' quarrel was not with the Pharians themselves, but with the
Adriatic dynast Demetrios of Pharos, who fled to the court of Philip V of
Macedon after the fall of the island. The city of Pharos seems to have been
rebuilt soon after the conclusion of the war, to judge from its appearance in
the treaty of 215 BC between Philip V and Carthage.[2]

The reconstruction of Pharos is described in a famous inscription from
Stari Grad, plausibly (if not quite definitively) dated to the immediate aftermath of the Second Illyrian War (c.218 BC).[3] The surviving part of the inscription begins with a decree of the city of Pharos (lines A3–21):

'[Since the sen]ate and people [of the Romans, being] fri[ends and well-
disposed] to the *polis* of the Pharians [(5) from ancestral times, having
restored] to us [our] city [and the ancestr]al laws and the p[art] of the territory [on] the island [which belonged to the city], have given us [- - fo]rty,
and have confirmed the allia[nce and friendship and oth]er benefits, [(10)
be it resolved by the *dē]mos* to send ambass[adors to our founders], the
Parians, and to the [kinsmen of the city (?), the Ath]enians,[4] to ren[ew their

---

[1] Polyb. 3.19.12; Appian *Ill.* 8.   [2] Polyb. 7.9.13.

[3] Robert, *Hellenica* XI–XII, 505–41; *SEG* 23, 489 (*SEG* 41, 545); English translation, Bagnall and
Derow 2004, no. 31. We translate the text as revised by Derow 1991, with a few minor modifications
noted below. The date of the inscription is not quite certain. Robert, while noting the attractions of a
link with the sack of 219, ultimately favoured a date in the late 170s or early 160s BC (537–41). The
earlier dating was vigorously defended by Derow 1991; Eckstein 1999 (esp. 415–18), while rejecting
Derow's interpretation of the 'alliance and friendship' between Pharos and Rome mentioned in the
inscription (not a matter of material significance for our purposes), nonetheless concludes that 219/18
remains the most attractive date for the inscription (cf. Burton 2011, 136–9).

[4] Restoring, with Robert (515), [πρὸς τοὺς οἰκιστὰς] Παρίους καὶ τοὺς συν[γενεῖς τῆς πόλεως
Ἀθην]αίους (lines A11–12); Paros was mother-city of Pharos, and the Athenians claimed to be the
mother-city of Paros (Rhodes and Osborne 2003, no. 29: 372 BC). Neither of the terms of relationship
are certain: for [οἰκιστάς], we could have [κτίστας] or even [πατέρας], as in **Document 1**, line A4, and
for συν[γενεῖς], we could have συν[οικιστάς], as in *IG* XII 4, 1, 222 (decree of Kamarina recognizing
Koan *asylia*, 242 BC), line 9 (thus implicitly Bagnall and Derow 2004, no. 31, translating 'co-
[founders]'). See also Curty 1995, 74–6, no. 37.

Teos and Abdera: Two Cities in Peace and War. Mustafa Adak and Peter Thonemann, Oxford University Press.
© Mustafa Adak and Peter Thonemann, 2022. DOI: 10.1093/oso/9780192845429.003.0008

previously exi]sting kinship with us, [and to call on them] to help in the (15)
reco[nstruction of our city] inasmuch as each of the [cities is in a position to
do so]; and to write up [a copy of the decree] that has been introd[uced on]
a stone *stēlē* and erect it [in the agora] so that the memory of those who helped
[the *dēmos* might be preserved in perpetuity], also for later generations. [(20)
There were chosen as am]bassadors: Athenas son of Dionys[ios, - -tylos son
of Polycharm]os, Antipatros son of Nikas.'

This is followed on the stone by a decree of the city of Paros in response to the
Pharian embassy. Precisely what kind of material assistance the Parians
decided to offer is unclear,[5] but there can be no doubt that they responded
positively to the Pharians' appeal (lines A29–41):

'Sin[ce the Pharians, being colonists] of our city, [have sent to us] both
letters and ambassad[ors, Athenas son of Dionysios, - -]tylos son of
Polycharmos, An[tipatros son of Nikas, in order to] make a speech concerning the [dis]asters [which have befallen the city] and to call [on us to help
th]em in the reconstruction of the [city inasmuch as] we are in a position to
do so,[6] and since [the ambassadors[7] have] come before the *boulē* [and the
dēmos and have made a speech accor]ding with the things [laid out] in the
[letters, lacking nothing] by way of enthusiasm and love of ho[nour]; concerning these things, be it resolved [by the *dēmos*...].'

The fate of Pharos bears a close and melancholy resemblance to that of Abdera
almost fifty years later. In 219, as in 170 BC, a Greek city which enjoyed
friendly relations with Rome was brutally destroyed by a Roman general in
pursuit of broader geopolitical objectives (the wars against Demetrios of
Pharos and Perseus of Macedon respectively).[8] On both occasions, the Roman

---

[5] On the Parian embassy to Delphi described in B16–26, see Robert, *Hellenica* XI–XII, 531–7: the
Parian Praxiepes sent to the Adriatic, perhaps as a 'second founder' of Pharos.

[6] Restoring, with Klaffenbach (*BE* 1964, 238; cf. Derow 1991, 264), [καθ' ὅσον ἂν εὐκ]αιρῶμες in
line A36. The language finds a reasonably close parallel in **Document 1**, line **B19** (see our commentary *ad loc.*).

[7] Restoring, with Robert (modified by Bousquet), ἐπελθόντες [δὲ καὶ οἱ πρεσβευταὶ ἐπί] τε τὴν
βουλὴν κτλ. in lines A36–7. The alternative restoration proposed by Derow 1991, 264 (ἐπελθόντες [δὲ
μετὰ του γραμματέως ἐπί] τε τὴν βουλὴν) cannot be right, since the subject here changes from the
Pharians to the ambassadors; the relative clause in lines A33–6 is still paraphrasing the original
Pharian decree, as demonstrated by the future indicatives ἀπολογίσονται...καὶ παρακαλ[έσουσιν]
(mistranslated by Bagnall and Derow 2004, no. 31).

[8] The careful euphemisms and strategic silences of both the Pharian and Abderite decrees tell their
own story: neither city felt able to identify by name the people responsible for their misery (the
Romans), the Abderites speaking merely of fortune being 'cruelly disposed' (**Document 1**, line **A16**),

senate promptly decreed that the city be restored to its former condition, but seems to have provided little practical assistance in the reconstruction of the devastated community. Both Pharos and Abdera were thus compelled to seek help elsewhere—but from whom? In neither case was it diplomatically feasible to seek assistance from one of the remaining 'great powers' of the Hellenistic world: the Pharians, now firmly back in Rome's orbit, could scarcely approach Philip V of Macedon for assistance, any more than the Abderites in 170 BC were in a position to turn to (say) Eumenes II of Pergamon or Antiochos IV of Syria.[9]

Both Pharos and Abdera chose to seek help from their mother-cities, Paros and Teos respectively.[10] As Diodoros puts it, 'when children are wronged, they turn to their fathers; when cities are wronged, they turn to the *dēmoi* who were their founders' ($\pi\alpha\hat{\imath}\delta\epsilon\varsigma$ $\mu\grave{\epsilon}\nu$ $o\hat{\upsilon}\nu$ $\dot{\alpha}\delta\iota\kappa o\acute{\upsilon}\mu\epsilon\nu o\iota$ $\pi\rho\grave{o}\varsigma$ $\pi\alpha\tau\acute{\epsilon}\rho\alpha\varsigma$ $\kappa\alpha\tau\alpha\phi\epsilon\acute{\upsilon}\gamma o\upsilon\sigma\iota$, $\pi\acute{o}\lambda\epsilon\iota\varsigma$ $\delta\grave{\epsilon}$ $\pi\rho\grave{o}\varsigma$ $\tau o\grave{\upsilon}\varsigma$ $\dot{\alpha}\pi o\iota\kappa\acute{\iota}\sigma\alpha\nu\tau\alpha\varsigma$ $\delta\acute{\eta}\mu o\upsilon\varsigma$, 10.34.3). The Pharians also appealed to the Athenians, as the mythological mother-city of Paros and hence 'kinsmen' to the Pharians; we do not know whether Athens too responded to the Pharians' call for help. Similarly, when the island-city of Aigina was captured by the Roman general P. Sulpicius Galba in 210 BC and the inhabitants enslaved, the Aiginetans' first thought was to appeal to their 'kinsmen' for assistance, to Sulpicius' profound contempt (Polybios 9.42.5–8):[11]

'When Aigina was captured by the Romans, those Aiginetans who failed to escape gathered together on the ships to ask the general to permit them to send ambassadors to cities that were their kin (*syngeneis*) to ask for ransom-money. At first, Publius gave a harsh refusal, saying that they ought to have sent their embassies to superior powers at a time when they were still their own masters, not now that they had become slaves. Not long ago, they had refused to give any reply to his own ambassadors; now that they had been subjected, it was absurd of them to ask permission to send embassies to their

---

and the Pharians focusing only on their 'restoration' by Rome (lines A5–6), not the destruction that preceded.

[9] In 208 BC, after the sack of Dyme and enslavement of the inhabitants by P. Sulpicius Galba, it was Philip V who restored the Dymaians to liberty (Livy 32.22.10). But royal restorations of this kind could be treated by Rome as aggressively expansionist acts, as in the case of Antiochos III's restoration of Lysimacheia in 196 BC: Polyb. 18.51.7–8; Livy 33.38.9–14 and 33.40.6.

[10] For the foundation of Pharos by Paros in 385 BC, Diod. Sic. 15.13.4, 15.14.1–2; also Strabo 7.5.5, Ephoros, *BNJ* 70 F 89, pseudo-Skymnos, *FGrHist* 2048 T1, lines 426–7; Hansen and Nielsen 2004, 333–4 (J. Wilkes and T. Fischer-Hansen).

[11] Erskine 2002, 97. It is unclear who these 'kinsmen' might have been: perhaps neighbouring Dorian cities (Walbank 1967, 186), or perhaps the Aiginetan colony of Kydonia on Crete (Strabo 8.6.6; Hansen and Nielsen 2004, 1170–2 [P. Perlman]). The appeal seems to have been unsuccessful (Polyb. 11.5.8, 22.8.9–10).

kinsmen. So on this occasion he sent away those who had approached him with these words; but on the following day he convened all the prisoners and said that he had no obligation to do any favours to the Aiginetans, but for the sake of the rest of the Greeks he would let them send ambassadors to ask for ransom-money, since this was customary among the Greeks.'

'Customary among the Greeks'—Polybios is here referring not to the specifics of this particular incident (seeking ransom-money), but the wider phenomenon known to us as 'kinship diplomacy'.[12] From the early Classical period to Late Antiquity, diplomatic relations between Greek cities (and, later, between Greek cities and Rome) were very often conceived in terms of the perpetuation or renewal of kinship-relations between communities. Appeals to kinship-links between cities could be (from our point of view) historical, as in the case of Teos and Abdera, or mythological, as in the case of Pharos and Athens; for the Greeks themselves, the line between the two was blurred at best.[13] The diplomatic contexts in which such links could be evoked are as varied as Greek international diplomacy itself: invitations to recognize the inviolability (*asylia*) of a city or sanctuary, arbitration of interstate disputes, pleas for *ad hoc* financial assistance, requests for foreign judges, and so forth.

Abdera's repeated appeals to Teos in the years following the sack of 170 BC are thus, in one sense, entirely in line with what we understand to have been the standard 'rules' of Greek diplomacy and inter-*polis* networks in the second century BC. The negotiations undertaken on Abdera's behalf by the Teian ambassadors Amymon and Megathymos at Rome in the winter of 167/6 BC (Chapter 5 above) find close parallels in other embassies to Rome performed by powerful cities on behalf of their weaker or less well-connected 'kinsmen'. For example, Polybios describes an extraordinary diplomatic intervention at Rome by the Rhodians in 189 BC, when the senate was in the process of settling affairs in Asia after the defeat of Antiochos (Polybios 21.24.10–12; cf. Livy 37.56.7):

'The Rhodians again came forward before the senate, to make a request concerning Soloi in Kilikia; for, they said, it was appropriate for them to

---

[12] The bibliography is huge: see e.g. Curty 1995; Jones 1999; Lücke 2000; Fromentin and Gotteland 2001; Erskine 2002; Battistoni 2010 (Rome and the Greeks); Prag 2010 (Sicily); Fragoulaki 2013 (Thucydides). For a contextualization of kinship diplomacy within wider interstate-relations in the Hellenistic world, see Ma 2003.

[13] Curty 1995, 215–23, argues for a distinction in the vocabulary used of mythological kinship and historical colonial relations, while acknowledging numerous exceptions.

promote that city's cause on account of their kinship (*syngeneia*). The Solians, they said, were colonists (*apoikoi*) of the Argives, as the Rhodians were too; as a result, they demonstrated that the two cities' kinship with one another was that of siblings (*adelphikē...syngeneia*). For this reason, they said that it was right that they should be granted freedom at the hands of the Romans as a reciprocal favour to the Rhodians.'

In the event, the Rhodian *démarche* (like the later mission of Amymon and Megathymos) came to nothing: when Rome proposed to detach Soloi (or, initially, all of Kilikia) from Seleukid control, Antiochos' representatives protested with such vehemence that the Rhodians prudently withdrew their request (Polyb. 21.24.13–15). But the incident nicely illustrates precisely the same cultural dynamics as the Teian embassy to Rome of 167/6 BC: the small city of Soloi had clearly called on their powerful sister-city of Rhodes to speak and act on their behalf, mindful that Rhodes was likely to be in Rome's good graces after their enthusiastic participation in the war against Antiochos.[14] A similar approach to Rome was made by the people of Ilion in 188 BC, requesting that the Lykians should be forgiven their support for Antiochos III on the basis of the mythological kinship-ties linking both Rome and Ilion and Ilion and the Lykians.[15] Much later, the city of Chersonesos in Tauris likewise appealed to their (historical) mother-city of Herakleia Pontike ('our most pious fathers...our ancestral metropolis') to send an embassy on their behalf to the emperor Antoninus Pius.[16]

Nonetheless, in the opening lines of the new decree in honour of the Teians (**Document 1**), the Abderites are passionately concerned to emphasize the distinctive—indeed unique—character of the Teians' support for Abdera in the years after 170 BC. Other cities, they acknowledge, have indeed 'dedicated themselves to comparable ends' (**A10**): there is (as we have seen) nothing intrinsically unusual about a mother-city supporting her daughter-city as the Teians have done. But the Teians have gone far beyond the normal duties

[14] For the mythological basis of this 'sibling' relationship between Rhodes and Soloi (the alleged colonial foundations of Rhodes and Soloi by Argos), see *SEG* 34, 282, with Stroud 1984, 199–202; Salmeri 2004, 199–203.

[15] Polyb. 22.5.3: the kinship-link between Ilion and Lykia no doubt derived from the Homeric Lykian heroes Sarpedon and Glaukos. In an unpublished treaty from Xanthos, the Xanthians swear not to act against the interests of Rome, Ilion, Rhodes, or any of their allies: Wiemer 2002, 264; Adak 2007, 258–65.

[16] *IOSPE*³ III 25 (previously *IOSPE* I² 362), lines 1.3–4, τοὶ εὐσεβέστατοι πατέρες; line 1.20, [τὰν πρό]γονον ἁ[μῶν ματρόπο]λιν. The Herakleotai are said to have 'displayed concern for our salvation out of familial sympathy' (lines 1.4–6, οἰκείωι πάθει τὰν ὑπὲρ τᾶς ἁμετέρας σωτηρίας ἐποάσαντο φροντίδα); the precise character of the crisis at Chersonesos is unclear. See also Robert, *OMS* I, 310–12; *Hellenica* XI–XII, 519–20, for more examples.

owed by kin to kin; they have, say the Abderites, left 'no opportunity for exceeding them in benefactions' to any other city (**A9**). The same point is repeated, with even more emphasis, at the end of the long narrative of the Teians' support for Abdera: the Teians have 'set up through their actions an eternal memorial for all men of their goodwill towards their kin...leaving space for no one else to surpass them in benefactions' (**B50–2**). As we saw in Chapter 6, the extraordinary benefactions of the Teians were reciprocated with equally extraordinary honours by the people of Abdera—a statue and cult of the *Dēmos* of the Teians unlike anything known to us from elsewhere in the Greek world.

The language used by the Abderites is hyperbolic, but also—so far as we can tell—justified. There are indeed no real analogies in the Hellenistic world for this kind of sustained, long-term, apparently disinterested support of one Greek city for another on grounds of kinship. What were the Teians' motives? Certainly not direct financial benefit: their monetary subsidies to Abdera were either gifts (**B18–19, B47–8**) or interest-free (**B29–30**). It is possible that they had an eye to longer-term benefits: for example, Teos may have hoped to become favoured recipients of Abderite grain-exports (see Chapter 2 above, on Teos' perpetual shortage of domestic grain), a hypothesis that receives some limited support from Teos' support for the purchase of draft-oxen at Abdera (**B24–31**) and the symbolic gift of 1,000 *medimnoi* of wheat—it is not clear whether one-off or annual—subsequently despatched by the grateful Abderites to Teos (**B79**). But ultimately there is no good reason not to take the Abderites' own presentation of the Teians' motives at face value: love of honour (*philotimia*, **A6**); the glory (*eudoxia*) deriving from the two cities' conspicuous like-mindedness (**A8–9**); 'care for their ancestral gods' (**B15–16**); the desire not to abandon the lands 'conquered and settled by their own ancestors' (**B36–7**). The Teians surely also had in mind the support provided by the Abderites in the aftermath of the battle of Lade in 494 BC, when the city of Teos was (in Pindar's words) 'struck down by enemy fire', and Abdera 'gave birth' to her own mother-city: in the early 160s, the Teians were at last able to return the favour.[17] We should also recall the (perhaps) unusually close institutional alignment of the two cities in the centuries following the Teian settlement at Abdera: as we saw in Chapter 3, it is quite possible that the early fifth-century 'Teian Dirae', proudly proclaiming the shared *nomima* of the two cities, were still visible (and in force) at Teos right down into the

---

[17] Pind. *Pae.* 2, lines 28–31, discussed in Chapter 2 above (where we tentatively attribute the destruction and refoundation of Teos to the late 490s BC).

Hellenistic period. The historical ties binding Teos and Abdera may well genuinely have been tighter than those linking most other mother-cities and colonies in the Hellenistic world.

Finally, it is worth evoking the peculiar character of the historical 'moment' at which the decrees of Abdera for Teos (**Document 1**) and Amymon and Megathymos (**Document 6**) were passed—that is to say, the year 166 BC, or at most a year or two later. In the years immediately following the Third Macedonian War, the Greek cities of the Aegean world must have felt the world shifting strangely around them. In the course of the preceding two years (168–166 BC), every single royal power in the eastern Mediterranean had suffered a more or less dramatic eclipse. The Antigonid kingdom of Macedon was no more, replaced with four nominally free Macedonian republics (the four *merides*); the Illyrian kingdom of Genthios was similarly dissolved by Roman *fiat* (Livy 45.18.1–7, 45.29–30). Ptolemaic Egypt was in chaos, wracked by local rebellions, the ongoing power-struggle between Ptolemy VI and Ptolemy VIII, and the aftermath of the devastating Seleukid invasions of 169 and 168 BC. The Seleukid king Antiochos IV had been summarily humiliated outside Alexandria in summer 168 BC (Polyb. 29.27), and his defiant military parade at Daphne in 166 (Polyb. 30.25–7) took place in the context of major revolts against the Seleukids in Judaea and the East. In late 167, the Romans abruptly broke off friendly relations with their former ally Eumenes II of Pergamon (Polyb. 30.19), who was already locked in a ferocious struggle in the eastern part of his kingdom against the Galatians (168–166 BC). The last major Greek imperial power in the Aegean, the Rhodians, had been stripped of the greater part of their mainland empire in Karia and Lykia by senatorial decree in the winter of 168/7 (Polyb. 30.5.12), and in 166 they also lost Kaunos and Stratonikeia (30.21).

For Polybios, famously, the year 168 marked the point at which Rome 'rendered the entire inhabited world subject to themselves...the increase and advance of the Romans' *dynasteia* was complete, and moreover it seemed to be universally agreed as a matter of necessity that what remained was to submit to the Romans and obey their orders' (3.3.9–3.4.3).[18] But is that really how it seemed to the Greek cities of the Aegean world in the mid-160s BC? In retrospect, of course, we know that Polybios was right, as the events of the 140s and 130s would show all too clearly (the crushing of the Achaian League, the destruction of Corinth, and the establishment of the first Roman provinces in the East). But in 166 BC, for very many Greek cities, the future may

---

[18] Derow 1979, 4–5; Millar 1987.

well have looked rather brighter than Polybios suggests. The Romans had withdrawn back across the Adriatic, leaving the former domains of Perseus as independent (albeit tributary) Macedonian republics; the cities of Abdera, Ainos, and Maroneia were recognized as free and autonomous.[19] In Asia Minor, the Greek cities of Karia and Lykia were free from hegemonic rule for perhaps the first time in their history, and Eumenes II of Pergamon was vigorously promoting himself as the 'common benefactor of the Greeks…applying all eagerness and foresight in order that the inhabitants of the Greek cities might continue to live in peace and the best state of affairs in perpetuity'.[20] In mainland Greece, the city of Athens was abundantly rewarded for her pro-Roman attitude during the war with Perseus, being granted possession of the territory of Haliartos in Boiotia, as well as the islands of Lemnos and Delos.[21] The new atmosphere of the mid-160s BC is perhaps most vividly seen in the dramatic transformation of Greek civic coinages at this period: between the mid-160s and early 140s BC, around forty Greek cities around the Aegean basin began striking new large-denomination silver coinages with ostentatiously local, civic types.[22]

In the event, this 'new beginning' for the Greek cities of the Aegean proved to be a false dawn. But the people of Teos and Abdera could not have foreseen that in 167/6 BC. For almost two centuries, the Abderites had lived in the shadow of the Argead and Antigonid monarchies. Over the same two centuries, the Teians had successively been subject to the Achaimenid kings, Alexander, Antigonos, Lysimachos; to the Seleukids, Ptolemies, Attalids, and at last to the Seleukids again. In the early 160s, for perhaps the first time in their four-centuries-long shared history, Teos and Abdera were both truly free and autonomous cities. At the midnight of Abdera's history, she called on her mother-city for help; and the Teians responded.

---

[19] Diod. Sic. 31.8.8; Livy 45.29.6; *IThrakAig* E168 (*StV* IV 664: Rome's treaty with Maroneia, 167 BC).

[20] *Milet* I 9, 306 (Welles, *RC* 52: letter of Eumenes II to the Ionian League, winter 167/6 BC), lines 7–13, with Thonemann 2013, 30–8.

[21] Habicht 1997, 214–19.   [22] Thonemann 2015, 56–61; Meadows 2018.

Bibliography

Adak, M. (2007) 'Die rhodische Herrschaft in Lykien und die rechtliche Stellung der Städte Xanthos, Phaselis und Melanippion', *Historia* 56, 251–79.

Adak, M. (2021) 'Teos und die hellenistischen Könige von Alexander bis Antiochos III', in *L'Asie Mineure occidentale au IIIe siècle a. C.*, ed. P. Brun, L. Capdetrey, and P. Fröhlich. Bordeaux, 231–57.

Adak, M. and Kadıoğlu, M. (2017) 'Die Steinbrüche von Teos und «marmor Luculleum»', *Philia* 3, 1–43.

Adak, M. and Stauner, K. (2018) 'Die Neoi und das Temenos des Dionysas: Eine hellenistische Pachturkunde aus Teos', *Philia* 4, 1–25.

Adak, M. and Thonemann, P. (2020) 'Teos und Abdera in hellenistischer Zeit: Der Jahreskalender, Kulte und neue Inschriften', *Philia* 6, 1–34.

Adams, J. P. (1986) 'Topeiros Thraciae, the Via Egnatia and the boundaries of Macedonia', *Ancient Macedonia* 4, 17–42.

Agelarakis, A. (2004) 'The Clazomenian colonization endeavor at Abdera in retrospect: evidence from the anthropological record', in Moustaka et al. 2004, 327–50.

Ager, S. L. (1994) 'Hellenistic Crete and *KOINOΔIKION*', *JHS* 114, 1–18.

Ager, S. L. (1996) *Interstate Arbitration in the Greek World, 337–90 B.C.* Berkeley, Los Angeles, and London.

Allen, J. (2006) *Hostages and Hostage-Taking in the Roman Empire.* Cambridge.

Allen, R. E. (1983) *The Attalid Kingdom: A Constitutional History.* Oxford.

Ameling, W. (2013) 'Ein Altar des Maussollos in Labraunda', *ZPE* 187, 215–19.

Aneziri, S. (2003) *Die Vereine der dionysischen Techniten im Kontext der hellenistischen Gesellschaft.* Stuttgart.

Anguissola, A. (2018) *Supports in Roman Marble Sculpture.* Cambridge.

Antonetti, C. and De Vido, S. (2017) *Iscrizioni greche: Un'antologia.* Rome.

Archibald, Z. H. (1998) *The Odrysian Kingdom of Thrace: Orpheus Unmasked.* Oxford.

Archibald, Z. H. (2013) *Ancient Economies of the Northern Aegean, Fifth to First Centuries BC.* Oxford.

Arnaoutoglou, I. (1998) *Ancient Greek Laws: A Sourcebook.* London and New York.

Arrington, N. T., Terzopoulou, D., Tasaklaki, M., Lawall, M. L., Brellas, D. J., and White, C. E. (2016) 'Molyvoti, Thrace, archaeological project: 2013 preliminary report', *Hesperia* 85, 1–64.

Atalay, E. and Türkoğlu, S. (1972–5) 'Ein frühhellenistischer Porträtkopf des Lysimachos aus Ephesos', *JÖAI* 50 (Beiblatt), 123–50.

Austin, M. (2006) *The Hellenistic World from Alexander to the Roman Conquest: A Selection of Ancient Sources in Translation* (2nd edn). Cambridge.

Badoud, N. (2011) 'Les colosses de Rhodes', *CRAI* 2011, I, 111–52.

Bagnall, R. S. and Derow, P. (2004) *The Hellenistic Period: Historical Sources in Translation.* Malden, MA and Oxford.

Baika, K. (2013) 'Abdera', in *Shipsheds of the Ancient Mediterranean*, ed. D. Blackman, B. Rankov, K. Baika, H. Gerding, and J. Pakkanen. Cambridge, 270–6.

Bailey, D. M. (2006) 'The Apries Amphora—another cartouche', in *Naukratis: Greek Diversity in Egypt. Studies on East Greek Pottery and Exchange in the Eastern Mediterranean*, ed. A. Villing and U. Schlotzhauer. London, 155–7.

Bakalakis, G. (1967) Ἀνασκαφή Στρύμης. Thessaloniki.

Baker, P. and Thériault, G. (2017) 'La vie agonistique xanthienne: Nouvel apport épigraphique (deuxième partie)', *REG* 130, 433–69.

Bannier, W. (1925) 'Zu griechischen Inschriften. II', *RhM* 74/3, 280–92.

Battistoni, F. (2010) *Parenti dei Romani: Mito troiano e diplomazia*. Bari.

Bechtel, F. (1887) *Die Inschriften des ionischen Dialekts*. Göttingen.

Bernabé, A. (2013) 'L'epiteto Εἰραφιώτης e la legittimità di Dioniso', in *Studium Sapientiae*, ed. A. Cosentino and M. Monaca. Soveria Mannelli, 57–73.

Bernand, A. (1992) *La prose sur pierre dans l'Égypte hellénistique et romaine* (2 vols). Paris.

Bernand, É. (1969) *Inscriptions métriques de l'Égypte gréco-romaine*. Paris.

Bernsdorff, H. (2020) *Anacreon of Teos: Testimonia and Fragments* (2 vols). Oxford.

Biard, G. (2010) 'Diplomatie et statues à l'époque hellénistique: À propos du décret de l'Amphictionie pyléo–delphique *CID* IV 99', *BCH* 134, 131–51.

Bielman, A. (1994) *Retour à la liberté: Libération et sauvetage des prisonniers en Grèce ancienne*. Lausanne.

Bikerman, E. (1937) 'Notes sur Polybe. I. Le statut des villes d'Asie après la paix d'Apamée', *REG* 50, 217–39.

Bingöl, O. (2012) 'Neue Erkenntnisse am Tempel der Artemis Leukophryene in Magnesia', in *Dipteros und Pseudodipteros: Bauhistorische und archäologische Forschungen*, ed. T. Schulz. İstanbul, 113–21.

Bingöl, O. (2013) 'From the dipteros of Polykrates to the pseudodipteros of Hermogenes', *Anadolu/Anatolia* 39, 107–19.

Blanshard, A. (2007) 'The problem with honouring Samos: an Athenian document relief and its interpretation', in *Art and Inscriptions in the Ancient World*, ed. Z. Newby and R. Leader–Newby. Cambridge, 19–37.

Bloy, D. (2012) 'Roman patrons of Greek communities before the title πάτρων', *Historia* 61, 168–201.

Boehm, R. (2018) *City and Empire in the Age of the Successors: Urbanization and Social Response in the Making of the Hellenistic Kingdoms*. Oakland, CA.

Boffo, L. (2012) 'L'archiviazione dei decreti nelle poleis ellenistiche', in *Il paesaggio e l'esperienza*, ed. R. Bargnesi and R. Scuderi. Pavia, 23–37.

Bogaert, R. (1968) *Banques et banquiers dans les cités grecques*. Leiden.

Boulay, Th. (2014) *Arès dans la cité: Les poleis et la guerre dans l'Asie Mineure hellénistique* (*Studi ellenistici* XXVIII). Pisa and Rome.

Boulay, Th. (2017) 'Cn. Manlius Vulso dans la vallée du Méandre en 189: À propos de Tite-Live, XXXVIII, 12, 8–13, 4', *Studi ellenistici* XXXI, 261–82.

Boulay, Th. (2018) 'La liberté de Téos et le soutien d'Attale II à Alexandre Balas', *Syria* 95, 133–54.

Bousquet, J. (1988) 'La stèle des Kyténiens à Xanthos de Lycie', *REG* 101, 12–53.

Braund, D. (2018) *Greek Religion and Cults in the Black Sea Region: Goddesses in the Bosporan Kingdom from the Archaic Period to the Byzantine Era*. Cambridge.

Bravo, B. (1984) 'Le commerce des céréales chez les Grecs de l'époque archaïque', in *Trade and Famine in Classical Antiquity*, ed. P. Garnsey and C. R. Whittaker. Cambridge, 17–29.

Brecoulaki, H. (2019) 'Truth, flattery, or good imitation? Aesthetic and moral value of representation in Greek painting', in *Περὶ γραφικῆς: Pittori, tecniche, trattati, contesti tra testimonianze e ricezione*, ed. G. Adornato, E. Falaschi, and A. Poggio. Milan, 45–66.

Bremmer, J. N. (1999) 'Transvestite Dionysos', in *Rites of Passage in Ancient Greece*, ed. M. W. Padilla. Lewisburg, 183–200.

Bresson, A. (2012) 'Painted portraits and statues: honors for Polystratos at Phrygian Apameia', in *Stephanèphoros: De l'économie antique à l'Asie Mineure*, ed. K. Konuk. Bordeaux, 203–20.

Bresson, A. (2016) *The Making of the Ancient Greek Economy: Institutions, Markets, and Growth in the City-States*. Princeton, NJ.

Bresson, A., Rousset, D., and Carbon, J.-M. (2007) 'Les estampages du Fonds Louis Robert', *CRAI* 2007, 643–60.

Briant, P. (1994) 'Prélèvements tributaires et échanges en Asie Mineure achéménide et hellénistique', in *Économie antique: Les échanges dans l'Antiquité: le rôle de l'État*, ed. J. Andreau, P. Briant, and R. Descat. Saint-Bertrand-de Comminges, 69–81.

Briant, P. (2002) *From Cyrus to Alexander: A History of the Persian Empire*. Translated by P. T. Daniels (French original, 1996). Winona Lake, IN.

Bringmann, K. and von Steuben, H. (1995) *Schenkungen hellenistischer Herrscher an griechische Städte und Heiligtümer* (2 vols in 3). Berlin.

Brock, R. (2009) 'Did the Athenian empire promote democracy?', in *Interpreting the Athenian Empire*, ed. J. Ma, N. Papazarkadas, and R. Parker. London, 149–66.

Brodersen, K., Günther, W., and Schmitt, H. H. (1992) *Historische griechische Inschriften in Übersetzung. Band I: Die archaische und klassische Zeit*. Darmstadt.

Bruneau, P. (1980) 'Le dromos et le temple C du Sarapieion C de Délos', *BCH* 104, 161–88.

Buck, C. D. (1955) *The Greek Dialects: Grammar, Selected Inscriptions, Glossary*. Chicago.

Burkert, W. (1983) *Homo Necans: The Anthropology of Ancient Greek Sacrificial Ritual and Myth*. Translated by P. Bing. Berkeley, Los Angeles, and London.

Burton, P. J. (2011) *Friendship and Empire: Roman Diplomacy and Imperialism in the Middle Republic (353–146 BC)*. Cambridge.

Burton, P. J. (2017) *Rome and the Third Macedonian War*. Cambridge.

Butz, P. A. (2010) *The Art of the Hekatompedon Inscription and the Birth of the Stoikhedon Style*. Leiden and Boston.

Camia, F. (2009) *Roma e le poleis. L'intervento di Roma nelle controversie territoriali tra le comunità greche di Grecia e d'Asia Minore nel secondo secolo a.C.: Le testimonianze epigrafiche*. Athens.

Canali de Rossi, F. (1997) *Le ambascerie dal mondo greco a Roma in età repubblicana*. Rome.

Canali de Rossi, F. (2001) *Il ruolo dei patroni nelle relazioni politiche fra il mondo greco e Roma in età repubblicana ed augustea*. Leipzig.

Canevaro, M. (2013) *The Documents in the Attic Orators: Laws and Decrees in the Public Speeches of the Demosthenic Corpus*. Oxford.

Canevaro, M. and Harris, E. M. (2012) 'The documents in Andocides' *On the Mysteries*', *CQ* 62/1, 98–129.

Carbon, M. (2014) 'A Hellenistic ritual calendar from Kyzikos', *EA* 47, 149–55.

Catling, R. W. V. and Canavou, N. (2007) 'Dionysikles son of Posideos from Teos', *ZPE* 163, 118–20.

Ceccarelli, P. (2010) 'Changing contexts: tragedy in the civic and cultural life of Hellenistic city-states', in *Beyond the Fifth Century: Interactions with Greek Tragedy from the Fourth Century BCE to the Middle Ages*, ed. I. Gildenhard and M. Revermann. Berlin and New York, 99–150.

Chandezon, Chr. (2003) *L'élevage en Grèce (fin V^e–fin Ier s. a.C.): L'apport des sources épigraphiques*. Bordeaux.

Chaniotis, A. (1988a) *Historie und Historiker in den griechischen Inschriften*. Stuttgart.

Chaniotis, A. (1988b) 'Als die Diplomaten noch tanzen und sangen: Zu zwei Dekreten kretischer Städte in Mylasa', *ZPE* 71, 154–6.

Chaniotis, A. (2004) 'Justifying territorial claims in Classical and Hellenistic Greece: the beginnings of international law', in *The Law and the Courts in Ancient Greece*, ed. E. M. Harris and L. Rubinstein. London, 185–213.

Chaniotis, A. (2005a) *War in the Hellenistic World*. Malden, MA and Oxford.

Chaniotis, A. (2005b) 'Akzeptanz von Herrschaft durch ritualisierte Dankbarkeit und Erinnerung', in *Die Welt der Rituale. Von der Antike bis heute*, ed. C. Ambos, S. Hotz, G. Schwedler, and S. Weinfurter. Darmstadt, 188–204.

Chaniotis, A. (2010) 'Aphrodite's rivals: devotion to local and other gods at Aphrodisias', *CCG* 21, 235–48.

Chaniotis, A. (2011) 'The ithyphallic hymn for Demetrios Poliorketes and Hellenistic religious mentality', in *More than Men, Less than Gods*, ed. P. P. Iossif, A. S. Chankowski, and C. C. Lorber. Leuven, 157–95.

Chankowski, A. S. (2010) *L'éphébie hellénistique: Étude d'une institution civique dans les cités grecques des îles de la Mer Égée et de l'Asie Mineure*. Paris.

Chankowski, A. S. (2018) 'Torch races in the Hellenistic world: the influence of an Athenian institution?', *JES* 1, 55–75.

Chiranky, G. (1982) 'Rome and Cotys: two problems', *Athenaeum* 60, 461–81.

Chishull, E. (1728) *Antiquitates Asiaticae christianam aeram antecedentes, ex primariis monumentis Graecis descriptae, Latine versae notisque et commentariis illustratae*. London.

Chistov, D. (2018) 'Amphorae assemblages of the second quarter – mid-6th century BC from the north-eastern part of the Berezan island site', in *Koinè et mobilité artisanale entre la Méditerranée et la Mer Noire dans l'antiquité: Hommage à Pierre Dupont*, ed. A. Avram, L. Buzoianu, and V. Lungu. Constanţa, 85–96.

Chrubasik, B. (2016) *Kings and Usurpers in the Seleukid Empire: The Men Who Would Be King*. Oxford.

Chryssanthaki, K. (2001) 'Les trois fondations d'Abdère', *REG* 114, 383–406.

Chryssanthaki-Nagle, K. (2007) *L'histoire monétaire d'Abdère en Thrace (VIᵉ s. av. J.-C.–IIᵉ s. ap. J.-C.) (ΜΕΛΕΤΗΜΑΤΑ 51)*. Athens.

Cohen, G. M. (2006) *The Hellenistic Settlements in Syria, the Red Sea Basin, and North Africa*. Berkeley, Los Angeles, and London.

Cole, S. G. (1995) 'Civic cult and civic identity', in *Sources for the Ancient Greek City-State*, ed. M. H. Hansen. Copenhagen, 292–325.

Collitz, H. (1884–1915) *Sammlung der griechischen Dialekt-Inschriften* (4 vols in 6). Göttingen.

Colvin, S. (2007) *A Historical Greek Reader: Mycenaean to the Koiné*. Oxford.

Condurachi, É. (1970) 'Kotys, Rome et Abdère', *Latomus* 29, 581–94.

Connor, W. R. (1993) 'The Ionian era of Athenian civic identity', *PAPhS* 137, 194–206.

Cousin, G. and Diehl, C. (1890) 'Inscriptions d'Halicarnasse', *BCH* 14, 90–121.

Crawford, M. (2003) 'William Sherard and the Prices Edict', *RN* 159, 83–107.

Crielaard, J. P. (2009) 'The Ionians in the Archaic period: shifting identities in a changing world', in *Ethnic Constructs in Antiquity*, ed. T. Derks and N. Roymans. Amsterdam, 37–84.

Crowther, C. V. (1997) 'Inscriptions from the Sparta and Larissa museums', *ABSA* 92, 345–58.

Curty, O. (1995) *Les parentés légendaires entre cités grecques*. Geneva.

Curty, O. (2015) *Gymnasiarchika. Recueil et analyse des inscriptions de l'époque hellénistique en l'honneur des gymnasiarques*. Paris.

D'Alessio, G. B. (1992) 'Immigrati a Teo e ad Abdera (*SEG* XXXI 985; Pind. fr. 52B Sn.–M.), *ZPE* 92, 73–80.

Dan, A., Gehrke, H.-J., Kelterbaum, D., Schlotzhauer, U., and Zhuravlev, D. (2016) 'Foundation patterns on the two Bosporus', in *Asian Bosporus and Kuban Region in Pre-Roman Time*, ed. D. Zhuravlev and U. Schlotzhauer. Moscow: 109–20.

Daubner, F. (2006) *Bellum Asiaticum: Der Krieg der Römer gegen Aristonikos von Pergamon und die Einrichtung der Provinz Asia* (2nd rev. edn). Munich.

Davesnes, A. (1987) 'Numismatique et archéologie: Le temple de Dionysos à Téos', *RN* 29, 15–20.

Debord, P. and Varinlioğlu, E. (2018) *Hyllarima de Carie: État de la question*. Bordeaux.

Delev, P. (2015) 'From Koroupedion to the Third Mithridatic War (281–73 BCE)', in *A Companion to Ancient Thrace*, ed. J. Valeva, E. Nankov, and D. Graninger. Malden, MA and Oxford, 59–74.

Delev, P. (2018) 'Did a "late" Odrysian kingdom ever exist?', in *Stephanos Archaeologicos ad 80 annum Professoris Ludmili Getov* (Studia Archaeologica Universitatis Serdicensis Suppl. VI). Sofia, 191–6.

Demangel, R. and Laumonier, A. (1922) 'Inscriptions d'Ionie', *BCH* 46, 307–55.

Demetriou, D. (2017) 'Beyond *polis* religion: religious practices in the cosmopolitan *emporion* of Naukratis', *BABESCH* 92, 49–66.

Denniston, J. D. (1954) *The Greek Particles* (2nd edn). Oxford.

Derow, P. (1979) 'Polybius, Rome, and the East', *JRS* 69, 1–15.

Derow, P. (1991) 'Pharos and Rome', *ZPE* 88, 261–70; reprinted in *Rome, Polybius, & the East*. Oxford, 2015, 265–78.

Deubner, F. (1932) *Attische Feste*. Berlin.

Dickie, M. W. (1996) 'What is a *kolossos* and how were *kolossoi* made in the Hellenistic period?', *GRBS* 37, 237–57.

Dillon, S. (2006) *Ancient Greek Portrait Sculpture: Contexts, Subjects, and Styles*. Cambridge.

Dillon, S. (2010) *The Female Portrait Statue in the Greek World*. Cambridge.

Dmitriev, S. (2010) 'Attalus' request for the cities of Aenus and Maronea in 167 B.C.', *Historia* 59, 106–14.

Donnellan, L., Nizzo, V., and Burgers, G.-J. (eds) (2016) *Conceptualising Early Colonisation* (*Artes* 6). Brussels.

Dössel, A. (2003) *Die Beilegung innerstaatlicher Konflikte in den griechischen Poleis vom 5.–3. Jahrhundert v.Chr.* Frankfurt am Main.

Dougherty, C. (1994) 'Pindar's second Paean: civic identity on parade', *CP* 89, 205–18.

Dragoumis, E. (1895) 'Inscription de Téos', *BCH* 19, 554–5.

Drew-Bear, Th. (1972) 'Deux décrets hellénistiques d'Asie Mineure', *BCH* 96, 435–71.

Dubois, L. (1980) 'Un nouveau nom de magistrat à Tirynthe', *REG* 93, 250–6.

Ducrey, P. (1999) *Le traitement des prisonniers de guerre dans la Grèce antique des origins à la conquête romaine* (rev. edn). Paris.

Dumont, A. and Homolle, Th. (1892) *Mélanges d'archéologie et d'épigraphie*. Paris.

Dupont, P. and Skarlatidou, E. (2005) 'Le débuts de la colonisation grecque en mer Noire', in *Pont–Euxin et polis: Actes du Xe Symposium de Vani*, ed. D. Kacharava, M. Faudot, and E. Geny. Besançon, 77–82.

Duyrat, Fr. (2002) 'Les ateliers monétaires de Phénicie du Nord à l'époque hellénistique', in *Les monnayages syriens*, ed. Chr. Augé and Fr. Duyrat. Beirut, 21–69.

Eckstein, A. M. (1999) 'Pharos and the question of Roman treaties of alliance in the Greek East in the third century B.C.E.', *Classical Philology* 94, 395–418.

Effenterre, H. van and Ruzé, F. (1994–5) *Nomima: Recueil d'inscriptions politiques et juridiques de l'archaisme grec*. Rome.

Ehrhardt, N. (1988) *Milet und seine Kolonien* (2nd edn). Frankfurt am Main.

Eilers, C. (2002) *Roman Patrons of Greek Cities*. Oxford.

Ellsworth, J. D. (1976) 'Agamemnon's intentions, ἀγών, and the growth of an error', *Glotta* 54, 228–35.

Elsner, J. (2015) 'Visual culture and ancient history: issues of empiricism and ideology in the Samos stele at Athens', *Classical Antiquity* 34, 33–73.

Errington, M. (1987) 'Θεὰ Ῥώμη und römischer Einfluss südlich des Mäanders im 2. Jh. v. Chr.', *Chiron* 17, 97–118.

Erskine, A. (1994) 'Greek embassies and the city of Rome', *Classics Ireland* 1, 47–53.

Erskine, A. (2002) 'O brother where art thou? Tales of kinship and diplomacy', in *The Hellenistic World: New Perspectives*, ed. D. Ogden. Swansea, 97–115.

Fabiani, R. (2015) *I decreti onorari di Iasos: Cronologia e storia*. Munich.

Famerie, É. (2007) 'Papiers de Sherard, copies de Hochepied, schedae de Duker: Contribution à l'histoire des copies manuscrites des inscriptions de Téos', *Chiron* 37, 65–88.

Faraguna, M. (2005) 'La figura dell'aisymnetes tra realtà storica e teoria politica', in *Symposion 2001*, ed. R. W. Wallace and M. Gagarin. Vienna, 321–38.

Faraguna, M. (2015) 'I nomophylakes tra utopia e realtà istituzionale delle città greche', *Politica Antica* 5, 141–59.

Faraone, C. A. (1996) 'Taking the "Nestor's cup inscription" seriously: erotic magic and conditional curses in the earliest inscribed hexameters', *Classical Antiquity* 15/1, 77–112.

Fears, J. R. (1978) 'Ο ΔΗΜΟΣ Ο ΡΩΜΑΙΩΝ Genius Populi Romani: a note on the origin of Dea Roma', *Mnemosyne* 31, 274–86.

Ferrary, J.-L. (1988) *Philhellénisme et impérialisme: Aspects idéologiques de la conquête romaine du monde hellénistique*. Rome.

Ferrary, J.-L. (1997a) 'De l'évergétisme hellénistique à l'évergétisme romain', in *Actes du Xᵉ Congrès International d'épigraphie grecque et latine (Nîmes, 4–9 octobre 1992)*. Paris: 199–225; reprinted with addenda in *Rome et le monde grec: Choix d'écrits*. Paris, 2017, 197–228.

Ferrary, J.-L. (1997b) 'The Hellenistic world and Roman political patronage', in *Hellenistic Constructs*, ed. P. Cartledge, P. Garnsey, and E. Gruen. Berkeley, Los Angeles, and London, 105–19.

Ferrary, J.-L. (2018) 'Le passage de la Macédoine et des régions adjacentes sous la domination romaine (168–88 av. J.-C.)', in *Βορειοελλαδικά: Tales from the Lands of the ethne. Essays in Honour of Miltiades B. Hatzopoulos*, ed. M. Kalaitzi, P. Paschidis, C. Antonetti, and A.-M. Guimier-Sorbets (*ΜΕΛΕΤΗΜΑΤΑ* 78). Athens, 299–308.

Fleischer, R. (1983) 'Gott oder Herrscher? Zwei syrische Denkmäler der Kleinkunst severischer Zeit', *AA* 253–71.

Fontenrose, J. (1988) *Didyma: Apollo's Oracle, Cult, and Companions*. Berkeley, Los Angeles, and London.

Fornara, C. W. (1977) *Translated Documents of Greece & Rome*, Vol. 1: *Archaic Times to the End of the Peloponnesian War*. Cambridge.

Fornasier, J. (2016) *Die griechische Kolonisation im Nordschwarzmeerraum vom 7. bis 5. Jahrhundert v. Chr.* Bonn.

Foucault, J.-A. de (1972) *Recherches sur la langue et le style de Polybe*. Paris.

Fournier, J. (2007) 'Les *syndikoi*, représentants juridiques des cités grecques sous le haut-empire romain', *Cahiers Glotz* 18, 7–36.

Fowler, R. L. (2013) *Early Greek Mythography*, Vol. 2: *Commentary*. Oxford.

Fragoulaki, M. (2013) *Kinship in Thucydides: Intercommunal Ties and Historical Narrative*. Oxford.

Fröhlich, P. (2004) *Les cités grecques et le contrôle des magistrats (IVᵉ–Iᵉʳ siècle avant J.-C.)*. Geneva.

Fromentin, V. and Gotteland, S. (eds) (2001) *Origines gentium*. Pessac.

Fuchs, M. (2018) 'The Frieze of the Temple of Dionysos at Teos', in *Sculpture in Roman Asia Minor*, ed. M. Aurenhammer. Vienna, 147–60.

Führer, R. (1967) *Formproblem–Untersuchungen zu den Reden in der frühgriechischen Lyrik*. Munich.

Gagarin, M. and Perlman, P. (2016) *The Laws of Ancient Crete c.650–400 BCE*. Oxford.

Gauthier, Ph. (1989) *Nouvelles inscriptions de Sardes II*. Geneva.

Gauthier, Ph. (1990) 'Quorum et participation civique dans les démocraties grecques', *Cahiers Glotz* 1, 73–99.

Gauthier, Ph. (1993) 'Décrets d'Érétrie en l'honneur de juges étrangers', *REG* 106, 589–98.

Gauthier, Ph. (1995) 'Du nouveau sur les courses aux flambeaux d'après deux inscriptions de Kos', *REG* 108, 576–85.

Gauthier, Ph. (2006) 'Les décrets de Colophon-sur-Mer en l'honneur des Attalides Athènaios et Philétairos', *REG* 119, 473–503.

Gauthier, Ph. and Hatzopoulos, M. (1993) *La loi gymnasiarchique de Beroia (ΜΕΛΕΤΗΜΑΤΑ 16)*. Athens.

Gelzer, M. (1912) *Die Nobilität der römischen Republik*. Leipzig and Berlin.

Georges, P. B. (2000) 'Persian Ionia under Darius: The Revolt Reconsidered', *Historia* 49, 1–39.

Glowacki, K. (2003) 'A personification of Demos on a new Attic document relief', *Hesperia* 72, 447–66.

Goldbeck, F. (2010) *Salutationes: Die Morgenbegrüssungen in Rom in der Republik und der frühen Kaiserzeit*. Berlin.

Gottlieb, G. (1967) *Timuchen: Ein Beitrag zum griechischen Staatsrecht*. Heidelberg.

Graf, F. (1985) *Nordionische Kulte. Religionsgeschichtliche und epigraphische Untersuchungen zu den Kulten von Chios, Erythrai, Klazomenai und Phokaia*. Rome.

Graham, A. J. (1991) '"Adopted Teians": a passage in the new inscription of Public Imprecations from Teos', *JHS* 111, 176–8; reprinted in Graham 2001, 263–8.

Graham, A. J. (1992) 'Abdera and Teos', *JHS* 112, 44–73; reprinted in Graham 2001, 269–314.

Graham, A. J. (2001) *Collected Papers on Greek Colonization*. Leiden, Boston, and Cologne.

Grainger, J. D. (2002) *The Roman War of Antiochos the Great*. Leiden and Boston.

Gray, B. J. (2013) 'Philosophy of education and the later Hellenistic *polis*', in *Epigraphical Approaches to the Post-Classical Polis*, ed. P. Martzavou and N. Papazarkadas. Oxford, 233–53.

Gray, B. J. (2015) *Stasis and Stability: Exile, the Polis, and Political Thought, c.404–146 BC*. Oxford.

Gruen, E. S. (1984) *The Hellenistic World and the Coming of Rome* (2 vols). Berkeley and London.

Gschnitzer, F. (1983) 'Zur Normenhierarchie im öffentlichen Recht der Griechen', in *Symposion 1979*, ed. P. Dimakis. Cologne, 143–64.

Gutzwiller, K. (2002) 'Art's echo: the tradition of Hellenistic ecphrastic epigram', in *Hellenistic Epigrams*, ed. M. A. Harder, R. Regtuit, and G. W. Wakker. Leuven, 85–112.

Habicht, Chr. (1982) *Studien zur Geschichte Athens in hellenistischer Zeit*. Göttingen.

Habicht, Chr. (1990) 'Samos weiht eine Statue des *Populus Romanus*', *MDAI(A)* 105, 259–68.

Habicht, Chr. (1997) *Athens from Alexander to Antony*. Translated by D. L. Schneider. Cambridge, MA and London.

Hagedorn, A. C. (2005) 'Wie flucht man im östlichen Mittelmeer? Kulturanthropologische Einsichten in die *Dirae Teiae* und das Deuteronomium', in *Kodifizierung und Legitimierung des Rechts in der Antike und im Alten Orient*, ed. M. Witte and M. T. Fögen. Wiesbaden, 117–50.

Hahland, W. (1950) 'Der Fries des Dionysostempels in Teos', *ÖJh* 38, 66–109.

Hamon, P. (2018) 'Tout l'or et l'argent de Téos: Au sujet d'une nouvelle édition des décrets sur les pirates et l'emprunt pour la liberation des otages', *Chiron* 48, 333–74.

Hansen, M. H. and Nielsen, T. H. (2004) *An Inventory of Archaic and Classical Poleis*. Oxford.

Harder, A. (2012) *Callimachus: Aetia* (2 vols). Oxford.

Harland, P. A. (2014) *Greco-Roman Associations: Texts, Translations and Commentary*, Vol. 2: *North Coast of the Black Sea, Asia Minor*. Berlin and Boston.

Harris, E. M. (2013–14) 'The authenticity of the document at Andocides *On the Mysteries* 96–98', *Tekmeria* 12, 121–53.

Harris, E. M. (2015) 'The family, the community and murder: the role of pollution in Athenian homicide law', in *Public and Private in Ancient Mediterranean Law and Religion*, ed. C. Ando and J. Rüpke. Berlin, Munich, and Boston, 11–35.

Hatzopoulos, M. B. (1996) *Macedonian Institutions under the Kings* (*ΜΕΛΕΤΗΜΑΤΑ* 22, 2 vols). Athens.

Hatzopoulos, M. B. (2001) *L'organisation de l'armée macedonienne sous les Antigonides: Problèmes anciens et documents nouveaux* (*ΜΕΛΕΤΗΜΑΤΑ* 30). Athens.

Hatzopoulos, M. B. (2008) 'Retour à la vallée du Strymon', in *Thrakika Zetemeta I*, ed. L. D. Loukopoulou and S. Psoma (*ΜΕΛΕΤΗΜΑΤΑ* 58). Athens, 13–54.

Hatzopoulos, M. B. (2015–16) 'Comprendre la loi ephebarchique d'Amphipolis', *Tekmeria* 13, 145–71.

Hatzopoulos, M. B. and Loukopoulou, L. D. (1987) *Two Studies in Ancient Macedonian Topography* (*ΜΕΛΕΤΗΜΑΤΑ* 3). Athens.

Hatzopoulos, M. B. and Loukopoulou, L. D. (1989) *Morrylos, cité de la Crestonie* (*ΜΕΛΕΤΗΜΑΤΑ* 7). Athens.

Hatzopoulos, M. B. and Loukopoulou, L. D. (1992–6) *Recherches sur les marches orientales des Téménides* (*ΜΕΛΕΤΗΜΑΤΑ* 11) (2 vols). Athens.

Hauken, T. (1998) *Petition and Response: An Epigraphic Study of Petitions to Roman Emperors 181–249*. Bergen.

Haussoulier, B. (1900) Review of W. Dittenberger, *Sylloge inscriptionum graecarum*[2], *Revue critique d'histoire et de littérature* 28 (9 July), 21–30.

Hawke, J. (2011) *Writing Authority: Elite Competition and Written Law in Early Greece*. DeKalb, IL.

Helly, B. (1971) 'Décrets de Démétrias pour les juges étrangers', *BCH* 95, 543–59.

Henrichs, A. (1978) 'Greek maenadism from Olympias to Messalina', *HSCP* 82, 121–60.

Herda, A. (2006) *Der Apollon-Delphinios-Kult in Milet und die Neujahrsprozession nach Didyma. Ein neuer Kommentar der sog. Molpoi-Satzung*. Mainz.

Herrmann, P. (1965) 'Antiochos der Grosse und Teos', *Anadolu* 9, 29–159.

Herrmann, P. (1971) 'Zum Beschluss von Abdera aus Teos *Syll.*[3] 656', *ZPE* 7, 72–7; reprinted in Herrmann 2016, 515–19.

Herrmann, P. (1979) 'Die Stadt Temnos und ihre auswärtigen Beziehungen in hellenistischer Zeit', *MDAI(I)* 29, 239–71; reprinted in Herrmann 2016, 543–79.

Herrmann, P. (1981) 'Teos und Abdera im 5. Jahrhundert v. Chr.: Ein neues Fragment der Teiorum Dirae', *Chiron* 11, 1–30.

Herrmann, P. (2000) 'Eine berühmte Familie in Teos', in *Studien zur Religion und Kultur Kleinasiens und des ägäischen Bereiches. Festschrift für Baki Öğun* (*Asia Minor Studien* 39), ed. C. Işık. Bonn, 87–97; reprinted in Herrmann 2016, 521–31.

Herrmann, P. (2016) *Kleinasien im Spiegel epigraphischer Zeugnisse: Ausgewählte kleine Schriften*, ed. W. Blümel. Berlin and Boston.

Hessel, F. (1731) *Antiquae inscriptiones quum Graecae, tum Latinae, olim a Marquardo Gudio collectae . . . nunc a Francesco Hesselio editae cum adnotationibus eorum.* Leeuwarden.

Höghammar, K. (1993) *Sculpture and Society: A Study of the Connection between the Free-Standing Sculpture and Society on Kos in the Hellenistic and Augustan Periods.* Uppsala.

Hoepfner, W. and Schwandner, E.-L. (eds) (1990) *Hermogenes und die hochhellenistische Architektur.* Mainz.

Hoffmann, O. (1891–8) *Die griechischen Dialekte in ihrem historischen Zusammenhange mit den wichtigsten ihrer Quellen* (3 vols). Göttingen.

Holleaux, M. (1901) 'Curae epigraphicae', *REA* 3, 115–30; reprinted (pp. 119–30) in *Études d'épigraphie et d'histoire grecques, Tome I.* Paris, 1938, 313–24.

Holleaux, M. (1907) 'Inscriptions de Priène', *BCH* 31, 382–8; reprinted in *Études d'épigraphie et d'histoire grecques, Tome I.* Paris, 1938, 302–12.

Holleaux, M. (1914) 'Note sur deux décrets d'Abdère', *BCH* 38, 63–70; reprinted in *Études d'épigraphie et d'histoire grecques, Tome I.* Paris, 1938, 277–84.

Holleaux, M. (1924) 'Inscription trouvée a Brousse', *BCH* 48, 1–57; reprinted in *Études d'épigraphie et d'histoire grecques, Tome II.* Paris, 1938, 73–125.

Hornblower, S. (2013) *Herodotus: Histories Book V.* Cambridge.

Howgego, C. J. (1985) *Greek Imperial Countermarks.* London.

Hülden, O. (2020) *Das griechische Befestigungswesen der archaischen Zeit: Entwicklungen—Formen—Funktion.* Vienna.

Humphreys, S. C. (2004) *The Strangeness of Gods: Historical Perspectives on the Interpretation of Athenian Religion.* Oxford.

Humphreys, S. C. (2018) *Kinship in Ancient Athens: An Anthropological Analysis* (2 vols). Oxford.

Iossif, P. P. (2018) 'Divine attributes on Hellenistic coinages', in *ΤΥΠΟΙ: Greek and Roman Coins Seen through their Images*, ed. P. P. Iossif, F. de Callataÿ, and R. Veymiers. Liège, 269–95.

İren, K. and Ünlü, A. (2012) 'Burning in Geometric Teos', in *Stephanèphoros: De l'économie antique à l'Asie Mineure. Hommages à Raymond Descat*, ed. K. Konuk. Bordeaux, 309–33.

Isaac, B. H. (1986) *The Greek Settlements in Thrace until the Macedonian Conquest.* Leiden.

Isager, S. and Karlsson, L. (2008) 'A new inscription from Labraunda. Honorary decree for Olympichos: *I.Labraunda* no. 134 (and no. 49)', *EA* 41, 39–52.

Isayev, E. (2017) *Migration, Mobility and Place in Ancient Italy.* Cambridge.

Jacobsthal, P. (1908) 'Die Arbeiten zu Pergamon 1906–1907. II. Die Inschriften', *MDAI(A)* 33, 375–420.

Jacquemin, A., Mulliez, D., and Rougemont, G. (2012) *Choix d'inscriptions de Delphes, traduites et commentées.* Athens.

Jeffery, L. H. (1956) 'The courts of justice in archaic Chios', *ABSA* 51, 157–67.

Jeffery, L. H. (1990) *The Local Scripts of Archaic Greece* (rev. edn with a Supplement by A. W. Johnston). Oxford.

Jones, C. P. (1999) *Kinship Diplomacy in the Ancient World.* Cambridge, MA and London.

Jones, C. P. (2011) 'Cleopatra VII in Teos?', *Chiron* 41, 41–53.

Jones, C. P. (2019) 'The lease of a heroic τέμενος at Teos', *ZPE* 212, 109–14.

Jones, C. P. (2020) 'Altars of Cleopatra VII and Ptolemy XV Caesarion at Teos', *Philia* 6, 85–92.

Kadıoğlu, M. (2019) 'Teos'ta Seramik ve Mermer Üretimi ile Dağılımı', in *Kültürlerin Bağlantısı: Başlangıcından Roma Dönemi Sonuna Kadar Eski Yakın Doğu'da Ticaret ve Bölgelerarası İlişkiler*, ed. V. Şahoğlu, M. Şevketoğlu, and Y. H. Erbil. Ankara, 293–320.

Kadıoğlu, M. (2020) 'Vorbericht über das Dionysos-Heiligtum von Teos im Licht der neuen Grabungen', in *Zwischen Bruch und Kontinuität: Architektur in Kleinasien am Übergang vom Hellenismus zur römischen Kaiserzeit* (BYZAS 25), ed. U. Lohner-Urban and U. Quatember. Istanbul, 171–93.

Kadıoğlu, M., Özbil, C., Adak, M., Vapur, Ö., Gençler Güray, Ç., Kılıç, Y., and Kopçuk, İ. (2019) '2017 yılı Teos kazı çalışmları (8. sezon)', *KST* 40/3, 45–70.

Kadıoğlu, M., Özbil, C., Kerschner, M., and Mommsen, H. (2015) 'Teos im Licht der neuen Forschungen', in *Anatolien—Brücke der Kulturen*, ed. Ü. Yalçın and H.-D. Bienert. Bochum, 345–66.

Kagan, J. H. (2006) 'Small Change and the Beginning of Coinage at Abdera', in *Agoranomia: Studies in Money and Exchange presented to John H. Kroll*, ed. P. van Alfen. New York, 49–60.

Kallet-Marx, R. M. (1995) *Hegemony to Empire: The Development of the Roman Imperium in the East from 148 to 62 B.C.* Berkeley, Los Angeles, and Oxford.

Kallintzi, D. and Veligianni, Chr. (1996) 'Eine neue Weihinschrift aus Abdera', *AHB* 10, 51–65.

Kallintzi, K. (2004) 'Abdera: organization and utilization of the area *extra muros*', in Moustaka et al. 2004, 271–89.

Kallintzi, K. (2006) 'Les nécropoles d'Abdère: Organisation de l'espace et rites funéraires', in *Rois, cités, nécropoles: Institutions, rites et monuments en Macédoine*, ed. M. Guimier-Sorbets, M. B. Hatzopoulos, and Y. Morizot. Athens, 143–53.

Kallintzi, K. (2012) 'Ἐπίθεση καὶ ἄμυνα στὴν πόλη τῶν Ἀβδήρων', in *ΔΙΝΗΕΣΣΑ: Τιμητικός τόμος για την Κατερίνα Ρωμιοπούλου*, ed. P. Adam–Veleni and K. Tzanavari. Thessaloniki, 131–40.

Kallintzi, K. (2018) 'The Roman city of Abdera and its territory', in *Proceedings of the First International Roman and Late Antique Thrace Conference (Plovdiv, 3rd-7th October 2016). Bulletin of the National Archaeological Institute*, 44. Plovdiv, 21–30.

Kallintzi, K. and Papaikonomou, I.-D. (2010) 'La présence des enfants dans les nécropoles d'Abdère', in *L'enfant et la mort dans l'antiquité*, Vol. I: *Nouvelles recherches dans les nécropoles grecques: Le signalement des tombes d'enfants*, ed. A.-M. Guimier-Sorbets and Y. Morizot. Paris, 129–59.

Kaye, N. (forthcoming) *Overnight Empire: The Attalids of Pergamon.* Cambridge.

Keesling, C. M. (2017) *Early Greek Portraiture: Monuments and Histories.* Cambridge.

Keil, J. (1912) 'Forschungen in der Erythraia II', *JÖAI* 15, Beibl. 49–76.

Kennell, N. M. (2013) 'Who were the *neoi*?', in *Epigraphical Approaches to the Post-Classical Polis*, ed. P. Martzavou and N. Papazarkadas. Oxford, 217–32.

Kerschner, M. (2006) 'Zum Beginn und zu den Phasen der griechischen Kolonisation am Schwarzen Meer: Die Evidenz der ostgriechischen Keramik', *Eurasia Antiqua* 12, 227–50.

Kerschner, M. (2014) 'Euboean imports to the Eastern Aegean and Eastern Aegean production of pottery in the Euboean style: new evidence from Neutron Activation Analyses', in *Archaeometric Analyses of Euboean and Euboean Related Pottery: New Results and their Interpretations*, ed. M. Kerschner and I. S. Lemos. Vienna, 109–40.

Killen, S. (2017) *Parasema: Offizielle Symbole griechischer Poleis und Bundesstaaten.* Berlin.

Kinns, P. (1980) *Studies in the Coinage of Ionia: Erythrae, Teos, Lebedus, Colophon, c.400–30 B.C.* Unpublished Cambridge PhD thesis.

Kirchhoff, A. (1887) *Studien zur Geschichte des griechischen Alphabets.* Vierte umgearbeitete Auflage. Gütersloh.

Knäpper, K. (2018) *Hieros kai asylos: Territoriale Asylie im Hellenismus in ihrem historischen Kontext.* Stuttgart.

Knoepfler, D. (2001) *Eretria XI: Décrets ététriens de proxénie et de citoyenneté.* Lausanne.

Koerner, R. (1987) 'Beamtenvergehen und deren Bestrafung nach frühen griechischen Inschriften', *KLIO* 69, 459–98.

Koerner, R. (1993) *Inschriftliche Gesetzestexte der frühen griechischen Polis.* Cologne.

Koparal, E. (2013) 'Teos and Kyrbissos', *Olba* 21, 45–70.

Kotsidu, H. (2000) *ΤΙΜΗ ΚΑΙ ΔΟΞΑ: Ehrungen für hellenistische Herrscher im griechischen Mutterland und in Kleinasien unter besonderer Berücksichtigung der archäologischen Denkmäler.* Berlin.

Koukouli-Chrysanthaki, C. (1990) 'Τα "μέταλλα" της Θασιακής περαίας', in *Μνήμη Δ. Λαζαρίδη: Πόλις και χώρα στην αρχαία Μακεδονία και Θράκη.* Thessaloniki, 493–532.

Koukouli-Chrysanthaki, C. (2004) 'The archaic city of Abdera', in Moustaka et al. 2004, 235–48.

Krauskopf, I. (1981) 'Leukothea nach den antiken Quellen', in *Akten des Kolloquiums zum Thema 'Die Göttin von Pyrgi'.* Florence, 137–48.

Kremydi, S. (2018) *'Autonomous' Coinages under the Late Antigonids (ΜΕΛΕΤΗΜΑΤΑ 79).* Athens.

Kropp, A. J. M. (2011) 'Anatomy of a Phoenician goddess: the Tyche of Berytus and her acolytes', *JRA* 24, 389–407.

Kuznetsov, V. D. (2000–1) 'Phanagoria and its metropolis', *Talanta* 32–3, 67–77.

Lambert, S. D. (1993) *The Phratries of Attica.* Ann Arbor.

Lambert, S. D. (2006) 'Athenian state laws and decrees, 352/1–322/1: III Decrees honouring foreigners. A. Citizenship, proxeny and euergesy', *ZPE* 158, 115–58.

Lambert, S. D. (2019) *Attic Inscriptions in UK Collections: British Museum: Cult Provisions* (AIUK 4.1), <https://www.atticinscriptions.com/papers/aiuk-41/>.

Lambrinudakis, W. and Wörrle, M. (1983) 'Ein hellenistisches Reformgesetz über das öffentliche Urkundenwesen von Paros', *Chiron* 13, 283–678.

Larson, J. (1992) *Greek Heroine Cults.* Madison, WI.

Latte, K. (1920) *Heiliges Recht: Untersuchungen zur Geschichte der sakralen Rechtsformen in Griechenland.* Tübingen.

Lawton, C. L. (1995) *Attic Document Reliefs.* Oxford.

Lawton, C. L. (2017) *The Athenian Agora XXXVIII: Votive Reliefs.* Princeton, NJ.

Lazaridou, C. (2015) 'Ἐφηβαρχικὸς νόμος ἀπὸ τὴν Ἀμφίπολη', *ArchEph* 2015, 1–45.

Le Bas, P. and Waddington, W. H. (1870) *Inscriptions grecques et latines recueillies en Grèce et en Asie Mineure, Tome III* (2 vols). Paris.

Le Guen, B. (2001) *Les associations des technites dionysiaques à l'époque hellénistique* (2 vols). Paris.

Le Guen, B. (2007) 'Kraton, son of Zotichos: artists' associations and monarchic power in the Hellenistic period', in *The Greek Theatre and Festivals: Documentary Studies*, ed. P. Wilson. Oxford, 246–78.

Le Rider, G. (1979) 'Un tétradrachme hellénistique de Cnide', in *Greek Numismatics and Archaeology: Essays in Honor of Margaret Thompson*, ed. O. Mørkholm and N. Waggoner. Wetteren, 155–7.

Le Rider, G. (2001) 'Sur un aspect du comportement monétaire des villes libres d'Asie Mineure occidentale au IIe siècle', in *Les cités d'Asie Mineure occidentale au IIe siècle a.C.*, ed. A. Bresson et R. Descat. Paris and Bordeaux, 37–63.

Lehmann, G. A. (1998) *'Römischer Tod' in Kolophon/Klaros: Neue Quellen zum Status der 'freien' Polisstaaten an der Westküste Kleinasiens im späten zweiten Jahrhundert v. Chr.* Göttingen.

Lehmann, G. A. (2000) 'Polis-Autonomie und römische Herrschaft an der Westküste Kleinasiens: Kolophon/Klaros nach der Aufrichtung der *provincia Asia*', in *Politics, Administration and Society in the Hellenistic and Roman World*, ed. L. Mooren. Leuven, 215–38.

Lenfant, D. (2002) 'Pourquoi Xerxès détacha son ceinture (Hérodote, VIII.120)', *ARTA* 2002, note 4.

Lewis, D. M. (1982) 'On the new text of Teos', *ZPE* 47, 71–2; reprinted in *Selected Papers in Greek and Near Eastern History*. Cambridge, 1997, 7–8.

Lewis, D. M. (1984) 'Democratic institutions and their diffusion', in Πρακτικὰ τοῦ Η΄ Διεθνοῦς Συνεδρίου Ἑλληνικῆς καὶ Λατινικῆς Ἐπιγραφικῆς, *1982*. Athens, 55–61; reprinted in *Selected Papers in Greek and Near Eastern History*. Cambridge, 1997, 51–9.

Linderski, J. (1995) 'Ambassadors go to Rome', in *Les relations internationales: Actes du Colloque de Strasbourg 15–17 juin 1993*, ed. E. Frézouls and A. Jacquemin. Paris, 453–78.

Lorber, C. C. and Hoover, O. D. (2003) 'An unpublished tetradrachm issued by the Artists of Dionysos', *NC* 163, 59–68.

Loukopoulou, L. D. and Parissaki, M.-G. (2004) 'Teos and Abdera: the epigraphic evidence', in Moustaka et al. 2004, 305–10.

Loukopoulou, L. D. and Psoma, S. (2008) 'Maroneia and Stryme revisited: some problems of historical topography', in *Thrakika Zetemata I* (*ΜΕΛΕΤΗΜΑΤΑ* 58). Athens, 55–86.

Lücke, S. (2000) *Syngeneia: Epigraphisch-historische Studien zu einem Phänomen der antiken griechischen Diplomatie*. Frankfurt.

Lund, H. S. (1992) *Lysimachus: A Study in Early Hellenistic Kingship*. London and New York.

Ma, J. (2002) *Antiochos III and the Cities of Western Asia Minor* (rev. edn). Oxford.

Ma, J. (2003) 'Peer polity interaction in the Hellenistic age', *Past & Present* 180, 9–39.

Ma, J. (2007a) 'Observations on honorific statues at Oropos (and elsewhere)', *ZPE* 160, 89–96.

Ma, J. (2007b) 'A *Horse* from Teos: epigraphical notes on the Ionian–Hellespontine association of Dionysiac Artists', in *The Greek Theatre and Festivals: Documentary Studies*, ed. P. Wilson. Oxford, 215–45.

Ma, J. (2013) *Statues and Cities: Honorific Portraits and Civic Identity in the Hellenistic World*. Oxford.

Ma, J. (2018) 'Seeing the invisible', in *Visual Histories of the Classical World: Essays in Honour of R. R. R. Smith*, ed. C. M. Draycott, R. Raja, K. Welch, and W. T. Wootton. Turnhout, 149–58.

Macdonald, D. (1992) *The Coinage of Aphrodisias*. London.

Mack, W. (2015) *Proxeny and Polis: Institutional Networks in the Ancient Greek World*. Oxford.

Mack, W. (2018) 'Vox populi, vox deorum? Athenian document reliefs and the theologies of public inscription', *ABSA* 113, 365–98.

Magie, D. (1950) *Roman Rule in Asia Minor* (2 vols). Princeton, NJ.

Magnetto, A. (2008) *L'arbitrato di Rodi fra Samo e Priene*. Pisa.

Malkin, I. (1985) 'What's in a name? The eponymous founders of Greek colonies', *Athenaeum* 63, 115–30.

Manov, M. (2002) 'Once again on the date of *Sylloge*³, 656', *Arheologia* 43/3, 28–34.

Marek, Chr. (1993) *Stadt, Ära und Territorium in Pontus–Bithynia und Nord–Galatia.* Tübingen.

Marek, Chr. (1997) 'Teos under Abdera nach dem Dritten Makedonischen Krieg: Eine neue Ehreninschrift für den Demos von Teos', *Tyche* 12, 169–77.

Marek, Chr. and Zingg, E. (2018) *Die Versinschrift des Hyssaldomos und die Inschriften von Uzunyuva (Milas/Mylasa). Asia Minor Studien* 90. Bonn.

Martin, K. (2013) *Demos, Boule, Gerousia: Personifikationen städtischer Institutionen auf kaiserzeitlichen Münzen aus Kleinasien* (2 vols). Bonn.

Masséglia, J. (2015) *Body Language in Hellenistic Art and Society.* Oxford.

Masson, O. (1984) 'Quelques noms de magistrats monétaires grecs, IV: Noms de monétaires à Abdère et Maronée', *Rev. Num.* 26, 48–60.

Matthaiou, A. P. (2006) '*Τρεῖς ἐπιγραφὲς Χίου*', in *Χιακὸν Συμπόσιον εἰς Μνήμην W. G. Forrest*, ed. G. E. Malouchou and A. P. Matthaiou. Athens, 103–36.

Matthaiou, A. P. (2011) *Τὰ ἐν τῆι στήληι γεγραμμένα: Six Greek Historical Inscriptions of the Fifth Century B.C.* Athens.

Matzke, M. (2002) 'Die frühe Münzprägung von Teos in Ionien: Chronologische und metrologische Untersuchungen um die Frühzeit der Silbermünzprägung', *JNG* 50, 21–53.

May, J. M. F. (1965) 'The coinage of Dicaea-by-Abdera', *NC*, 1–25.

May, J. M. F. (1966) *The Coinage of Abdera (540–345 B.C.).* London.

McNicoll, A. W. (1997) *Hellenistic Fortifications from the Aegean to the Euphrates.* Oxford.

Meadows, A. (2013) 'The closed currency system of the Attalid kingdom', in *Attalid Asia Minor*, ed. P. Thonemann. Oxford, 149–205.

Meadows, A. (2018) 'The great transformation: civic coin design in the second century BC', in *TYΠOI: Greek and Roman Coins Seen through their Images*, ed. P. P. Iossif, F. de Callataÿ, and R. Veymiers. Liège, 297–318.

Megow, W.-R. (1994) 'Zwei Köpfe im Rijksmuseum van Oudheden in Leiden', *AntPl* 23, 65–79.

Meier, L. (2012) *Die Finanzierung öffentlicher Bauten in der hellenistischen Polis.* Berlin.

Meier, L. (2017) 'Der sogenannte Piratenüberfall auf Teos und die Diadochen: Eine Neuedition der Inschrift SEG 44, 949', *Chiron* 47, 115–88.

Meier, L. (2019) *Kibyra in hellenistischer Zeit: Neue Staatsverträge und Ehreninschriften.* Vienna.

Meiggs, R. and Lewis, D. (1969) *A Selection of Greek Historical Inscriptions to the End of the Fifth Century B.C.* Oxford.

Mellor, R. (1975) *ΘΕΑ ΡΩΜΗ: The Worship of the Goddess Roma in the Greek World.* Göttingen.

Meritt, B. D. (1945) 'Attic inscriptions of the fifth century', *Hesperia* 14, 61–133.

Merkelbach, R. (1982) 'Zu dem neuen Text aus Teos', *ZPE* 46, 212–13.

Merkelbach, R. (1988) *Die Hirten des Dionysos.* Stuttgart.

Messerschmidt, W. (2003) *Prosopopoiia: Personifikationen politischen Charakters in spätklassischer und hellenistischer Kunst.* Cologne.

Meyer, E. A. (2016) 'Posts, *kurbeis*, metopes: the origins of the Athenian "documentary" stele', *Hesperia* 85, 323–83.

Meyer, K. M. (2012) 'Die Binde des Dionysos als Vorbild für das Königsdiadem?', in *Das Diadem der hellenistischen Herrscher*, ed. A. Lichtenberger, K. Martin, H.-H. Nieswandt, and D. Salzmann. Bonn, 209–31.

Meyer, M. (2006) *Die Personifikation der Stadt Antiocheia.* Berlin and New York.

Michel, C. (1900) *Recueil d'inscriptions grecques*. Paris.

Migeotte, L. (1980) 'Note sur l'emploi de *prodaneizein*', *Phoenix* 34, 219–26.

Migeotte, L. (1984) *L'emprunt public dans les cités grecques*. Québec and Paris.

Migeotte, L. (1992) *Les souscriptions publiques dans les cités grecques*. Geneva and Québec.

Mikalson, J. D. (1975) *The Sacred and Civil Calendar of the Athenian Year*. Princeton, NJ.

Mikalson, J. D. (1998) *Religion in Hellenistic Athens*. Berkeley, Los Angeles, and London.

Millar, F. (1987) 'Polybius between Greece and Rome', in *Greek Connections: Essays on Culture and Diplomacy*, ed. J. A. T. Koumoulides. Bloomington, IN, 1–18; reprinted in *Rome, the Greek World, and the East*, Vol. 3: *The Greek World, the Jews, & the East*, ed. H. M. Cotton and G. M. Rogers. Chapel Hill, 2006, 91–105.

Miller, M. (1970) *The Sicilian Colony Dates*. Albany.

Milner, N. P. and Eilers, C. F. (2006) 'L. Calpurnius Piso, Moles son of Moles, and emperor worship: statue bases from the upper agora at Oinoanda', *AS* 56, 61–76.

Minon, S. (2007) *Les inscriptions éléennes dialectales (VIᵉ–IIᵉ siècles avant J.-C.)* (2 vols). Geneva.

Mirón, D. (2018) 'From family to politics: Queen Apollonis as agent of dynastic/political loyalty', in *Royal Women and Dynastic Loyalty*, ed. C. Dunn and E. Carney. Cham, 31–48.

Möller, A. (2001) *Naukratis: Trade in Archaic Greece*. Oxford.

Moltesen, M. (2002) *Catalogue: Imperial Rome II: Statues: Ny Carlsberg Glyptotek*. Copenhagen.

Monakhov, S. Iu. and Kuznetsova, E. V. (2017) 'Overseas trade in the Black Sea region from the Archaic to the Hellenistic period', in *The Northern Black Sea in Antiquity*, ed. V. Kozlovskaya. Cambridge, 59–99.

Moreno, A. (2007) *Feeding the Democracy: The Athenian Grain Supply in the Fifth and Fourth Centuries BC*. Oxford.

Morgan, C. (2004) *Phanagoria Studies*, Vol. 1: *Attic Fine Pottery of the Archaic to Hellenistic Periods in Phanagoria*. Leiden and Boston.

Moroo, A. (2014) 'The Erythrai decrees reconsidered: *IG* I³ 14, 15 & 16', in *ΑΘΗΝΑΙΩΝ ΕΠΙΣΚΟΠΟΣ: Studies in Honour of Harold B. Mattingly*, ed. A. P. Matthaiou and R. K. Pitt. Athens, 97–119.

Moustaka, A., Skarlatidou, E., Tzannes, M.-C., and Ersoy, Y. (eds) (2004) *Klazomenai, Teos and Abdera: Metropoleis and Colony*. Thessaloniki.

Müller, H. (1989) 'Ein neues hellenistisches Weihepigramm aus Pergamon', *Chiron* 19, 449–53.

Nevett, L. (2000) 'A real estate "market" in Classical Greece? The example of town housing', *ABSA* 95, 329–43.

Nixon, L. and Price, S. (1990) 'The size and resources of Greek cities', in *The Greek City from Homer to Alexander*, ed. O. Murray and S. Price. Oxford, 137–70.

Olding, G. (2007) 'Ion the wineman: the manipulation of myth', in *The World of Ion of Chios*, ed. V. Jennings and A. Katsaros. Leiden and Boston, 139–54.

Osborne, R. (1998) 'Early Greek colonisation? The nature of Greek settlement in the West', in *Archaic Greece: New Approaches and New Evidence*, ed. N. Fisher and H. van Wees. London, 251–70.

Osborne, R. (2009) 'The politics of an epigraphic habit: the case of Thasos', in *Greek History and Epigraphy: Essays in Honour of P. J. Rhodes*, ed. L. Mitchell and L. Rubinstein. Swansea, 103–14.

Osborne, R. and Rhodes, P. J. (2017) *Greek Historical Inscriptions 478–404 BC*. Oxford.

Ostwald, M. (1955) 'The Athenian legislation against tyranny and subversion', *TAPA* 86, 103–28.

Palmisciano, R. (2019) 'On drinking wine in Anacreon fr. 356 *PMG* (= 33 Gent.)', *AION* 41, 17–30.

Paneris, J. R. (1983) 'Die eigenhändige Tötung des Räubers bei Demokrit und des nächtlichen Einbrechers bei Platon', *Philologus* 127/2, 298–302.

Parker, R. (1996) *Athenian Religion: A History*. Oxford.

Parker, R. (2005) *Polytheism and Society at Athens*. Oxford.

Parissaki, M.-G. (2000–3) 'Τὰ στενὰ τῶν Κορπίλων καὶ τῶν Σαπαίων. Ἡ ἐπανεξέταση ἑνὸς τοπογραφικοῦ προβλήματος', *Horos* 14–16, 345–62.

Paul, S. (2013) *Cultes et sanctuaires de l'île de Cos*. Liège.

Paul, S. (2018) 'Sharing the civic sacrifice', in *Feasting and Polis Institutions*, ed. F. van den Eijnde, J. H. Blok, and R. Strootman. Leiden and Boston, 315–39.

Pochmarski, E. (1974) *Das Bild des Dionysos in der Rundplastik der klassischen Zeit Griechenlands*. Vienna.

Pottier, E. and Hauvette–Besnault, A. (1880) 'Décret des Abdéritains trouvé à Téos', *BCH* 4, 47–59.

Pouilloux, J. (1989) 'Akèratos de Thasos: poésie et histoire', in *Architecture et poésie dans le monde grec. Hommage à G. Roux*, ed. R. Etienne, M.-T. Le Dinahet, and M. Yon. Lyon, 193–204.

Poulsen, F. (1951) *Catalogue of Ancient Sculpture in the Ny Carslberg Glyptotek*. Copenhagen.

Povalahev, N. (2008) *Die Griechen am Nordpontos: Die nordpontische Kolonisation im Kontext der Großen Griechischen Kolonisationsbewegung vom 8. bis 6. Jahrhundert v. Chr.* Munich.

Povalahev, N. (ed.) (2014) *Phanagoreia und darüber hinaus . . . Festschrift für Vladimir Kuznetsov*. Göttingen.

Povalahev, N. and Kuznetsov, V. (eds) (2011) *Phanagoreia, Kimmerischer Bosporos, Pontos Euxeinos*. Göttingen.

Povalahev, N. and Kuznetsov, V. (2012) *Phanagoreia und seine historische Umwelt*. Göttingen.

Prag, J. (2010) 'Kinship diplomacy between Sicily and Rome', in *Alleanze e parentela: Le 'affinità elettive' nella storiografia sulla Sicilia antica*, ed. D. Bonanno, C. Bonnet, N. Cusumao, and S. Péré-Noguès. Caltanissetta and Rome, 179–206.

Price, M. J. (1991) *The Coinage in the Name of Alexander the Great and Philip Arrhidaeus* (2 vols). Zürich and London.

Procopé, J. F. (1990) 'Democritus on politics and the care of the soul: appendix', *CQ* 40/1, 21–45.

Psoma, S. (2007) 'Profitable networks: coinages, panegyris and Dionysiac Artists', *MHR* 22/2, 237–55.

Psoma, S. (2015) 'Did the so-called Thraco-Macedonian standard exist?', in *ΚΑΙΡΟΣ: Contributions to Numismatics in Honor of Basil Demetriadi*, ed. U. Wartenberg and M. Amandry. New York, 167–90.

Psoma, S. (2016) 'Choosing and changing monetary standards in the Greek world during the Archaic and the Classical periods', in *The Ancient Greek Economy: Markets, Households and City-States*, ed. E. M. Harris, D. M. Lewis, and M. Woolmer. Cambridge, 90–115.

Psoma, S., Karadima, C., and Terzopoulou, D. (2008) *The Coins from Maroneia and the Classical City at Molyvoti* (*ΜΕΛΕΤΗΜΑΤΑ* 62). Athens.

Pugliese Carratelli, G. (1960) '*ΦΑΡΜΑΚΑ ΔΗΛΗΤΗΡΙΑ*', *PP* 15, 58–9.

Radt, S. L. (1958) *Pindars zweiter und sechster Paian: Text, Scholien und Kommentar*. Amsterdam.

Reger, G. (2004) '*Sympoliteiai* in Hellenistic Asia Minor', in *The Greco-Roman East: Politics, Culture, Society* (*Yale Classical Studies* 31), ed. S. Colvin. Cambridge, 145–80.

Reiche, F. (2006) *Grammateis und Mnamones: Schreiber und Rechtsbewahrer in archaischer und frühklassischer Zeit*. Unpublished Dissertation, Universität Münster.

Reynolds, J. (1982) *Aphrodisias and Rome*. London.

Rhodes, P. J. (1972) *The Athenian Boule*. Oxford.

Rhodes, P. J. (1981) *A Commentary on the Aristotelian* Athenaion Politeia. Oxford.

Rhodes, P. J. (2007) 'διοίκησις', *Chiron* 37, 349–62.

Rhodes, P. J. with Lewis, D. M. (1997) *The Decrees of the Greek States*. Oxford.

Rhodes, P. J. and Osborne, R. (2003) *Greek Historical Inscriptions 404–323 BC*. Oxford.

Rigsby, K. J. (1996) *Asylia: Territorial Inviolability in the Hellenistic World*. Berkeley, Los Angeles, and London.

Robert, L. (1935) 'Inscription hellénistique de Dalmatie', *BCH* 59, 489–513; reprinted in *OMS* I, 302–26.

Robert, L. (1936) *Collection Froehner I: Inscriptions grecques*. Paris.

Robert, L. (1937) *Études anatoliennes: recherches sur les inscriptions grecques d'Asie Mineure*. Paris.

Robert, L. (1938) *Études épigraphiques et philologiques*. Paris.

Robert, L. (1945) *Le sanctuaire de Sinuri près de Mylasa, première partie: Les inscriptions grecques*. Paris.

Robert, L. (1960) 'Recherches épigraphiques', *REA* 62, 276–361; reprinted in *OMS* II, 792–877.

Robert, L. (1962) *Villes d'Asie Mineure: Études de géographie ancienne* (2nd edn). Paris.

Robert, L. (1967) *Monnaies grecques: Types, légendes, magistrats monétaires et géographie*. Geneva and Paris.

Robert, L. (1969) 'Les inscriptions', in *Laodicée du Lycos: Le Nymphée. Campagnes 1961–1963*, ed. J. des Gagniers et al. Quebec and Paris, 247–389.

Robert, L. (1987) *Documents d'Asie Mineure*. Athens and Paris.

Robert, L. and Robert, J. (1976) 'Une inscription grecque de Téos en Ionie: L'union de Téos et de Kyrbissos', *JSav*, 154–235; reprinted in *OMS* VII, 297–379.

Robert, L. and Robert, J. (1983) *Fouilles d'Amyzon en Carie*, Vol. I: *Exploration, histoire, monnaies et inscriptions*. Paris.

Robert, L. and Robert, J. (1989) *Claros I: Décrets hellénistiques, fasc. I*. Paris.

Roberts, E. S. (1887) *An Introduction to Greek Epigraphy*, Part I: *The Archaic Inscriptions and the Greek Alphabet*. Cambridge.

Robinson, E. W. (1997) *The First Democracies: Early Popular Government outside Athens*. Stuttgart.

Robinson, E. W. (2011) *Democracy beyond Athens: Popular Government in the Greek Classical Age*. Cambridge.

Roehl, H. (1882) *Inscriptiones Graecae antiquissimae praeter Atticas in Attica repertas*. Berlin.

Roisman, J. and Edwards, M. J. (2019) *Lycurgus: Against Leocrates*. Oxford.

Rosivach, V. J. (1994) *The System of Public Sacrifice in Fourth-Century Athens*. Atlanta, GA.

Rostovtzeff, M. (1941) *The Social & Economic History of the Hellenistic World* (3 vols). Oxford.

Roueché, C. (1993) *Performers and Partisans at Aphrodisias*. London.

Rousset, D. (2002) *Le territoire de Delphes et la terre d'Apollon*. Athens and Paris.

Rousset, D. (2010) *Fouilles de Xanthos X. De Lycie en Cabalide: La convention entre les Lyciens et Termessos près d'Oinoanda*. Geneva.

Rubinstein, L. (2007) '"*ARAI*" in Greek laws in the Classical and Hellenistic periods', in *Symposion 2005*, ed. E. Cantarella. Vienna, 269–86.

Rubinstein, L. (2016) 'Reward and deterrence in Classical and Hellenistic enactments', in *Symposion 2015*, ed. D. F. Leão and G. Thür. Vienna, 419–49.

Russell, T. (2017) *Byzantium and the Bosporus: A Historical Study, from the Seventh Century BC until the Foundation of Constantinople*. Oxford.

Rutherford, I. (2001) *Pindar's Paeans: A Reading of the Fragments with a Survey of the Genre*. Oxford.

Rutherford, I. (2013) *State Pilgrims and Sacred Observers in Ancient Greece*. Cambridge.

Saba, S. (2018) 'A problem of historical geography: Orthagoreia in Thrace reconsidered', *Ancient Society* 48, 103–13.

Şahin, S. (1985) 'Ein neues Dekret der Symmoria zu Ehren ihrer Prostatai in Teos', *EA* 5, 13–17.

Şahin, S. (1994) 'Piratenüberfall auf Teos: Volksbeschluss über die Finanzierung der Erpressungsgelder', *EA* 23, 1–40.

Salmeri, G. (2004) 'Hellenism on the periphery: the case of Cilicia and an etymology of *soloikismos*', in *The Greco-Roman East: Politics, Culture, Society* (*Yale Classical Studies* 31), ed. S. Colvin. Cambridge, 181–206.

Salviat, F. (1992) 'Calendrier de Paros et calendrier de Thasos', in *Mélanges Pierre Lévêque*, Vol. 6: *Religion*, ed. M.-M. Mactoux and E. Geny. Paris, 261–7.

Samitz, Chr. (2019) 'Advances of money made by financial magistrates in Hellenistic cities', in *Debt in Ancient Mediterranean Societies: A Documentary Approach*, ed. S. Démare-Lafont. Geneva, 269–325.

Santiago Álvarez, R.-A. (1990–1) 'Sobre las «Teiorum dirae»', *Faventia* 12–13, 327–36.

Savalli-Lestrade, I. (2012) 'ΥΠΕΡ ΤΗΣ ΠΟΛΕΩΣ: Les intervenants étrangers dans la justice et dans la diplomatie des cités hellénistiques', *CCG* 23, 141–80.

Schipporeit, S. T. (2013) *Kulte und Heiligtümer der Demeter und Kore in Ionien* (BYZAS 16). Istanbul.

Schlotzhauer, U. and Villing, A. (2006) 'East Greek pottery from Naukratis: the current state of research', in *Naukratis: Greek Diversity in Egypt. Studies on East Greek Pottery and Exchange in the Eastern Mediterranean*, ed. A. Villing and U. Schlotzhauer. London, 53–68.

Schlotzhauer, U. and Zhuravlev, D. V. (2013) 'Forschungen in der antiken Siedlung "Golubickaja-2" auf der südrussischen Taman'-Halbinsel', *Eurasia Antiqua* 19, 105–25.

Schmalz, G. C. R. (2009) *Augustan and Julio-Claudian Athens: A New Epigraphy and Prosopography*. Leiden and Boston.

Schmitt Pantel, P. (1997) *La cité au banquet: Histoire des repas publics dans les cités grecques*. Paris and Rome.

Schönert-Geiss, E. (1975) *Griechisches Münzwerk: Die Münzprägung von Bisanthe—Dikaia—Selymbria*. Berlin.

Schuler, Chr. (1998) *Ländliche Siedlungen und Gemeinden im hellenistischen und römischen Kleinasien*. Munich.

Schuler, Chr. (2005) 'Die διοίκησις im öffentlichen Finanzwesen der hellenistischen Poleis', *Chiron* 35, 387–403.

Schuler, Chr. (2010) 'Sympolitien im Lykien und Karien', in *Hellenistic Karia*, ed. R. van Bremen and J.-M. Carbon. Bordeaux, 393–413.

Schwyzer, E. (1921) 'Kleine Bemerkungen zu griechischen Dialektinschriften', *Glotta* 11, 75–9.

Schwyzer, E. (1923) *Dialectorum Graecarum exempla epigraphica potiora*. Leipzig.

Seibert, J. (1963) *Metropolis und Apoikie: Historische Beiträge zur Geschichte ihrer gegenseitigen Beziehungen*. Würzburg.

Sève, M. (1979) 'Un décret de consolation à Cyzique', *BCH* 103, 327–59.

Sezgin, Y. (2012) *Arkaik Dönem İonia Üretimi Ticari Amphoralar*. Istanbul.

Sezgin, Y. (2017) 'Arkaik Dönemde Teos'ta ticari amphora üretimi: sorunlar ve gözlemler', *Anadolu/Anatolia* 43, 15–36.

Shaverbi, E. (2019) 'An inscription of Darius I from Phanagoria (DFa): Preliminary report of a work in progress', *ARTA* 2019.005, <http://www.achemenet.com/pdf/arta/ARTA_2019_005_Shavarebi.pdf>.

Sherk, R. K. (1969) *Roman Documents from the Greek East: Senatus Consulta and Epistulae to the Age of Augustus*. Baltimore, MD.

Sherk, R. K. (1984) *Translated Documents of Greece & Rome*, Vol. 4: *Rome and the Greek East to the Death of Augustus*. Cambridge.

Sherk, R. K. (1991) 'The eponymous officials of Greek cities III', *ZPE* 88, 225–60.

Sherk, R. K. (1992) 'The eponymous officials of Greek cities IV', *ZPE* 93, 223–72.

Shipley, G. (2019) *Pseudo-Skylax's Periplous: The Circumnavigation of the Inhabited World. Text, Translation and Commentary* (2nd edn). Liverpool.

Skarlatidou, E. (1990) 'Οἰκισμοί καὶ ἐγκαταστάσεις ἱστορικῶν χρόνων μέσα στα ὅρια τῆς "χώρας" τῶν Ἀβδήρων', in *Μνήμη Δ. Λαζαρίδη: Πόλις καὶ χώρα στην αρχαία Μακεδονία καὶ Θράκη*. Thessaloniki, 611–28.

Skarlatidou, E. (2004) 'The archaic cemetery of the Clazomenian colony at Abdera', in Moustaka et al. 2004, 249–60.

Skarlatidou, E. (2010) *Τὸ Ἀρχαϊκό Νεκροταφείο τῶν Ἀβδήρων*. Thessaloniki.

Slawisch, A. (2011) 'Aus unruhigen Zeiten: Die ›Ächtungsinschrift‹ aus Milet, ein Erlass aus dem frühesten 5. Jahrhundert v. Chr.', *Ist. Mitt.* 61, 425–32.

Smith, A. C. (2011) *Polis and Personification in Athenian Art*. Leiden and Boston.

Smith, R. R. R. (1988) *Hellenistic Royal Portraits*. Oxford.

Smith, R. R. R. (1993) *Aphrodisias I: The Monument of C. Julius Zoilos*. Mainz am Rhein.

Smith, R. R. R. (2006) *Aphrodisias II: Roman Portrait Statuary from Aphrodisias*. Mainz am Rhein.

Smith, R. R. R. (2013) *Aphrodisias VI: The Marble Reliefs from the Julio-Claudian Sebasteion at Aphrodisias*. Darmstadt.

Smith, R. R. R. (2019) 'Diadems, royal hairstyles, and the Berlin Attalos', in *Art of the Hellenistic Kingdoms: From Pergamon to Rome*, ed. S. Hemingway and K. Karoglou. New York, 75–82.

Sokolowski, F. (1962) *Lois sacrées des cités grecques: Supplément*. Paris.

Sokolowski, F. (1965) *Lois sacrées de l'Asie Mineure*. Paris.

Sommerstein, A. H. and Bayliss, A. J. (2013) *Oath and State in Ancient Greece*. Berlin and Boston.

Spier, J., Potts, T., and Cole, S. E. (eds) (2018) *Beyond the Nile: Egypt and the Classical World*. Los Angeles.

Strang, J. R. (2007) *The City of Dionysos: A Social and Historical Study of the Ionian City of Teos*. Unpublished PhD thesis, State University of New York at Buffalo.

Stroud, R. S. (1984) 'An Argive decree from Nemea concerning Aspendos', *Hesperia* 53, 193–216.

Sullivan, R. D. (1990) *Near Eastern Royalty and Rome*. Toronto, Buffalo, and London.

Taşdelen, E. and Polat, Y. (2018) 'New investigations, finds and discoveries concerning the city walls of Teos', *Philia* 4, 173–99.

Theotikou, M. (2013) *Die ekecheiria zwischen Religion und Politik*. Berlin.

Thériault, G. (1996) *Le culte d'Homonoia dans les cités grecques*. Lyon and Québec.

Thomas, R. (1996) 'Written in stone? Liberty, equality, orality, and the codification of law', in *Greek Law in its Political Setting*, ed. L. Foxhall and A. D. E. Lewis. Oxford, 9–31.

Thomas, R. (2019) *Polis Histories, Collective Memories and the Greek World*. Cambridge.

Thonemann, P. (2011) *The Maeander Valley: A Historical Geography from Antiquity to Byzantium*. Cambridge.

Thonemann, P. (2013) 'The Attalid state, 188–133 BC', in *Attalid Asia Minor: Money, International Relations, and the State*, ed. P. Thonemann. Oxford, 1–47.

Thonemann, P. (2015) *The Hellenistic World: Using Coins as Sources*. Cambridge.

Thonemann, P. (2020) 'Inscriptions from Abdera and Maroneia', *Tekmeria* 15, 1–26.

Thür, G. and Taeuber, H. (1994) *Prozessrechtliche Inschriften der griechischen Poleis: Arkadien*. Vienna.

Tiede, M. (1990) 'Hellenistische Pfeilermonumente im Heraion von Samos und in Magnesia am Maeander', *MDAI(A)* 105, 213–58.

Tiverios, M. (2008) 'Greek colonisation of the northern Aegean', in *Greek Colonisation: An Account of Greek Colonies and Other Settlements Overseas*, vol. 2, ed. G. R. Tsetskhladze. Leiden and Boston, 1–154.

Tod, M. N. (1946) *A Selection of Greek Historical Inscriptions to the End of the Fifth Century B.C.* (2nd edn). Oxford.

Touloumakos, J. (1988) 'Zum römischen Gemeindepatronat im griechischen Osten', *Hermes* 116, 304–24.

Tracy, S. V. (1990) *Attic Letter-Cutters of 229 to 86 B.C.* Berkeley, Los Angeles, and Oxford.

Triandaphyllos, D. (2004) 'Abdera: the Classical and Hellenistic cities', in Moustaka et al. 2004, 261–9.

Trümpy, C. (1997) *Untersuchungen zu den altgriechischen Monatsnamen und Monatsfolgen*. Heidelberg.

Tsakirgis, B. (2015) 'Tools from the house of Mikion and Menon', in *Autopsy in Athens*, ed. M. M. Miles. Oxford, 9–17.

Tsetskhladze, G. R. (2007) 'The Ionian colonies and their territories in the Taman peninsula in the Archaic period', in *Frühes Ionien: Eine Bestandsaufnahme* (*Milesische Forschungen* 5), ed. J. Cobet, V. von Graeve, W.-D. Niemeier, and K. Zimmermann. Mainz am Rhein, 551–65.

Tuna, N. (1997) 'Teos Araştırmaları, 1995', *AST* 14/1, 219–33.

Tuna, N. (1998) 'Teos Araştırmaları, 1996', *AST* 15/2, 323–32.

Tuplin, C. J. (2003) 'Xerxes' march from Doriscus to Therme', *Historia* 52, 385–409.

Tybout, R. (1993) 'Malerei und Raumfunktion im zweiten Stil', in *Functional and Spatial Analysis of Wall Painting*, ed. E. M. Moormann. Leiden, 38–50.

Uz, D. M. (2013) *Teos'taki Dionysos Tapınağı*. Ankara.

van Alfen, P. (2014) '*Metoikêsis* and Archaic monetary coordination: Teos-Abdera and Phokaia-Velia', in *First International Congress of the Anatolian Monetary History and Numismatics*, ed. K. Dörtlük, O. Tekin, and R. Boyraz Seyhan. İstanbul, 632–52.

van Bremen, R. (1996) *The Limits of Participation: Women and Civic Life in the Greek East in the Hellenistic and Roman Periods*. Amsterdam.

van Bremen, R. (2008) 'The date and context of the Kymaian decrees for Archippe', *REA* 110, 357–82.

Vasilev, M. I. (2015) *The Policy of Darius and Xerxes towards Thrace and Macedonia*. Leiden and Boston.

Veligianni, Chr. (1995) 'Abdera, Maroneia, Ainos und der Odrysenstaat', *Tekmeria* 1, 136–72.

Vollgraff, W. (1918) 'De lege collegii cantorum Milesii', *Mnemosyne* 46/4, 415–27.

Walbank, F. W. (1967) *A Historical Commentary on Polybius*, Vol. II: *Commentary on Books VII–XVIII*. Oxford.

Walbank, F. W. (1979) *A Historical Commentary on Polybius*, Vol. III: *Commentary on Books XIX–XL*. Oxford.

Walbank, F. W. (1985) 'The via Egnatia: its original scope and date', in *Studia in honorem Christo M. Danov*, ed. A. Fol, M. Tatcheva, and N. Nedjalkov (*Terra Antiqua Balcanica* 2). Sofia, 458–64.

Walser, A. (2009) 'Sympolitien und Siedlungsentwicklung', in *Stadtbilder im Hellenismus*, ed. A. Matthaei and M. Zimmermann. Berlin, 135–55.

Wartenberg, U. (2015) 'Thraco-Macedonian bullion coinage in the fifth century B.C.: the case of Ichnai', in *KAIPOΣ: Contributions to Numismatics in Honor of Basil Demetriadi*, ed. U. Wartenberg and M. Amandry. New York, 347–64.

West, M. L. (2001) 'The fragmentary Homeric Hymn to Dionysus', *ZPE* 134, 1–11.

Wiemer, H.-U. (2002) *Krieg, Handel und Piraterie: Untersuchungen zur Geschichte des hellenistischen Rhodos*. Berlin.

Wilhelm, A. (1898) Review of C. Michel, *Recueil d'inscriptions grecques* Fasc. I/II, *GGA* 160, 201–35; reprinted in *Kleine Schriften, Abteilung II: Abhandlungen und Beiträge zur griechischen Inschriftenkunde, Teil IV*. Vienna, 2002, 213–47.

Wilhelm, A. (1912) 'Παρατηρήσεις', *AE* 1912, 250–3; reprinted in *Kleine Schriften, Abteilung II: Abhandlungen und Beiträge zur griechischen Inschriftenkunde, Teil III*. Vienna, 2000, 154–7.

Wilhelm, A. (1914a) 'Berichtigungen', *AM* 39, 177–88; reprinted in *Kleine Schriften, Abteilung II: Abhandlungen und Beiträge zur griechischen Inschriftenkunde, Teil III*. Vienna, 2000, 563–74.

Wilhelm, A. (1914b) 'Urkunden aus Messene', *JÖAI* 17, 1–120; reprinted in *Kleine Schriften, Abteilung II: Abhandlungen und Beiträge zur griechischen Inschriftenkunde, Teil I*. Leipzig, 1984, 467–586.

Wilhelm, A. (1915) 'Neue Beiträge zur griechischen Inschriftenkunde, IV. Teil', *SB Wien* 179/6, 1–70; reprinted in *Akademieschriften zur griechischen Inschriftenkunde, Teil I*. Leipzig, 1974, 177–244.

Wilhelm, A. (1921a) 'Neue Beiträge zur griechischen Inschriftenkunde, VI. Teil', *SB Wien* 183/3, 1–79; reprinted in *Akademieschriften zur griechischen Inschriftenkunde, Teil I*. Leipzig, 1974, 294–370.

Wilhelm, A. (1921b) 'Hellenistisches', *Anz. Wien* 1921, 70–83; reprinted in *Akademieschriften zur griechischen Inschriftenkunde, Teil II*. Leipzig, 1974, 57–70.

Wilhelm, A. (1925) 'Attische Urkunden, III. Teil', *SB Wien* 202/5, 3–64; reprinted in *Akademieschriften zur griechischen Inschriftenkunde, Teil I*. Leipzig, 1974, 463–524.

Wilhelm, A. (1932) 'Neue Beiträge zur griechischen Inschriftenkunde, V. Teil', *SB Wien* 214/4, 1–51; reprinted in *Akademieschriften zur griechischen Inschriftenkunde, Teil I*. Leipzig, 1974, 245–93.

Wilhelm, A. (1942) 'Attische Urkunden, V. Teil', *SB Wien* 220/5, 3–192; reprinted in *Akademieschriften zur griechischen Inschriftenkunde, Teil I*. Leipzig, 1974, 619–808.

Williams, D. (2004) 'Captain Donnelly's altar and the Delian Prytaneion', *RA* 37, 51–68.

Yon, M. (2004) *Kition–Bamboula V: Kition dans les textes*. Paris.

Youni, M. S. (2007) 'An inscription from Teos concerning Abdera', in *Thrace in the Graeco-Roman World*, ed. A. Lakovidou. Athens, 724–36.

Zannis, A. G. (2014) *Le pays entre le Strymon et le Nestos: géographie et histoire (VIIe–IVe siècle avant J.-C.)* (*ΜΕΛΕΤΗΜΑΤΑ* 71). Athens.

Ziebarth, E. (1895) 'Der Fluch im griechischen Recht', *Hermes* 30/1, 57–70.

Index of Greek Terms

This index includes all Greek words that appear in the inscriptions published or republished in this volume (**Documents 1–6**), omitting only very common particles, connectives and suchlike (δέ, καί, ὁ, etc.). References in the form 1.A6 are to lines of the relevant inscriptions; references in square brackets are to terms which are wholly or partially restored.

Subject Index